Ecce Mulier

Ecce Mulier

Nietzsche and the Eternal Feminine

An Analytical Psychological Perspective

GERTRUDIS OSTFELD DE BENDAYAN, PH.D.

CHIRON PUBLICATIONS
WILMETTE, ILLINOIS

Cover image by Mariano Fernandez-Porras

Library of Congress Cataloging-in-Publication Data

Ostfeld de Bendayan, Gertrudis.
  Ecce mulier : Nietzsche and the eternal feminine : an analytical psychological per-
spective / Gertrudis Ostfeld de Bendayan.
      p. cm.
  Includes bibliographical references (p.   ) and index.
  ISBN-13: 978-1-888602-43-2 (pbk. : alk. paper)
  ISBN-10: 1-888602-36-8 (pbk.)
  1. Nietzsche, Friedrich Wilhelm, 1844—1900. 2. Femininity (Philosophy) 3.
Woman (Philosophy) I. Title.

  B3318.F45O88 2007
  193—dc22

To my parents, Hillo and Klara Ostfeld, survivors of the Holocaust, with everlasting gratitude for having instilled in me the will to struggle and persevere.

To Frank, my husband, friend, and destiny.

Contents

ACKNOWLEDGMENTS

MY GREATEST DEBT IS TO my doctoral tutor, Dr. Roderick Main, who with great devotion has been an unerring psychopomp in this solo transatlantic crossing between the Old and the New Worlds.

I give special acknowledgment to Dr. Paul Bishop, a model to emulate, whose valuable feedback and support provided me with the necessary courage to present my manuscript for publication.

My eternal gratitude to Dr. Luis Sanz, the wise alchemist who motivated me to transmute my internal lead into gold.

My thankfulness to Eyra Marcano, whose Eros accompanied me throughout the long course of *coagulatio* of the present work.

ABBREVIATIONS

NIETZSCHE'S WRITINGS

Quotations are cited with reference to the following abbreviations.

AC   *The Antichrist: Curse of Christianity.* 2000. Translated by A. M. Ludovici. New York: Prometheus Books. Cited in the text with aphorism number.

AML   *De mi vida (About My Life).* 1997. Madrid: Valdemar. Cited in the text with page reference.

AOM   *Assorted Opinions and Maxims.* 1992. Translated and edited by W. Kaufmann in *Basic Writings of Nietzsche.* New York: The Modern Library. Cited in the text with aphorism number.

BGE   *Beyond Good and Evil: Prelude to a Philosophy of the Future.* 1992. Translated and edited by W. Kaufmann in *Basic Writings of Nietzsche.* New York: The Modern Library. Cited in the text with aphorism number.

BT   *The Birth of Tragedy, Out of the Spirit of Music.* 1992. Translated and edited by W. Kaufmann in *Basic Writings of Nietzsche.* New York: The Modern Library. Cited in the text with section reference.

D   *Daybreak: Reflections on Moral Prejudices.* 2000. Translated by R. J. Hollingdale. Edited by M. Clark and B. Leiter. Cambridge: Cambridge University Press. Cited in the text with aphorism number.

EH   *Ecce Homo: How One Becomes What One Is.* 1992. Translated and edited by W. Kaufmann in *Basic Writings of*

Nietzsche. New York: The Modern Library. Cited in the text with section number plus subtitle abbreviation and section number.

GM   *On the Genealogy of Morals: A Polemic*. 1992. Translated and edited by W. Kaufmann in *Basic Writings of Nietzsche*. New York: The Modern Library. Cited in the text with essay number plus aphorism number.

GS   *The Gay Science*. 1974. Translated by W. Kaufmann. New York: Vintage Books. Cited in the text with aphorism number.

HATH   *Human, All Too Human: A Book for Free Spirits*. 1996. Translated by M. Faber and S. Lehman. Lincoln: University of Nebraska Press. Cited in the text with aphorism number.

LNB   *Writings from the Late Notebooks*. 2003. Translated by K. Sturge. Edited by R. Bittner. Cambridge: Cambridge University Press. Cited in the text with notebook number and note number.

NCW   *Nietzsche contra Wagner* (1968). Translated by W. Kaufmann in *The Portable Nietzsche*. New York: Viking Press.

PN   *The Poetry of Friedrich Nietzsche*. 1986. Translated by P. Grundlehner. New York and Oxford: Oxford University Press.

PTAG   *Philosophy in the Tragic Age of the Greeks*. 1962. Translated by M. Cowan. Washington, D.C.: Regnery Publishing, Inc. Cited in the text with section reference.

TCW   *The Case of Wagner: A Musician's Problem*. 1992. Translated and edited by W. Kaufmann in *Basic Writings of Nietzsche*. New York: The Modern Library. Cited in the text with aphorism number.

TI   *Twilight of the Idols, or How One Philosophizes with a Hammer*. 1998. Translated by D. Large. Oxford and New York: Oxford University Press. Cited in the text with aphorism number.

TLNS   *On the Truth and Lies in a Nonmoral Sense*. 1994. Translated and edited by D. Breazeale in *Philosophy and Truth*. Atlantic Highlands, NJ: Humanities Press International, Inc. Cited in the text with page reference.

UM (I–IV) *Untimely Meditations.* 1991. Translated by R. J. Hollingdale. Cambridge: Cambridge University Press. Cited in the text with essay number plus section reference.

WP *Will to Power.* 1968. Translated by W. Kaufmann and R. J. Hollingdale. Edited by W. Kaufmann. New York: Vintage Books. Cited in the text with aphorism number.[1]

WS *The Wanderer and His Shadow.* 1992. Translated and edited by W. Kaufmann in *Basic Writings of Nietzsche.* New York: The Modern Library. Cited in the text with aphorism number.

Z (I–IV) *Thus Spoke Zarathustra: A Book for All and None.* 1978. Translated by W. Kaufmann. New York: Penguin Books. Cited in the text with part number plus sub-part title and section.

Jung's Writings

Quotations are cited with reference to the following abbreviations.

CW *Collected Works.* 1979. Edited by Sir H. Read, M. Fordham, G. Adler and W. McGuire, 20 vols. Bollingen Series XX. Princeton: Princeton University Press. Cited in the text with volume number and paragraph number.

LJ *Letters: 1906–61* in two volumes. Edited by G. Adler and A. Jaffé. Translated by R. F. C. Hull. Princeton: Princeton University Press. Cited in the text with volume number and page reference.

MDR *Memories, Dreams, Reflections.* 1965. Fourth edition. Recorded and edited by A. Jaffé. Translated by R. and C. Winston. New York: Vintage Books. Cited in the text with page reference.

---

[1] It is important to highlight that the notes contained in *The Will to Power* are of great interest as background for achieving a better understanding of Nietzsche's finished books. Nevertheless, *The Will to Power*, presented under false pretenses by Nietzsche's sister as his final philosophical treatise, creates a false impression, as its "unconnected connections" differ considerably from the aphorisms of his other works. For this reason, this work should not be overestimated.

SNZ   *Nietzsche's Zarathustra: Notes from the Seminar Given in 1934–1939* in two volumes. 1988. Edited by J. L. Jarrett. Bollingen Series XCIX. Princeton: Princeton University Press. Cited in the text with volume number and page reference.

VS   *Visions: Notes of the Seminar Given in 1930–1934* in two volumes. 1997. Edited by Claire Douglas. Bollingen Series XCIX. Princeton: Princeton University Press. Cited in the text with volume number and page reference.

Not everything will have been said when it is recalled that Nietzsche never forgot what was, for him, that strange, lost paradise of a Protestant presbytery filled with feminine presence. Nietzsche's femininity is deeper for being more hidden. Who is there under the super-masculine mask of Zarathustra? With regard to women, there are in Nietzsche's work petty shows of disdain, in bad taste. Beneath all these coverings and compensations, who will discover the feminine Nietzsche for us? And who will find the Nietzscheism of the feminine?

—Gaston Bachelard, *The Poetics of Reverie*

INTRODUCTION

But I should think that today we are at least far from the ridiculous immodesty that would be involved in decreeing from our
corner that perspectives are permitted only from this corner.
Rather has the world become "infinite" for us all over again,
inasmuch as we cannot reject the possibility that "it may
include infinite interpretations."

—F. Nietzsche, *The Gay Science*

Psychobiography [is] a still-developing field. . . . We should be
encouraging the efforts of anyone who can make important addi-
tions to our understanding of the subjects chosen for study. . . . We
need the contributions of as many explorers as we can send out,
with as many ways to look at the terrain as they can bring to bear.

—Alan C. Elms, *Uncovering Lives*

MANY WORKS HAVE BEEN WRITTEN about Friedrich Nietzsche's
(1844–1900) life and opus, yet, as he defined himself as a posthumous
thinker, he tacitly authorized us to repeatedly approach his philosophical
and human facets, to reinterpret them with each new present, with each
new *Zeitgeist*, and with the endless variety of individual perspectives.

The present work focuses on the question, or challenge, posed by the
French philosopher Gaston Bachelard: "Who will discover the feminine
Nietzsche for us?" I consider that unless we address this issue both
Nietzsche's creativity and his madness will remain imperfectly under-

stood. "The creative process," wrote Jung, "has a feminine quality, and the creative work arises from unconscious depths—we may truly say from the realm of the Mothers" (CW 15:158). Madness also stems from the same feminine depths: in both cases there occurs an intrusion of unconscious symbolism.[1] In Jung's imagery, madness is the result of possession by the Terrible Mother, with her "mantic and orgiastic characteristics." The dissolution of the personality forms part of the sphere of the Great Mother (the unconscious): "Insanity," writes the Jungian analyst Erich Neumann, "is an ever-recurrent symptom of possession by [the Mother] or by her representatives" (1991, 61). The outcome, creativity or madness, depends on the strength of the ego when confronted with the onslaught of unconscious contents.[2]

Let us then explore the world of the feminine in Nietzsche, its role in creating the "topography" of his soul—looking in particular at his relationship with women, the feminine, and the maternal, whether it be called the unconscious, maternal complex, or anima.

Previous studies have approached Nietzsche's relationship to the feminine through the lens of philosophy. Because Nietzsche employed "woman" as a trope for such absolute transcendental values as Truth, Life, Beauty, Eternity, Wisdom, Happiness, etc., numerous philosophers have taken his theoretical approach to women and sexuality as a key to understanding his philosophy. Though this book will refer to several of these studies, it is with the understanding that they are oriented more toward the thinker than toward the man.

The present work is a psychobiographical study from the perspective of analytical psychology.[3] Thanks to the theories proposed by C. G. Jung (1875–1961) and enhanced by his followers regarding the collective unconscious and its contents—the eternal archetypes, the compensatory attitude of the psyche, the psychological (personality) types, the phenomena of synchronicity, and the method of amplification—we are now able to understand in greater depth a personality such as Nietzsche's, a complex tapestry of mythos and pathos.

I utilize the term "analytical psychology" in its broadest sense, as I intend to make use of the classical, archetypalist, and developmental approaches (see Samuels 1985, 15). Taking all three schools into consideration, I will interpret events in Nietzsche's life from the perspective of analytical psychology in its plurality, positioning this study in as vast a critical space as possible. This falls in line with Nietzsche's spirit, as we cannot forget that his proposal regarding the "death of God," which implies the human impossibility of a discourse of absolute truth, also implies that the desire for the Absolute is severed and gives way to the appearance of an agonistic worldview.[4]

The investigation progresses by interlacing two temporal levels. On the one hand, there is linear, masculine, objective, solar time—the time of consciousness that acts as "Ariadne's thread," capable of following the chronological order of the determining factors and the development of the philosopher's subjectivity. On the other hand, I will focus on circular time, feminine, subjective, lunar time—the time of the unconscious, of the creative source. In this way, we will position ourselves in an eternal present. The fusion of both times will offer us a holistic view of the psychic life of the philosopher: a simultaneous image of potentiality (*dunamis*) and actuality (*energeia*), giving rise to a uroboric circle in which beginning and end shall meet: "Every ring strives and turns to reach itself again" (Z II:5).

At this point I would like to recall Nietzsche's words: "Everybody knows nowadays that the ability to accept contradiction is a sign of high culture" (GS 279). Taking my cue from this, I will embrace the diversity among the postulates of the various Jungian schools as a resource for enriching the topic to be investigated. "Pluralism," as Samuels points out, "is an attitude to conflict that tries to reconcile differences *without* imposing false resolution on them *or* losing sight of the unique value of each position" (1989, 1). Samuels likewise considered that this posture is based on the inherent plurality of the psyche: "Psyche brings with it its own plurality, fluidity, and the existence of relatively autonomous entities therein" (ibid., 2). A pluralistic standpoint was also considered by the French philosopher Gilles Deleuze as "the properly philosophical way of thinking . . . the only guarantor of freedom in the concrete spirit" (1983, 4).

In accordance with Jung's viewpoint and that of the followers of the classical approach, I will highlight the dialogue between Nietzsche's consciousness and the unconscious and the conflict of opposites inherent to this dialectic, which includes the compensatory tendency of the psyche in its search to fulfill a given teleology. I will likewise attempt to analyze and highlight the relationship of the ego with the anima, observed from the perspective of the constellation of Nietzsche's innate resources manifested through archetypal imagery, emphasizing the last period of the thinker's lucid life.

In order to evidence the compensatory function operative in the psychological process, I will focus on the purpose and meaning of Nietzsche's states of mind, his emotional life, his dominant patterns of behavior, his recurrent fantasy motifs, his interests and choices, and his symptoms, as well as the manifestations of the Self. Particular emphasis will be given to the images that appear in dreams, visual and auditory hallucinations, and poems, all rich sources of psychological insight.

Additionally, following Jung's method of amplification, enriching contributions from alchemy, religion, philosophy, literature, and archetypal symbolism will be employed to broaden the context of a dream, an experience, an idea, an image, or a fantasy, thus following Nietzsche's own spirit when he points out the need for many and different eyes: "The *more* eyes, different eyes, we can use to observe one thing, the more complete will our 'concept' of this thing, our 'objectivity' be" (GM III:12). A pluralistic approach will help prevent the imposition of our own historical, social, and cultural environment onto Nietzsche's life, and counteract any tendency toward entrapment in circular logic when attempting to select or adjust the data to fit a given theoretical current.[5]

We are fortunate enough to have extensive data from primary sources (autobiographies; plentiful correspondence; personal reports of dreams, visions and states of mind, yearnings, and health conditions; in addition to firsthand testimonies from family, friends, colleagues, and relatives) that offer us detailed pictures of the thinker's life from his infancy to his death in 1900. But from a psychological perspective, the importance lies not in distinguishing the historical veracity of the events reported, but in the fact that for Nietzsche they are subjectively true: they have psychic reality (cf. Jung, CW 11:6).

The same approach applies for historical facts. If the historical facts are relevant, I consider that it is not important to discern whether or not the descriptions Nietzsche offered of the persons who played a significant role in his life are faithful images: what seems of basic importance when preparing a psychoanalytic study is the imago Nietzsche had of these personalities.[6] Nonetheless, the greater the number of sources available when writing a psychobiography, the less need there will be to resort to reconstructions and inferences (although it is not feasible to free oneself completely from such resources) in order to fill in the gaps in the life of the person being studied.

Of course, as Nietzsche stated in *The Gay Science,*

> How far the perspective character of existence extends . . . all existence is essentially actively engaged in *interpretation* . . . it cannot be decided [even] by the most industrious and most scrupulously conscientious analysis and self-examination of the intellect; for in the course of this analysis the human intellect cannot avoid seeing itself in its own perspectives, and only in these. (GS 374)

Wherever possible, I will make an effort to minimize the contamination stemming from projective elements by amplifying symbolic meaning rather than analyzing unconscious motivations. This method offers infinite possibilities, which it became necessary to limit: I will restrict Jung's method of amplification to Western world mythology (particularly to Greek myths),[7] religion, and culture.

Since I am trying to understand Nietzsche through his symbolic configurations, I would suggest that the reader approach this material open-mindedly, assuming an attitude similar to that required for symbols; that is, that the interpretations offered can never be final or total: "The symbol is never explained at once and for all, but has always to be deciphered anew, just like a music score" (Corbin 1964, 10). Like a symbol, psychobiography must be a living thing and can never be conceptually exhausted. It is important to point out that the task of interpretation is infinite and any given interpretation cannot claim to hit "bedrock."

Following the Nietzschean precept according to which there exist only interpretations, not facts or explanations (cf. WP 481, 477), when all is said and done, this project is just another interpretation and, consequently, liable to be included among those qualified by the philosopher as belonging to the order of "devilry, stupidity, and foolishness of interpretation—even our own human, all too human folly, which we know" (GS 374).

Part One

Part One

CHAPTER I

Incipit tragoedia:
realm of the Mothers

I was born on a day
that God was ill. . . .
There is an emptiness
in my metaphysical air
that no one will ever fill:
The cloister of a silence
that spoke on the fluttering of fire.
I was born on a day
that God was ill,
seriously ill.

—César Vallejo, "Espergesia"

It is not only interesting but also necessary to examine the past . . .
especially the years of childhood . . . we will never be able to come
to a clear judgment about ourselves without first studying the circumstances of our upbringing and measuring their impact on us.

—F. Nietzsche (AML, 1860)

UNDER THE APPROVING GAZE OF Euterpe, the muse of music, a daily
scene: Fritz,[1] the firstborn of the Lutheran minister from Röcken, Karl
Ludwig, is seated on his father's lap at the piano or the church organ, lis-

tening enraptured to the minister's masterly improvisations and interpretations. This child, who remained for hours, fascinated, near the performer and composer (cf. Janz 1987, I:40), was endowed with an erotica of the soul alien to both his sister Elisabeth, two years younger, and his brother, little Joseph. The melodies articulated Nietzsche's intimate and sublime feelings. Music, followed by poetry, became his most deeply felt passion and his preferred means of expression.[2]

Unluckily, in 1849, when he was not yet five years old, little Fritz suffered a severe blow: his father died of what was diagnosed as "softening of the brain" (cf. ibid., 41). The illness was very painful, and the little one intensely shared those terrible moments at the bedside of his beloved protector: "For eleven months the young Friedrich watched his father endure agonies which, as his mother put it, 'pierced her to the quick'—agonies of paralysis, of convulsions, of failing eyesight and finally of dementia" (Köhler 1998, 15).

Soon after his father's death, little Fritz left his beloved home to move to his paternal grandmother's house in Naumburg (cf. Janz 1987, I:43). With the early departure of this venerated figure, the child remained trapped in the "realm of the Mothers," which included the paternal grandmother, the mother, the sister, and two unmarried aunts: dry, severe, and castrating women who found their life's meaning in an excessive and suffocating overprotection of that "divine child."

Janz writes:

> [The mother] was a cold woman, with an emotional life of very little depth and amplitude. . . . She was, no doubt, proud of her son, but much more so because he was a good student rather than a budding thinker. . . . She focused on his conduct and his success. . . . But she never stopped advising her son not to ever do things that differed from . . . others. (1987, I:44)

The resultant damage to her son's discriminatory capacity was significant. "The experience of 'being different,' which is the primary fact of nascent ego consciousness and which occurs in the dawnlight of discrimination, divides the world into subject and object," suggests Neumann (1993, 109). According to Andrew Samuels, the Self is first experienced by the individual "in terms of the presence and feeling of his mother as she accepts him as an integrated whole; he experiences his personal wholeness in her perception of his wholeness, in her relating eye" (1999b, 133). Samuels adds: "Her capacity to hold together his multiplicity of being and to give him a sense of meaning provides him with a base for subsequent psychic integration. He, in turn, brings to the situation an innate potential to feel whole in himself" (ibid.).

With the reiterative command of "Don't be different!" Nietzsche's mother was incapable of "holding together his multiplicity of being"; consequently, neither was the son capable of "feeling whole in himself." Nietzsche's history indicates a perpetual internal struggle among his multiple dissonant voices, incapable of integrating under a unifying personality. Perhaps he referred to his own existential condition when he wrote: "The grossest error in judging a person is made by his parents; this is a fact, but how is one to explain it? Do the parents have too much experience of the child, and can *they no longer compose it into unity?*" (HATH 423, emphasis added).

The animus of the mother (and of the substitutes) acted as a pseudo-logos, and through severe discipline it imposed structures, limits, rules, and order. Furthermore, by way of manipulation, and in the absence of the real father, the figure of God-judge-chastiser was constantly invoked at home. In an environment saturated with religiosity, the threat of divine wrath, brought on by disobeying established precepts, was an omnipresent reality in Fritz's mind and in that of his sister, as has been suggested in various biographical testimonies. "Naumburg's terrifying bourgeois conventionality, conformism, and religious conservatism seeped into his being as afflictions he called 'Naumburger Tugend,' a superficial decorum or respectability against which he was to rebel strenuously or meekly accept all his life," wrote the philosopher Siegfried Mandel (in Salomé 2001, xiv).[3]

Such an animus attempted to elucidate for the little boy the image of Jehovah: primitive, archaic, and fierce. The development of Nietzsche's entire philosophy would be based on this particular confrontation and on the unconscious hostility he felt toward the severe and castrating God presented by his mother, as well as the abandoning God represented by the early departure of the father. From the "daybreak" of his life,

Nietzsche was confronted with questions on the meaning of life, of death, of the nature of a God who took his father and brother from him, and of the world itself.

> The father . . . is a powerful archetype dwelling in the psyche of the child. At first he is *the* father, an all-encompassing God-image, a dynamic principle. In the course of life this authoritarian imago recedes into the background: the father turns into a limited and often all-too-human personality. (Jung, CW 10:67)

For Nietzsche, the father's imago could not be humanized through experience with the real father, so the minister remained an idealized figure, omnipresent and omniscient like a God who must be redeemed: "Now the tombs stammer, 'Redeem the dead!' " (Z IV:19.5). Thus the archetype split into two polarities: the benevolent and shadowless Father[4] and the tyrannical and castigating Father, the animus of the mother, which was cast into the shadow. The psychic condition of entrapment in the (M)other, due to the absence of the necessary masculine figure, and its nefarious outcome were manifested at an early stage in a dream little Fritz had the day before the death of his younger brother Joseph, not yet two years old, and just a few months after the death of his father:

> I dreamed that I heard the sounds of an organ coming from the church, as if at a burial. When I tried to find out what was happening, I saw a grave open suddenly and saw my father emerge in his shroud. He hurried toward the church and almost immediately came back with a small child in his arms. He went back into the grave, and the tombstone fell on it. The organ music ceased immediately and I awakened. The following day, little Joseph began to have spasms and died after a few hours. Our pain was immeasurable. My dream had been fulfilled completely. (AML 45)

Jung believed that "the initial dreams which appear at the very outset of the treatment" or are remembered from earliest childhood often have prognostic value: they reveal, "in broad perspective, the whole program of the unconscious" (CW 16:343). Since this is the first dream Nietzsche remembered, and is recalled twice (in 1858 and 1861) in his autobiographical sketch many years after, I will assume it as an "initial" dream.

Due to the abundance of symbols that the dream contains, it can be read from diverse angles and at different levels. First, as the dreamer himself concluded, the precognitive nature of the dream is apparent. This indicates "medium" capabilities, perhaps enhanced by the psychic preeminence of the matriarchal dynamics and the concomitant closeness of the nascent ego to the collective unconscious ambit (with its relativization of time and space, and where the law of causality loses its absolute validity) in the early stages of development.[5] Approaching the dream through a subjective level of interpretation, it is relevant to regard all of the images of the dream—the church, the tomb, the music, the child, the father, etc.—"as personified features of the dreamer's own personality" (Jung, CW 8:509).[6] Also, the dream would appear to enter the category of prospective or anticipatory dreams; that is, it anticipates some possibility in the future.[7]

From a symbolic point of view it is possible to decipher in the dream signs of fatality, since, in addition to announcing the imminent loss of the youngest child of the Nietzsche-Oehler family, the dream also heralded Nietzsche's own tragic destiny: the past, personified by the dead father, comes to claim the future, embodied by the child. Thus the child seems to be condemned from the beginning: "The past must be left behind if it is not to become the gravedigger of the present" (UM II:1). Though Nietzsche's Zarathustra visited the lost isle of his youth to try to recover the past that threatened to become a tomb for him (cf. Z II:11), Nietzsche himself could never overcome his past: he encrypted his father's imago and installed his tomb in himself.

The same fatalistic situation reflected in the initial dream is confirmed in another dream reported by the adult Nietzsche in his *Zarathustra*:

> I had turned my back on all life, thus I dreamed. I had become a night watchman and a guardian of tombs upon the lonely mountain castle of death. Up there I guarded his coffins: the musty vaults were full of such marks of triumph. Life that had been overcome looked at me out of glass coffins. (Z II:19)

And in *Ecce Homo,* Nietzsche expressed the fatality of his existence in these words: "I am, to express it in the form of a riddle, already dead as my father" (EH I:1).

For his part, Hillman suggested that *"The senex is there at the beginning as an archetypal root of ego-formation.* It makes consolidation of the ego possible, giving its rule as an identity within fixed borders" (1994, 20). He concluded: "The *senex* as *spiritus rector* bestows the certainty of the spirit, so that one is led to state that ego-development is a phenomenon of the *senex* spirit" (ibid.). Nonetheless, the father appeared in the initial dream not as a loving and guiding figure, but as a dead man "with waking eyes": a frightening, demonic *senex* who robbed the fragile ego (represented by the little child) of the capacity for development.

Moreover, the dream seems to announce a latently psychotic potential future in Nietzsche. Given the fact that consciousness is symbolically of a masculine nature and that the unconscious is thought of as having a feminine nature, we can see how the dream foreshadows the immersion of consciousness (psychosis) in the recess of the feminine-unconscious (tomb).[8] "When the great mother dominates her son-lover," wrote Neumann, "he is condemned to an early [psychic] death; the unconscious assimilates all the activities of the ego, employing them for its own purpose, and prevents it from ripening the reality of an independent world of consciousness" (1974, 60). Using Jung's method of amplification, we can interpret the dream's images in comparison to similar images from other sources. I esteem that this situation evokes the myth of Uranus, the most ancient and primitive of the patriarchal deities in Greek mythology, god of the heavens and son of Gaea, Mother Earth. Unable to tolerate his progeny, the Titans begotten incestuously with his mother, Uranus[9] returned them, reediting the incestuous condition, to the womb of living magma where they were forced to remain (Titanomachy).[10] Thus Nietzsche's *nous* (spirit) remained trapped in the *physis* (matter) represented by the (bowels of the) earth.[11] In his adolescent years Nietzsche wrote: "Ah, Nature! How strong are the ties with which you imprison me!" (AML 112).

Uranus's myth also embodies a drama that does not take place in the psyche but in the *physis*: the smothered son (ego) materializes or manifests himself through the soma (mother-body-matter). This condition is evident throughout the entire life of the thinker, whose reactions to psychological distress caused numerous psychosomatic manifestations. Due to his strong identification with the father, and his mother's incapacity to provide even basic emotional care, immediately after his father's death he began to have problems with his eyesight that resulted in an early quasi-blindness, similar to that which his father had suffered during the long, agonizing months before his death (cf. Janz 1987, I:42). When nearing his psychological decline, Nietzsche recognized the psychosomatic origin of the problem: "My eye trouble . . . though at times dangerously close to blindness, is only a consequence and not a cause: with every increase in vitality, my ability to see has also increased again" (EH I:1).

Under the aegis of Uranian consciousness the ego remains primordially in a psychic condition we could call that of "mother's son," described as follows by Neumann: "With mother's sons the father-god is eclipsed by the Terrible Mother, and they themselves are unconsciously held fast in the womb and cut off from the . . . solar side" (1991, 189). The spirit encapsulated within the (M)other (matter) leads the ego to act in blind repetition. This psychic condition is reflected in Nietzsche's latter years in his seminal doctrine of the eternal recurrence: "Time itself is a circle. . . . Must not all things that *can* happen *have* already happened?" he asked through the dramatis persona of Zarathustra (Z III:2).

In turn, in view of the terrible fear of the castrating Father—embodied in the primitive animus of the phallic Mother—the person with a Uranian consciousness tends to be docile, complacent, and obstinately attached to the status quo, in order to free himself from the threat of the frightening punishment that might be imposed by the wrathful and primitive god (anxiety of castration). This is the case with the boy Nietzsche, whose extreme docility, affability, and discipline contributed to his being called "little pastor."[12] Like a wild beast, Nietzsche was tamed by the rigid rules and precepts of the mother and surrogates. Nietzsche's sister recounts the following:

> [My brother] was exceedingly strong, and, as a child, very hot-tempered—a characteristic which he did not like to hear mentioned in later years, because, in accordance with the family tra-

dition of the Nietzsches, he soon learned to control himself. When he was older, if he did anything awkward or broke something, for which he had to be scolded, he would grow very red, say nothing, and withdraw silently into solitude. After a while he would reappear with modest dignity, and would either beg for forgiveness, if he had convinced himself of his fault, or else say nothing. (Förster-Nietzsche 1912, 12–13)

On the other hand, one might ask, how would Nietzsche, the child, interpret at such an early age the ephemeral survival of the masculine while the feminine radically held fast to life? The feminine would appear to him later in life as the master of life and death, and in his conception of love as an "eternal war of the sexes" he tended to portray the female as the strongest antagonist.

Furthermore, the appearance of the feminine in a non-humanized or anthropomorphized form (church and tomb) imparts tremendous primitive archetypal force to the dream. The existential conditions of the thinker generate the constellation of the Great Mother archetype in its devouring aspect, and the nourishing and protective feminine aspect (*Mater Ecclesia*) is vanquished in the end by the negative aspect of the archetype (tomb). It is clear in the dream that the child was not taken from his house—he was taken from the church, a place that did not seem to offer the sustenance necessary to nourish and protect him.[13] Echoes of that reality can be found in a sentence uttered by the madman who announces the death of God: "What after all are these churches now if they are not the tombs or sepulchers of God?" (GS 125).

With regard to the dark aspect of the Mother archetype, Neumann suggested:

Behind the archetype of the terrible Earth Mother looms the experience of death, when the earth takes back her progeny as the dead, divides and dissolves them in order to make herself fruitful. This experience has been preserved in the rites of the Terrible Mother, who, in her earth projection, becomes the flesh eater and finally the sarcophagus. . . . Castration, death, and dismemberment on this level are all equivalent. (1991, 58)

If the dream can be interpreted on an objective level regarding its images as reference to objects in external reality, it could reflect the well-known theme of sibling rivalry. However, reading it within the whole context of his life seems to indicate also Nietzsche's desire to meet once again with his beloved father in the place where he would lie until the end of time: in the bowels of the devouring earth. Although little Joseph was "elected" to embody the desire of his older brother, Nietzsche lived this wish symbolically. The psychotherapist Alfred Collins writes that this wish could be understood if we consider that the "Father-Son unity implies that the father's death is also the son's" (1994, 41). At the same time, the death of the father stimulates intense activity in the Father-Son archetype. Collins remarks:

> In India there is an elaborate series of rituals . . . lasting years which serve to work out relations between dead father and son. . . . At the time of the father's death, the son is instructed to lie on top of the father, and one by one the father's vital essences are transferred into the son's being. (ibid., 110)

Perhaps as the result of a transference of the "father's vital essences" to the "son's being," the young Nietzsche dedicated himself enthusiastically to composing music,[14] writing poetry, and reading biblical verses and religious poems.

Nietzsche remembered this period of his life as one of loneliness:

> Even then my personality began to reveal itself. Despite having lived for such a short time, I had already experienced a great deal of pain and affliction and, consequently, I wasn't as vivacious and confident as children usually are. My schoolmates used to make fun of me because of my seriousness. . . . From my early childhood I sought solitude. I felt best in those places where, without being disturbed, I could abandon myself to my thoughts. This usually occurred in the open temple of Nature. (AML, 48)

And in his autobiographical work *Ecce Homo*, Nietzsche confessed:

"At an absurdly early age, at seven, I already knew that no human word would ever reach me" (EH II:10).

It would seem that the mother and substitute mothers, so strongly directed toward academic achievements, were unable to offer him the possibility of constellating a relational Eros.

> The basis of human capacity for relationship is the primal rela-
> tionship with the mother. A successful primal relationship
> makes the child capable of love and of mutual relationships. . . .
> An unsatisfactory primal relationship leads to a negative over-
> stressing of the mother archetype, which endangers . . . the
> child's capacity for love and community. (Neumann 1979, 214)

There was never any sign of camaraderie with his peers. He was able to establish a close friendship with only two boys of similar demeanor, manners, and cultural interests: one was Clemens Felix Gustav Krug, son of a great music lover. The other friend was Eduard Wilhelm Pinder, son of a pious and erudite prelate and royal counselor of the Court of Appeals in Naumburg (cf. Janz 1987, I:46). The fathers of both these friends seemed to combine the most salient characteristics of Fritz's deceased father: love of music and theology.

Pinder gave the following account of Nietzsche's character at this time:

> The fundamental trait of [Nietzsche's] character was a certain
> melancholy, which manifested itself in his whole being. From his
> earliest childhood he loved solitude in which he could give him-
> self up to his own thoughts. To a certain extent he avoided com-
> pany, and would search out the spots where Nature displayed her
> sublimest beauty. . . . His principal virtues were modesty and
> gratitude, which he displayed in the most unmistakable manner
> on every occasion. (cited in Förster-Nietzsche, 1912, I:42–3)

The "modesty and gratitude" of a "little pastor" were the characteristics of a persona with which Nietzsche would identify for the rest of his lucid life.

CHAPTER 2

Pater severitas:
locus melancholicus

Unresolved dissonances in the relation of the character and disposition of the parents continue to reverberate in the nature of the child, and constitute his inner sufferings.

—F. NIETZSCHE, *Human, All Too Human*

Youth and childhood have a value in themselves and by no means only as passageways and bridges.

—F. NIETZSCHE, *Human, All Too Human*

THE CHAPTER OF NIETZSCHE'S CHILDHOOD came to an end when he reached fourteen years of age. On October 5, 1858, he entered the Royal Provincial School of Pforta as a boarder. As soon as he crossed the threshold of the school, the youngster left behind feminine overprotection. In this institution, with its rigors and austerities similar to those of a military academy, students were immersed in the world of the spirit, of erudite knowledge, and particularly of antiquity (cf. Janz, 1987, I:60, 61). Here Nietzsche was to spend the next six years of his life.

His initial impression of this new world was recorded in a letter written to his friend Pinder in February 1859: "When I saw Pforta before me, I thought it was more a jail than an *alma mater*. . . . My heart was beating, full of sacred sentiments: I approached God with a silent prayer, and a profound peace filled my soul." At that time, he still sought support and metaphysical consolation in the idealized Father of the Gospels.[1] There is evidence of belief in divine intervention in autobiographical notes from his youth:

> There is no such a thing as chance; everything that happens has a significance, and the more that science searches out and researches, the more illuminating the thought will be that everything that is, or happens, is a link in a hidden chain. . . . Whatever happens does not happen by chance: a higher being knowingly and meaningfully guides all creation. (AML 182)

Nonetheless, with the inexorable passing of time, the bitter experiences of a painful past impossible for him to overcome, represented by the loss of his father and the subsequent separation from his home, slowly transformed Nietzsche into an ever lonelier, more melancholic and skeptical being. In his infancy he had begun his passage through that "pathos of distance" which he subsequently predicated in his philosophy. The new separation reedited the previous loss and exacerbated his taciturn and reflexive nature, arguably due to what Jung described as "the specific inertia of the libido, which will relinquish no object of the past, but would like to hold it fast forever . . . [an] original passive state where the libido is arrested in the objects of childhood" (CW 5:253).

Even in the search for identity characteristic of adolescence, the boy yearned to have his father reborn in him in order to fulfill his mother's expectations. Following this line of thought, we can see how Nietzsche early in life attempted to incorporate attributes, interests, and the vocation associated with the paternal imago. The magnitude of this identification was in proportion to the Eros linked to the lost object. Consequently, he endeavored to follow an ecclesiastical career. One of his writings from 1858, among others, gives proof of this: "God has led me with the same assurance of a father toward his small son . . . I have taken the firm determination to dedicate myself forever to His service."

The traumatic separation from his father, his "love object," introduced great suffering (*mortificatio*) that is decisively engraved in the structure of his personality. Consequently, the archetypal field formed in his personality would throughout his life attract recapitulations, new editions, of the personal and archetypal constellation of the initial abandonment and subsequent suffering.[2]

Although the alchemical operation of *mortificatio*, with its fateful images of "darkness, defeat, torture, mutilation, death and rotting" (Edinger 1996, 148), is necessary for psychological development in offering awareness of one's own shadow, and consequently is not pathological in itself, fixation or identification with the mortification process leads to a state of entrapment in suffering (martyrdom). "When literalization and exclusive identification [with *mortificatio*] happens," writes the Jungian analyst Lyn Cowan, "[we are] stuck in the mortar which is the mixed ingredients of our life: as the suffering hero, the rejected lover, the hairshirted ascetic, the misunderstood rebel, the unappreciated martyr, the sufferer-on-automatic" (1997, 73). As will be demonstrated throughout this work, Nietzsche seemed possessed by the feeling of being the most deserving man, and, at the same time, the one receiving the least reward. Nietzsche's natural setting was always the *locus melancholicus*. In 1871, he could articulate his psychic condition in a poem titled "To Melancholy":

> Do not reproach me, Melancholy
> That I sharpen my quill to extol you
> And that I, praising you, my head bow to my knee
> Sit like a hermit on a tree stump. . . .
> Thus I sat often in the deep wilderness
> Hideously bent, like a savage at a sacrifice
> My mind on you, Melancholy
> A penitent, though of youthful years!
> Thus sitting I enjoy the vulture flight
> The thundering course of rolling avalanches. . . .
>
> You harsh goddess of the wild Alpine nature
> Mistress, you love to appear near me
> You show me then the vulture's course
> And the laughter of avalanches in order to repel me.

All around breathes a savage lust to murder
Torturous desire to seize life by force!
Seductively there on a rigid cliff
The flower longs for butterflies. . . .

Do not reproach me, evil deity
That I plait rhymes delicately around you
You terrifying phantom—whomever you approach trembles
And quivers when you extend your evil right hand. . . .

Now goddess, goddess, let me—let me rule! (PN 52–3)[3]

The strength of Nietzsche's "I" (constituted gradually by early conflicts) would depend on how his childhood episodes of grief were handled. He was incapable of coping with this grief, and consequently remained in a state of pathological mourning. In his youthful memoirs he wrote: "It is a strange peculiarity of the human heart, that after the loss of a loved one, instead of making efforts to forget the person, we visualize that person as often as possible in our soul."[4]

At this point, it should be underlined that one of the characteristics of pathological mourning is the resentment experienced toward a loved one, who is reproached for the emotional misery brought about by his death. While Nietzsche tried to redeem his father for the pain and guilt he had caused by his departure, this would only be possible after confrontation with the archetypal father, who constitutes the outer mantle, the ontogenic aspect of the archetypal image. Nietzsche never achieved this confrontation and redemption.

In his essay "Mourning and Melancholy" (1917), Freud stressed the differences between the normal grieving process (mourning) and the pathological condition known as "melancholia." Although in both cases he found similar traits such as painful dejection, diminished interest in the outside world, loss of the capacity to love, and inhibition of all activities, in melancholia there is additionally a loss of self-esteem, a self-reproach often culminating in a delusional expectation of punishment, which is absent in the mourning process. Freud likewise considered that grief involved the loss of the "I" due to the strong identification of the ego with the lost object. As in the case of the mourner, the melancholic experiences the painful loss of an object, but the idealization of the object results in concomitant unconscious losses along with the object: "This would suggest that melancholia is in some way related to an unconscious loss of a love-object, in contradistinction to mourning, in which there is nothing unconscious about the loss" (1953, 155). Freud also considered that, unlike mourning, where the object is finally relinquished, in melancholia the release of the object is very difficult because the object has become completely self-identified, meaning that the melancholic is unconscious of the causes of his pathology.

The melancholic, unlike the mourner, experiences the loss of his idealized object in an ambivalent manner. In melancholia, there are "countless single conflicts in which love and hate wrestle together" (ibid., 168). Hate emerges from the feeling that the object has abandoned one,[5] more painful than the feeling in grief, where the loved object has been "taken away." Nietzsche seems to have felt this ambivalence vis-à-vis the idealized father figure elevated to the condition of a divinity: by abandoning him, Nietzsche's father left him at the mercy of the castrating and neurotic women who, with their narrow, pious, moralistic, and sadistic teaching, limited, in the name of God, his freedom and individuality.

The melancholic, according to Freud, exists in a "state of revolt," which implies that he manifests vengeful feelings toward the lost object. This "state of revolt" began to manifest itself at an early stage in Nietzsche's philosophical writings: he reached the point where he aimed to destroy the entire structure of western civilization and its meaning, as a result of the projection of the internalization of the wounding world in which he was raised. His final proclamation was the death of the "Father-God" and, concomitantly, his own disintegration.

Unable to free his libido from the lost object, Nietzsche, like the Fisher King, had a wound that could not be healed. "The shadow of the object fell upon the ego," Freud pointed out (1953, 159), and for Nietzsche that shadow became insurmountable. The melancholy of the *senex*[6] gradually took possession of his being, as is reflected in his early poetry: "I am old like a coin, have become green with verdigris, covered with moss, wrinkles on the figure which once served as adornment" (PN

22). This suggests the kind of situation noted by the Jungian analyst Irene Gad: "The tragic wound that forces a child to become a premature pseudo-adult will, paradoxically, keep the crippled child alive, behind the unbreakable walls of his defensive fortress" (1996, 45).

A negative, saturnine nature, characterized by autocracy and rigidity, by dogmatism, and by depression and rejection of life, became increasingly evident in Nietzsche.[7] He adopted an adult persona as a consequence of his identification with the deceased father. We find an example of this saturnine permeation in a few lines written while his classmates secretly shared the Dionysian nectar:

> With no other company than my own,
> let them surrender themselves to their libations in the cellars
> until they fall to the ground.
> I will dedicate myself to my occupation of gentleman.
> —F. NIETZSCHE (cited in Janz 1987, I:74)

When the *senex* is split from its own *puer* aspect, "Folly and immaturity are projected onto others," writes Hillman (1994c, 21).[8]

In his autobiographical notes, Nietzsche wrote continuously, in reflexive prose or poems, about the serious consequences caused by the irreparable loss of his love object, so necessary at that stage in his life to encourage the breaking away from the familiar protection (the endogamic world) and to set him out on the "hero's journey." The Father is the promoter par excellence of the constellation of the *puer* archetype as hero, the other side of the *senex*. It is the archetype needed to learn to conquer the fear of leaving home and discovering something new and unfamiliar, the Other that triggers individuality and independence in the exogamic world.

For the young Nietzsche, the exogamic world was the school at Pforta, where he continually showed signs of being overcome by the desolate feeling of homelessness.[9] "In memory of my home," he wrote in 1859, "I tried to imagine what a person with no homeland must feel."

> Wild horses take me
> without fear and hesitation

through the wide world.
And whoever sees me knows me,
and whoever knows me calls me
the homeless man.
—F. NIETZSCHE, *Without a Homeland* (NP 13)

On a psychological level, the poem also reflects the feelings of alien-ation and fear characteristic of the ego when it is forced by circum-stances to separate itself from the totality of the unconscious. Thus the poem articulates the symbolic exile from the endogamic world, from the paradisiacal uroboric condition of his childhood. "Thrown out into the world," writes Erich Neumann, "the young man always laments the loss of happiness of the childlike state without anxiety" (1995, 403). And "when paradise is abandoned, the voice of God that spoke in the Garden is abandoned too, and the values of the collective, of the fathers, of law and conscience, of the current morality, etc., must be accepted as the supreme values in order to make social adaptation pos-sible" (ibid.).

Nietzsche never rid himself of this early and painful feeling of uproot-ing. Although he outwardly seemed to act to the contrary by rejecting the God of the "shalt's" and "shalt not's" as well as his German citizenship, living instead from "port to port" as a "roving philosopher," the interior uprooting, as will be shown over time, was in fact devastating.

Around this time, he also wrote the poem "Return" (1859), dedicated to the memory of his father:

That was a painful day,
the day of our farewell . . .
all my hope
destroyed in one fell swoop.
Oh, unfortunate moment!
Oh, fateful day!

I have cried abundantly
at my father's grave;
many, many are the tears

shed on the tomb.
The beloved paternal home
was so empty and sad
that I have abandoned it
to retreat into the *dark forest*.
Hidden in its shadows
I have forgotten all pain,
the quiet stillness brings peace to my heart.
The golden flower of youth,
the roses and the flight of the lark
seem to me to emerge
from the quiet sleep beneath the shadows.
—F. NIETZSCHE (AML 130, emphasis added)

From a classical Jungian perspective, the forest is also a suitable metaphor for the entrance into the unknown world of the unconscious. It should be pointed out that the imaginal scenarios are extremely significant symbols. Thus, as Marie-Louise von Franz, an analyst and close collaborator with Jung, related in her findings, "the forest is especially associated with the bodily unconscious . . . it has to do with the psychosomatic realm of the psyche. . . . The forest . . . has to do with vegetation . . . generally symbolizes the vegetative realms of the psyche where it melts with the material process of the body" (1998, 63). It is another image that reflects the entrapment of the spirit in Mother Earth and the expression of such entrapment through psychosomatic symptoms. Furthermore, it is worth noting that the forests were the first places of worship consecrated to the gods. "The forest, dark and impenetrable to the eye, like deep water and the sea, is the container of the unknown and the mysterious. It is an appropriate synonym for the unconscious," concluded Jung (CW 13:241).

The emotional rending caused by the traumatic "expulsion" from his overprotective feminine home to the boarding school sets Nietzsche on a journey from innocence to suspicion, as his own life and work will progressively reveal.[10] Cast out of the Paradise of childhood, he attempted to penetrate the wilderness, represented by the "dark forest" of the "realm of the Mothers": a sheltering reality into which the adolescent could withdraw. There he tried, without success, to forget "all pain" caused by the irreplaceable lost object, submerging himself in the silence and regressive tranquility of the *Magna Mater*, "the quiet sleep beneath the shadows."

The "homelessness" he felt at school reflected the loss of the boundaries that surrounded his "I am": " 'Fatherland' implies boundaries," suggested Jung, "a definitive localization in space, whereas the land itself is Mother Earth" (CW 19:65). Such "boundaries" are needed to achieve the configuration of an ego differentiated from the (M)other. Lacking the masculine differentiating element needed to provide him a heroic withdrawal from the maternal, as a compensatory act, the psyche of the adolescent manifested a determination to free the son-lover from the innermost recesses of the *Magna Mater*. This determination becomes evident through the emergence of an image—Prometheus and the light of his fire—in which the young man showed an obsessive interest. This seems to reflect an attempt at self-regulation on the part of the psyche:[11] through a necessary state of inflation, it tried to promote the development of the ego by liberating the libido trapped in the unconscious, in the primal beginnings. The Titanic character is a representation of the *puer*, "the Promethean dynamos of the Hero" (Hillman 1994c, 20), the polarity that must be incorporated by the disassociated spirit of the *senex* with which the young man's ego was identified.

At fifteen years of age and subjugated by the Promethean theme, Nietzsche planned a meticulous and vast study of the mythical character. He persuaded his classmate and friend Pinder, member of the elite youthful trio of cultural research self-denominated "Germania,"[12] to dedicate himself to this task:

> Prometheus has become a very interesting topic for me, and it would please me very much if we could both take notes of our ideas on the subject. I am, first of all, trying to conjure up an image as complete as possible of his life, as well as of his entire mythological ambit, with the help of dictionaries, books, treatises on mythology. . . . Write down all the ideas that occur to you when you analyze and study this matter more closely; I will do the same. Immediately afterwards, we can divide the subject

matter: I. Titans. II. Prometheus. III. Epimetheus and Pandora. IV. The last destinies of Prometheus. V. Epimetheus and Prometheus, Pandora (relationship with both). VI. The end of Zeus. (cited in Janz 1987, I:79)

Why Prometheus? Nietzsche considered that a man can free himself from all dependence only by becoming a god, and that rebellion is the way to attain this goal. By interpreting the Promethean myth from a classical Jungian perspective, it is possible to conclude that Prometheus is the archetype of the rebel, the transgressor par excellence, who refused to submit to existing structures. Prometheus represents the principle of rebelliousness within the society of the gods. His sympathy and his complicity are directed to those who, under the order of Zeus, came to occupy an inferior position and were condemned to limitation and suffering. His search, like that of the solar heroes, seemed to have been motivated by his wish to conquer the sterile past on behalf of his vital needs, and at the same time to dominate a present that, like Saturn, tried to "devour him." Prometheus was the bearer of a new order, and the fire stolen from the gods and given to man represents a new form of consciousness.

Another dream of a premonitory nature that Nietzsche had during this time and reported to his sister,[13] in which he foreshadowed his maternal grandfather's death in a vision of the parsonage destroyed and his grandmother sitting among the ruins, shows signs of the Promethean spirit needed to confront that which represents the feared punitive God of the Mother embodied in the maternal grandfather: "Like grass and red poppies, I love to sit in broken churches" (Z III: 16.2).[14] Like his father, Nietzsche's grandfather, David Ernst Oehler, was a pastor. The dream, in addition to bringing Nietzsche into intimate contact with the atemporality of the unconscious, portrays the embryonic stage of one of his most famous subsequent statements: "God is dead!" On an archetypal level, the *mortificatio* of the King, as bearer of the collective God-image, "refers to the death and transformation of a collective dominant or ruling principle" (Edinger 1996, 151), so as to allow the emergence of a new center. At the same time, the indestructible Great Mother personified in the dream by his grandmother is a reminder of his inherent connection to the earth, to the body, to his biological roots.

However, to confront the primitive, omnipotent, wrathful, and castrating God—the intransigent spirit, Uranus, Cronus, or Yahweh, distant from the "human, all too human" in its amoral condition (undifferentiated)—not only courage is needed, but also boundless pride or inflation (hubris) and violence (*atasthalié*). Inflation leads man to believe in his own powers: to be a creator. Consequently, psychologically, the Promethean myth gives rise to the birth and development of the individual ego.

The history of Prometheus is the history of the awakening of consciousness. Although during his last two years at Pforta young Nietzsche showed an emerging and liberating consciousness, the constellated archetype was not integrated with his consciousness so as to "coagulate" into a strong ego. As a result, the *puer et senex* archetype remained separate. The *puer* is formed in the unconscious under the guise of a Promethean complex, as described by Gaston Bachelard, manifested in his compulsion "to know as much as our fathers, more than our fathers, as much as our masters, more than our masters" (1968, 12). On multiple occasions we find proof of this Faustian desire for knowledge. Nietzsche grouped his interests under a categorical imperative defined as an "interior impulse toward universal knowledge": he confessed in his autobiographical notes that "The period from nine to fifteen years of age [was] characterized by a true yearning for 'universal knowledge.' " As a complex, the Promethean spirit would accompany Nietzsche until his declining years. From the unconscious, it gradually acquired a tremendous force.

In 1862, Nietzsche showed the first sign of his loss of faith (cf. Janz 1987, I:83): "I have broken with the legacy of old times . . . with whatever held me in my childhood faith" (GS, "Now and Formerly").[15] And, as always, Nietzsche's psychic drama manifested itself particularly through the *physis*. There exists factual evidence to support this interpretation. The year 1862 was especially important for Nietzsche's mental and physical health (ibid., 115). The medical diary of that time reveals the intensification of his recurring migraines. When Nietzsche was taken to the school physician because of his acute headaches, the doctor noted that Nietzsche's father had died from softening of the brain and that "the son is of the age at which his father was already ill" (Pletsch 1991, 54).

Plestch comments in this respect: "It is . . . particularly striking that Friedrich should have told Dr. Zimmerman about his father's death and especially that he was of an age at which his father was already ill (which of course he was not). He apparently associated his suffering with his father's, and feared he was fated to die in the same fashion" (ibid., 55). Therefore Pletsch raises "the question of whether his headaches might not have been psychosomatic" (ibid.).

Perhaps the psychosomatic symptoms arose due to his guilt feelings for beginning to lose his faith in God. Another consequence of this loss of faith appears in the pronounced nostalgia for death that is evident in various poems from that period.[16] Although the allegory of death is common during adolescence, this stage of "storm and stress" is linked to the fear of castration, and the Oedipal disposition is reactivated due the "killing of the father" through his loss of faith. Fear of death is in turn resolved through the voyage of the hero who conquers death (death-resurrection). Nonetheless, the conditions required to activate the hero archetype do not seem to be present in Nietzsche.

The "death of God" began to be projected by Nietzsche, first of all, in his literary endeavors and poems.[17] Let us recall that the last chapter of his Promethean project refers to "the death of Zeus." In his early essays "Fatum and History" and "Free Will and Fatum," included in his autobiographical notes, Nietzsche, possessed by a Titanic consciousness, defies the cultural canon of the times: he questions religious dogmas and their consequences in an attempt to achieve autonomy.

The ideas in his essays contain, in embryonic form, what would become his subsequent philosophy. In these writings he questions the "truths of the church," attributing to them the "power of habit, the need for something superior, the doubt as to whether during two millennia, mankind might not have let itself be misled by a false image . . . all this maintains an unresolved struggle, until, ultimately, a series of painful experiences . . . leads us once again to the old childish faith." He continues:

> To risk plunging into an ocean of doubt, without guide or compass, is loss and madness for a young brain; most of those who venture to do so are destroyed by the hurricane; only very few discover new regions . . . we must expect great upheavals on the

day when the multitude understands that all of Christianity is founded on gratuitous statements. The existence of God, immortality, the authority of the Bible, revelation, all these will eternally continue to be problems. (cited in Halévy 2000, 21)

The doubts contained in his early essays reflect his restrained anger toward the tyrannical God of the Mother and the abandoning Father-God, imagos incapable of providing him with the psychic resources required to confront the new challenges he faced. He found no support in those transcendent images for his existential journey.

The undifferentiated world of *natura* would win Nietzsche over increasingly as time goes on. Evidence of this is found in the fragment of the unfinished novella "Euphorion" (1862), where Nietzsche portrayed the Euphorion character of Goethe's *Faust II*:[18]

A flood of soft and tranquil harmonies washes over my soul—I do not know what made me feel so melancholy; I would like to weep and then die. It's no good anymore! I am played out, my hand trembles. The crimson dawn plays its multichrome upon the sky, fizzling fireworks, how boring. . . . I feel I am outside the chrysalis. I know me through and through, and would only like to find now the head of my doppelgänger in order to vivisect his brain, or perhaps my own little boy's head all goldilocks. . . . And now, like a beast tied to the millstone, I slowly pull on the rope that men call *fatum*. And this will go on until I end up putrid, or until the butcher cuts me up in pieces and only a few botflies ensure me a bit of immortality. . . . Meanwhile, I'm embarrassed by another idea—perhaps tiny blossoms will burst from my bones, maybe a "violet of the heart" or even—if only the Torturer will aim his micturition upon my grave—a forget-me-not. . . . While I savor all of these ideas about my future—because it is more pleasant to decompose in the moist of the earth than to vegetate under the blue sky, to scrabble as a fat worm is far sweeter than to be a human being—a walking question mark. . . . A silence of death reigns in my room . . . I would like to write the story of my life. . . .Who should read it? *My*

other I's, many of which still wander through the valley of tears.
(AML 197, emphasis added)

These lines overflow with symbols derived from the alchemical oper-
ations of *mortificatio* and *putrefactio*—symbols also related to Saturn,
"black bile," the planet associated with depression and melancholy.
Furthermore, the image of "a beast tied to the millstone" brings to mind
the figure of the mythical Ixion. And "to be put on the wheel in punishment," as in the case of the mythical character, "is to be put into an
archetypal place, tied to the turns of fortune, the turns of the moon and
fate, and the endless repetitions of coming eternally back to the same
experiences without release. Everything moving and nothing changing;
all life as déjà vu" (Hillman 1979, 161).[19] Sacrifice and self-torture are
not equivalent symbols. Although the sacrifice of the ego is a necessary
condition for individuation, at a certain stage of development, torture is
an entrapment in a vicious, compulsive, repetitive circle. It is the impris-
onment of the ego in the snares of the unconscious as blind fate or
fatum. Consequently, Nietzsche's being was left as a mere project, as a
"question mark" or unsolved enigma. The intuitive young man recognized this reality when he himself pointed out his existential situation.

Additionally, those "other I's" are the complexes that, as relatively
autonomous entities within the psyche—"independent beings," according to Jung—offer the conscious personality the experience of many
selves.[20] The essay shows the conflict between the ego-complex and the
other complexes.

Nietzsche's "Euphorion" announced, at an early stage, the risk of the
dominion of the personality due to the splitting of an activated complex.
This risk goes from the possibility of a state of inflation, when the ego
identifies itself with the complex, to the overwhelming of the ego by an
autonomous complex, as in the case of a psychosis.

Without the differentiation or consciousness contributed by the
Father, the boundaries between the "I" and the world are indistinct, and
something important and necessary for the development of the ego is
lost: "Without the father we lose also the capacity . . . recognized as 'discrimination of the spirits': the ability to know a call when we hear one
and to discriminate between the voices" (Hillman 1990, 173–74).

For Nietzsche it was impossible to distinguish the voices coming from his persona, identified by the *senex*, from those coming from his shadow, possessed by the *puer*. This psychic reality created a permanent conflict between the dissonant voices claiming their respective authority in his psyche. The disassociated archetypes of the *puer* and the *senex* are likewise reflected in his autobiographical notes from that time:

> Imagine me seated in my room in the afternoon of the first day of Easter, wrapped in a robe; it's raining softly outside, there is no one else in the room. For a long time I contemplate the blank sheet of paper before me, pen in hand, annoyed at the Babel of topics, events, and thoughts that cry out to be written; some in a very tenacious manner, because they're still young and frothy like mist; but, on the other hand, the mature and aged thoughts that coexist with the young ones rebel like an old man who, contemplating with a skeptical eye, looks down on the anxieties of youth. Let's speak frankly: our spiritual disposition is conditioned by the struggle between those two worlds, the young and the old; we call the succeeding stages of conflict, states of mind or, somewhat derogatorily, humor. (AML 227–28)

What Pforta finally represented as a paternal substitute was presented, years later (1868), by the young man in the following reflections on this topic:

> My father . . . died all too soon; I missed the strict and superior guidance of a masculine intellect. When I came to Schulpforta, I found only a surrogate for a father's education, the uniforming discipline of an orderly school. But precisely this almost military compulsion, which, because it has to affect the mass, treats coolly and superficially what is individual, made me fall back on my own resources. I have rescued my private inclinations and endeavors from the uniform law; I lived a secret cult of certain arts. . . . The external chances were lacking, or I might at that time have ventured to become a musician. For, since my ninth year, music was what attracted me most of all, in that happy state

in which one does not yet know the limits of one's gift and thinks all objects of love are attainable. (cited in Middleton 1996, 47)

As we can see, the philosopher who called himself a "transgressor" was incapable of transgressing the maternal and the paternal symbolic "prosthesis" represented by Schulpforta, despite the fact that this meant going against his own desire and inclination to be a musician. In May 1863, he wrote to his mother:

> My future worries me. . . . What shall I study?. . . How quickly one goes astray due to a momentary preference, a family tradi- tion. . . . There is no question that I must suppress many tastes and, at the same time, acquire new ones. But which will be the unfortunate ones that I will throw overboard? Possibly the crea- tures dearest to me!

The so-called "external chance occurrences" (which one can interpret to be the mother's desire) had already predetermined Nietzsche's indis- putable destiny: he was to be a clergyman like his father. The Promethean spirit, bearer of new visions and values, had been silenced by chaining it, by means of a complex, in the depths of the unconscious. The psyche's attempts at self-regulation had failed, perhaps because the maternal imago still seemed constellated by a specter more threatening than that of Zeus deceived by the rebel Titan. The maternal imago car- ried with it the threat of emasculation. Consequently, the repressed hos- tility toward the mother was compensated by a masochistic, submissive adaptation to her demands, and Nietzsche momentarily kept silent with regard to his criticisms and doubts concerning Christianity in the pres- ence of his mother (cf. Janz, 1987, I:83) so as to avoid a conflict that, in time, would be inevitable. Thus, after graduating from Pforta, he regis- tered at the School of Theology in Bonn.

It is possible to surmise that giving up the musical career he so dear- ly longed for brought about a "transvaluation" of Nietzsche's own typolo- gy. Thus an intuition-feeling was forced to orient itself from the perspec- tive of an intuition-thinking. Music and life were for Nietzsche synony- mous terms. Life, for him, was understood only through music: "Life without music is nothing but an error, exhausting toil, an exile," Nietzsche wrote to Peter Gast in January 1888 (cf. also TI 33). In a letter to his mother, he confessed, "When I don't hear music, everything seems dead to me." If we add that music was to be the bearer of the Eros principle incarnated in his lost father, we can then understand the extent of this vocational renunciation.

CHAPTER 3

The road not taken

Christianity is a conjecture.

—F. NIETZSCHE, *Fatum and History*

God is conjecture.

—F. NIETZSCHE, *Thus Spoke Zarathustra*

NIETZSCHE ARRIVED IN BONN IN mid-October 1864 to commence his studies in theology. The new university student felt impelled, more because of his wish to overcome his misanthropic tendency than because of the cultural ethos, to form part of a student association. Together with his classmate Paul Deussen, he decided to join the fraternity known as Franconia (cf. Janz, 1978, I:120). In addition to his urgent need for belonging, he wished to please his mother and sister: "Most courteous bows to the right and to the left: introducing myself to you as a member of the German student fraternity Franconia!" (Letter to his mother, October 1864).

Confronted with this broad and free "new world," far from the Spartan strictness and constriction of the boarding school, Nietzsche attempted to take on a spirit of camaraderie and to establish contact with the mundane. For several weeks, he let himself be carried away, together with his fellow students, by the environment impregnated with smoke fumes, ethylic vapors, and the din characteristic of the local inns. Nonetheless, these experiences seemed alien to his nature. To mitigate his interior uneasiness, he reproached himself for the hours wasted in this trivial merriment and once again decided to be the austere, discreet, and modest "little pastor":

> At first, I strove to adapt to the norms, to become what is called a "happy student." . . . [However,] the only thing I saw after the excessive drinking, revelry, and debts typical of a student's life was nothing more than the appearance of a very conventional form of the most vulgar philistinism. . . . Little by little I felt stranger in those circles from which, nonetheless, it was not easy to escape. Furthermore, I began to suffer constant rheumatic pains. (AML 262–63)[1]

The student's happiness was a state of mind alien to Nietzsche's nature, which was more in harmony with a significant amount of *mortificatio*; therefore, the pleasure obtained from suffering allowed him to maintain his psychic equilibrium and give his mind coherence. "Pain is also a joy," said Nietzsche as Zarathustra, "For all joy wants itself, therefore, it also wants heart's agony! O happiness! O pain!" (Z IV:19.12).[2] His existential condition made him incapable of adapting himself to his changing circumstances, with their potential to bring about a *joie de vivre*. As a consequence, his libido regressed once more to the unconscious. The (M)other (unconscious) hurled the son (ego) once again into the abysmal vertigo of her irrational magma.

It was that saturnine conscience which Nietzsche hoped would become the *spiritus rector* of the fraternity; consequently, he proposed a reform to achieve this end: the replacement of the hedonistic life with one more committed to erudition. It is not difficult to imagine how such a proposal was received by those young men, eager for adventure and enjoying their newly acquired freedom. Their reply can be summarized in one word: alienation. "My young comrades," he confessed in the autobiographical sketch of his youth, "withdrew from me." Once again, the known archetypal field, described by the Jungian analyst Michael Conforti (1999), characteristic of one abandoned by divine Providence, was constellated, a field consonant with the melancholic character of the young man.

In a dreamlike account titled "A St. Sylvester's Night Dream," there is evidence of the need in his soul at the time when he was to determine his destiny, implied in his first New Year in the "free world":

> All is quiet in my room. . . . It is just a few hours to midnight. . . . My spirit begins to soar over its beloved places. It stops in Naumburg, then in Pforta and Plauen and, finally, returns to my room. In my room? But what is it I see on my bed? There is someone there. He moans very quietly, he is in the throes of death. . . . A dying man! And he is not alone! There are floating shadows around him. And the shadows speak:
>
> "You, wicked year, what did you promise me and what have you given me? I'm poorer than before, and you assured me that I would have good fortune. Damn you!" . . .
>
> Suddenly, everything became bright. The walls of the room disappeared, the roof rose. I looked toward the bed. The bed was empty. I heard a voice:
>
> "You, crazy mad people of these times, who have nothing in your heads and what you have is only in them! I ask you: What have you done? If you want to be and have that to which you aspire, that to which you cling, do what the gods have imposed on you as a test before the prize which will come after the struggle. When you are ripe, the fruit will fall. Not before!"
>
> At that moment, the hands of the clock clicked softly; everything disappeared, the clock struck twelve and in the street someone shouted: "Long live the new year!" (AML 239–41)

As a result of a new libidinal regression, the "I," de-energized, became "moribund," and the autonomous and blaspheming "floating shadows" appeared. This is evidence of a level of consciousness called by Pierre Janet an *abaissement du niveau mental*, a state of relaxation of the psychic restraints, which produces a decrease of the intensity of consciousness. In this uninhibited state of consciousness, the libido, previously in a progressive state, reverses its direction in view of the obstacles that cannot be managed by the ego, with a simultaneous intensification of the unconscious contents. With the "lowering of the guard" brought about by the reversal of the energetic flow, the unconscious contents break into consciousness and assume control of the total personality, at least temporarily. Consequently, the ego's free will is suppressed. Jung described this psychic condition as follows:

> The forward-striving libido which rules the conscious mind of the son demands separation from the mother, but his childish longing for her prevents this by setting up a psychic resistance that manifests itself in all kinds of neurotic fears—that is to say, in a general fear of life. The more a person shrinks from adapting himself to reality, the greater becomes the fear which increasingly besets his paths in every point. Thus a vicious circle is formed: fear of life and people causes more shrinking back, and this in turn leads to infantilism and finally "into the mother." The reasons for this are generally projected outside oneself: the fault lies with the external circumstances. (CW 5:456)

In the St. Sylvester's Night vision,[3] the shadows seemed to be morally inferior personifications, capable of blaspheming, representations of Nietzsche's contained anger. With the lowering of the threshold of consciousness, a relative reversal of "egotic" values occurred and the disassociated anger emerged.

Nonetheless, a disembodied voice from "on high" (the voice of the Self?) issued a supreme decree: "Do what the gods have imposed on you as a test." Marie-Louise von Franz suggested the following in this regard: it is only "when the shadow is partially integrated that the I will be able to contribute to compliance with its destiny." When the shadow is not integrated with consciousness, that is, when the symbolic images that have emerged from the unconscious have not been understood by the experiencing subject, "another factor present in the unconscious, the Self, will assume the major part of this function" (1993, 170).[4]

Strongly identified with the deceased father, Nietzsche experienced his self as moribund. This situation seems to be reflected in the disappearance of the "other dying man" at the end of the vision, which the taciturn young man did not attribute to his own internal being but only to the death of the "old year," without realizing that an archetypal drama was taking place, a ritual drama of renewal that emerged spontaneously from the psychic depths.[5]

The religion historian Mircea Eliade, in *The Myth of Eternal Return,* perceived that the ancient New Year rites or dramas symbolize the periodic effort to escape from the profane to the sacred, an attempt to abolish the past and destroy the old year, in order to begin the new year with a state of consciousness that is outside time altogether. Such rites offered the individual the possibility of escaping from the vicissitudes and miseries of temporal existence through contact with the archetypal substratum: "Ritual projects him into the mythical epoch of the beginning" (1991, 22). Nietzsche's psyche seemed to update this ancient rite on St. Sylvester's night.[6]

In a strong activation of the unconscious contents that may reflect the fragility of the ego and its proclivity toward psychic disassociation (shattered ego), Nietzsche decided "to get to know the human being empirically, without letting myself be influenced in my task by any known belief or doctrine" (AML, 246). His search was driven by a psychic need for knowledge of his own identity. At the same time, he seemed to be impelled by the unconscious Promethean complex to feel a general dissatisfaction with collective and cultural values. In order to achieve what appeared to him to be a goal projected toward the general human aspect, he undertook an exercise we could describe as "active imagination." Protected by the gloomy darkness of his room, he gave free rein to the emergence of images without the "intervention of the will." He proceeded to draw all that emerged spontaneously from his psyche: "images and figures are produced unintentionally" (ibid.).

The symbols that emerged from this research were not preserved. Nietzsche seems to have been unable to establish a dialogue with his fantasy-images or to integrate them in his consciousness, as the continuous and subsequent appearance of autonomous complexes indicates. What does seem clear is the fact that Nietzsche tried to "unregister himself," to free himself from inherited truths, from collective beliefs or doctrines, "currency without value,"[7] in order to find his own individuality. As a result, his discontent with his academic choice, the dogma-related discipline, grew *in crescendo.* The Christian symbols no longer mediated psychic power. "As regards theology," he wrote, "I occupied myself solely with the philological aspect of biblical criticism and the issue of researching the sources of the New Testament" (cited by Janz, 1987, I:125).

With the regression of the libido, the Promethean complex was let loose, taking over Nietzsche's consciousness, and he lent it his voice in order to openly violate his family's expectations. His firm decision provoked the crumbling of his mother's dreams; a violent scene took place within the symbiotic dyad (cf. Janz, 1987, I:128). From that moment, following an intrinsic and symbolic need, the young man unsuccessfully attempted to distance himself spiritually from his mother, literalizing a *separatio* that should be resolved in a symbolic ambit. Separating *de facto* from the mother does not imply the separation from the maternal archetype that makes it possible to exercise the free will; thus his act of transgression in becoming "a humanist rather than a believer" (Pletsch 1991, 68) was not sufficient to allow his own differentiation from the (M)other.

This confrontation also did not spare him the enormous suffering caused by his mother's lack of understanding and her subsequent tendency to meddle, in a violative and reiterative manner, in his life. It was at this time that the figure of his sister Elisabeth, his erstwhile playmate, permanent confidante, and ally, came on the scene: Elisabeth, who later had such a nefarious and decisive influence both on Nietzsche's personal life and on his work. In an attempt to bring the "lost sheep" back to the fold, she wrote to her beloved brother: "It is necessary to search for the truth in that which is most painful, and it is not possible to believe in the mysteries of Christianity without hard work. Consequently, the mysteries of Christianity are true."[8] Nonetheless, the young man was eager to know his own "truths" and would dedicate the rest of his existence to searching for them. Realizing the sterility of any attempt at "reconversion," and perhaps fearing that in retaliation she might be separated from the object of her adoration, as had happened with her mother, Elisabeth stopped persisting.

During the time Nietzsche spent in Bonn, there was no evidence of an amorous or erotic relationship (cf. Janz, 1987, 121). With his lack of knowledge of any image of anima except the incestuous one, any actual approach to the feminine, excluding the mother and sister, could awaken a threat of emasculation. Respecting Nietzsche's incapacity to show disloyalty to the maternal imago, his friend Deussen described an episode that later inspired the writer Thomas Mann to create his well-known work *Doktor Faustus* (1947). In February 1865, when Nietzsche was twenty years old, he traveled to Cologne alone. There he asked a coachman to show him all the sights of the city worth seeing. The coachman interpreted this as a very refined way of asking to be taken to a brothel. The next day, Nietzsche told his friend:

> I saw myself suddenly surrounded by half a dozen apparitions attired in gauze and sequins, who looked at me expectantly. For a while, I didn't know what to say or do. Almost instinctively, I immediately walked toward the piano, as the only being with a soul in that entire group, and played a few chords. I was then able to free myself from my stupefaction, and walked out to the street. (cited by Janz, 1987, I:121)

Deussen's comment was that during the time they were together *"mulierem nunquam attigit"*—Nietzsche "never touched a woman" (ibid.)

Indeed, the "Eternal Feminine" incarnate in a woman represented his greatest fear: "Eternal-Feminine is designed to induce fear in men" (BGE 163). In an attempt to free himself from that dreaded ensnaring object, the feminine body (see GS 59), Nietzsche took refuge in music, so as to "elevate his spirit and lead it to goodness."

As for his academic choice, it was suspended while awaiting the outcome of his dilemma: music or philology? Both possibilities were presented to him, embodied in two very close, relevant figures, in frank opposition in Bonn's academic milieu: Otto Jahn and Friedrich Ritschl. Although Nietzsche gave signs of being more affectionately inclined toward Mozart's biographer, Jahn, he opted for Ritschl, his philology professor: "And how easily men like Ritschl can influence us, how easily can they draw us toward paths that are far from those of our own nature," he confessed in a letter to his friend Muschacke in August 1865.

Ritschl seemed to echo the "you must" of the maternal imago, dissuading Nietzsche from any other field of study, such as music: "If you want to become a strong man," he advised his student, "you must specialize" (Halévy 2000, 32). Philology, an orthodox career, would provide a prestigious position as a university professor, and Nietzsche, fearful of being carried away by his passions, "Sirens' songs," felt the need to tie himself, like Odysseus, to the firm mast of the solar world represented by academe: "The feeling of being unable to delve into the deepest part of the universe throws me into the arms of scientific rigor. Thus, there remains the longing to know that one is safe from the constantly changing feelings of the world of artistic inclinations, in the safe haven of objectivity," he wrote in his autobiographical notes on his youth.

Urged by the growing dissatisfaction of his fraternity brothers, Nietzsche tried to find his way in another city. Thus his friend Carl von Gersdorff's suggestion in favor of Leipzig "had a strong effect on him," writes Janz. "He made a firm decision to move to this city, joining the project. When not much later Ritschl accepted the professorship at the University of Leipzig, Nietzsche felt totally justified with regard to his decision" (1987, I:135).[9]

His conflict with the other Franconians, projection screens of his own internal conflicts, led him to abandon the city as a haunted fugitive on August 9, 1865:

> I left Bonn like a fugitive. I was at the Rhine pier by midnight. . . . I didn't feel even the slightest impression that I was leaving such a beautiful place, a countryside covered with flowers, and a group of young comrades. On the contrary, I was running away from them. . . . My temperament found absolutely no satisfaction among them . . . I was still too timidly caught up in myself and had no strength to keep up my role. . . . Everything was imposed on me. . . . I felt in an anguished way that I had done nothing for science, little for life, and that I had only known how to make mistakes. . . . While I watched the slowly dimming lights that indicated the city's bank, everything conspired to give me an impression of flight. (AML 262)

Was he really fleeing from his comrades or from the implacable "interior law" of his moral conscience, desirous of separating him from life? "The content of our [moral] conscience," wrote Nietzsche, "consists of

all that which, in our childhood, was demanded from us, without explanation and regularity, from persons we respected or feared" (WS 52). He
trusted his steps to the father-mentor Ritschl, the orthodox scholar—
"his scientific conscience," as he described him—to protect him from
the dangers inherent in a new course.

On May 29, 1865, Nietzsche wrote to his mother about his plans to
leave for Leipzig to begin his studies in philology, hoping to "make her
happy with the news" and yearning to evoke in her a feeling capable of
assuring his expiation. Having abandoned his dream of becoming a musician—a dream his mother never would have approved—he was still
unaware that his decision simply implied the imposition of another
mask. He had again positioned himself in the psychic place in which he
became the object his mother desired.

Still, he did not fail to let his mother and sister know how much it had
upset him to give up his genuine wishes. In a letter addressed to them,
dated November 1865, he wrote:

> Do your duty! Very well, I do, or try to, but where does my duty
> end? . . . Have the demands of our human character been satis-
> fied by complying with the demands of the situation in which we
> have been born? And if we didn't want to act in this manner, if
> we decided only to follow ourselves and to force others to accept
> us as we are, then what?

These questions were left pending, and only Nietzsche, not his mother or sister, would have to answer them.

CHAPTER 4

The demons whisper in Leipzig

There is no such thing as coincidence;
everything that happens has a meaning.

—F. NIETZSCHE (1861)

A man may keep the commandments but be far from God.

—HERMAN HESSE

ON OCTOBER 17, 1865, NIETZSCHE ARRIVED IN Leipzig. The following day
he presented himself before the university council. If he had any doubts
concerning his new destination, an event that could be considered an
omen cleared his mind of them: the day he registered, the institution was
celebrating the one hundredth anniversary of Goethe's registration at the
university. "I can't tell you how much this casual coincidence has meant
to me. . . . It was certainly a good omen for my years in Leipzig, and the
future certainly proved it right" (AML 267). In addition to this notable
coincidence, public recognition as the anointed one of the "patriarch"
Ritschl filled his soul completely with the joy of victory:[1]

> According to academic custom, Ritschl was expected to present
> his inaugural lesson publicly in the main lecture hall. . . . While
> he walked toward the rear of the hall, he suddenly exclaimed,

"Oh, Mr. Nietzsche is here with us!" and greeted me enthusiastically with a wave of his hand. (ibid., 268–69)

Furthermore, the enthusiasm shown by the famous professor for
Nietzsche's work on Teognis encouraged him to persevere on the chosen
path: "[Ritschl] stated that he had never seen, in the work of a third-
semester student, such scientific rigor. . . . I had already experienced the
taste of fame" (ibid., 276).

The young disciple had projected the imago of the kind father on the
mature man of letters whose presence allowed him to sustain his ego
ideal. After the public and notorious acknowledgment, a relationship of
intimacy was established between the fatherless Nietzsche and the
childless Ritschl (cf. Janz 1987, I:177). As will become evident,
Nietzsche, until his early adulthood, repeatedly showed a strong psychological need to find a surrogate father, to fulfill the paternal function
which he lacked, and to promote his role identification. Ritschl was one
among many in this lifelong search.

In a letter dated April 1867, addressed to his friend Deussen,
Nietzsche still seemed, or wished to be, convinced of having made the
right choice: he confessed that he felt like a man who "returns from the
labyrinth of theological scruples to celebrate his marriage to philology" in
a dignified Apollonian wedding.

Nonetheless, at the beginning of his first trimester in Leipzig, in a letter to his aunt, he manifested certain metaphysical concerns that had
arisen in his new and unfamiliar surroundings and which indicated that
the enigma of his existence, his true identity and scholarly vocation, had
yet to be solved:

You know well that every seven years, the human body renews
itself totally and completely; hence the importance of the numbers seven, fourteen, and twenty-one. Consequently, I begin to
see myself for the fourth time in a new body. But what happens
to our soul? Has it also transformed itself three times? Does it
have our characteristics, our capacities, and such scarce consis-
tency that it likewise disappears every seven years, leaving a new
one in its place? . . . But what is going to happen to me in this

fourth circle of seven years? Everything must be decided there; once it has concluded, man will have been completed; the structure of his building will already be there, consummated; we can continue to embellish it, but the building will remain. (cited in Janz 1987, I:149)[2]

In his autobiographical notes dated from September 1867 to April 1868, there is evidence of Nietzsche's indecision regarding his identity:

At that time, as a result of several painful experiences and cruel disillusions, I felt as though I were drifting, alone, without solid principles, without hope and without even a pleasant memory. The only desire that set me aflame from morning till night was to build a life for myself that would adapt to my nature. (AML 272)

"When an inner situation is not made conscious, it happens outside, as fate," stated Jung (CW 9, II:126). As if following this "mysterious sequence," there occurred to Nietzsche what appears to have been an epiphany of Hermes, god of synchronicity, a decisive event in his life: the discovery of Schopenhauer: "Now, imagine the impact on me when I read Schopenhauer's main work under those circumstances" (AML 272). This discovery was wrapped in a mysterious atmosphere, which Nietzsche described as follows:

I picked up this totally unfamiliar book [*The World as Will and Representation*] and began to leaf through it. I don't know what demon whispered to me: "Take this book home with you." In any case, this occurred contrary to my usual custom of not rushing into the purchase of books. . . . There, in every line, renunciation, negation, resignation cried out; here I saw a mirror in which I beheld the world, life, and my own soul in terrifying magnificence. . . . I was seized by a powerful need for self-knowing—and even for "self-gnawing." (ibid., 272–73)

In addition to Nietzsche's encounter with a philosophical theory that opened up for him the world of the irrational and could explain the origin of his strong feelings of identification with natural phenomena,[3] what seemed to attract the young philosopher most about the Schopenhauerian vision was the redemption of man through art and particularly through music.[4] Both thinkers shared the same psychic perspective, and their views interlaced under the aegis of the same Eros incarnated in music. For Nietzsche, music remained the direct path to the tragic emotion that profoundly moves the body without needing the intervention of resources such as the figures and concepts used in other forms of art. The mythopoeic power of music arises, according to Nietzsche, as a direct expression of the essence of being, the Dionysian world (see BT 17).

Moreover, in Schopenhauer's weltanschauung Nietzsche found a reflection of his own tragic and secret worldview. His most intimate fibers vibrated at the sound of the tragic sense of life. Nietzsche found in Schopenhauer a kindred spirit hurled into a world abandoned by Providence, a world without God. Despite its pessimism, he found Schopenhauer's world liberating, because by depriving man through the "death of God" of the theological pillars, there was no longer any room for the collective morality against which Nietzsche had intimately and secretly struggled since his late adolescent years.

In a letter dated October 1868, addressed to his friend Erwin Rohde, Nietzsche furthermore stated that what fascinated him about Schopenhauer was the "ethical air, the Faustian odor, Cross, Death, grave."[5] "You ask me for an apology on Schopenhauer?" he inquired in a letter to his friend Deussen. "I feel on home ground in these obscure regions."[6] Contrary to the father-surrogate Ritschl, the pessimistic philosopher validated Nietzsche's own Dionysian nature and would become the "Spirit-Father" toward whom the passionate young man would direct his soul for some time.

In antiquity, the demonic served as spiritual and divine mediator, driving man's actions toward the fulfillment of his assigned destiny. In moments of conflict, confusion, and doubt, at the crossroads of our existence, "something" manifests itself within us, a something possessed of foreseeable knowledge and resources capable of pointing out the direction to follow or the options available. That "something" is Hermes, an Agathos Daimon capable of offering a solution through a dream or fantasy or some object or person we find in our path, some incident that can attract our attention and indicate the right way: "whatever marks an epoch in [me] came in my way by accident," declared Nietzsche (EH II:3).[7]

God's imago underwent a protean metamorphosis, appearing embodied in Schopenhauer. Idealizing the pessimistic philosopher whom he called his father,[8] Nietzsche literalized the Hermetic message and initiated a "conversion." He resorted to asceticism as a means of salvation. Deep inside, and in what appears to be a compensatory mechanism, he wanted to silence blind will in an attempt to escape from his inner turmoil. As a melancholic he was also satisfying his sense of denigration and his unconscious need for self-punishment. Consequently, the new disciple and "son" directed "an unbridled hate" toward his own self. For fourteen uninterrupted days he submitted himself to various physical tortures, limiting his hours of sleep and his intake of food to a minimum. These exercises in "self-flagellation" produced a state of "constant nervous excitement" that threatened to lead to madness, as Nietzsche himself confessed (AML 273). Through such severe corporal punishment, he was perhaps attempting to free himself from the captivity of the "Mother-dragon," the Schopenhauerian unconscious will. Paradoxically, this kind of attitude can only bring about greater submission and suffering. "The non-liberation of the captive," Neumann considers, "expresses itself in the continued dominance of the Great Mother under her deadly aspect, and the final result is alienation from the body and from the earth, hatred of life, and world negation" (1991, 206). Nonetheless, "the demands of everyday life, the ambition and imposition of regular studies," as Nietzsche concluded, served as a mast to which he could cling, momentarily saving himself from the danger of madness (cf. AML 274).

The new apostle attempted to proselytize in order to convert his closest friends to the recently acquired Schopenhauerian "religion." He thus became the prophet of the new Gospel and replaced, although temporarily, the dying Judeo-Christian God with Schopenhauer. With his tragic vision of life, Schopenhauer came to be considered by Nietzsche as a consolation for all the fatalities inherent to existence.[9]

As a result of his "conversion," the initial enthusiasm of "his nuptials with philology" hastily began to crumble. The following lines addressed to Carl von Gersdorff in April 1867 showed signs of existential unrest: "The hundred books on the table in front of me are so many tongs which pinch out the nerve of independent thought. . . . One cannot go one's own way independently enough. Truth seldom dwells where people have built temples for it and have ordained priests." Nietzsche subsequently confessed to the same friend his idea that philology was the result of a "faulty childbirth of the goddess Philosophy. A creature engendered by an idiot or a cretin."

Nonetheless, Nietzsche found it difficult to commit a new and necessary transgression in order to "remain true to [his] spirit." An ego, only slightly differentiated from the (M)other, tends to adhere strictly to the status quo, identifying with the persona. This identification led Nietzsche to carry out actions and adopt attitudes that reflected collective expectations. All other aspects of the personality that differed from dominating cultural precepts were thrown back toward the shadow. Consequently, the demons of yore constellated once again, because the more the shadow is ignored, the greater its tendency to activate itself and to exercise its autonomous nature. From the shadow, the split-off contents will lie in wait to catch the ego by surprise, because the greater the persona, the greater the "shadow" it will project.

With a decrease in conscious will, the shadow, as an autonomous complex, may take possession of the ego. Subsequently, the individual will be surprised by the negative effects of this possession, since, according to the Episcopal priest and Jungian analyst J. A. Sanford, "the disdained qualities do not cease to exist simply because their direct expression has been denied. Instead, they live within us and form a second personality" (1998, 50). Under appropriate circumstances, they emerge with a strength equivalent to the degree of repression. Control of the shadow produces a dangerous subworld, capable of exploding destructively. This type of condition manifested itself in Nietzsche through a strange episode, described in his notes, dated between the fall of 1868 and the spring of 1869: "What I am afraid of is not the terrible shape behind my chair but its voice; also not the words but the horrible unarticulated and inhuman tone of that shape. Yes, if only it spoke as human beings do" (AML 301).

From a psychological viewpoint, Jung pointed out that demons are nothing more than intruders from the unconscious: spontaneous outbursts of unconscious complexes within the specter of consciousness. Concerning this, von Franz stated:

> Jung emphasized that the demonic works, with negative effect, mainly at the moment when an unconscious content of seemingly overwhelming power appears on the threshold of consciousnesses; then it will lay hold of the personality in the form of a possession. Before such content is integrated into consciousness, it will always *appear physically*, because it "forces the subject into its own form." (1995, 105)[10]

The demonic seems to contain the creative seeds for our own regeneration or redemption. Consequently, as in the case of the shadow, the constructive integration of the demonic into our conscious personality could make us participants in the creative process through self-assertion: "The daemonic, therefore, would be the creative *in statu nascendi*, not yet realized, or 'made real' by the ego" (von Franz 1995, 105).

However, demons can be benign allies, as in Socrates' case,[11] or malignant enemies, who for example did everything possible to deceive Descartes during his eager search for the truth. Therefore the conscious ego must assume the final word.

The content of the words spoken by Nietzsche's demon is unknown. Yet the inhuman and terrifyingly inarticulate tone of voice frightened him terribly. After this episode, there is no recorded evidence of any other similar psychopathological manifestation during this period of his life.[12] Nonetheless, if one is to judge by various early writings, as well as by his letters and subsequent works, the experience of "hearing" voices was not alien to him (see Ross 1994, 206). Even in his *Zarathustra*, Nietzsche wrote: "O my brothers, I heard a laugher that was no human laughter; and now a thirst gnaws at me, a longing that never grows still. . . . Oh, how do I bear to go on living! And how could I bear to die now!" (Z III:2.2).

The cause of these hallucinations could be found in the continuous denial of his own truth, and "for every truth that departs from the world, there arrives a ghost" (Heller 1976, 37). However, whatever that ghostly voice uttered, Nietzsche remained faithful to the learning and teaching of philology until 1879. This seems to indicate that the psychological defense mechanisms had been triggered, in order to avoid new persecution anxieties: "But to keep me from whirling, my friends tie me tight to this column" (Z II:7). Thus Nietzsche tied himself to the column of academe.

Yet, by denying the somber contents rather than integrating them into consciousness so as to reduce their demonic autonomous power, Nietzsche only worsened his situation. As a result, we can say that Nietzsche unquestionably became a man with a "haunted mind." According to Jung, the more unconscious the Self is for the ego, the more it will correspond to the Freudian superego.[13] At the same time, it will be "a source of perpetual moral conflict" (CW 11:396). The Jungian analyst Mario Jacoby agrees with this opinion when he considers the emergence of a disembodied voice a manifestation of a "conflict between an imposed moral code and a personal conscience" (1985, 148).

Nietzsche's excessive sense of duty also kept him morally tied to the figure of his mentor, Ritschl. In 1867 he wrote to Deussen: "You cannot imagine how personally tied I am to Ritschl, so much so that I don't want to, and cannot, free myself."

Free will, according to the psychologist S. A. Diamond, is determined by how we become aware of and respond to the consequences generated by the blind urges of the demonic that act upon the ego. The individual's response "to the blind, obliging, psychobiological urgings of the daimonic; and [the way he is] willing to assume the responsibility for the consequences" (1996, 103) becomes an ethical act. Although Nietzsche reached a point where he understood his suffering as a result of his own alienation, he inhibited the exercise of his free will, of his "will to power," letting himself be dragged by "unconscious actions": "Our acts," he admitted at that time, "have to occur in an unconscious manner" (AML 301). Thus he let himself be seduced once again by the paternal imago of Ritschl, coinciding with his ego ideal, and accepted a teaching position at the University of Basel.

In January 1869, a professorship became available in classical philology at the prestigious Swiss university, and the counselor for academic affairs contacted Ritschl, requesting information on an appropriate candidate. Nietzsche's professor and protector responded with the following note:

Although there are many young men whom I have seen develop before my eyes in almost thirty-nine years, I have never known one who, so soon and at such an early age, could achieve such a high degree of maturity as this Nietzsche. . . . I foresee that he will some day occupy one of the most prominent positions in German philology. . . . You probably think I am describing some type of phenomenon, and in truth that is what he is. (cited by Janz, 1987, I:219)

Such a superlative recommendation from a scholar as renowned as Ritschl was, of course, decisive, and at twenty-four years of age Nietzsche was named professor at the University of Basel. He was awarded a doctoral degree without having to submit a formal dissertation, a unique case in the German academic world (cf. ibid.). With this appointment, Nietzsche "tightened the bonds" so as to cling even more painfully to the mast of collective expectations, and consequently augmented the repression of his Dionysian nature.

In various letters, Nietzsche confessed how the "laurel wreath" represented by the new appointment was received as a "crown of thorns": "We are undoubtedly toys of destiny; just last week I thought I would write you and propose that we study chemistry. . . . And now the demon of 'destiny' seduces me with a chair in philology" (Letter to Rohde, 1869).

At around that same time, once again Nietzsche wrote to his friend von Gersdorff concerning the new position: "Now the stern goddess rules, the daily dutiful task. . . . One does not enter professional work and dignities with impunity—it just depends on whether the bonds are of iron or of thread . . . may Zeus and all the muses protect me." Words like "demon," "destiny" and the "stern goddess" who rules denote once again Nietzsche's fatalist view: the domination of the ego by the world of the (M)other.

According to Jung, the strength of the ego is measured based on how much will is exercised to face opposition and resistance, manifesting a will to power (cf. CW 16:109). Nietzsche proved to be incapable of exercising his self-proclaimed "will to power"; renouncing freedom and his newly acquired love of philosophy, as before he took on a mask, hoping "to thus bring happiness" to the implacable maternal-filial imago. As soon as they heard of his prestigious appointment, mother and sister ran all about Naumburg to spread the news (cf. Janz, 1987, I:222). Consequently, Nietzsche's "I" was increasingly diluted in the desire of the Other and, as in a game of mirrors, would reflect collective ideals. " 'You must suffer privations, you have to suffer privations,' is a motto valid everywhere, in all human life," Nietzsche stated in a letter sent to Marie Baumgartner in August 1877 and applied fervently to his own self.

"My formula for greatness in a human being is *amor fati*: that one wants nothing to be different, not forward, not backward, not in all eternity" (EH II:10). How far the thinker is still from converting his demonic fate into his desired *amor fati*, his love for Nemesis: "It is certainly a painful experience to have to renounce one's own autonomy for the unconscious acceptance of external impressions, to repress capacities of the soul for the power of habit, and, against all will," he wrote in "Fatum and History" (1862).

What the "good pastor" seems to lack is the "most necessary agent of liberation from the harmful mother bond," that is, anger. The Jungian analyst J. W. Perry suggested in this regard:

> The proper function of anger is to rise up and protest against the annihilative aspect of the mother. The anger itself tends toward this function, to give vent to the long-accumulated emotions of resentment[14] and thus introduce some saving consciousness into the relationship with the mother. On the archetypal level the anger appears as the aggressive fight of the hero (the prototype of the ego's self-assertion) against the Terrible Mother monster; his aim is to force her to yield up the vital treasure she hoards, the symbol of the self, that is, to grant him his first experience of selfhood. . . . Hostility is the great separator or differentiating agent, just as its opposite, love. (1976, 50)

But in Nietzsche's case, anger was not assimilated by consciousness. Anthony Storr suggested: "It has been generally recognized that [melancholics] have a particular difficulty in handling their aggressive impulses. Instead of being able to express aggression against others who frus-

trate or deprive them, they turn their aggression inwards against themselves in self-reproach, punish themselves for the hostility they feel"
(1993, 106). This psychic situation was confirmed by Nietzsche himself
when he stated in his work *On the Genealogy of Morals* that "the instinct
of the wild, free man, could no longer be discharged outwardly and thus
had to be turned inwardly. This was the origin of guilt feelings." Only in
his later writings did Nietzsche use his pen as a weapon and paper as his
battlefield: he attacked everything established with strong hammer
blows, be it philosophy, science, religion, or morality.[15]

MANIFESTATIONS OF NIETZSCHE'S EROS IN LEIPZIG

Only that which is similar
seeks to attract the soul.
—F. NIETZSCHE (1862)

IN ADDITION TO THE EROS linked to his professor Ritschl and to his new
god-Schopenhauer, Nietzsche established an emotional relationship
with only one other person while in Leipzig: Erwin Rohde,[16] a faithful
and devoted friend for many years.

Nietzsche adorned his new comrade with the most sublime attributes,
because he was "incapable of loving without admiring" (Halévy 2000,
43).[17] The idealization process, described by Nietzsche himself as a kind
of Dionysian intoxication, was an unmistakable seal of his personality.

Rohde had also been a disciple of Ritschl's in Bonn and, like
Nietzsche, had followed him to Leipzig. Even if the two friends were
separated by "a great distance . . . in the scientific field"—Nietzsche
being more intuitive and passionate and Rohde more rational
(Nietzsche, AML 296)—they were linked by indefectible ties: love for
solitude, for music, and for Schopenhauer; a passionate character; a similar disciplinary path; and an innate curiosity to go beyond the confines
of academic erudition. Nietzsche established with Rohde what seems to
be a specular relationship. Unlike the kinship with Ritschl, in which the
mentor placed his ideal over Nietzsche's "I," Nietzsche's friendship with
Rohde was more like a relationship between twins. Ritschl used to call

Nietzsche and Rohde "the Dioscuri," Castor and Pollux (see Cardew, 2004, 458). "There is no sense of what has lately been called 'otherness' in this duality [Castor and Pollux]" (ibid., 460).

Janz described the new comrade as a young man with "a rich spiritual life [that] closed itself to the world and withdrew behind a protective wall of brusqueness. His passionate nature prevented him from exercising restraint; he was extraordinarily vulnerable and, deep inside, he had an almost feminine overwhelming need for love and sweetness" (Janz 1987, I:182). Rohde was one of the first to recognize Nietzsche's genius, and followed his career very closely. With this kindred spirit Nietzsche developed an intense relationship, until their particular circumstances brought about a separation that, in 1887, would become final.[18]

Nietzsche's Eros, an Eros with a masculine source,[19] constellated with Rohde. James Hillman established a distinction between the Eros originating in the feminine and that originating in the masculine:

> The contemporary analytical confusion of soul with Eros has its source,[20] I believe, in the archetypal perspective of Aphrodite. She would insist that we look at phenomena through the eyes of Eros, her son. By maintaining this perspective she would perpetually be reclaiming this son to serve a Venusian and venereal view of soul and femininity. She above all has an interest in keeping Eros on the feminine side of the *coniunctio*. If Eros is kept on her side, his eroticism will be stimulated in an aphrodisiac fashion, giving that cast to Eros in our consciousness today which is so highly sexualized. Socratic/Platonic Eros . . . is definitely masculine.[21] This Eros had Hermes in his genealogy. (1996a, 29)

In Nietzsche's case, it would seem that the second origin is the most appropriate: an Apollonian, masculine Eros, a nonsexualized connecting principle capable of elevating him to a higher sphere.

In January 1869, Nietzsche wrote a few lines, an ode to his friendship with Rohde, emphasizing its sublime character:[22]

Whoever is . . . lonely because of the caprice of nature, because of a curiously brewed mixture of wishes, gifts, and endeavors of the will, he knows what an "incomprehensible lofty marvel" a *friend* is; and if he is an idolater, he must first and foremost erect an altar to the "unknown god who created a friend." . . . To those exhausted travelers whose way through life leads through the desert; a friendly spirit consoles them when they lie in the sand, and he moistens their parched lips with the divine nectar of friendship.

Nietzsche and Rohde shared the fullness of a private world: "We both enjoyed ourselves like artists who momentarily withdrew from the impulse of the stimulating will to live, and abandoned themselves to pure contemplation" (AML 296). Jung, in turn, described the Eros shared by same-sex partners, and its relationship with the maternal complex, as follows:

Thus a man with a mother complex may have a finely differentiated Eros instead of, or in addition to, homosexuality. . . . This gives him a great capacity for friendship, which often creates ties of astonishing tenderness between men and may even rescue friendship between the sexes from the limbo of the impossible. . . . Often he is endowed with a wealth of religious feelings, which help to bring the "ecclesia spiritualis" into reality; and a spiritual receptivity which makes him responsive to revelation. (CW 9, I:164)

The constellation of Eros in the figure of Rohde thus seemed to compensate Nietzsche for the frustration generated by following the path of "Thou shalt!" rather than his inner calling.

This was also the best period of Nietzsche's life with regard to his physical and mental health: "The second year [Nietzsche] spends in Leipzig is perhaps the happiest in his life," Halévy declares (2000, 41). And this fact is confirmed by Janz, who writes: "From the point of view of health, those first two years in Leipzig were extraordinarily good for Nietzsche, much better than at any other time in his life" (1978, I:192).

It is worth highlighting that during this period Nietzsche began to show a peculiar characteristic that remained throughout most of his life: his tendency to gravitate toward older women, bearers of the "motherly" aspect of his anima, who offered him a model different from that provided by his mother and maiden aunts. Among these women we find the wife of his admired mentor, Sophie Ritschl, a converted Jew, who was almost twenty-five years older than Nietzsche. That relationship could be characterized as the encounter of the "prodigal son" with the "good mother" (cf. Janz 1987, II:383; Diethe 1996, 30). A basic factor served as the attracting element: the passion for music manifested by Sophie, an excellent pianist. Attracted by Madame Ritschl's musical soul, Nietzsche spent most of his social life during his stay in Leipzig in the Ritschls' home. Thus Nietzsche's father's Eros seemed to be the basis of this friendship.

An additional link between Sophie and Nietzsche was their common admiration for Wagner, whom Sophie met through the composer's sister (cf. ibid., I:213). When Wagner arrived in Leipzig in 1868 to visit his sister, it was through Sophie that Nietzsche came into personal contact with the "music phenomenon of the time" and formed a relationship that would prove a determining factor in his life.

Part Two

CHAPTER 5

Spirit of the camel: ten years in Basel (1869–1879)

A completely radical institution for truth is not possible here. Above all, from here nothing really revolutionary can come.

—F. NIETZSCHE (1870)

THE NEXT PHASE IN NIETZSCHE'S life can be recorded under the aegis of the spirit of the camel, proclaimed by his Zarathustra. "What is difficult? asks the spirit that would bear much, and kneels down like a camel waiting to be well loaded. . . . All these most difficult things the spirit that would bear much takes upon itself" (Z I:1). In the desert, in a sterile space, the camel lives the intensification of its fate, parallel to Nietzsche's experience beginning on April 19, 1869.

Apparently incapable of imposing his will, Nietzsche surrendered passively to what he saw as the capricious designs of fate. He wrote to Rohde in November 1867: "Fate has with a sudden wrench torn the Leipzig page out of my life, and what I see next in this sibylline book is covered from top to bottom with an inkblot." He adopted the rhetoric of victimhood, seeing himself as subject to the whim of chance.

Nietzsche's stay and activities in Basel had profound repercussions on his development, personally and professionally. This period could be considered the "rise and twilight of the gods"—and the list of those gods who, in the end, were found to have feet of clay included the names of Wagner and Ritschl.

During his first year in Basel, Nietzsche was unable to establish any friendships. Always attracted by paternal images, he approached in particular two personalities who were well known outside of the philological ambit. J. J. Bachofen at that time had already published his main works, *Oknos* (1858), *Symbolic of the Tombs* (1859), and *Das Mutterrecht*, "Mother's Right" (1861). Despite admiring him for his intellectual capacity, Nietzsche was not able to establish a connection of intimacy and affection, particularly given "the markedly Christian bases of Bachofen's view of the world" (Janz 1987, II:42). The other intellectual to whom he felt initially attracted was Jacob Burckhardt, professor of history and art history at Basel University. In addition to sharing Nietzsche's passion for Schopenhauer—"our philosopher," he called him in conversations with Nietzsche—Professor Burckhardt was also musically gifted. Both inclinations served to bring them together initially. Nietzsche had described this sarcastic old bachelor as "an eccentric with a wit." Nonetheless, the fact that the mature professor considered Wagner an abomination, rejecting the famous composer's personality and music, soon brought about a parting of the ways. Nietzsche's marked enthusiasm and blind passion for Wagner provoked in the elderly scholar an attitude of reserve and, finally, of silence (see ibid., 45–49).

With no one with whom to share the profound loneliness of his soul, Nietzsche begged for the return of his distant Eros: he sent out an anguished cry to Rohde, asking him to help a "sick man." Nietzsche needed his companion in order to emerge from his schizoid self-absorption. Perhaps inspired by this experience, a subsequent insight was expressed thus in his *Zarathustra*: "I and me are always too deep in conversation: how could one stand that if there were no friend? For the hermit the friend is always the third person . . . that prevents the conversation of the two from sinking into the depths" (Z I:14).

So as to avoid "sinking into the depths," he wrote to Rohde in early 1870, proposing the following:

> Consider living with me for a while. . . . It is incredible how much I miss you. . . . It really is a new feeling for me to have

absolutely nobody on the spot to whom one can speak about the best and the most difficult things of life. . . . My friendship is assuming, under such hermetic conditions, in such young and hard years, a veritable pathological character. I implore you, as a sick man might: "Come to Basel."

Rohde answered the heartrending call and spent two weeks with his comrade in Basel. Nietzsche took him to the mythical Olympic land, Tribschen, to meet his god-Wagner (cf. Köhler, 1998, 104). The short visit of his dear friend left in the eternal sufferer the urgent desire to arrange for Rohde to remain permanently at his side, in order to jointly found a "monastery for free spirits" where they could "reach an island on which we shall not need to plug our ears with wax anymore." Thus, in a letter dated December 15, 1870, he expressed a wish that emulates the image of Achilles and his lover Patroclus in the "Isles of the Blessed." In this state of mind, in January 1871, he recommended Rohde as a philology professor (cf. Letter to Vischer, January 1871).

At the same time, Nietzsche offered to cover a chair in philosophy, alleging that his choice of career had been motivated mainly by the fact that he had been exposed to a "truly exciting philology professor." Nonetheless, he confessed, his true vocation was philosophy, a field for which he considered himself well prepared: "I possess the capacity . . . and even feel myself to be better qualified for that office than a purely philological one" (ibid.). Yet he lacked credentials as a philosopher, and all his publications were in the field of philology; hence his bold proposal was rejected (cf. Janz, 1987, II:110). His disappointment was so great that he told his sister he might give up his position at the university so as to join Wagner in his campaign to collect funds for the Bayreuth festival (cf. Förster-Nietzsche, 1912, 355; Peters 1997, 31).

Having lost his hope of sharing a common existence with Rohde, he felt trapped in his circumstances and was prone to explode in anger. He wrote to Rohde: "My whole concern is first to get rid of all polemical, negative stuff in me; I want to sing assiduously the whole scale of my hostile feelings, up and down, really outrageously" (March 1874). And two weeks later to Carl von Gersdorff: "I defend myself and revolt against the quantity—the unspeakable quantity—of unfreedom which clings to me. There can be no talk or real productivity as long as one is still to a large extent confined in unfreedom, in the suffering and burdensome feeling of constraint."[1]

It was only after the arrival in 1870 of his new neighbor, Franz Overbeck, who was to take over the theology chair, that Nietzsche was able to obtain partial relief with the meeting of a kindred spirit (cf. Janz 1987, II:77).[2] In March 1873, in a letter sent to Rohde, he summarized Overbeck's personality as follows: "Overbeck is the most serious, openminded, and personally kind and simple man and scholar whom one could wish to have for a friend."

Nietzsche's rejection of theological topics did not prevent him from establishing a close relationship with Overbeck, since the scholar did not manifest a pietistic approach to theology, nor was it his intention to promulgate the divine word (cf. Janz 1987, II:75).[3] Nietzsche shared lodgings with his new companion until 1875. In 1876, Overbeck married Ida Rothpelz, who became Nietzsche's friend and confidante.

Despite having given up his Prussian citizenship to become "a free Swiss," Nietzsche decided to join the German army as a volunteer when the Franco-Prussian War began a year after his arrival in Basel (cf. Janz, 1987, II: 86). He filed a request at the Council of Education to be released from his position, alleging the need to "offer his small donation or contribution to the coffers of the fatherland" (Letter to Vischer, August 1870). However, since he had previously manifested his sense of homelessness and his disdain for everything German, his decision seemed more an escape from the misery of feeling like a caged bird at the university than an act of loyalty and solidarity with his country.

Once the dispensation was granted, he began to offer his services at a medical station (taking into consideration Swiss neutrality). He occupied this position for only a week and was discharged due to dysentery and a diphtherial infection (cf. Janz, 1987, II:88). In this short time, however, Nietzsche was profoundly impressed by what he saw of the war, which affected him considerably for a prolonged period:

> I have seen the war and continued my meditations uninterrupt-
> edly, in the presence of the most horrendous scenes. . . . I
> remember one night when, alone, stretched out in a flatcar with
> the wounded under my care, I couldn't stop thinking about the
> three abysses of tragedy, called *Wahn, Wille, Wehe*: illusion, will,
> and pain. How did I then arrive at the certainty that the future
> hero of tragic knowledge and Greek joy would undergo such a
> test at birth? (cited in Halévy 2000, 76)

It seemed impossible for Nietzsche to transmute black misery into
"Greek joy." The unchanged *prima materia* was expressed in his physical
ailments: neuralgias, insomnia, stomachaches, hemorrhoidal problems,
diminished eyesight, and a growing dependence on chloral hydrate. His
impulse toward the infinite and the vehemence of his spirit were suffo-
cated by the asphyxiating atmosphere of Basel. Once again, illness would
rescue him from his unconditional surrender to fatalism;[4] once again, his
nous would be expressed through the *physis*. "Whether or not his illness
had a palpable medical-physiological basis," concluded Janz, "the fact is
that it also took hold, at least in the same proportion, in the psychic
aspect, in the irresistible tension between profession and vocation,
between appearance and being. This tension essentially formed part of
Nietzsche's destiny and nature" (1987, II:113–14).

Taking advantage of Nietzsche's precarious physical state,
Elisabeth offered to move in with him in Basel and care for him (cf.
Peters 1997, 31). As history testifies, her offer arose in part from her
wish to perpetuate her incestuous attachment to her brother, and
from her longing to live a cosmopolitan life and fulfill her own social
ambitions. But even she could not have imagined how easy it would
be to win the consent of her "prey," thanks to his poor physical and
mental condition. As was to be expected, Nietzsche accepted her "sacrifice" and Elisabeth was able to put into practice what she had
yearned to do for so long. She took her "pots and pans" and went to
Basel. Thus the place left vacant for a wife was occupied and
Nietzsche remained trapped in a kinship libido. It could be said that
the Elisabeth-Friedrich couple had practically formed a sibling mar-

riage: "Even their frequent quarrels followed by tearful reconciliations exhibit a conjugal pattern" (Peters 1974, 84).

In contrast to her markedly introverted brother, Elisabeth had the practicality required to handle the difficulties of everyday life, with its worldly obligations and chores: "A simple household, a completely regulated daily routine . . . the life with my sister (which makes every-thing around me so *Nietzschean* and strangely tranquil), this is what makes my life at present" (Letter to von Gersdorff, December 15, 1875). Meanwhile, Elisabeth, who devoted her entire being to an incestuous attachment to her venerated brother, came in time to demand a price equivalent to the magnitude of such devotion: life itself.

NIETSZSCHE'S EROS IN BASEL
Richard and Cosima Wagner

> I searched for great human beings but always found only the apes of their ideals.
> —F. NIETZSCHE, *Twilight of the Idols*

The first period of Nietzsche's life in Switzerland can be divided into experiences of two antithetical worlds: on the one hand, Basel, locus of his academic life, which seemed to cause in Nietzsche's spirit a contin-uous reediting of Tantalus's torment; on the other, Tribschen, on Lake Lucerne, locus of a mythical world inhabited by the "gods" Richard and Cosima Wagner.[5] He found in Tribschen the "Blessed Isle" that he yearned for. "Dearest friend," he wrote to Rohde in 1869, "everything I learn and see, hear and understand there [in Tribschen] is indescribable. Believe me, Schopenhauer and Goethe, Aeschylus and Pindar, still live."[6] Thus "between his bourgeois existence and Tribschen, there was a magic door, through which he let in the irrational" (Janz 1987, II:31). Basel and Tribschen are antagonistic images that reflect the philosopher's own con-tradictions between his rigid adherence to existing conventions and his radical and Dionysian philosophy.

The encounter with the Wagners, particularly with Richard Wagner, was a determining factor in Nietzsche's life. The famed composer was born in 1813, the same year as Nietzsche's father, and was "said to resemble him facially" (Magee 2000, 288). Of course, music remained Nietzsche's emotional tie to his deceased father. Nietzsche seemed to see in Wagner the incarnation in flesh and blood of an idealized patriarchal figure,[7] before whom he prostrated himself: "Let us think of Schopenhauer and Richard Wagner," he wrote to Rohde in November 1868: "The two eccentrics of one heart and mind are a happy spectacle for the gods." The tragic philosopher fused Schopenhauer and Wagner in one single god and started a new private religion presided over by this twin deity.

As he had discovered in the pessimistic philosopher, Nietzsche found in Wagner the "ethical air, the Faustian odor, Cross, Death, Grave." Besides their common interest in Schopenhauer's worldview and their passionate love of music, Nietzsche and Wagner also shared an outstanding interest in Greek drama: through "the art of Wagner . . . I feel so much closer to the Greeks than ever before" (Letter to Mathilde Maier, July 15, 1878).

The projection on Wagner of the mana personality[8] is shown, among other ways, in Nietzsche's correspondence: "In Wagner there dominates such an unconditioned ideality, such a profound and exciting humanity, such an elevated vital rigor, that in his proximity I feel close to the divine!" (Letter to von Gersdorff in 1869). In view of this, he gave Wagner the name of Jupiter. He addressed a letter, dated May 1879, to this new god, with a phrase taken from the end of Goethe's *Faust*—*Pater Seraphicus*—and declared his complete submission: "I am never far; my thoughts always circle around you. If it is true, as you once wrote, to my pride, that music is my conductor, then you are at all events the conductor of this music of mine." The "wish to gratify him," he confessed to Rohde, "impels me more powerfully than any other force." In this respect Nietzsche's sister declared: "All my brother's plans in those days were conceived in connection with Wagner: in regard to everything he did, [Nietzsche] asked himself the question: 'Will this do Wagner any good?' He was prepared to make any sacrifice" (Förster-Nietzsche 1912, I:355).

Apparently, this fascination was not to the liking of Cosima, who, on August 2, 1871, wrote in her diary: "[Nietzsche] is certainly the most gifted of our young friends, but a not quite natural reserve makes his behavior in many respects most displeasing. It is as if he were trying to resist the overwhelming effect of Wagner's personality" (1997, 111).

For his part, Nietzsche not only found Cosima the "most charming woman," with "the highest aesthetical sense he had met in his life," as he described her in *Ecce Homo*, but he shared with her total surrender and loyalty to the god-hero-genius that was Wagner. Cosima's devotion toward Wagner was almost as pathological as Elisabeth's toward Nietzsche. Like Elisabeth, Cosima devoted herself totally to the man she worshipped.

To the young Nietzsche, Richard and Cosima Wagner seemed to represent a divinized parental couple: Jupiter (Zeus) and Juno (Hera). Welcomed into their home, he felt himself to be the chosen of the gods, even though he occupied "the lower ranks of a family hierarchy" (Köhler 1998, 46).[9] The Wagners thought it natural that the young philologist should be at their complete disposal, and Cosima often asked him to perform the services of an errand boy, which Nietzsche diligently carried out (cf. Köhler 1998, 59–67; Magee 2001, 295).

With the publication of his first work, *The Birth of Tragedy*, dedicated to Wagner, Nietzsche achieved a higher rank in Wagner's circle. The entire book is addressed to the composer. In a letter sent to the musician together with a copy of the book he wrote:

> On every page you will find that I am only trying to thank you for everything you have given me; only doubt overcomes me as to whether I have always correctly received what you gave. . . . Meanwhile I feel proud that I have now marked myself out and the people will now always link my name with yours. (January 2, 1872)

In response, the "celestial father" told Nietzsche that he was next to Cosima in his heart, and that he had raised him to the rank of genius, fulfilling one of Nietzsche's long-cherished dreams. "A more beautiful book," he would write to Nietzsche after having received the advance copy, "I have never read! Everything is wonderful! . . . To Cosima I said, you come right after her, and after that no one else until Lenbach, who just painted a fascinating picture of me" (cited in Köhler 1998, 80).

Cosima, Nietzsche, and Lenbach had satisfied Wagner's narcissistic character; they were planets that gravitated around his solar figure. At that time, Cosima was transcribing his autobiography, *Mein Leben*, and Nietzsche, in addition to providing unconditional publicity for Wagner's works through his first publication, in his letters granted the composer the title of the "German Aeschylus." And Franz Lenbach, a painter from Munich, had done exalted portraits of the luminous hero.

Nietzsche was trapped in a state of total fascination, continuously fed by Wagner.[10] Wishing to flatter Nietzsche, the composer decided that "his chosen one" would be little Siegfried's tutor, while he, the father, would remain at a distance, observing the process, "as Wotan watches the education of Siegfried" (Wagner 1997, 43). Nietzsche, however, had to comply with one condition: he must devote himself exclusively to the child and give up his teaching position at the university (cf. Köhler 1998, 65).[11] As it happened, Wagner's plan could not be carried out before he and Nietzsche experienced a parting of the ways.

Despite the esteem he manifested toward Nietzsche, Wagner arrogated to himself the intellectual paternity of *The Birth of Tragedy*: "It was my lead that he followed," he wrote to his nephew Clemens Brockhaus, "so no one can judge better than I how deeply my ideas have penetrated the mind of this man" (cited in Köhler 1998, 81). As for Cosima, she stated in her diary that the work took shape "almost before our eyes . . . a work virtually created for us." She gloried in the way in which "Richard's ideas can be extended in this field" (1997, 85).

In his reverence for the beloved genius-father, Nietzsche not only became the spokesman for the Wagnerian cause through his first creative work; he also contributed with his scarce resources to the titanic project of constructing an opera house in Bayreuth, dedicated exclusively to the mise-en-scène of Wagner's works (cf. Förster-Nietzsche 1912, I:356). Thus the Wagners made the most of the fanaticism shown by the young acolyte, and of his privileged position in the academic world, to further their own cause.

Yet Nietzsche also benefited. In Wagner, he found a surrogate father, an "informing spirit," capable of stimulating his creativity and self-confidence. In this respect Pletsch wrote the following:

Living in closest association with Wagner, Nietzsche learned to measure himself against an authentic genius. Their antagonistic relationship was the matrix in which Nietzsche wrote his first book. In his struggle to please Wagner, Nietzsche discovered his own creativity and learned many of the psychological characteristics of genius: audacity, narcissism, and single-mindedness. Eventually he would be able to practice these virtues of genius. (1991, 125)

"How many purely scientific problems," wrote Nietzsche to Wagner in May 1869, "have been gradually clarified for me by contemplating your personality."

Although the relationship with Wagner was decisive in Nietzsche's life, it was not in the life of the famous composer. In this respect the philosopher Bryan Magee states: "Nietzsche had no perceptible influence on Wagner's operas, but Wagner was the greatest influence on Nietzsche in the whole of his life" (2000, 286). For this reason, Pletsch concludes: "The lives of these two great men necessarily appear as chapters in each other's biographies—Nietzsche naturally occupying a smaller chapter in Wagner's life than Wagner does in Nietzsche's" (1991, 117).[12]

For Wagner, Nietzsche's musical skill was not the main attractive element. When Nietzsche played the piano for him on one occasion, "Richard Wagner left the room, barely able to contain his laughter" (Safranski 2002, 58). Rather, he knew how to take advantage of those of Nietzsche's abilities that could be of great use to him for his own ends. In February 1870, he requested of Nietzsche: "Now you must demonstrate the purpose of philology and help me to usher in the 'Renaissance' in which Plato embraces Homer, and Homer, filled with Plato's ideas, really does become the greatest possible Homer" (cited in ibid.).

The main reason for the ending of their relationship, according to Nietzsche, was his inability to tolerate Wagner's entrance into the *Parsifal* stage; his need for confession, contrition, and absolution provoked total rejection in Nietzsche. "It is all too Christian," he wrote to Rohde in January 1878, "time-bound, limited; sheer fantastic psychology; no flesh and much too much blood." The twilight of the gods Richard and Cosima began with this "conversion."

Nietzsche narrated the following incident in *Ecce Homo*: At the same time that he sent a copy of his work *Human, All Too Human: A Book for Free Spirits* to Wagner, the latter sent him a copy of the *Parsifal* text. Both works crossed each other on the way: "This crossing of the two books—I felt as if I heard an ominous sound—as if two swords had crossed" (EH III: HATH 5). Even though this meaningful coincidence is historically inaccurate, Nietzsche experienced it so at the threshold of madness.[13] On his part, Wagner also began to show signs of contempt for Nietzsche's work. On June 24, 1878, Cosima recorded in her diary: "R[ichard] read some of Nietzsche's latest book and is astonished by its pretentious ordinariness" (1997, 312).

In fact, in this book, which represented Nietzsche's intellectual emancipation, Wagner perceived the desertion of his most fervent admirer and disciple. The author made evident the notorious contradiction between the fascinating, idealized projection and the ordinary reality of the other person, to which he had been blind. The book was the result of the "twilight of a god" who, after all, ended up being "human, alas, all too human." His entire experience in the mythical Olympus seemed to suddenly go up in smoke like a mere illusion: "Tribschen—a distant isle of the blessed: not a trace of any similarity" (EH III: HATH 2).

Wagner demanded of his friends and admirers an absolute loyalty and surrender, and Nietzsche was not exempted from this criteria. With this liberation, Wagner received a narcissistic wound that he was unwilling to tolerate. Nietzsche wrote: "Friend!—nothing binds us now. But we have taken pleasure in one another up to the point where one advanced the ideas of the other, even though these were diametrically opposed to his own." "But Wagner," stated Elisabeth, "had no intention of interpreting the book after this fashion. He saw therein nothing but the apostasy of his former disciple . . . and therefore this occurrence had the effect of a blow and an insult" (1949, 38).

Nietzsche also was unable to bear Wagner's total surrender to German nationalism. This was another case of an attack against his ideals projected on the venerated figure: "What did I never forgive Wagner? That he *condescended* to the Germans—that he became *reichs-deutsch*" (EH II:5).

Finally, in *Ecce Homo*, Nietzsche's posthumous self-portrayal and last confession, he concluded that Wagner's work served only as a narcotic for those who, like himself, "are condemned to choose vocations too early, and then to waste away under a burden they can no longer shake off—Those people require Wagner as an *opium*; they forget themselves, they get rid of themselves for a moment" (EH P:2).

After the crashing downfall of this ideal, Nietzsche would no longer project the imago of the wise man on any other external figure.[14] However, Wagner's image continued to be a perturbing and determining element throughout the remainder of his life: "I call Wagner the great benefactor of my life" (EH II:6).

It is only fair to ask whether Nietzsche was really able to free himself from Wagner in order to take possession of himself. There is evidence that he was not: as the personification of an aspect that belonged to Nietzsche, Wagner remained part of Nietzsche's nature, although this part was not consciously integrated.

Using the above argument we can understand how all of Nietzsche's works, beginning with *The Birth of Tragedy*, appear to revolve around Wagner, either to exalt him as an example to be followed, as when at the beginning he embodied a way of life and thought admired by Nietzsche, or, as occurred later, to use Wagner as a model to be repudiated in favor of an affirmative philosophy of life.

Nietzsche's thoughts regarding Wagner reflected the projections of his positive and negative shadow. The philosopher Bryan Magee wrote the following in this regard:

> Nietzsche was never able, to the end of his days, to cast off Wagner's spell. Some of the rage he expressed against the composer in his later years may have been due to this. His obsession with Wagner makes Wagner a presence in literally all his books, even when he is not named—in *Human, All Too Human* he is "the artist," in *Thus Spake Zarathustra* he is "the Sorcerer." In other books whole sections are openly devoted to him—for example, Wagner is altogether the foremost name in *Ecce Homo*. . . . Two books [by Nietzsche] are specifically about [Wagner]. Another is titled cunningly after one of his operas. Another consists largely of his ideas. There is nothing remotely comparable with this situation to be found anywhere else in the literature of philosophy. (2000, 341)

On his part, Jung concluded: "Nietzsche had Wagner *in himself,* and that is why he envied him *Parsifal.*[15] . . . Therefore Nietzsche became one stigmatized by the spirit; like Saul he had to experience Christification, when the 'other' whispered the 'Ecce Homo' in his ear" (CW 7:43).

The Birth of Tragedy from the Spirit of Music

> *The Birth of Tragedy* was my first revaluation of all values: so again I am taking myself back to the ground from which my willing, my ability grows—I, the last disciple of the philosopher Dionysus—I, the teacher of the eternal recurrence.
>
> —F. NIETZSCHE, *Twilight of the Idols*

Nietzsche was a confessional writer, and his first work, *The Birth of Tragedy from the Spirit of Music,* was a symbolic expression of an inner reality. He even warned his readers in his autobiographical work *Ecce Homo* that *The Birth of Tragedy* was the result of a study based on the "strangest objectivity": "The absolute certainty about what I am was projected on some accidental reality—the truth about me was spoken from some gruesome depth" (EH III: BT 4). Consequently, when casting a retrospective glance in the "Attempt at Self-Criticism" added to the third edition (1886), Nietzsche admitted an essential fault: the book had been written using an inadequate reflective language. It should have been presented in a poetic language, capable of permitting him to release the "mystical, almost maenadic soul that stammered with difficulty," because what is intuitive cannot be explained through words. It is best expressed through artistic creation.

Nietzsche pointed out that his mistake in relation to *The Birth of Tragedy* could have been brought about by his pretensions and the pressures he felt to produce a scholarly treatise molded by the philological demands of his academic milieu. He should have followed the path of his own inspiration: "What finds expression [in *The Birth of Tragedy*] in any case was a *strange* voice, the disciple of a still 'unknown God,' one who concealed himself for the time being under the scholar's hood."

Having betrayed the expression of his inner voice, he concluded: "It should have *sung*, this 'new soul'—and not spoken!" (BT: ASC).

Nonetheless, Nietzsche paid a very high price for his "firstborn": the book was stigmatized from the beginning. The reaction of the academic world was totally negative: they considered him an apostate and questioned the total absence of any historical-documentary justification of the views expressed on the birth, constitution, and death of tragedy (cf. Janz 1987, II:157).[16]

The most venomous critic of his work was Ulrich von Wilamowitz, professor of philology in Berlin and also an alumnus of the boarding school at Pforta, where he had met Nietzsche. In his "Response to Friedrich Nietzsche's *Birth of Tragedy*," he recommended "that Mr. Nietzsche . . . give up his chair at the university, where he should teach science; that he gather tigers and panthers at his feet, but not the young philology students of Germany, whom he should teach ascetically with a work in which one renounces oneself" (cited in ibid., 161). As a result of the poison thus instilled in the academic milieu, Nietzsche was abandoned by his students and his colleagues. Once again, the archetypal figure of "the abandoned one" came into play.

However, the most heartfelt disappointment for Nietzsche came from Ritschl, to whom he sent his book. The reply was absolute silence. Nevertheless, in his diary, Ritschl commented upon the book as "an inspired waste of energy" with an "intelligent rakish dissoluteness" (cited in Middleton 1996, 93). Incapable of bearing his mentor's silence, Nietzsche wrote him a letter, dated January 1872, asking for a reply:

> You will not grudge me my astonishment that I have not heard a word from you about my recently published book, and I hope you will also not grudge me my frankness in expressing this astonishment to you. For this book surely is by way of being a manifesto, and surely it challenges one least of all to keep silence.

Nietzsche went on to claim that his book was promising for the new generation of classical philologists and for Germany. Once again, Ritschl wrote an entry in his diary referring to an "Amazing letter from Nietzsche—megalomania" and "His *Birth of Tragedy*, conceived by

Mamma" (cited in Middleton 1996, 93). The mature mentor's intuition was not far from the truth: *The Birth of Tragedy* was conceived by the creative powers of the (M)other. The old and orthodox teacher could not accept the subversive character of his protégé. For him, as for his university colleagues, Nietzsche was academically dead:

> Our winter semester has begun, and I have no students at all! . . . To you, beloved master, I tell it because you should know it all. The fact is, indeed, so easy to explain—I have suddenly acquired such a bad name in my field that our small university suffers from it! This agonizes me. . . . Until last semester the number of students in classical philology was constantly growing—now, suddenly, they are all blown away! . . . A professor of classical philology at Bonn, whom I highly regard, has simply told his students that my book is "sheer nonsense" and is quite useless: a person who writes such things is dead to scholarship. (Letter to Wagner dated mid-November, 1872)

Only two people showed their support publicly: Richard Wagner and Erwin Rohde. Wagner published an article against Wilamowitz in the *Norddeutsche Allgemeine Zeitung.* Given his great prestige, it had a favorable influence on public opinion, and Nietzsche was forever grateful for this gesture. In his autobiographical work, *Ecce Homo,* he stated that only one man, and no other, had understood his first work: Richard Wagner. As for Erwin Rohde, he also published an article against the corrosive critic, in which he refuted the majority of Wilamowitz's philological objections. "What you have done for me is beyond words," wrote Nietzsche to Rohde on October 25, 1872. "I would be quite incapable of doing it for myself, and I know of no other person from whom I could hope for such a gift of friendship."

THE LOSS OF HIS EROS

When, in 1876, Erwin Rohde informed Nietzsche of his engagement to Valentine Framm, loneliness began to weigh more than ever on the soul of the tragic philosopher.[17] In a letter dated July 18, 1876, he wrote to his friend congratulating him on his engagement, with words that exude a melancholic air. "Last night," Nietzsche wrote to Rohde, "it occurred to me to make a poem out of this."

> A wanderer walks through the night . . .
>
> The night is beautiful—
> He does not know where his path will lead.
> Through the night there sings a bird:
> "O bird, what have you done?
> Why do you arrest my senses and stride
> and pour sweet chagrin of the heart
> into my ear, so that I must stop
> and listen—
> Why do you entice me with your sound and greeting?"[18]
>
> The good bird stops singing and speaks:
> "No, wanderer, no! It's not you whom I am luring
> with my song—
> I am luring a woman from the heights—
>
> . . .What's that to you? For you should go:
> and never, never stop!
> Why are you still standing? . . .
>
> The good bird was quiet and pondered:
> "What did my piping do to him?
> Why is he still standing now?—
> the poor, poor, wandering man!"
> —F. NIETZSCHE, fragment of the poem "The Wanderer" (1876)

Rohde, the bird in the poem, would no longer sing for Nietzsche the wanderer but for a female friend, his beloved. Like the poet, Nietzsche must continue his journey alone without a known destination: "At this time, Nietzsche began work on the section of *Human, All Too Human* entitled 'The Wanderer and His Shadow,' and in his letters to Rohde in the subsequent years Nietzsche played the role of the solitary outcast, the anchorite, and the well-worn romantic role of the Wanderer" (Cardew 2004, 462).[19]

Nietzsche's melancholy increased to such a degree that he became ill in December 1876 and did not recuperate for several months. We can find a description of his condition in the following lines written to von Gersdorff on February 18, 1876:

> I will be brief, because it is an effort for me to write. I have never had such a sad, such a painful, such a fearfully ominous Christmas! I can no longer doubt: my illness is cerebral; my stomach and my eyes make me suffer because of another ailment, the center of which is somewhere else. My father died at thirty-six years of age from an inflammation of the brain. It may be that with me things may go even more quickly.

Rohde's "abandonment" seemed to mirror the "abandonment" of his father with his Eros.

Even a year after Rohde announced his engagement, Nietzsche was unable to overcome the pain of separation. Rohde did not hear from him for a year (cf. Janz 2987, II:394).[20] In August 1877, he manifested his lacerating pain to his "dear, dear friend":

> How shall I put it into words? Whenever I think of you, emotion comes over me . . . I even shed tears—I know no tenable reason why.[21] Let us ask the psychologists one day; they will explain in the end that it is envy that makes me grudge you your happiness, or annoyance that someone has taken my friend away and is now keeping him hidden.

In addition to the envy he might have felt for his friend's happiness, he also experienced the pain of having lost his mirror image and, consequently, the hope of picking up his reflection in the waters: "Have you ever seen your friend asleep—and found out how he looks? What is the face of your friend anyway? It is your own face in a rough and imperfect mirror" (Z I:14).

Nonetheless, when they met again in 1886 in Leipzig, they reacted like two strangers. "I saw Nietzsche," Rohde stated. "His entire person showed signs of an indescribable strangeness, which was profoundly disquieting. There was something in him that I had never known, and of the Nietzsche I once knew, several traits had disappeared. It seemed as if he came from an uninhabited country" (cited in Halévy 2000, 283). This portrayal evokes the clinical description of a depersonalization experience,[22] not alien to Nietzsche.[23] However, a year before his mental collapse, once again Nietzsche pleaded with his dearest friend: "No, do not let yourself be estranged from me so easily! I at least shall not lose now, at my age and in my isolation, the few human beings in whom I once placed my trust" (Letter to Rohde, November 11, 1887).[24]

A Desperate Plea for Human Contact

As a result of the publication of his first work, Nietzsche was abandoned by his mentor Ritschl, his colleagues, and his students. When Wagner then moved to Bayreuth, just a few weeks after the publication of *The Birth of Tragedy*, Nietzsche was left totally alone and forsaken in Basel. In 1875, on a trip with his friend Carl von Gersdorff, who had moved to Vienna, he decided to remain in Veytaux a little longer. He went to Geneva to visit Hugo von Senger, director general of the Geneva orchestra and another admirer of Wagner's whom he had met in Bayreuth. It was Senger who introduced him to the first woman to whom Nietzsche made a marriage proposal: Mathilde Trampedach, a piano student of Senger's. Mathilde was a beautiful young woman, not yet twenty-three years of age, who loved music and had a well-rounded education. But most of all Nietzsche was extremely taken by her love of poetry. After a second meeting, in less than a week, he abruptly proposed marriage in a letter dated April 1876: "Muster all the courage of your heart, so as not to be afraid of the question I am going to ask you: Will you be my wife? I love you and feel that you already belong to me." Upon receiving her negative reply, Nietzsche excused himself for "the unexpected shock caused." What he had not perceived was the fact that there existed a bond of affection between Senger, forty years of age and married for the second time, and his pupil, who eventually became his third wife (see Janz 1870 II:286–88; Ross 1994, 471–76; Pletsch 1991, 184–85). From Pletsch's point of view, "Nietzsche's considerations of marriage were only too rational. . . . He seemed to lack any emotional, romantic, or sexual interest in women. . . . Nietzsche reached out to Mathilde Trampedach as if for salvation from his fate, or simply toward a new beginning. He may even have seen a potential disciple in her, for she was intellectually acute" (1991, 185).

Return to the Realm of the Mothers

Disheartened by his losses, as on other occasions, Nietzsche decided to lessen his feelings of loneliness by taking refuge in the bosoms of two saving maternal figures.

One of the women who came to Nietzsche's aid during this period was Marie Baumgartner, the mother of one of his students, a well-educated, cosmopolitan woman with an open mind and a refined spirituality, and who admired Schopenhauer. Marie's dedication to Nietzsche became more than maternal, as she cared for him during the distressing time of his intense suffering. Fascinated by the personality of her son's mentor, she offered to translate his works into French (see Janz 1987, II:300–06; Diethe 1996, 36).

The other mother figure was the likewise cosmopolitan Malwida von Meysenbug, writer and feminist, author of *Memoirs of an Idealist* (1876) and *An Idealist's Autumn of Life* (1898). She was a member of the exclusive circle of Wagner's most intimate friends and patroness of young intellectuals like Nietzsche, whom she met through Cosima. Nietzsche established the most valuable of his friendships with her (see Janz ibid., 324–38). She knew how to offer him "human kindness, of such magnitude, that she was able to triumph always over all his changes of mood and indisposition, and also over their divergences" (ibid., 324). Even when Nietzsche tried to destroy this relationship during his mental breakdown, the noble lady knew how to justify him in the name of the affection he had always shown her.

Finally, when Nietzsche left his teaching position at Basel after his physical breakdown in the spring of 1879, he turned once again to his mother. "He continues ever more attached to that bond and dependence until, with his intellectual breakdown, he falls completely into her solicitous arms" (ibid., 371).

New Friendships

> Don't shut your gates: new friends may come along.
> Let old ones go.
> —F. NIETZSCHE, *Aftersong*

Paul Rée

In 1873, the critical moral philosopher Paul Rée (1849–1901), son of a Jewish landowner in Pomerania and author of *Psychological Observations* (1875) and *The Origin of the Moral Sensations* (1877), came into contact with Nietzsche through a common friend, the classicist and Kantian Heinrich Romundt (cf. Janz 1987, II:297). Rée was a student in Nietzsche's course on the pre-Platonic philosophers. After obtaining a law degree, he went into the field of philosophy. In addition to their shared interest in this discipline, a common character trait seemed to bring Rée and Nietzsche together: self-torment. Lou Salomé described Rée as a man marked by "self-hate" and whose "melancholy and pessimism led him to toy with the idea of suicide even as an adolescent" (1991, 54).

Nietzsche's friendship with Rée was strongly criticized by his sister, and by the Wagnerian circle in Bayreuth, because of Rée's Jewish origin (cf. Köhler 1998, 126). Nietzsche ignored these pernicious prejudices, considering that Rée helped him to free himself definitely "from the odors and vapors of Wagnerian idealism" (Ross 1994, 477). In helping Nietzsche to disencumber himself from the Wagnerian and Schopenhauerian restrictions, Rée aided in letting Nietzsche's voice be heard as a "free spirit" when he began *Human, All Too Human* in 1878. Rée was a philosophical spirit at the level of Nietzsche's genius: "If Nietzsche's relation to Wagner consisted of a discipleship," considered Lou Salomé, "his friendship with Rée formed more of an intellectual companionship" (2001, 60). For Nietzsche, this friendship represented a new choice marked by a desire to free himself from Wagner's possessive imago. The philosopher Tomas Abraham wrote in this regard:

> Nietzsche debated between his wish to satisfy the desire of the master and the distance he saw increase day by day with regard to what he represented. . . . He perceived a genius who imminently needed the servile praise of others, a parade of shadows, as much as he needed air to breathe. In search of an escape from this profound inner dilemma, he threw himself into the relationship with Paul Rée, a faithful follower as well of Schopenhauer's doctrine, in order to "flee from the Lucifer-like persecution of the Maestro." (1996, 55)

With Rée Nietzsche abandoned idealism to enter completely into "Réealism," as he put it: "With all the good things you are preparing my table too is set and I have a lively appetite for Réealism, as you know," confessed Nietzsche. *Human, All Too Human* is the result of the emancipated positivist view. Consequently, the book sent to his friend was accompanied by the following note: "It belongs to you . . . to the others it is sent as a gift! . . . All my friends are now of one opinion—that my book was written by you and originated with you: therefore, I congratulate you on your paternity! Long live Réealism!" (April 24, 1878).

Nietzsche and Rée could be considered two kindred spirits and, at the same time, contradictory or rather complementary ones. Whereas Rée's tendency was to aseptically separate thought from emotion, the thoughts presented by Nietzsche in his writings emerged from the exuberant fire of his emotions. Consequently, Lou Salomé concluded, "The danger for Nietzsche resided in his unlimited capacity for empathy and a dependence upon stimuli and excitations for his moods. . . . Rée, on the other hand, rejected every intrusion of sentiment into his quest for knowledge, to avoid distortions" (ibid., 74–75).

Nietzsche collaborated on Rée's second work, *The Origin of Moral Sentiments* (1877). It served him as inspiration in the search for the origins of the moral phenomenon, which he would subsequently develop in his work *On the Genealogy of Morals*. As a sign of his appreciation for the help received, Rée sent Nietzsche a gift copy of this second book, the birth of which had been a joint effort, with the following inscription: "To the father of this work from its mother, most gratefully" (cited in Janz 1987, II:438).

At this time Nietzsche seemed to have transferred his Eros, previously projected onto Rohde, to Rée. He now addressed his new friend with the same affection shown before to Rohde: "Ten times a day, I wish to be at your side, with you," he writes to Rée (Basel, December 1878), and "I always tie the spirit of my future to yours" (Geneva, May 1879). Again, "I have had to relinquish many wishes but never *the wish for a life together* with you in my 'Epicurean garden' "(Naumburg, October 1879).

This relationship, however, came to a bitter end when the "Eternal Feminine," embodied in Lou Salomé, came between them.

Heinrich Köselitz (Peter Gast)

Having read *The Birth of Tragedy*, and having accidentally met Franz Overbeck at Nietzsche's publisher, the musician and composer Heinrich Köselitz (1854–1918) decided to travel to Basel to attend lectures by Nietzsche and Overbeck (cf. Janz 1987, II:339).

Köselitz was the one among Nietzsche's few friends who had the most uninterrupted contact with the philosopher. He became his most faithful disciple, dedicating himself to Nietzsche's genius and cooperating ardently with the publication of his works. He likewise acted as scrivener for the blind "Oedipus" and offered a secure handhold to this desolate being, trying constantly to console him.[25]

The total surrender of the famulus to the master, a relationship that echoes the relation between the literary figures of Don Quixote and Sancho Panza, was due to the fact that Köselitz, according to Janz, "had the sensation, as regards Nietzsche, of being before one of the great, before a visionary of his people, before a daimonic power whose voice he had to make immediately his own" (1987, II:339). Despite this, it appears that a profound friendship was not established between them. It was rather an asymmetrical relationship, similar to that between Nietzsche and Wagner, where Köselitz held "the subordinate position of a collaborator" (ibid.). In this case, the roles were reversed and the idealized one, for the first time, was Nietzsche.[26]

Nietzsche seemed to harbor a utopian dream: to make his faithful follower a composer who would surpass the now disdained Wagner in stature, perhaps to fulfill a desire for secret revenge: to supplant the "musical phenomenon" of his time. Nietzsche changed Köselitz's name to Peter Gast—or even sometimes to Pietro Gasti—believing that it would be more acceptable to a general European audience. Trusting that Gast would banish Wagner into the shade, he exalted Gast to the level of a second Mozart in a letter addressed to Overbeck in October 1882:

> Köselitz is the musical justification of my whole new praxis and rebirth . . . to put it all together egotistically. Here is a new Mozart—that is the sole feeling I have about him; beauty, warmth, serenity, fullness, superabundant inventiveness, and the light touch of mastery in counterpoint—such qualities were never combined before. . . . How poor, artificial, and histrionic all that Wagnerei now sounds to me.

However, Nietzsche's hopes were not fulfilled, as Gast could not live up to these great expectations. Instead, he was always overshadowed by Nietzsche, and his name has found its place in history only because of its connection with Nietzsche's life and works.[27]

The Wanderer and His Shadow

> Wanderer, who are you? I see you walking on your way without
>   scorn, without love, with unfathomable eyes . . . who are you?
> What have you done? Rest here: this spot is hospitable to all—
>   recuperate! And whoever you may be: what do you like now?
> What do you need for recreation? Name it: whatever I have I
>   offer you!
> "Recreation? Recreation? You are inquisitive! What are you say-
>   ing? But give me please—"
> What? What? Say it!

"Another mask! A second mask!"
—F. NIETZSCHE, *Beyond Good and Evil* (278)

Feeling betrayed in his ideals by *Pater* Wagner; denied a degree in philosophy; having been declared "academically dead" after the publication of *The Birth of Tragedy*, abandoned by colleagues and students, and moreover by his mentor Ritschl; grieved by the poor reception of his subsequent works, *Human, All Too Human* and *Untimely Meditations*; desolate in spirit because his Eros had been lost with Rohde's marriage; sad in view of the unfortunate loss of his good friend and confidant Carl von Gersdorff, who stopped all correspondence toward the end of 1877 "after Nietzsche interfered in his love life and in his engagement in a clumsy manner" (Janz 1987, II:423); lonely due to his inability to find solace in new relationships; his musical soul wounded and mocked by Hans von Bülow, who accused him of having violated the muse Euterpe with his interpretations (cf. EH II:4); Nietzsche deteriorated to the point that he was unable to fulfill his academic duties: "Monday, ill; Tuesday, attack; Wednesday, ill; Thursday and Friday, strong attack once again, unending; today, broken and tired," he wrote in January 1879 (cited in Janz 1987, II:454). "The body has gone mad" is the way the psychoanalyst Joyce McDougall describes the psychosomatic states in which "the *body* appears to be behaving in a 'delusional' fashion, often *overfunctioning* excessively . . . to a degree that appears physiologically senseless" (1989, 18).

On June 18, 1879, having requested retirement, Nietzsche left the University of Basel (cf. Janz 1987, II:459).[28] Once again, he was saved by his illness: "Sickness *detached me slowly*: it spared me any break, any violent and offensive step. . . . My sickness also gave me the right to change all my habits completely; it permitted me, it *commanded* me to forget" (EH III: HATH 4). Nietzsche seems to have preferred his illness a thousand times to "that unseemly 'selflessness' into which [he] had got [him]self originally in ignorance and youth and in which [he] had got stuck later on from inertia and a so-called 'sense of duty' " (ibid.).

Following the precepts of the Egyptian guide and god of mysteries and revelations, Hermes Trismegistus, "the thrice greatest" (who stated, "As above, so below"[29] and *mutatis mutandis*, "As outside, so within"), it is possible to assume that all these external vicissitudes were the cause of Nietzsche's mental and physical deterioration, as one of the ways in which the psyche urges man to follow his vocation or "inner call."[30] Psychic compensation can emerge not only from the psychic matrix but also through events from the outside world.[31] Jung observed that certain "events in the external world . . . have the same meaning as endopsychic events" (CW 8:870).

Nietzsche perceived the urgent need for a change in the course of his life, and at the same time, given the impossibility of finding the necessary guiding principle (inside and outside), the *spiritus rector,* he once again literalized the Hermetic message when he stated:

> My knowledge simply failed to include *realities,* and my "idealities" were not worth a damn. A truly burning thirst took hold of me: henceforth I really pursued nothing *more* than physiology, medicine, and natural sciences. . . . I first guessed how an activity chosen in defiance of one's instincts, a so-called "vocation" for which one does not have the least vocation, is related to the need for *deadening* the feeling of desolation and hunger of a narcotic art. (EH III: HATH 3)

The strong need to contact "realities" instead of "idealisms" seems to have been a reflection of his internal struggle of matter vs. spirit, between the outside world and the inner world (failure in adaptation).

As a result of the new literalization of the message from Hermes, "the God of revelation" (Jung, CW 13:256), Nietzsche did not start out from the wound but from rationality, hearkening to the "call" from the outside and not from the inside. And he acted out that exile without understanding that the problem stemmed from his own constitutional exile. Thus he continued living like a spirit in an alienated body. Paradoxically, it was his body that urged him to free himself from his imprisoned condition.

Like his admired Byron's Manfred, a character who wandered over desolate mountaintops in total isolation from society, Nietzsche condemned himself to wander for the rest of his lucid life. *Fugitivus errans* (a wandering fugitive), he called himself, abandoning his last place of residence to begin a peripatetic existence in hope of overcoming the loneliness, depression, and fear of failure resulting from the loss of significant others: "From all mountains I look out for fatherlands and motherlands. But home I found nowhere; a fugitive am I in all cities and a departer at all gates" (Z II:14). The analyst Ann Shearer writes: "The essence of the wanderer . . . is the quality of aimlessness, the want of direction or containment—the 'going idly or restlessly about' of the dictionary description. This is not 'journeying,' which has always a goal, however hidden that might be" (2001, 33). The author adds: "When we grieve we wander, searching for what is lost and that part of ourselves lost with it" (ibid., 41).

Carrying along his only possession, "a heavy and graceless wooden trunk," for the rest of his life the "good European"[32] led a reclusive existence in Swiss, French, German, and Italian cities,[33] never residing in any place longer than several months at a time due to an extreme physical and mental hypersensibility to landscape and climate. "[While] the external course of [Nietzsche's] life . . . appears closed and at the same time ended . . . his life as a thinker actually begins" (Salomé 2001, 8).

Chapter 6

Lou Salomé: *femme inspiratrice*

If it is not the eternal feminine which draws this pseudo-
maiden ever onward, then perhaps it is—the eternal masculine.

—F. NIETZSCHE (To Overbeck regarding Lou, October 17, 1885)

No mother gave me birth.
I honor the male, in all things but marriage.
Yes, with all my heart I am my Father's child.

—Athena in Aeschylus's *Eumenides*

DESPITE THE BREVITY OF THE relationship established between Nietzsche and Lou Salomé (April–November 1882), she had a profound impact on him, to the point that their final breakup, in which he also lost his closest friend, Paul Rée, practically led him to self-annihilation. With this loss Nietzsche for the first time became fully aware of the nefarious influence of his mother and sister regarding both his relationship with Lou and his life in general.

"In order to understand the course taken by one life, we need to develop some understanding of the other lives that intersect with it in important ways in crucial moments" (Elms 1994, 206). Following this guideline offered by the psychobiographer Alan C. Elms, it seems important to point out some relevant aspects of the life of Louise Salomé. After five sons, the Salomé couple enthusiastically received their daughter, Louise, born on February 12, 1861.[1] Descended from an aristocratic German family, Lou was brought up in the Russian city of St. Petersburg. She was described as a free spirit, of outstanding intelligence, and of a subversive character (cf. Janz 1987, III:90). Extremely spoiled by her father, a general of a passionate temperament, she grew up, unlike Nietzsche, in a markedly masculine environment. Driven by an evident Athenian spirit, the "father's child" showed, from a very early age, that she was clearly aware of the road she was to follow. Lou evidenced signs of sharing many of the attributes traditionally associated with the goddess Pallas Athena, such as competitiveness, decisive and reflective capacity, civilizing intellect, wisdom and intelligence, a will to win, perfectionism, impenetrability, defiance, pride, and rationality.

Lou manifested the tenacity required to follow her own path despite every possible type of family coercion. By way of an emancipation manifesto, she wrote in her memoirs: "I can't live according to some model, and I could never be a model for anyone else; but I intend to shape my life for myself, no matter how it turns out" (1991, 46). Her statement evokes the concept of virginity, in its psychological connotation, offered by the Jungian analyst Esther Harding: "The woman who is virgin, one-in-herself, does what she does—not because of any desire to please, not to be liked, or to be approved, even by herself; not because of any desire to gain power over another, to catch his interest or love, but because what she does is true" (1971, 125). Lou, with her Athenian consciousness, was at the same time warrior and virgin.

Having been raised in a very pious family, she admitted that one of the most traumatic events in her life was the loss of her faith in God: "[God not only] disappeared just for me, he disappeared totally—he was lost to the entire universe as well" (Andreas-Salomé 1991, 5). Although Lou subsequently showed interest in theological studies, her motivation was purely intellectual, as she herself confessed in her autobiography.

Sheltered first under the wings of the Dutch Pastor Hendrik Gillot, the eighteen-year-old Lou received private and secret lessons from the fascinating and liberal orator in comparative history of religions, philosophy, logic, metaphysics, theory of knowledge, etc. (cf. Janz 1987, III:93). Thus, under the guidance of Gillot, not only did Lou become a kind of Enlightenment heroine, but also "the shades of Héloïse and Abelard hovered over them" (Peters 1974, 56).[2]

Upon the death of her father, Lou moved with her mother to Zurich in 1880, for health reasons and due to her wish to expand her cultural horizon at the university (cf. ibid., 66). At that time "Lou was already as cerebral, bewitching, and heartless as ever she was to be" (Binion 1968, 32). "Her vitality was too cerebral," suggests Peters, "and her will too masculine" (1974, 67).

Even though Lou did not have the necessary credentials to register at the university, Professor Biedermann, Gillot's theology professor, was so impressed by the young woman's erudition and enthusiastic tempera-ment that he accepted her in his course on the General History of Religion, Logic, and Metaphysics. She likewise took courses in art histo-ry and archaeology, given by Gottfried Kinkel,[3] and in history with Nietzsche's disciple Baumgartner (cf. Peters 1974, 66).

In 1881, she was forced to interrupt her studies due to a worsening of previous pulmonary problems, and, following her doctor's orders to search for warmer climates, she moved to Rome in 1882. Thanks to Kinkel's rec-ommendation, she was received in the intimate circle of the cosmopoli-tan intellectual Malwida von Meysenbug, a close friend of Nietzsche and of Rée (cf. ibid., 68). It was at this lady's home that she first met Rée.[4]

An almost immediate attraction sparked between Lou Salomé and Paul Rée. "The same evening [we met], and every day thereafter," recalls Lou, "we continued talking excitedly. . . . The walks through the streets of Rome beneath the moon and stars soon brought us so close to one another that I began to devise a wonderful plan by means of which we could continue this way" (Andreas-Salomé 1991, 44). The plan consist-ed in establishing an Apollonian fraternal couple, alien to all social con-ventions, devoted in a spiritual brotherhood to intellectual pursuits. Her intellectual pursuits coincided with Nietzsche's "Blessed Isles" project.

Rée, astounded at Lou's intelligence, audacity, and beauty, wrote to Nietzsche, inviting him to come to Rome to meet this disconcerting young woman. Malwida, always anxious to find an adequate wife for the eternally lonely one, also wrote to Nietzsche pointing out Lou's philo-sophical talents, exempt from metaphysical assumptions. She closed the letter manifesting an intimate yearning: "Rée and I coincide in our desire to see you some day with this extraordinary being" (cited in Janz 1987, III:98). Nietzsche sent his reply to Rée in March 1882, from Genoa:

> Please greet this Russian lady in my name . . . I long for this type of soul. Yes, I shall soon leave in search of this prey: in view of what I want to do in the next ten years, I need her. Marriage is another matter: the most I could consider would be a two-year marriage, and only in the light of what I will do in the next ten years.

Nietzsche seemed more interested in acquiring a disciple than in taking a wife. In a letter dated June 1882, Nietzsche would subsequently confess to Lou:

> Back in Orta I conceived the plan of leading you step by step to the final consequence of my philosophy—*you,* as the first person I took to be fit for this. Oh, you cannot imagine what resolve, what determination, this took. As a teacher I have always done much for my students . . . but what I meant to do *here, now,* given my continuing physical deterioration, went beyond everything earlier. A procreated building, building up! I never thought of first asking your consent: you were barely to notice it as you entered upon this work. I trusted those higher impulses I believed to be yours. I thought of you as my heiress. (cited in Binion 1968, 69)

To Peter Gast he wrote, concerning Lou, admitting how wonderful it was for him to see "to what extent she is ready for my way of thinking and my ideas. . . . She is also extremely firm of character and knows very well what she wants—without asking the world and without concerning herself about it." In December 1882 he wrote again to Gast: "I have felt the strongest and most genuine emotions for Lou and there was nothing erotic in my love."

Toward the end of April, Nietzsche the wanderer arrived in Rome from Messina to meet his "prey." After several hours of conversation with the young Lou, sixteen years younger than he, the thirty-seven-year-old Nietzsche was totally subjugated by her magnetic personality. Lou recalled the first words that Nietzsche said to her: "From what star have we fallen together here?" (Andreas-Salomé 1991, 47). As for Lou, she described her impression of their first encounter thus:

> I remember that when I first spoke with Nietzsche . . . in St. Peter's in Rome, his studied, elegant posture surprised and deceived me. But not for long was one deceived by this recluse who wore his mask so awkwardly, like someone who has come out of the wilderness and mountains and who dressed conventionally. (Salomé 2001, 9–10)

Lou, as a knowledge-hunter, seemed to be attracted to Nietzsche (as to the other men in her life) just by the challenge of getting to know his inner treasures.

With the same awkwardness and precipitation with which he had proposed marriage to Mathilde Trampendach six years before, Nietzsche charged Rée with the embarrassing mission of asking for Lou's hand in his name (cf. ibid., 47). On this occasion, as on the previous one, he had not perceived the lady's feelings for another man, in this case his best friend.

Lou considered Nietzsche a man of passionate intelligence, yet she confessed to her friend Gillot that she definitely felt attracted to Rée (cf. Nietzsche, Salomé and Rée 1982, 73). But when Rée asked Mme. Salomé for her daughter's hand in marriage, he seemed not to have understood the plan prepared by the emancipated young lady regarding their relationship:

> To my sorrow and rage, suggesting a totally different plan to my mother—that we get married—which made her agreement to my own plan that much more difficult. First of all I had to make [Rée] envision and understand that the "self-contained" love life I had settled upon as a permanent condition meant in combination with my impulse toward a totally unconstrained freedom. (Andreas-Salomé 1991, 44–45)

Lou defended a freedom which neither Gillot nor Rée nor Nietzsche could persuade her to give up.

Continuing with Harding's description of psychological virginity, one might add that "the virgin can also present unconventional behavior. She may have to say no, when it would be easier to say yes. But as a virgin she is not influenced by the considerations that make the nonvirgin woman . . . trim her sails and adapt herself to expediency" (1971, 125).[5] The author adds that the virgin would never lend herself to act as the "female counterpart or syzygy to some male" (ibid.): "Lou's commitment to the laws of her own nature ruled out the possibility of her becoming any man's follower" (Peters 1974, 146).

Lou and Rée agreed to maintain Nietzsche's ignorance of their secretive and intimate liaison. Resigned, or perhaps liberated by her negative response, Nietzsche "made himself a third member of our alliance," thus forming what Lou called the "trinity" (cf. Andreas-Salomé 1991, 47). Once more Nietzsche seems to have been the "disembodied third person or entity" (Mandel in Salomé 2001, lxii), *tertium quid*, as he once described himself. As a memento of this "unholy" trinity, Nietzsche planned the well-known portrait of the three members who made up this very unique brotherhood, in a gesture totally alien to his introverted personality. Lou recalls this episode thus in her memoirs:

> [Nietzsche] arranged a photograph of the three of us in spite of strong objections on the part of Paul Rée, who suffered throughout his life from a pathological aversion to the reproduction of his features. Nietzsche, who was in a playful mood, not only insisted on the photo, but took a personal hand in the details— for example the little (far too little!) cart, and even a touch of kitsch with the sprig of lilacs on the whip. (ibid., 48)[6]

Against all current social customs, Lou had planned to live under the same roof with the two men, who, like her, were hungry for knowledge: a "chaste *ménage à trois*," as described by Binion (1968, 53):

> A simple dream first convinced me of the feasibility of my plan, which flew directly in the face of all social conventions. In it I saw a pleasant study filled with books and flowers, flanked by two bedrooms, and us walking back and forth between them, colleagues, working together in a joyful and earnest bond. (ibid., 45)

Lou's bold proposal was an affront to the puritanical customs of both friends, who nonetheless, seduced by the multiple charms of this muse-hetaera-mediatrix, agreed to accept it, although Nietzsche warned Lou of the need to carry out this audacious plan in absolute secrecy. Possibly fearing especially the reaction of his mother and sister, in a letter dated June 1882 he subtly advised that they limit "the people who must of necessity be initiated into what we intend."

Lou's appearance and the trinity plans immediately introduced the phantom of deceit and pretense between the two friends, who had now become rivals.[7] Although Nietzsche suggested to Rée that he marry "that admirable woman," the development of events made it clear that he had other wishes. "When I am completely alone," Nietzsche wrote to Lou in May 1882, "I frequently, very frequently pronounce your name, which constitutes a great joy to me." And in other correspondence sent around that same date, he wrote to Lou: "You have reached my *heart* directly (and also my eyes). Yes, I believe in you: help me to believe always in myself. . . . People say that I have never been as happy as I am now. I trust in my destiny." And in August of that same year, he confessed: "I would have liked to live alone. But then the dear bird Lou[8] flew in my path, and I thought it was an eagle and I wanted the eagle to stay with me."[9]

At the same time, although Rée had already proposed marriage to Lou, he kept this fact from his friend and responded thus with regard to Nietzsche's suggestion about marriage: "No, I am a pessimist; the idea of propagating human life is detestable to me. You are the one who should marry her; she is the companion you need" (cited in Halévy 2000, 218). This advice, of course, contradicted Rée's own desires: "When the train began to move, taking me away from you. . . . I thought I would die of pain and nostalgia," Rée confessed in a letter sent to Lou in May 1882. Thus the two men were affected, whereas Lou continued to be, as in the subtitle of *Zarathustra*, "For None and All." Just as in the photograph, two brilliant and stimulating minds were prostrate at her feet. For Lou, both thinkers proved to be a means of transition but not of destiny.

During the following months, the three characters met in different places, such as Lucerne, Tautenburg, and Tribschen (cf. Janz 1987, III:103–04). In the last, driven by his memories, Nietzsche took Lou to the place where he had lived the happiest moments with Wagner. Lou recalled how Nietzsche remained seated for a long time in silence on the shore of the lake. She saw how tears ran down his cheeks when he spoke to her of the time spent in that mythical land (cf. ibid., 104).

Nietzsche's relation with Lou continued to be marked by an intense exchange of existential philosophical ideas, as well as the discussion of the shared experience of the loss of God. In this regard, Lou confessed to Rée in a diary written for him in Tautenburg, when Lou remained alone with Nietzsche:

> We've talked ourselves to death these past three weeks, and strange-ly enough, he is now able to talk almost ten hours a day. . . . It's strange, but our conversations have led us automatically toward those chasms, those dizzying places, where one once climbed alone, to gaze into the abyss. We've constantly chosen the moun-tain goats, and if anyone had heard us, he would have thought two devils were conversing. (Andreas-Salomé 1991, 50)

Nietzsche seemed to perceive Lou as an outcast of the same idyllic world that he fervently yearned for, and it appears that in this profound affinity there was no place for any sensuous feeling. His thoughts always tended upward, toward the spiritual sphere. It was a totally intel-lectual eroticism that nonetheless awakened jealousy in Rée (cf. Janz 1987, III:115).

In the triangular situations lived throughout Lou's life (Lou-Rée-Nietzsche; Lou-Andreas-Rilke; Lou-Freud-Adler, to mention some), she seemed to find certain protection against any emotional risk. As a worthy "daughter" of Pallas Athena, the emotional function was not fully devel-oped in her, as opposed to her marked rational capacity: "Her power of rationalization protected her inwardly as she strove to master the man's world that was hers" (Binion 1968, 30). The only kind of relationship that she could admit with a man was that of competitiveness or of ownership.

The eternal recurrence, one of Nietzsche's fundamental doctrines, was enhanced considerably through the discussions held with Lou on walks to the mountain sacred to Franciscans, the Monte Sacro in Rome (cf. ibid., 54). Nietzsche seemed to find in Lou a philosophically kindred spirit, his *soror mystica*,[10] a muse or a spiritualized form of the Eternal Feminine:

> The most useful activity this summer was walking with Lou. There is a deep affinity between us in intellect and taste—and there are in other ways so many differences that we are the most instructive objects and subjects of observation for each other. I have never met anyone who could derive so many *objective insights* from experience, who knows how to deduce so much from all she has learnt. (Letter to Overbeck, September 1882)

In May 1882, Nietzsche wrote to Lou: "When I think for minutes about what I want, I look for words for a melody that I have and a melody for words that I have, and both things, which I have, do not agree, despite the fact that they stem from the same soul. That is my fate!" (cited in Ross, 1994, 81). Lou supplied the words for his melody, and together they produced the musical piece that bears the title of the poem written by Lou, "Gebet an das Leben" ("Hymn to Life"). "If you have no more happiness to give: / Give me your pain," the last lines read. Nietzsche was also highly moved by Lou's poem "An den Schmerz" ("To Sorrow"), in which she wrote: "Give me only one thing: pain which lends true greatness. . . . Do come and dip into the heart's deepest interior / and rummage through the depths of life . . . although we collapse in death / you are the pedestal for our soul's greatness" (cited by Mandel in Salomé 2002, xlix). Nietzsche sent this poem to his friend Peter Gast with a letter (July 1882) in which he confessed: "This poem has such power over me that I have never been able to read it without shedding tears; it is like a voice for which I have waited since my childhood." Pain, death, sorrow—words that reflect Nietzsche's own tragic nature. It is easy to understand the fascination produced by these words for a man who lived trapped in a state of *mortificatio*: "We can catch nothing at all except that which allows itself to be caught in precisely *our* net," concluded Nietzsche (D 117).

In May, while strolling alone in a park in Lucerne, Nietzsche solemnly proposed marriage to Lou—in person this time—and equally solemnly she refused, alluding that she wanted to remain free: "It seemed to

Lou that he was almost relieved when she turned him down" (Peters 1974, 101). They left the brief episode behind and continued with their friendship and with their study plan.[11]

In her memoirs, Lou described the impression caused in her by the presence of Nietzsche as a paradoxical mixture of "fascination, and, at the same time, an inner aversion" (Andreas-Salomé 1991, 50). What seemed to cause the most aversion was the evangelical zeal shown by Nietzsche to "recruit heroes as disciples." In her diary written for Rée, she described this difference between the two friends:

> Your style aims at convincing the reader in an intellectual man-
> ner; consequently, it is scientific and clear, and avoids all emo-
> tion. Nietzsche wants to convince totally, he wants his words to
> penetrate the deepest recesses of the soul and agitate its depths;
> he does not wish to instruct but rather to convert. (Nietzsche,
> Salomé and Rée 1982, 128)

Lou intuitively perceived Nietzsche's intentions towards her; on a certain occasion he had confessed: "I had the best intention of remaking her into the image I had formed of her" (Letter to Ida Overbeck dated July 24, 1882). However, having abandoned all religious dogmatism, Lou was able to become that "free spirit" that Nietzsche so yearned to be and never became.[12] She embodied his own desire for freedom of thought and action, unattainable for one who only dared transgress with his pen. "She is self-assured and knows just what she wants, without asking the world for permission, not caring what the world thinks of her," wrote Nietzsche to Gast (cited in Peters 1974, 112). Nietzsche thanked Malwida for procuring him that "young, truly heroic soul."

Referring to Nietzsche, Lou asked herself:

> Are we very close to each other? No, despite everything, no, we
> are not . . . in some hidden recess of our being, we are immense-
> ly apart one from the other. Comparing him with an old fortress,
> Nietzsche has some dungeons and secret caves that vanish upon
> a superficial observation and which, nonetheless, constitute his
> character. (Nietzsche, Salomé and Rée 1982, 126–27)

And with accurate insight, she finished with the following: "It is strange: the idea that some day we could become enemies struck me with a sudden force" (ibid.). However, the violent intrusion of Elisabeth and his mother in the relationship was the main cause of their final separation.

KINSHIP LIBIDO *vs.* EXOGAMIC LIBIDO

> The tie that binds sister to brother
> is strongest of all ties, I hold:
> They're riveted to one another
> more firmly than by lines of gold.
> —F. NIETZSCHE, Stanza written to his sister

Although it was initially possible to maintain the Nietzsche-Lou-Rée trinity given the secrecy of the ties between Lou and Rée, the triad began to crumble once Elisabeth appeared. Still single and with no affectionate perspectives at thirty-six years of age, Elisabeth was consumed by jealousy when she met this emancipated twenty-one-year-old so totally opposed to her own provincial and prudish nature.[13]

Nietzsche, totally unconscious of the scope of the dark feminine, had sent Elisabeth ahead to Jena to meet Lou at the temporary residence of Heinrich Gelzer, a Basel Byzantinist, while he looked for a place in Tautenburg to stay with his sister and his friend. Nietzsche had informed Elisabeth of everything concerning the young lady, except their plan to live together (cf. Binion 1968, 76), and in Elisabeth's view Lou's bold and cosmopolitan behavior was nothing short of "scandalous." She had met the young woman before in Bayreuth (at the premiere of Wagner's *Parsifal*), where Lou had become enthused with a third philosopher and metaphysician, the twenty-five-year-old Baron Heinrich von Stein. She had also established an acquaintance with a fellow countryman, Paul Joukowsky, a friend of Wagner's and a painter who had collaborated on the sets for *Parsifal*. Taken with Lou, Paul Joukowsky had invited her to participate in a séance (cf. Ross 1994, 655–56).

Elisabeth had written to her brother to report her experiences in

Bayreuth: a tangle of lies and half-truths intended to plant the demon of doubt in her jealously guarded "property." She openly manifested all her destructive capacity, however, after a new encounter with Lou in Jena, where she was informed by the lady herself about the plans of the trinity (cf. Janz 1987, III:115).

While the Gelzers were attending other friends of Nietzsche who were visiting them, Nietzsche's sister led Lou to a separate room where there took place an ominous duel of words (cf. ibid.). Like a jealous Hera, Elisabeth proceeded to start a campaign to discredit Lou, the "lovely sister" of Nietzsche, with the intention of provoking a final separation from her brother. Full of vengeful and hysterical rage, Elisabeth subsequently told Mme. Gelzer, perhaps distorting what had taken place in the room,

> Lou burst forth with a flood of invective against my brother: he's a madman who doesn't know what he wants, he's a common egoist who wanted only to exploit her mental gifts, she doesn't care a hoot for him but if now they didn't go to a city together it would mean she wasn't "great," that's why Fritz doesn't want to study with her—so as to shame her. What's more, Fritz would be crazy to think she should sacrifice herself to his aims or that they had the same aims at all, she knew nothing of his aims. Besides, were they to pursue any aims together, two weeks wouldn't go by before they were sleeping together, men all wanted only that, pooh to mental friendship! And she knew firsthand what she was talking about, she had been caught *twice* already in that kind of relationship. (cited in Binion 1968, 66–7)

With profound sorrow, Nietzsche confessed to Franz Overbeck, in a letter dated September 1882:

> Unfortunately, my sister has become a deadly enemy of Lou; she was morally outraged form start to finish. . . . In brief, I have the Naumburg "virtuousness" against me; there is a real *break* between us—and even my mother at one point forgot herself so far as to say one thing which made me pack my bags and leave

early the next day for Leipzig. My sister . . . quotes ironically in this regard, "Thus began Zarathustra's Fall."[14]

Since Elisabeth saw no disposition on Fritz's part to put an end to the relationship with Lou, she sent a long letter to Clara Gelzer in October 1882, in which she urged her not to read her brother's books: "You cannot imagine with what zeal that Russian has taken over his philosophy; it has been for her the most adequate adornment for her evil, selfish, and immoral nature. At that time she completely subdued Rée and Fritz."
Wishing to broaden the radius of her vengeance among all those closest to her brother, she concluded the letter with these lines:

Dearest Clara, I beg you *to speak* to the Overbecks. . . . Ah! Naturally, the Overbecks can do nothing! Who is it that is not taken with this Russian woman! In any case, if you hear it said that Fritz and I have broken up, let them say that I am jealous, it sounds more decorous than the truth. (Nietzsche, Salomé and Rée 1982, 177–82)

And, she proudly confessed, "I wrote accordingly to Dr. Rée's mother, trying to persuade her to use her influence towards securing Lou's return to her people in Russia" (Förster-Nietzsche 1912, II:173).
What Elisabeth had as yet not realized was that the poison instilled through her continuous intrigues, nasty words, and insults was already working its way into her brother's psychic system, and the ludic mood initially apparent was changing into black bitterness. A diabolic doubt began to show its effects, and Nietzsche discharged the bitter bile among the members of his own trinity. The shadow of jealousy and uncertainty led him to tell Lou about Rée's negative dispositions, about his pessimism and suicidal tendencies. This was a wrong tactic, because he achieved contrary results with Lou. This is evident from the following passage written by Lou in her memoirs:

If I ask myself what it was that began to affect my inner feelings toward Nietzsche, it was his increasing tendency to imply things with the intention of making me think less of Paul Rée, and also my astonishment that he could think such a method might work. Only after our departure for Leipzig did hostility toward me emerge as well, hateful reproaches, which I know only from one subsequent letter.[15] . . . But I was protected from much of the ugliness of this period by Paul Rée, who simply covered it up. . . . Paul Rée also concealed the extent to which the current stir had incited his family against me, to the point where they hated me, which of course was particularly evident on the part of his mother, who was pathologically jealous and wanted to keep her son all to herself. (Andreas-Salomé 1991, 50–1)

Paul and Lou left for Berlin and set up their residence. There "the communal life we'd dreamed of was fully realized," wrote Lou, "including a circle of young academics, several of them university lecturers" (Nietzsche, Salomé and Rée 1982, 51). Nietzsche once again occupied the familiar place of the abandoned one, the outcast.[16] In anguish he wrote to Lou, who was by December 1882 with Rée in Berlin:

Don't worry yourselves too much over my outbreaks of "megalomania" and "wounded vanity"—and if by chance some feeling drove me to take my life, there wouldn't be much to mourn over there either. What business of yours are my fantasies! . . . Only you might care together to dwell on the fact that ultimately I am a semi-lunatic with head trouble, one whom long loneliness has completely distracted.

In the course of her celibate relationship with "brother" Rée Lou wrote her first work, *Struggling for God*, which she signed with the pseudonym "Henri Lou." At the same time, Rée wrote his philosophic treatise *The Origin of Conscience*.[17] It was also during her relationship with Rée that Lou, aged twenty-six, married the Orientalist scholar Friedrich Carl Andreas, forty-one: "When I became engaged, it was not supposed to result in any change in our relationship. My husband had declared that he understood and accepted this as an irrevocable fact" (ibid., 55).[18] He likewise subsequently accepted several other of his wife's intimate relationships, the most notorious of which was her not-so-celibate illicit affair with the poet Rainer Maria Rilke.[19] This platonic (celibate) marriage lasted for forty-three years (cf. Peters 1987, 168–79). To those men she considered remarkable, Lou offered unlimited understanding,[20] admiration, and encouragement. However, she showed herself to be *une dame sans merci* when she abandoned, without guilt or compassion, those persons who loved her, when she considered that the relationship had exhausted itself.[21] The "father's daughter" always felt particularly attracted to "mother's sons," possibly because of those "feminine" qualities alien to an Athenian consciousness. In the end, what Nietzsche was unable to achieve was attained by the father of psychoanalysis, Sigmund Freud. Lou became his faithful disciple, and later his colleague and close collaborator.[22]

Athena was never in a woman's womb, and seemed to have no womb herself.[23] Although Lou's womb was fruitless, her intellect was not, and she became known to the world as a prominent writer and practicing psychoanalyst. Lou died in 1937.

Rée subsequently studied medicine and dedicated himself to his practice, taking care of the poor in the town of Celerina, located in the Swiss Engadine: "There, in the surrounding mountains, he accidentally fell to his death" in 1901 (Andreas-Salomé 1991, 56). However, the circumstances of his fall do not exclude the suspicion of suicide. Not long before this fatal event, Rée had stated: "I must philosophize, and when I no longer have the material to do so, the best thing for me would be to die" (cited in Janz 1987, II:299).

As for Nietzsche, the final separation brought upon him a deep state of depression, and during the somber winter days of 1882 he tried to take refuge from his despair in the "artificial paradises" provided by a "huge dose of opium," as he himself admitted (to Salomé and Rée, mid-December, 1882). This was clear proof of his incapacity to tolerate the abandonment of the disciple and his beloved friend who best seemed to understand the twists and turns of his soul and of his thoughts. "When I show you great rage," Nietzsche wrote to his sister (mid-May 1885), "it is because you forced me to relinquish the last human beings [Lou and Rée] with whom I could speak without Tartuffery. Now—I am alone. With them, I had been able to converse without mask about things which interest me" (cited by Mandel, Salomé 2001, lix).

In December 1882, Nietzsche informed Franz Overbeck of his immersion in the state of *nigredo* as a result of this abandonment:

> This last *morsel of life* has been the hardest I have ever chewed, and it is still possible that I might *choke* on it. I have suffered from the humiliating, tormenting memories of this past summer as from a bout of madness. . . . I am exerting every ounce of my self-mastery; but I have lived in solitude too long and fed too long off my "own fat," so that I am now being broken, as no other man could be, on the wheel of my own passions. . . . Unless I discover the alchemist's trick of turning this—muck into *gold*, I am lost.

In Overbeck's opinion, it was this alchemical goal that Nietzsche set for himself that saved him from suicide.

The appearance of his sister could have represented an opportunity for Nietzsche to establish contact with his anima, the mediator between the unconscious and the conscious. But for this to occur, the "incestuous" condition with the sister, writes Neumann, should have been solved through repression: "It is only after this repression has taken place that a man can achieve a personal attachment to a partner" (1979, 139–40). Neumann added:

> Owing to the repression of the incestuous attachment to the sister, this unconscious soul-image [different from that of the mother] is activated in the psyche of the man and in this way becomes ready for projection, so that it can be projected outwards on the feminine principle and can help to determine the man's relationship to it. (ibid., 202)

Nonetheless, in Nietzsche's case, it seems that neither the mother nor the sister (personal and suprapersonal) provided the necessary space for a projection to occur on a different real figure. We find examples of the nonrepression of the filial imago on several occasions.[24]

Elisabeth continuously encouraged the nonrepression of the filial imago. In response to a passage in a work by Schopenhauer (*Parerga and*

Paralipomena), for example, in which the pessimistic philosopher suggests that human life moves in a causal chain, she advised her brother of her conclusion: "Should that chain end with me as an old maid—and I almost think it will because from inner necessity I have recently rejected three worthy suitors—then, my dear Fritz, do not think badly of me and love me also in my old age" (Peters 1977, 19). Such a statement bears the guarantee of the unconditionality of her love and total dedication, with the possible hope of this being reciprocated. If at that time she was subtle and affectionate, with the appearance of Lou Elisabeth would openly show her hostility, so as to preserve what she considered her exclusive property: her brother.

Nietzsche blamed his mother and sister for his breakup with Lou and Rée, and from that moment he openly showed an anger that had previously been consciously denied (cf. Janz 1987, III:122). Proof of this is available in his correspondence of that time[25] and in pages recently discovered[26] of *Ecce Homo*, in which he declared that if the eternal recurrence—one of his most prominent doctrines—implied the return to the mother and to the sister, he would prefer to eliminate that experience totally.

According to Jung, when we disqualify the mother, when she is seen as "a wicked witch," we must translate it as: "the son is unable to detach his libido from the mother-imago, he suffered from resistances because he is tied to the mother" (CW 5:329).

> My dear Lou, the old, deep, heartfelt plea: *become who you are!* First, one has the difficulty of emancipating oneself from one's chains; and, ultimately, one has to emancipate oneself from this emancipation too! . . . In fond devotion to your destiny—for in you I love also my *hopes*. (Letter to Lou, end of August 1882)

"What do you love in others?" asked Nietzsche in *The Gay Science*. And he responds: "My hopes." What attracted Nietzsche about Lou seemed to be the "eternal masculine" element in her psyche. Emancipation and freedom are considered traditionally masculine attributes.

Emancipation from the chains represented by kinship libido requires an act of transgression, and the conscious Athenian anima, projected on Lou, could have been capable of overcoming the dark feminine repre-

sented both by the maternal-filial imago and by the irrational forces of
the unconscious. "Athena claims the power of the dark feminine represented by Medusa; consequently," suggests James Hillman, "she carries
on her breast the Gorgon, that terrifying image of irrationality" (1980,
27). Hillman also suggests that to locate Athena, from a psychological
viewpoint, "we must go close to what we call the ego (and Athena was
counselor of many heroes)" (ibid.). The solar hero requires the assistance
of Athena, who, since she combines feminine and masculine elements
in her psyche, does not constitute a menace to him. Athena is the appropriate mediator for all solar figures, to connect with the repressed or
denied feminine aspect.

Psychologically, the Athena woman acts "as self-restraining voice or
insight within our reflections. She is the internal Mentor—and it is as
Mentor-bird[27] that she appears so often in the Odyssey. When one takes
counsel with oneself, the act is itself Athenian" (Hillman 1980, 31).
Athena is the goddess of civilization and, as such, of consciousness.

At the same time, Athena represents victory over motherhood.[28]
Nietzsche thanked Malwida for having procured him, in the person of
Lou, a "young, truly heroic soul." The realization of Lou's imago personifying his inner Athenian energy could have helped Nietzsche
achieve the heroic ego, so as to differentiate himself from the
(M)other, because, as occurs with any other complex, the anima oper-
ates in a relationship compensatory to consciousness: it represents,
according to Jung, "those tendencies and contents hitherto excluded
from conscious life."

Nietzsche identified his transcendental soul with its temporary
incarnation represented by Lou. Due to the fact that the anima is projected, it is difficult to recognize it as one's own because it seems
rather like something outside of the individual. I believe that is why
Nietzsche fell under the spell of Lou, the woman bearer of the anima
for him: "Formerly I was inclined to take you for a vision, for the earthly apparition of my ideal," Nietzsche confessed in a letter to Lou. In
Nietzsche's case, as we can see, various archetypal figures emerged
from the animated unconscious in order to provide the energy
required for the act of separation or differentiation from the mother's complex. Nonetheless, Nietzsche either identified himself with

these figures or they remained projected in the world. Not integrated in his consciousness, the "Mentor-bird" returned once again to the unconscious, taking his "hopes" of emancipation. Thus Nietzsche continued suckling the "bilious milk offered him by the maternal disposition." With evident pride, Elisabeth stated in her work that Nietzsche finally and definitely gave up all marriage plans because all he needed was to be found exclusively in her. "No, it isn't a wife that I want. . . . Best of all it would be to have my old Lama again. A sister is an admirable institution for a philosopher, especially when she is cheerful, plucky and affectionate" (cited in Förster-Nietzsche 1912, II:315). As a result of the tragic outcome of the brief, albeit intense, affair with Lou, Nietzsche definitely discarded the idea of marriage, resentfully considering it "a poverty of the soul in pair" (Z I:20). With this statement, Elisabeth had finally won the battle. Nietzsche had proved himself incapable of becoming conscious of his dominating Athenian warlike anima, and lost the opportunity to differentiate the anima figure from the mother archetype.

Finally, in an unsuccessful attempt to free himself from the effects of Lou, Nietzsche tried to demolish her imago. He composed a long list enumerating her defects, a result of a projective intercrossing of his own shadows (negative and positive). Nietzsche presented Lou as an orally sadistic mother ready to destroy and devour (as his own mother and sister):

> [Lou has the] character of a cat—of an animal of prey that presents itself as a domestic animal. . . . / without application or cleanliness, without bourgeois honesty / horribly repressed sensuality / delay in maternity—due to atrophy and sexual delay. . . . / astute and full of self-control with respect to male sensuality / heartless and incapable of loving / as to the emotional aspect, always sickly and close to madness / ungrateful, immodest vis-à-vis the benefactor / unfaithful and dedicated to each person in the relationship with any other / without modesty of thought, always nude against herself / violent on a particular level / not very reliable / not "docile" / coarse in matters of honor. (cited in Ross 1994, 677)

Once Nietzsche's anima was imprisoned once again inside him, his insurmountable rancor toward Lou was definitively projected on phallic-emancipated women in general. We find numerous examples of this in his oeuvre. In *Beyond Good and Evil* he declared:

> Woman wants to become self-reliant—and for that reason she is beginning to enlighten men about "woman as such": this is one of the worst developments of the general *uglification* of Europe. For what must these clumsy attempts of women at scientific self-exposure bring to light! Woman has much reason for shame; so much pedantry, superficiality, schoolmarmishness, petty presumption, petty licentiousness and immodesty lies concealed in woman. . . . Even now female voices are heard which—holy Aristophanes!—are frightening: they threaten with medical explicitness what a woman *wants* from man, first and last. Is it not the worst taste when woman sets about becoming scientific that way? Unless a woman seeks a new adornment for herself that way—I do think adorning herself is part of the Eternal-Feminine?—she surely wants to inspire fear of herself—perhaps she seeks mastery. . . . We men wish that woman should not go on compromising herself through enlightenment. (BGE 232)

Again: "When a woman has scholarly inclinations there is usually something wrong with her sexually" (BGE 144). Perhaps inspired by eagle-Lou, he wrote: "Men have so far treated woman like birds who had strayed to them from the height: as something more refined and vulnerable, wilder, stranger, sweeter, and more soulful—but as something one has to lock up lest it fly away" (BGE 237a). In the following paragraph, we read: "To go wrong on the fundamental problem of 'man and woman,' to deny the most abysmal antagonism between them and the necessity of an eternally hostile tension, to dream perhaps of equal rights, equal education, equal claims and obligations—that is a *typical* sign of shallowness." And in a passage of *Ecce Homo*, we find the following: "Perhaps I am the first psychologist of the eternally feminine. They all love me—an old story—not counting *abortive* females, the 'emancipated' who lack the stuff for children" (EH III:5). Nietzsche considered that the only women who were not menacing were those who had been mothers. He identified with them, because, according to him, "pregnancy has made women kinder, more patient, more timid, more pleased to submit" (GS 72).

Although after a few months Nietzsche reconciled himself first with Elisabeth and later with his mother, the wounds resulting from the affair with Lou remained tacitly open, particularly between brother and sister. Elisabeth, perhaps reacting to that very same wound, and after she could have been considered eliminated from the list of marriageable candidates at almost forty years of age, in 1885 decided to marry Dr. Bernhard Förster, a well-known Wagnerian admirer and virulent anti-Semite (cf. Macintyre 1992, 99). This gentleman embodied all those aspects that Nietzsche most repudiated and hated in a human being. It would seem that it was now Elisabeth's turn to take revenge, since with her choice of partner Nietzsche felt betrayed in his own ideals and refused to attend the wedding (cf. ibid., 116). Nietzsche observed in this regard: "People like my sister must be irreconcilable enemies of my thoughts and my philosophy. That lies in the nature of things" (cited in Peters 1977, 76). In the same trend of feelings and ideas, Elisabeth, in her work *The Life of Nietzsche*, strongly attacked Lou and the Overbecks, whom she considered accomplices to "all the vexation she [Lou] has caused my dear brother and myself" (1912, II:142).

The newly wed couple left for Paraguay, together with other German patriots who shared Förster's convictions, to found a Teutonic colony and a pure German race, away from any Jewish influences (cf. Macintyre 1992, 116). The Aryan colony in Paraguay failed: the people who had invested in the project and trusted in the endeavor lost all their capital, and the Promised Land turned out to be a precarious, wild, and inhospitable place. While the Förster-Nietzsche couple lived in a spacious and comfortable home, the other colonists found themselves living in miserable huts (cf. ibid., 130). Intimidated by the general discontent, the colonists' request to be reimbursed for their investment, and the bad publicity that spread in Germany with regard to the project, Bernhard Förster took his life on June 3, 1889 (cf. ibid., 139), the same year as Nietzsche's mental breakdown. Like her mother, Elisabeth experienced a single, short marriage.

CHAPTER 7

Zarathustra: a dithyramb of solitude

Here I sat waiting, waiting—yet for nothing,
beyond good and evil, enjoying now the light,
now the shadows, all only a game,
all the sea, all noon, all time without a goal.
Then, suddenly, Lady Friend![1] One turned into two—
and Zarathustra passed me by.

—F. NIETZSCHE, "Sils-Maria" (1882)

Zarathustra is a mirror of Nietzsche's own cryptic autobiography.

—JOACHIM KÖHLER, *Zarathustra's Secret*

Zarathustra . . . is an *unintelligible* book, because it is based on
experiences which I share with nobody.

—F. NIETZSCHE (Letter to Overbeck, August 1886)

FOR NIETZSCHE, CREATION WAS "THE great redemption from suffering.
. . . Indeed, there must be much bitter dying in your life, you cre-
ators" (Z II:2).[2] Creation was the means he found to overcome his
profound depression; the greater the adversity and interior conflict,
the greater his creative capacity. He believed that inner chaos was a
necessary precondition for human creativity: "I tell you: one must have
chaos in one, to give birth to a dancing star" (Z P:5).

With depression, there occurs a lowering of the frontiers between consciousness and unconsciousness (*abaissement du niveau mental*). Thus consciousness is invaded by unconscious psychic contents, now energized. This chaotic invasion of feelings, impulses, desires, and attitudes—alien to our consciousness and therefore unmanageable—can be extremely painful. Nonetheless, depression also has a positive aspect: the appearance of hidden or forbidden contents that bring into consciousness unknown potentialities, unperceived until that moment.

Becoming aware of the positive aspect of pain can allow its transformation into a creative, germinating quality and a broadening of consciousness. In Nietzsche's case we can say that he tried to transform the suffering caused by the Lou-Rée affair, including his family's involvement, into his magnum opus, *Thus Spoke Zarathustra*. In this way he created a rope over the "veritable abyss of emotions" into which he felt thrown by personal betrayals, in order to reach his compensatory ideal: the *Übermensch*. *Thus Spoke Zarathustra* can be considered Nietzsche's *opus alchymicum*:[3] he wanted to slay "the Great Dragon," the monster that embodied the " 'mother' as the symbol of an unconscious that holds the son fast into the collective world of drives" (Neumann 1974, 21).[4] " 'Thou shalt' is the name of the Great Dragon. But the Lion-spirit [*leo viridis*] says, 'I will' " (Z I:1). The victory over the dragon, according to Jung, is equivalent to the sacrificing of the regressive (incestuous) fantasies (cf. CW 5:316ff).

Thus Spoke Zarathustra is a provocative book in which we encounter radical concepts rarely found in Nietzsche's other published works. Among these concepts are those of the *Übermensch*, the "will to power," and the doctrine of eternal recurrence. *Zarathustra* also stands completely separate from the rest of Nietzsche's oeuvre because of its biblical style. The numerous parallels between *Zarathustra* and the Old and New Testaments are not only ideological and doctrinal, but also stylistic. Subsequent works seem to be a profane exegesis of this seminal book. Parables, myths, hymns, allegories, sermons, poems, dreams, songs, enigmas, elegies, panegyrics, and apocalyptic revelations all form an amalgam of styles that provide this vertiginous work with an exuberant richness of tones and nuances.

Nietzsche wrote the first part of *Zarathustra* in ten days,[5] as if under the effects of a heady spell. The dithyrambic rhapsodist related that practically the whole of the book was whispered in his ear while he marched over the mountains in a mood of ecstasy. "[*Zarathustra*] overtook me," he confessed in *Ecce Homo* (EH III:1).

Nietzsche's *Zarathustra* would be the result of the emerging of his own creative *daimonion*, which manifested itself under the aegis of inspiration. "If you gaze long enough into the abyss, the abyss will gaze back into you" (BGE 146), and Nietzsche's "abyss began to speak." For him, the animated unconscious was perceived as an autonomous force governing the conscious psyche and that force could be experienced by him as inspiration and rapture:[6]

> If one had the slightest residue of superstition left in one's system, one could hardly reject altogether the idea that one is merely incarnation, merely mouthpiece, merely a medium of overpowering forces. The concept of revelation—in the sense that suddenly, with indescribable certainty and subtlety, something becomes *visible*, audible, something that shakes one to the last depths and throws one down—that merely describes the facts. One hears, one does not seek; one accepts, one does not ask who gives; like lightning, a thought flashes up, with necessity, without hesitation regarding its form—I never had any choice. A rapture whose tremendous tension occasionally discharges itself in a flood of tears—now the pace quickens involuntarily, now it becomes slow; one is altogether beside oneself, with the distinct consciousness of subtle shudders and of one's skin creeping down to one's toes; a depth of happiness in which even what is most painful and gloomy does not seem something opposite but rather conditioned, provoked, a *necessary* color in such a superabundance of light; an instinct for rhythmic relationship that arches over wide spaces and forms—length, the need for a rhythm with wide arches, is almost the measure of the force of inspiration, a kind of compensation for its pressure and tension. Everything happens involuntarily in the highest degree but as in a gale of a feeling of freedom, of absoluteness, of power, of divinity—The involuntariness of image and metaphor is strangest of

all; one no longer has any notion of what is an image or a metaphor; everything offers itself as the nearest, most obvious, simplest expression. It actually seems, to allude to something Zarathustra says, as if the things themselves approached and offered themselves as metaphors. . . . This is my experience of inspiration; I do not doubt that one has to go back thousands of years in order to find anyone who could say to me, "it is mine as well." (EH III: TSZ 3)

The author's nonordinary, altered state of consciousness suggests that we are dealing here with a raw material that allows the underlying psychological process to become directly visible. Jung called *Zarathustra* the "*drame intérieur* of the author himself" (SNZ I:112): each figure that appears in his poetic drama (the Tightrope Walker, the Clown, the Wanderer, the Shadow, the Shepherd, the Ugliest Man, etc.) is a representation of different aspects of Nietzsche's psyche. Jung suggested that each chapter of the book represents "a stage in a process of initiation," and every personification represents "a new image in the process of initiation" (SNZ I: 459, 461). Graham Parks concludes that "*Thus Spoke Zarathustra* is a play of images constituting a consummate picture of the most comprehensive soul, of psyche in totality. It is possible, and enlightening, to read the entire text as a complex image of a single soul" (1994, 360).

The central theme of the first part of *Thus Spoke Zarathustra* is the announcement of the death of God.[7] With this great parricide, connoting the elimination of the transpersonal world, Nietzsche established himself subversively as the "I" of the *ego cogito*, which implies, "I am the measure of all things." Only based on this premise did he conceive the possibility of being a creator, of experimenting with such grandeur as to create *ex nihilo* his new Gospel. Jung suggested that "wise men or prophets appear in times of trouble, when mankind is in a state of confusion, when an old orientation has been lost and a new one is needed" (SNZ I:24). Indeed in such a state of confusion, and looking for a new orientation, Nietzsche was "overcome by that archetypal situation" (ibid., 10). The "transvaluation of all values" after the death of God was an expression of Nietzsche's enantiodromia.[8] Having fallen completely into a nihilistic state (ego alienation), Nietzsche's psyche must have constellated the archetype of the wise prophet, a personification of the Self,[9] so as to find a compensatory meaning for his meaningless existence.[10] Through *Zarathustra*, Nietzsche attempted to forge a new set of values in order to replace those he had lost.

Studying the phenomenon of inflation, Jung stated:

> It is a psychological rule that when an archetype has lost its metaphysical hypostasis, it becomes identified with the conscious mind of the individual, which it influences and refashions in its own form. And since an archetype always possesses certain numinosity, the integration of the numen generally produces an inflation of the subject. (CW 11:315)

Instead of recognizing the transpersonal forces of the collective unconscious (archetypes), Nietzsche's ego identified itself with those forces. Thus he deified himself through Zarathustra, a clear phenomenon of inflation through the archetype of the Wise Old Man. In a godlike state, as Zarathustra, Nietzsche wanted to bend all things to his will.[11]

For Jung, Nietzsche's encounter with Zarathustra was a classic example of broadening of consciousness through the ego's encounter with the Self.[12] According to Jung, "When a summit of life is reached, when the bud unfolds and from the lesser the greater emerges, then, as Nietzsche says, 'One becomes Two' and the greater figure—which one always was, but which remained invisible—appears to the lesser personality with the force of revelation" (CW 9, I:121). According to Jung, Nietzsche himself is defined as Personality No. 1, and we can observe the emergence of Personality No. 2 in the figure of the semi-legendary Persian prophet Zarathustra, the one responsible for the good-evil fission and for the "transportation of morality into the metaphysical realm" (EH IV:3). The radical shift of beliefs is evident in the voice of Personality No. 2,[13] which emerged from Nietzsche's animated unconscious.

With regard to the appearance of the figure of Zarathustra, Jung is of the opinion that Nietzsche "obviously felt quite clear that the experience of that figure was archetypal. It brought something of the breath of centuries with it, and it filled him with a peculiar sense of destiny: he felt that he was called to mend a damage done in the remote past" (SNZ I:10).

One might add that the figure, on a personal level, attempted to mend the damage implicit in Nietzsche's own history. While the young Nietzsche felt that with the death of his father he remained as a "tree deprived of its crown [whose] branches languished toward the earth" without any sign of life, possessed by Zarathustra's spirit he felt like a pine: "long, silent, hard, alone, of the best and most resilient wood, magnificent—and in the end reaching out with strong branches for his *own* dominion." As a pine, Nietzsche-Zarathustra "refreshes even the gloomy ones, the failures; [whose] sight reassures and heals the heart even of the restless" (Z IV:11).

Following the death of God, Zarathustra, at thirty years of age,[14] climbs a mountain and confines himself in a cave,[15] rejoicing at the superabundance of the new knowledge that he must go deeper into himself and empty himself of what he knows, so that he can be renewed. "Who is going up to the mountain?" asks Hillman. "Is it the unconscious do-gooder Christian in us, he who has lost his historical Christianity and is an unconscious crusader, knight, missionary, savior?" (2000, 126). Nietzsche-Zarathustra began the ascent, unmindful of the fact that he bore within him the shadow of God, who would reappear after a Protean transformation, personified by the *Übermensch*.[16]

After ten years, Zarathustra decides to come down to the human world, evoking the image of Moses descending from Mount Sinai, to offer humankind the new tablets of the law.[17] With this descending movement, Nietzsche would have had the opportunity to humanize the constellated archetypal force: "I must *go under*—go down, as it is said by man, to whom I want to descend . . . Zarathustra wants to become man again" (Z P:1).[18] Hillman reminds us of a pertinent phrase in this regard: "come down from the mountains, monks . . . come into the vale of soul-making" (2000, 131).

This descent of Zarathustra, in the opinion of the philosopher David Farrell Krell, "is perhaps the most important step, but it is not a homecoming, for Zarathustra regarded his cave in the mountains, his solitude, as his uncanny home" (1996, 20). After four failed attempts at staying down (in each of the four parts of the book), the hermit sage goes back up the mountain alone, that is, he loses himself once again in the collective unconscious: "Down there . . . all speech is in vain. . . . He who grasps everything human would have to grapple with everything. But for that my hands are too clean. I do not even want to inhale their breath" (Z III:9). As a result, in the end Nietzsche was incapable of making "soul."[19]

In a way, Zarathustra is a solar hero, a Promethean hero who emerged in Sils-Maria at "six thousand feet beyond man and time": a consciousness saturated by the superabundance of light shed by the sun, which, like the titanic mythical character, aims at destroying the status quo. J. W. Perry has assumed the emergence of a sunlike figure in the psyche as a compensatory fantasy in view of a weak ego trapped in the (M)other. He wrote: "When the ego is too demoralized to take on this responsibility, and settles into its weakness as a way of life, playing a part of the sick or handicapped personality, then the only outlet for the hero image is in compensatory fantasy" (1976, 51–52).

As Jung points out, *Thus Spoke Zarathustra* is "the story of an initiation process that failed" (cf. SNZ I:460). What Nietzsche seems to have been looking for primarily was to escape, through a vertical-spiritual axis, from the suffering caused by his entrapment in the horizontal-material axis: Nietzsche-Zarathustra's battle was against "disgust with existence" (Z III:13).[20] So Nietzsche moved from the secular realm of matter to the sacred realm of the spirit.[21] If we are to follow Hillman's interpretations of peaks and vales, the vale can be related to the horizontal axis and the mountain peak to the vertical. Hillman explains that the peaks belong to the spiritual ambit, and that "the climber up the peaks is in search of spirit or is the drive of the spirit in search of itself" (2000, 118). The vale, in turn, can be considered, "in the usual religious language of our culture, [as] a depressed emotional place—the vale of tears" (ibid.). Hillman adds: "The meanings of the vale and valley include entire subcategories referring to such sad things as the decline of years and old age, the world regarded as a place of troubles, sorrow, and weeping, and the world regarded as the scene of the mortal, the earthly, the lowly" (ibid.).

With Zarathustra, Nietzsche abandoned the "feminine valley," the world of "troubles, sorrow, and weeping," to take flight toward the most elevated peaks in search of freedom: "I am a wanderer and a mountain climber . . . I do not like the plains" (Z III:1). And he explained: "Whoever climbs the highest mountains laughs at all tragic plays and tragic seriousness" (Z I:7).

Writing to Overbeck in February 1883, Nietzsche asserted: "Before I was in an authentic abyss of sentiment but I have known how to raise myself in a considerable 'vertical' manner toward my own heights." He shot himself like an antigravitational arrow toward the world of the spirit: "My most hidden will [is to be] a bow lusting for its arrow, an arrow lusting for its star—a star ready and ripe in its noon, glowing, pierced, enraptured by annihilating sun arrows—a sun itself and an inexorable solar will" (Z III:12–30). With the constellation of the archetype of the Wise Old Man, Nietzsche was snared in a state of *sublimatio*. Trapped in the hyperborean regions,[22] identified with the *fictio* of his own *poesis*, his ego took on an attitude of supreme grandeur. It is the grandiose "I," possessed by the transpersonal meaning of the archetype, who declares in *Ecce Homo*:

> Among my writings, my *Zarathustra* stands to my mind by itself. With that I have given mankind the greatest present that has ever been made to it so far. This book, with a voice bridging centuries, is not the highest book there is, the book that is truly characterized by the air of the heights—the whole fact of man lies *beneath* it at a tremendous distance. . . . Such things reach only the most select.

It is also possible to appreciate his megalopsychia (Aristotle) in the following declaration: "Zarathustra possesses an eternal right to say: 'I draw circles around me and sacred boundaries; fewer and fewer men climb with me on ever higher mountains: I am building a mountain range out of ever more sacred mountains'" (EH 3: Z 6).

Jung commented: "We are bound to admit that Nietzsche lived beyond instinct, in the lofty heights of heroic sublimity. . . . Nietzsche got stuck in a state of high tension . . . one cannot avoid foreseeing that this joyful intensification of mood to heroic and godlike heights is dead certain to be followed by an equally deep plunge into the abyss" (CW 7:39). "This is my alpha and omega," declared Nietzsche-Zarathustra, "that all that is heavy and grave should become light; all that is body, dancer; all that is spirit, bird" (Z III:16–6). According to Jung, "you cannot individuate if you are spirit. . . . If you speak of individuation at all, it necessarily means the individuation of beings who are in the flesh, in the living body" (SNZ I:202).

The "spirit of gravity" eventually took revenge on Nietzsche as the spiritual being. His supreme and most powerful enemy reminded him of the fateful fall: " 'O Zarathustra,' he whispered mockingly, syllable by syllable; 'you philosopher's stone! You threw yourself up high, but every stone that is thrown must fall' " (Z III:11.1). To the spirit of gravity, Zarathustra opposed the bird's way (cf. ibid.). Therefore it is possible to conclude that Nietzsche "was tragically caught in the archetypal dynamism of *sublimatio* as an autonomous process of dissociation. It impelled him further and further from the personal, earthly reality until the inevitable enantiodromia sent him crashing to the ground" (Edinger 1996, 126). Thus, finally, Nietzsche-Zarathustra fell and drowned in the sea (the unconscious) like the mythical Icarus, who, escaping with his father from the labyrinth (the horizontal-material axis) with wings made by Daedalus out of feathers and fastened with wax, flew too close to the sun, and, once the wax melted, plunged to his death in the sea.

Although when Nietzsche wrote the poem "Sils-Maria" he perceived Zarathustra as something separate from his ego, something similar to a second personality, later, with the total abandonment of his feeling of relatedness and the suffering that ensued, the Promethean consciousness took hold of him completely. Nietzsche was no longer the father and Zarathustra the son: Nietzsche became Zarathustra, the prophet who offered the new tablets of the law and his doctrine of will to power, the driving element in all life: "I stood in the foothills today—beyond the world, held scales and weighed the world" (Z III:10).

Jung considered that Nietzsche identified with Zarathustra "naively." And he added:

> He [was] so swallowed up by the archetype from the collective unconscious. [Nietzsche] intuited it because it is a figure of such mighty attraction: his whole life was sucked in by it and the body could go by the board. That special body, the man Nietzsche, simply disappeared behind it. Therefore, there [was] nobody left to receive Zarathustra's message. Zarathustra [spoke] his own message, using the means of the body of Nietzsche, and the ordinary human being, Nietzsche, [did] not exist.

[Nietzsche] could not stand up against Zarathustra; he was completely dissolved. (SNZ I:203)

The emergence of Nietzsche's second personality exacerbated his
mania for solitude and isolation, yet nothing was harder for him to bear
than loneliness of the spirit, lack of affection.[23] As his state of inflation
intensified, little by little he lost the few friends on whom he had projected his unrealized shadows. He felt that they did not understand him,
even that they had betrayed him.

Identified with the numinous figure, Nietzsche lost the opportunity to
integrate the energy of the "wise prophet with his consciousness, so as to
offer meaning and overcome his nihilistic state." The energy emanating
from the archetype that possessed him did not act as a psychopomp and
initiator capable of accompanying Nietzsche on the uncharted journey
through the hidden inner realms of his spirit, as Virgil did with Dante:[24]

> Throughout *The Divine Comedy*, the guiding principle explains
> the logic of the labyrinth,[25] the meanings of the wonders and the
> horrors, and of their relationship to the moral life. Perhaps most
> important, Virgil keeps Dante *moving* through the realm, keeps
> him on a journey rather than transfixed at one of its situations
> like the many human sufferings they encounter. . . . The guide
> did not necessarily design the labyrinth, but he becomes its rev-
> elator and spokesman, implying a secret affinity with the archi-
> tect. (Larsen 1996, 210)

Nietzsche, incapable of consciously incorporating the constellated
archetype of the wise prophet, did not consider this experience as part of
his subjectivity; rather, he invested it with a mystical air and buried his
conscious personality under the shelter of this great shadow. Thus he
lived and addressed the world convinced that he was the herald of a
divine revelation. Jung concluded:

> Nietzsche [was] so interwoven with Zarathustra that it is
> almost impossible to separate the two. . . . You see, the old man
> would tell him something about the inner world; he would be

the psychopompos, the great initiator who would lead Nietzsche to the understanding, or to the vision at least, of pleromatic things, the things which are below our level of consciousness. And then Nietzsche might have made a record of what he had experienced and would perhaps have presented it to the world. But it would then be a story of a traveler on uncharted seas, and not a book of new values or philosophic thought. Or if he wrote a book of philosophical thought, it would not be Zarathustra who was speaking. [Nietzsche] would take the responsibility for what he said. He [did] not, however. He [said] that Zarathustra [was] speaking, and there is the entanglement. (SNZ I:222)

Consequently, Jung stressed the importance of the need for a critical discrimination and a renunciation of the demands of the spiritual power. The "I," called Personality No. 1 by Jung, must be the ultimate meaning of our existence, even though Personality No. 2 should not be forgotten, because it allows the broadening of consciousness.

ZARATHUSTRA'S SHADOW

> I am a wanderer who has already walked a great deal at your heels. . . . I have already sat on every surface; like weary dust, I have gone to sleep in mirrors and windowpanes; everything takes away from me, nothing gives, I become thin—I am almost like a shadow.
> But after you, O Zarathustra, I flew and blew the longest. And even when I hid from you I was still your best shadow; wherever you sat, I sat too.
> *The Shadow* (Z IV: 9)

Just as Nietzsche had the opportunity to come into contact with the archetype of the wise prophet, he also had several opportunities during his lifetime to establish contact with the shadow. When he reached the same age at which his father had died, for example—a time that coincid-

ed with Rohde's engagement—his "vitality went down to a minimum."
Nietzsche described this experience:

> My father died at the age of thirty-six. . . . In the same year in
> which his life went downward, mine too went downward: at
> thirty-six, I reached the lowest point of my vitality—I still lived,
> but without being able to see three steps ahead. Then—it was
> 1879—I retired from my professorship at Basel, spent the sum-
> mer in St. Moritz like a shadow, and the next winter, than which
> not one in my life has been poorer in sunshine, in Naumburg as
> a shadow. This was my minimum: *The Wanderer and His Shadow*
> originated at this time. Doubtless, I then knew about shadows.
> (EH II:1)

By that time, Nietzsche seemed to have already acknowledged the
shadow, as he declared that less darkness would cling to humankind if
the shadows were omnipresent. Both the Shadow and the Wanderer in
his work express a desire for union in order to acquire completion:

> The Wanderer: Only now do I notice how impolite I am, my
> beloved shadow: I have not said a word about how *pleased* I am
> to see you as well as hear you. You should know that I love the
> shadow as much as I cherish the light. For facial beauty, clarity
> of speech, quality and firmness of character, shadow is as neces-
> sary as light. They are not opponents: they are rather affection-
> ate, holding hands—and if the light disappears, the shadow slips
> away after it (WS: P).

In turn, the Shadow, uttering, "When man shuns the light, we shun
man: our freedom extends that far," asserts its autonomy. Nietzsche had
the right intuition when he wrote that the Shadow was "greedy for
knowledge," because understanding something about one's shadow side
is the beginning of the most important knowledge of all: self-knowledge.

However, when he wrote his *Zarathustra*, Nietzsche, possessed by the
persona of the Persian prophet, sent the Shadow back to his cave (unconscious) so he could leave unencumbered for the "bliss of Noontide": "I

will run alone, so that it may grow bright around me." He envisioned his perfect *Übermensch* without shadow: "The sun of [the overman's] knowledge will stand at noontide," says Nietzsche-Zarathustra at the end of Part I of the book. When he banished his shadow, Nietzsche could assume the creation of the ideal, of the *Übermensch*, no longer as a work of God but as man's concern, derived from the theogonic powers inherent to his Promethean nature: "The beauty of the overman came to me as a shadow.[26] O my brothers, what are gods to me now?" (EH III: TSZ 8). The *Übermensch* is a Promethean man who has assumed the attributes of the deity: he is "the amoral worshipper of instinct, whose God is dead, and who presumes to be God himself, or rather a demon 'six thousand feet beyond good and evil' " (Jung, CW 10:434).

To Jung, who pointed out Zarathustra's inability to accept his shadow (embodied in the Ugliest Man), it was evident that Nietzsche was incapable of integrating his own shadow as well. When the Ugliest Man prompts Zarathustra to decipher the riddle of his being, the latter responds: "I recognize you well . . . *you are the murderer of God!* Let me go. You could not bear *him* who saw *you*—who always saw you through and through, you ugliest man!" (Z IV:7).

The Ugliest Man justifies his great crime in terms that reflect his imago of a persecuting God (cf. Z IV:7).[27] The Self as "eye" carries the disturbing connotation of "judgment." "But see how the eye of God is on those who fear him" (Psalm 33:18). This is because the Self, as the center of the psyche, "searches the hearts of men, laying bare the truth and pitilessly exposing every cranny of the soul. It is a reflection of one's insight into the total reality of one's own being" (Jung, CW 10:639). Yet "The Ugliest Man," says Hillman, "is at the same time the redeemer in disguise" (1994b, 77). Unfortunately, Nietzsche-Zarathustra was unable to perceive the redeeming potentiality in this terrible personification of the shadow. Incapable of assuming his feelings of guilt, of self-contempt and of shame, brought about by his declaration of the death of God, Zarathustra flees from the Ugliest Man, for in his presence he feels "frozen down to his very entrails" (Z IV:7).

Nietzsche-Zarathustra sends the disdained character embodied in the Ugliest Man to his cave so that he may meet the noontide, a moment perfectly unshadowed: "Mid-day; moment of the shortest shadow; end of

the longest error; zenith of mankind; *INCIPIT ZARATHUSTRA*" (TI 4).
Yet before meeting the noontide Zarathustra has to face and deal with
other characters, personifications of Nietzsche's shadow. One is the
Voluntary Beggar, who embodies the intolerable feelings of rage, anger,
and hate that arose in Nietzsche-Zarathustra due to his fellow men's failure to recognize the valuable gift he had presented them with in his previous works.[28] "Away, away with you," Zarathustra shouts at the Voluntary
Beggar (Z IV:8).[29] Nonetheless, this character comes to him in his cave.

The next character invited to rest in Zarathustra's cave is the Shadow
itself, from whom the new lawgiver tried to run away but who manifested his strengths and weaknesses to Zarathustra: "and if there is anything
in me that is virtue, it is that I had no fear of any forbiddance . . . nothing is true, all is permitted" (Z IV:9). Nietzsche-Zarathustra projected
onto this figure his frustrated longings to love and be loved, his concomitant feelings of self-denigration, and his despair at not having fulfilled his
most intimate yearnings, represented by his need for belonging and his
sense of destiny.

For Nietzsche-Zarathustra, it is not the human being but the Shadow,
the Wanderer, who desires homecoming.[30] So speaks the Shadow:
"Trying thus to find my home—O Zarathustra, do you know it?—trying
this was my trial; it consumes me. 'Where is—*my* home?' I ask and
search and have searched for it, but I have not found it. O eternal everywhere, O eternal nowhere, O eternal—in vain" (Z IV:9). Yet, even though
Zarathustra recognizes the Shadow as his own shadow,[31] he denies it in
order to finally enter alone into the luminosity of noontime, returning to
the spirit world.

Jung gave emphasis to another episode of Nietzsche-Zarathustra's
denial of the unconscious: the rejection of "the enormous black snake
hanging from the shepherd's mouth," which takes place in the riddle of
the shepherd and the snake (Z III:2).[32] The snake, due to its chthonic
qualities, is an agent of the unconscious: it "appears in mythology as an
agent of darkness [unconscious] that may at the same time be the awak-
ener of consciousness" (Geer 1996, 162). In this regard, Jung points out:

> The unconscious insinuates itself in the form of a snake if the
> conscious mind is afraid of the compensating tendency of the

unconscious, as is generally the case in regression. But if the compensation is accepted in principle, there is no regression, and the unconscious can meet halfway through introversion. (CW 5:587)

Thus the snake becomes another redeemer in disguise that Nietzsche is incapable of recognizing.[33]

Finally, in his cave, the place of beginning and ending, Nietzsche-Zarathustra confronts all the shadow personifications of his own deepest needs: the one that demands pity from him (the Soothsayer), the lack of recognition (the two kings), the one trampled by man who wants to be assured that he is indeed a great expert (the Leech), the one who requires flattery (the Magician), the one whom God disappointed, and who wants a new ideal (the Last Pope), the murderer of God who is burdened with the despair of endless guilt which he wants to get rid of (the Ugliest Man), the one who gave up searching for happiness on earth and is sick of endless giving (the Voluntary Beggar), the one who aspires to achieve all that is forbidden (the Shadow). All are weighted down by the past. However, even after inviting his dark brothers to his cave, and having the opportunity to recognize them as parts of himself, Zarathustra finally rejects them all because he only wants beside him those men who are capable of reflecting his own pristine image: "Nor are you beautiful and wellborn enough for me. I need clean, smooth mirrors . . . on your surface even my own image is distorted . . . much in you is crooked and misshapen. There is no smith in the world who could hammer you right and straight for me" (Z IV:11).

We may conclude from this that Nietzsche lacked body (material existence) and did not achieve the integration of the shadow; consequently, he could not impregnate the spirit and carry out the indispensable *coagulatio*. As occurred with the *Übermensch*, he preached about the body without having attained it:

Nietzsche preaches any amount about the body, but ask the man Nietzsche what he thinks about the body and he will tell a different story. It is a possession when people preach things which they don't make true in their lives. They simply run away with the disembodied spirit who talks marvelous high stuff, but they are not confronted with it in their lives. (Jung, SNZ II:222)

According to Edinger, "As long as an individual does not function out of substance, as long as he or she does not demonstrate material weight but exists as a kind of flimsy, gypsy, transparent, indefinitive entity, there'll be no shadow. . . . The only way to avoid casting a real shadow is not to have any materiality" (1995, 88). Nietzsche-Zarathustra avoided casting his real shadow and maintained the appearance of "a disembodied spirit": Nietzsche "became a ghost that wanders over glaciers" (BGE 243).

Having failed to recognize his own shadow as a living part of his personality, Nietzsche could not effect the necessary integration to consciousness of his own dark side. As a result, he tended to project it on the other, converting him or her into a scapegoat, guilty of all his misfortune. Strongly identified with the ego ideal, the shadow was separated from his consciousness and projected on the surrounding world: Nietzsche first looked for the contradictor in Wagner, and then concentrated his wrath on the philosophers, whom he attacked in their rationality; on the moralists, attacked for their ethical sense; on the priests, whom he considered "castrated and castrating"; on Christianity in general, and in particular on St. Paul; on emancipated women, maenadic destroyers; and on the individual, in whom he perceived the danger of his ruin.

Nietzsche's incapacity to realize his shadow led Jung to write the following regarding the "fatal omen" inherent in the return of the shadow: "You will see how the Shadow comes back at Nietzsche with vengeance: that is the tragedy of *Zarathustra*" (SNZ II:1114). And Nietzsche's shadow came back to claim his due: " 'O Zarathustra,' the child said to me, 'look at yourself in the mirror.' " But when I looked into the mirror I cried out, and my heart was shaken: for it was not myself I saw but a devil's grimace and scornful laughter" (Z II:1).

Part Three

CHAPTER 8

Now his wars on God begin

He with the body waged a fight,
but the body won; it walks upright.
Then he struggled with the heart:
innocence and peace depart.
Then he struggled with the mind;
his proud heart he left behind.
Now his wars on God begin;
at stroke of midnight God shall win.

—W. B. Yeats, "The Four Ages of Man"

From the time of his beloved father's death, Nietzsche's entire life seems to have centered on compensating for this abandonment. The loss was absolute and his "I" inhibited. Echoes of pathological mourning permeate all his life and works.

Nietzsche's madman, carrying a lamp in the midday sun, evoking the image of the *Sol niger* and reminiscent of the Greek Diogenes, cries incessantly to the people congregated in the marketplace, "I seek God! I seek God!" (GS 125). Like that tragic figure, Nietzsche, from early adolescence, searched for a surrogate father figure to "lead [him] with the same assurance of a father toward his small son" and, moreover, to validate him as a subject. When the loss is transformed into a state of mind, the "I" itself becomes the lost object: "My misfortune is this: that I have no model and I am in danger of making a fool of myself all on my own" (Letter to Rohde, January 1879).

His life gives indications of disturbances of the primal relationship: the Self (*imago Dei*), molded through the relationship with the Father-God, did not operate independently as a guiding principle. Therefore, he always searched for guidance in the external world through surrogate father figures.[1] The father remained as an archetypal image, a suprapersonal spiritual power largely unrealized in the ambit of the eternal forms,[2] and ready to be activated and projected onto suitable personalities, particularly Richard Wagner.

For three years the maestro filled the fatherless void that tormented Nietzsche. Under the spell of the composer's demonic/charismatic personality, Nietzsche lived the illusion that his wound had finally healed. Through a primitive idealization defensive process, he saw in the famous composer a redeemer[3] (see TCW 2, 3, 4, 11) and the spokesman par excellence of a radically Dionysian conception of the world. He perceived in the weltanschauung and artistic expression of this living demiurge the epiphany of a god who, like Dionysus, was capable of affirming all the irreconcilable contradictions inherent in Nietzsche's personality, particularly through his music, which Nietzsche considered to be a primordial language (*Ursprache*).[4] Wagner became for Nietzsche the bearer of his Dionysian Self; consequently, he was capable not only of providing freedom from the castrating effects attributed to the wrathful and punitive God of Nietzsche's mother, the God of "shalt's" and "shalt not's," but also, most importantly, of validating his "Dionysian nature," as Nietzsche described himself (EH IV:2). We can find evidence of this in a letter addressed to Wagner, his surrogate father, on his sixty-first birthday: "It is an incomparable good fortune for one who has been feeling and stumbling along on dark and foreign paths to be led gradually into the light, as you have done with me. I cannot therefore honor you in any other way than as a father. *So I celebrate your birthday also as a celebration of my own birth*" (emphasis added). In May 1873, he wrote again to Wagner confessing that "If I had not known you, what would I be other than a stillborn creature. . . . I always tremble with fear when I think that I could well have remained apart from you: in that case life would truly not have been worth living." In a letter addressed to Rohde dated December 1868, Nietzsche wrote: "My listening to Wagnerian music is a jubilant intuition to the point of being an overwhelming discovery of myself."

Nevertheless, when Wagner decided to place his musical art at the service of the Christian ideals (*Parsifal*) and German interests (Bayreuth Festivals), Nietzsche fell into a primitive devaluation defensive process.[5] He observed with astonishment what he considered the submission to God of his anointed celestial father, whom he had thought to be "beyond good and evil": "Incredible! Wagner had become pious" (EH III: HATH 5).[6] For Nietzsche, music had to have a redemptive task; however, expecting to meet a king, a cultural reformer, and a genius legislator in Bayreuth, he found a theatre manager, an actor, and a scene director (cf. NCW 8–11). Nietzsche noticed how his master's musical opus was moving closer and closer to the "moral" and the "rational," and farther and farther from the Greek ideal, particularly from the Dionysian worldview. Finally he implored "Redemption *from* the redeemer" (NCW P:1).[7] For the second time, God "took away" his father. Nietzsche felt betrayed in those ideals which he had thought his venerated *Pater Seraphicus* embodied: "It is in the ideals where the offense is most deeply felt," he once confessed to Malwida von Meysenbug (cf. Letter dated December, 1882).[8]

Finally, Nietzsche lost all hope of finding a substitute outside of his selfhood: "No new idols are erected by me; let the old ones learn what feet of clay mean" (EH P:2).

Oh, you have also fallen from the Cross,
you too, you, a subjected one!
I have stood before this scene for a long time
breathing tombs, rancor, prisons and sorrows
among the scent of church whores and clouds of incense
that frighten me.
Dancing, I throw the buffoon's cap into the air
because I escaped from this.
—F. NIETZSCHE, fragment from a poem dedicated "To Richard
Wagner" (1884)[9]

Disillusioned by the obstreperous downfall of the last of the father-surrogate figures, Wagner, Nietzsche had to sacrifice God himself. "Once one sacrificed human beings to one's god," wrote Nietzsche, "perhaps those whom one loved most. . . . Then, during the moral epoch of mankind, one sacrificed to one's god one's own strongest instincts, one's 'nature.' . . . Finally, what remained to be sacrificed? . . . God himself" (BGE 55).

Nietzsche also projected his conflict with the idealized father onto the celestial realm in a kind of cosmic (archetypal) transference:[10] he directed his hammer toward Christianity in particular, since Christianity is the religion of the Father and the Son. Understandably, Nietzsche seemed to perceive himself as the son of an abandoning father. With the absence of God, the Absolute Object is lost and the betrayed love turns into hate.[11] Like the dying Christ on the cross, Nietzsche seems to have asked himself: "My God, my God, why hast thou forsaken me?" (Matthew 27:46).

Therefore, after the fall of Wagner's imago, Nietzsche could not find God and with a heartrending cry pronounced, through the voice of the madman, his most famous phrase: "God is dead." But who has killed God? Projecting his own inner experience onto the collective man, Nietzsche has his grieving madman say, "I will tell you. *We have killed him*—you and I. All of us are his murderers" (GS 125).[12] Incapable of finding empathy among the groups congregated in the marketplace, Nietzsche's madman directs his steps to the churches to intone a *requiem aeternam Deo* (eternal rest for God). As he is thrown out of the holy places he reflects with pain: "What after all are these churches now if they are not the tombs and sepulchers of God?" (GS 125).

When Nietzsche refers to "The greatest recent event—that 'God is dead,' that the belief in the Christian God has become unbelievable" (GS 343), we understand that the dead God is the God of his ideal, the *Pater* of the Gospels. But the cry "God is dead" turned out not to be a theological phrase for Nietzsche. With it, he seemed to desire the elimination of the suprasensible world of ideals, so as to find the possibility of freedom from judgment, from guilt, from prohibition/inhibition, and from loss and depressive suffering, in order to reflect on the truth, his truth. He believed that the collective certainty inherent to religion requires the sacrifice of the intellect: "God is a gross answer, an indelicacy against us thinkers—at bottom merely a gross prohibition for us: you shall not think!" (EH II:1) and "Every 'thou shalt' has been directed against us" (D 13).[13] His reasoning reminds us of that used by Fyodor Dostoevsky, who, through one of his characters, the ancient father Karamazov, concluded: "If there is no God, everything is permitted."[14] With the deicide Nietzsche seems to look for a way to follow his own self-created values, rooted within his "will to power,"[15] his leitmotif, which was undermined by the notion of God.[16]

In spite of the alienation brought about by the rejection of God, a new possibility, like a sea, opened up before Nietzsche: "*Our* sea lies open again; perhaps there has never been such an 'open sea' "[17] (GS 343). Now he was able to observe the horizon toward the infinite (cf. ibid., 124). However, Nietzsche seems to have intuited that this situation would lead him directly to anarchy, adding: "But hours will come when you will realize that it is infinite and there is nothing more awesome than infinity" (ibid.). The individual needs certain restrictions to avoid diluting himself in the infinite ocean, in the chaotic superabundance of meanings of the collective unconscious.[18]

With the announcement of the death of God, Nietzsche sealed his fate. He eliminated from his life everything that could have performed the functions of *arkhé* (fundament), *telos* (finality) of action, and *nomos* (law). If God is dead there is no executioner, but neither is there hope of any divine protection. With the death of God came the "advent of nihilism" and the overthrow of previous certainties: the logos, the spirit represented by the disembodied mind, the dominion of man over nature, normative principles, categorizations, hierarchies, laws, order or pattern, values, and established truths. History was replaced by genealogy, temporality by infinity, and teleological bases by fate, destiny, and chance. Goals and collective ideals likewise disappeared in order to take the final leap toward the primordial, enigmatic, fascinating, and frightening Dionysian world of chaos represented by the body and the unconscious with its plurality of opposite drives, affects, or passions (narcissistic regression): "Body I am entirely, and nothing else; and soul is only a word for something of the body. The body is a great reason, a plurality . . . a war and a peace" (Z I:4).

In the opinion of the French philosopher Pierre Klossowski,

Nietzsche necessarily lost his identity when he wrote that God was dead. The absolute guarantor of the identity of the responsible "I" disappeared from Nietzsche's consciousness, and with this disappearance he became confused (cf. 1963, 220–21). By eliminating God, Nietzsche was trying to recover himself as a subject; however, his decision had the opposite effect, because the death of God is an ontological emptying.[19] Consequently, Nietzsche remained "a walking question mark," an *increatum* who must create himself starting from the absence of reference, from the *tohu wa bohu* (Genesis 1:2), the formless void or primordial chaos.[20] To the declaration "God is dead," one is tempted to add Unamuno's heartrending lament: "Because, Lord, if you existed, I would also truly exist."

Under the aegis of Zarathustra Nietzsche showed that he wanted to be the very thunderclap of creation: "Every wisdom . . . is yet to give birth to lightning bolts" (Z IV:13.7). A narcissistic desire to achieve the identity he lacked and longed for appears to have been the driving force behind the creative act. Through creation Nietzsche seemed to overcome the wound produced by the hiatus between the ego and the ideal, between Being (essence) and appearance. Through a hubristic *imitatio dei*, Nietzsche attempted to take God's place, to become, as Zarathustra, the Creator.[21] With Zarathustra's New Commandments, Nietzsche tried to occupy the place of the Law.

The idea of this *Übermensch* was directly opposed to the superego or moral conscience because it was placed beyond all laws of the human condition itself. Nietzsche's creation of the *Übermensch* would symbolize the phallus *in lacunae*: an autonomous and illusory phallus, created *ex nihilo*, which occupied a hyperdimensional place in Nietzsche's ego.[22] To his own fragile and hypersensitive condition Nietzsche opposed, in compensation, this superhuman condition, represented by the overman. Nonetheless, he mistook the symbol for what it symbolizes: the creator became identified with the creation itself, wanting to become the overman. However, it was a failed attempt: he was never able to meet his cherished ideal: "Never yet has there been an overman. Naked I saw both the greatest and the smallest man: they are still all too similar to each other" (Z II:4).

The primal crime of parricide committed by Nietzsche seems to have been compensatory to his strong identification with the father archetype, and to his ensuing inability to free the libido from the lost love object so that it could be used once again to enrich the ego. Perhaps Nietzsche was symbolically attempting to solve the parricide through his writing, to establish himself as a subject by way of his discourse. Nevertheless, because of his identification with the departed father, his search for freedom was doomed to fail, and his opus became a mausoleum for his missing father/God.

Even as the son-Nietzsche rebelled against the God-father until he destroyed him, the son-Nietzsche *was* the father, as the result of the introjection of the lost object, a means of thwarting the loss. Nietzsche's identification with the father permeated his whole life;[23] hence, in trying to destroy the father, Nietzsche was also annihilating himself. Paradoxically, he became both murderer and victim, "the sacrificer" and the "animal sacrificed."[24] Salomé denounced Nietzsche's sadomasochistic relationship with himself, saying he was "happy with the damage inflicted upon himself and with his own suffering" (2001, 42). His persistence in "auto-vivisection" evokes the image presented by the French poet Charles Baudelaire in his poem "L'héautontimorouménos" (*Les fleurs du mal*):

> I am the wound and the knife!
> I am the slap in the face and the cheek!
> I am the members and the wheel,
> and the victim and the executioner!

The case of Nietzsche is that of a conflictive subjective tension generated by two forces, one represented by the father-*senex* and the other by the son-*puer*, that constantly attempted to annul each other.[25] Jung wrote in this respect:

> Identification with the father means, in practice, adopting the entire father's ways of behaving, as though the son were the same as the father and not a separate individuality. . . . Identification can be beneficial so long as the individual cannot go his own way. But when a better possibility presents itself,

identification shows its morbid character by becoming just as great a hindrance as it was an unconscious help and support before. It now has a dissociative effect, splitting the individual into two mutually estranged personalities. (CW 6:742)[26]

"What was silent in the father speaks in the son; and often I found the son the unveiled secret of the father" (Z II: 7). Unable to reconcile these opposites, Nietzsche-Zarathustra remained trapped between them, Janus-faced: "Can you guess what is my heart's double will?" (Z II:21). The contradicting paths represented by the past (embodied by the father) and the future (embodied by the son) could never reach a reconciliation in the present "Moment," for "These paths [past and future] contradict each other eternally" (Z III:2.2).

As the father, Nietzsche showed a deeply rooted and intimate conviction of being condemned to the same tragic destiny as his progenitor. As he recognized in *Ecce Homo*, "At another point as well, I am merely my father once more, as it were, his continued life after an all-too-early death" (EH I:5). "*Schicksalsneurose*, neurosis of destiny. What appears as a clinical label becomes [for Nietzsche] the expression of a haunting reality" (Stern 1985, 98).

As the son, Nietzsche identified himself with the kenotic Christ[27] who experiences the incomprehension of man and the abandonment of God.[28] The imagery of Christ's Passion, a symbol of *mortificatio*, became for Nietzsche his own annihilating Passion (*imitatio Christi*). As Christ, he wanted to become "mankind's redeemer and savior" (Salomé 2001, 43). But what was the sense of his suffering when, unlike Christ, he had renounced being God's son? He experienced the suffering (sadistic superego) without any meaning (lack of the symbolic or paternal function). Perhaps motivated by his personal tragedy, in *The Birth of Tragedy* Nietzsche invoked the wisdom of Silenus, Dionysus's companion, who, when questioned by King Midas about "the best and most desirable of all things for man," answered that "the best of all is utterly beyond your reach: not to have been born, nor to be, to be nothing. But the second best for you is—to die soon" (BT 3). When Zarathustra saw himself overcome by sadness, "something unknown" around him, as an echo in the forest, asked him: "Are you still alive, Zarathustra? Why? What for? By

what? Whither? Where? How? Is it not folly still to be alive?" (Z II:10).
Also, among Nietzsche's posthumous writings there is a passage entitled
"The Innocence of Becoming," in which he confessed: "I do not want to
live again. How was I able to withstand life?"[29]

The tragic philosopher showed evidence of being conscious of the
nefarious consequences of the "death" of God when he wrote:

> What were we doing when we unchained this earth from its
> sun?[30] Whither is it moving now? Whither are we moving? Away
> from all suns? Are we not plunging continually? . . . Are we not
> straying as through an infinite nothing? Do we not feel the
> breath of empty space? Has it not become colder? Is not night
> continually closing in on us? (GS 125)

The madman who announces the death of God is hardly edified by
His end; rather, he is frightened by the emptiness. "Who loved and possessed Him most has also lost Him most," thinks Zarathustra when he
hears the laments of the Last Pope, whose God has died because He
became "old and soft" like Nietzsche's own father (Z IV:6). In *The Gay
Science*, Nietzsche describes the deicide as a "breakdown," a "destruction," a "ruin," a "cataclysm," a "monstrous logic of terror" (GS 343).
However, if God died as victim of his own cruelty, Nietzsche, whose ego
was so identified with that God, would have no way of freeing himself
from his own destruction; consequently, "God must not die." As a result
of such an existential dilemma, we can observe, throughout Nietzsche's
writings, his stormy relationship with God manifested as a continuous
alternation between his need of God and the compulsive need to deny
His existence, because he considers him a cruel demon.[31] This antagonistic situation is reflected in the lament poured out by the Magician in
Zarathustra (cf. Z IV: "The Magician"). In this moving poem we can
appreciate a "God-tormented" mind that curses and at the same time
invokes God with all the passion of a Christian soul.[32] Therefore, the
Ugliest Man after "killing" God had to resurrect Him: "The old god lives
again. . . . In the case of gods *death* is always a mere prejudice" (Z
IV:18.1)

Consequently, it is possible to conclude that despite having declared himself an atheist by instinct (cf. EH II:1), Nietzsche, whose biographers and contemporaries commented on his deep religious longings, never acted as such: "Man is a reverent animal" (GS 346). Lou Salomé called Nietzsche "the God-seeker." In her *Looking Back Memoirs,* she confessed: "Soon after I met Nietzsche I wrote to Malwida that his was a *religious* nature. . . . Today I would underline that twice" (1991, 50). Additionally, Lou rightly declared: "We will live to see him as a prophet of a new religion, one which recruits heroes and disciples" (ibid.). In her work *Nietzsche,* Lou also suggested: "Of all his great intellectual dispositions, none is bound more profoundly and unremittingly to his whole intellectual being than his religious genius. . . . All of Nietzsche's knowledge arose from a powerful religious mood" (2001, 24). On his part, Jung stated: "Nietzsche was no atheist, but his God was dead" (CW 11:142). Nietzsche replaced one God with another. Regarding this, the philosopher Jerry S. Clegg considers: "Nietzsche remained true to his dictum that no one can do battle about values without the aid of one's household gods. . . . As a result, all his battles are theological ones, he fights one god with the help of another. . . . His reader is always in the midst of a theological dispute" (2001, 161).

Nietzsche gave signs of constantly searching for a new god capable of supplanting the "abandoning" god. But he was no longer looking for a transcendent or incarnated God (e.g., Wagner); he yearned for a "personal" and immanent God. That is why Lou Salomé concluded: "The possibility of finding some substitutions for the lost God by means of the most varied forms of self-idolization constituted the story of his mind, his works, and his illness" (2001, 26). As for Jung, he considered that "The tragedy of Zarathustra [was] that, because his God died, Nietzsche himself became a god; and this happened because [Nietzsche] was no atheist" (CW 11:142).

CHAPTER 9

Nietzsche, a marauder of abysses

Do you realize the sort of danger to which you are going to
expose your soul?

—Plato, *Protagoras*

AFTER GIVING UP EVERY POSSIBILITY of finding a *spiritus rector* in some
other paternal ideal, and failing in his attempt to create himself after his
ideal overman—unable to be guided by the archetype of meaning and
wisdom, personified by Zarathustra, as an inner force that contained the
energy and potential that had been invested in the projection of the
father imago—Nietzsche found himself in the anguish of the void resulting from the absence of God. The accompanying sense of ego-alienation
was manifested by Nietzsche as abandonment (cf. HATH P:4).

Crying out for a god as violent as "Storm and rain!," "Lightning and
thunder!," Nietzsche recalled the epiphany, during his adolescence, of a
deity that could be considered as perilous as the mythical Dionysus
Zagreus: "When I was young I made contact with a dangerous deity, and
I would not like to repeat what things scarred my consciousness" (cited
in Köhler 1998, 17). Nietzsche seems to have felt so threatened and ter-
rified by this haunted image because the dark and unknown side of his
psyche represented by the mysterious deity was then denied and sent to
the shadow. However, the divinity that appeared to him had an emotional effect on him that could be described, employing the words of the religion phenomenologist Rudolf Otto, as the *mysterium tremendum et fasci-*

nans,[1] expressed as "a propulsion and urgency" that "rules over the younger soul and commands it like a master."[2] This tyrannical form of appearance of the "dangerous deity" indicates the constellation of an autonomous complex forcing Nietzsche's ego to obey in order to illuminate the rejected side of his psyche.

When the feelings of solitude, exile, and emptiness became omnipresent during Nietzsche's years as a solitary wanderer, the dangerous god of his adolescence emerged once again. The philosopher María Zambrano commented in this respect:

> In moments of solitude, of that absolute solitude that appears after experiencing the disillusionment of things and the ensuing emptiness, reality—or its absence—makes itself felt as if coming from a primary, living focal point. Only that focal point can restore confidence and life. Thus, when man drains his solitude and believes, at the same time, that he himself is reality, he needs to find that primary focal point of reality in himself or in something that he feels in a primary, immediate form. And when this reality is felt exclusively in the form of resistance, man finds himself again under the unknown God. But now within himself. (1993, 301)

With regard to Nietzsche, Zambrano commented: "The solitude of Nietzsche, the man, is not the solitude of consciousness but that of man in his intimate hell, who calls out to a nonexistent god—to the vacuum of God—and, wanting to definitely stop being the beggar,[3] engenders a god in his solitude" (ibid., 167–68).

This is an "Unknown God,"[4] whom in later years Nietzsche recognized as Dionysus, his personification of the shadow denied to the luminous Father, the Christian God:[5]

> For just as happens to everyone who from childhood has always been on his way and in foreign parts, many strange and not undangerous spirits have crossed my path, too, but above all he of whom I was speaking just now . . . namely, no less a one than the god *Dionysus*, that great ambiguous one and tempter god to whom I once offered, as you know, in all secrecy and reverence, my firstborn—as the last, it seems to me, who offered him a *sac-*

rifice: for I have found no one who understood what I was doing then. (BGE 295)[6]

Similar to the history of the tragic Christ, the Dionysian myth is a story of death and resurrection:[7] "Dionysus cut to pieces is a *promise* of life: it will be eternally reborn and return again from destruction" (WP 1052). The mysteries of life, suffering, death, and rebirth experienced by Dionysus constitute an eternal unity of the dual, paradoxical nature of the god, a necessary condition for self-overcoming.

Nietzsche had sought to free himself through his *Zarathustra* from the labyrinthine bowels of Mother Earth that had trapped him from the dawn of his life. In the ascensional world of the spirit, he sought to redeem his past through the will to power, "To recreate all 'it was' into a 'thus I willed it' " (Z II:20). However, Nietzsche-Zarathustra found that "the will itself is still a prisoner. . . . Powerless against what has been done, he is an angry spectator of all that is past. The will cannot will backwards [because] he cannot break time" (Z II:20). Having failed, with this limit to his power, to "ascend" to the world of the Spirit-Father as Zarathustra, Nietzsche fell into the "matriphallic," into the timeless realm of the mysterious Mothers,[8] the source of meaning, redemption, and creativity.[9] The vertical orientation remained but changed its direction.

When Nietzsche penetrated the zone where no answers were possible, he was driven back to the mystery represented by the *camera obscura*: the unconscious.[10] Determined by an irresistible desire to create himself (cf. Z II:2), he yearned to descend to those regions forbidden to reason, laws, rules, or conventions so that he might shape himself out of himself, the "Primordial One's" creative self-genesis out of the powers of wild nature: "Learn to become nature again yourselves and then with and in nature let yourself be transformed" (RWB 6). Submerged in nature, the primary unity, he would finally be subjugated by Dionysus, the "dangerous deity" of his adolescence.

While Apollo was a god who represented the Olympian sunlike powers and the world of form, Dionysus was a deity of the earth forces, and therefore represented the world of formless chthonic powers. Based on Nietzsche's approach to the Dionysian, it is possible to infer that, for the tragic philosopher, the ecstatic deity was ontologically the personification par excellence of the primordial substratum from which arises the entire world of phenomena (BT 25). His conclusion is validated by the very myth in which Dionysus, "the foreigner," represents otherness: even on Olympus Dionysus embodies the figure of the Other (cf. Vernant and Vidal-Naquet 2002, 231). Consequently, to see Dionysus, it becomes necessary to penetrate a different universe, where the Other (the unconscious) and not the Same (consciousness) reigns (cf. ibid., 235).

Dionysus, like the unconscious, wished to reveal himself, to be known, recognized, and understood (cf. ibid., 232), as is evident in Euripides' *Bacchae*. And Dionysus revealed himself through Nietzsche. In the fourth and last part of Nietzsche's magnum opus, we see an aged and convalescent Zarathustra, who gives an extravagant banquet in honor of the "higher men," a bizarre group made up of condemned, crippled, and grotesque beings, whom he piously accompanies in an act of adoration of an ass. Nietzsche as Zarathustra seems to have turned Christ's last supper into a Dionysian feast (cf. Z IV: "The Ass Festival").

When Nietzsche-Zarathustra wrote: "Better to adore God in this form [as an ass] than in no form at all" (ibid.), he had already succumbed to the terrific forces of the unconscious. The ass represented an "animality" related to the "instinctuality" inherent in the figure of Dionysus and denied to God. The ass was one of the animals that accompanied the frenzied god, symbolizing his lascivious aspect.

Liliane Frey-Rohn, a Jungian analyst and close collaborator of Jung, wrote the following with respect to the instinctive side of Dionysus: "The glorification of God in the form of the ass is a clear example of Nietzsche's soul succumbing to the instinctual aspect of the image of God" (1988, 161–62). She explained: "It represents the most forceful expression of compensation for Nietzsche identifying himself with the aspect of God's light. What he had frequently prophesied as the destiny of modern man was now his own: namely, God gradually becoming an animal" (ibid.).[11] It is thus possible to conclude that *Thus Spoke Zarathustra* paved the way for the return of Dionysus.[12]

If God is destroyed, the Goddess must return. The Jungian analyst E. F. Edinger points out that when the road to "salvation" cannot be followed through the Gnostic model of an elevation of consciousness, it is possible to find it through the Great Mother. This is a uroboric salvation that "demands the abandonment of the conscious principle and homecoming to the unconscious" (1995, 119); in other words, a sacrifice of the ego different from an accepting of the ego's abdication of the dominant role.[13]

Though in the early work *The Birth of Tragedy* Nietzsche urged us to take the way of the Mothers, according to the philosopher Farrell Krell, he "resist[ed] every step along the path" (1986, 37). "It is not the height, it is the abyss that is terrible," uttered Zarathustra (Z II:21). The constant struggle between abjecting the feminine (real and symbolic) and merging with it became emblematic in Nietzsche.[14]

Failing to find redemption in the luminous world of the Father, Nietzsche finally submitted himself to the somber world of the (M)other as a promise of resurrection and life in order to be reborn: he attempted a search for self-creation through rebirth from the eternal void (autogenesis of the subject).[15] In his state of abandonment, he fell inexorably into the vast primeval abyss, where vertigo and drowning—a lapse into insanity—ensued.

During his inward pilgrimage he became a "subterranean man . . . one who tunnels and undermines . . . as though he perhaps desires this prolonged obscurity, desires to be incomprehensible, concealed, enigmatic, because he knows what he will thereby also acquire: his own morning, his own redemption" (D P:1). This is a redemption through pathos: a Dionysian redemption.[16]

Nietzsche allowed himself to be totally subjugated by the (M)other, becoming her consort. In this he unconsciously attempted to recover his lost phallus, the castration wrought by his mother's wrathful and persecuting God, who then became his superego: "The saint, in whom God is well pleased, is the ideal castrato. . . . Life ends where the 'kingdom of God' *begins*" (TI V:4).[17]

Dionysus is the god of the tumescent and uncastratable phallus (death-rebirth), of the life force or libido (cf. Jung, CW 5:329).[18] In Latin, the *phallus* is the *fascinum*, that which fascinates. The phallus is a symbol of truth and meaning, and its loss indicates the loss of the being as truth. Nietzsche lets himself be fascinated and, ultimately, possessed by this phallic deity. His statement in his essay "On Moods" (1864), "Only that which is similar seeks to attract the soul," written while he anxiously sought a substitute for the Christian God, leads us to expect the epiphany of a divinity with characteristics similar to those of his own psychological condition.

Since the paternal function did not occur in Nietzsche, the imaginary dyad of (M)other-son could not be broken. The early disappearance of his father, and the incapacity shown by his mother (and substitutes) to introduce the metaphor of the father in the mind of the child, impeded Nietzsche from extricating himself from the power of the (M)other (unconscious) and thus generated an interdependent relationship. Consequently, his ego was not very differentiated from that of the (M)other, whose focus and greatest area of extension is found in primary identity with the self[19]—a Dionysian self ("matriarchal consciousness"). Therefore Nietzsche's psychic world was opposed to the Apollonian appearance governed by the congregational morality, and manifested through differentiated consciousness.

With his ego so close to the collective unconscious, Nietzsche felt linked to the surrounding world by a dark feeling of identification through Dionysian-matriarchal consciousness with its suffering and contradiction, where "the serious, the troubled, the sad, the gloomy, the sudden restraints, the tricks of accidents, anxious expectations, in short, the whole divine comedy of life, including the inferno, also passes before him, not like mere shadows on a wall—for he lives and suffers with these scenes" (BT 1). Since his early youth he yearned to "form a God according to [his] rudimentary character." This God, like Dionysus, rules a cyclical world: without beginning or end, as Nietzsche expressed it in a poem from his youth, "Fled Are the Lovely Dreams" (1860). He is entirely without moral scruples and his nature is capable of containing all contradictions: creation and destruction, good and evil, joy and suffering, horror and beauty (see BT P:5).

"If cows had religion their gods would have hooves." Updating Xenophanes' taunt, Nietzsche searched for a God after his own undifferentiated psychic condition.

"I obey my Dionysian nature" (EH IV:2)

Nietzsche, like Dionysus, had been a victim of a destructive (M)other.[20] His mother had raised him under the imposition of a castrating desire: Nietzsche was to be a clergyman, so as to fill the father's absence and fulfill the mother's sense of destiny. Thus there seemed to be a wish to "clone" the dead father's figure in that of the son. Nietzsche's mother seems to have loved him and cared for him as the future that embodied the past, in this way denying the child's own individuality: he never existed as a true subject. She lacked any awareness of her son's personal intentions: he became for her a depersonalized object, and consequently his real needs went unmet. In the mother's consciousness, Nietzsche's subjectivity did not seem to play a fundamental role: "Usually a mother loves *herself* in her son more than she loves the son himself" (HATH 385). Nietzsche also declared, "Some mothers need happy, respected children; some, unhappy children: otherwise they cannot demonstrate their goodness as mothers" (ibid. 387).

Lacking a paternal figure, Nietzsche depended on his mother to stimulate and mirror his own archetypal masculine potentials.[21] However, the mother inhibited the child's sense of his own authority, and as a result his self-esteem was seriously damaged: "Someone said: I have been prejudiced against myself from childhood upward, and hence I find some truth in every censure and some absurdity in every eulogy. Praise I generally value too low and blame too high" (HATH 262).

Feelings of worthlessness became apparent in Nietzsche when he failed to live up to his mother's expectations. "Our dear mother," Elisabeth confessed, "was not exactly an encouraging influence for her son" (1912, II:73). Consequently, Nietzsche did not feel worthy of maternal affection: "You mustn't believe that I was ever in my life spoiled by excess of love. . . . In this regard I bear about me ever since my earliest childhood some sort of resignation. However, it may be that I never deserved anything better," Nietzsche confessed to Marie Baumgartner in a letter written in August 1875. Even if this consideration was not totally true from a historical point of view, it would appear to be a subjective truth or psychic reality for Nietzsche: an experience that he felt as real. From a psychoanalytic point of view, it is not important to distinguish between the actual mother and the mother constituted out of unconscious fantasy: the important thing to take into account is Nietzsche's subjective image of the mother (imago).

For the child Fritz the order of the world must have seemed composed of precepts and rules without much sense. He seems to have become convinced that in order to live he must conform to the "shalt's" and "shalt not's" inculcated by his mother. The rigid norms and rules applied by Nietzsche's mother and substitutes, their constant invocation of the wrath of a severe and persecuting God, and the pain and guilt caused by depriving and impoverishing the "I" with the early departure of his father turned Nietzsche into a guilty person (one with a "bad conscience") with persecuting anxieties.[22] The conflict-avoidance approach used during his formative years turned him into a schizoid being through the dynamic of deprivation-intrusion. His early experiences of the feminine also crippled his ego and his imago of the feminine itself.

When Nietzsche wrote *Ecce Homo*, two months before his final breakdown, he would appear to have been trapped between Scylla and Charybdis—an insurmountable alternative: be like his father or identify with the (M)other. When he included in this work the riddle that enclosed the enigma of his own fatality—"As my father I already died: as my mother I am still alive and am growing old" (EH I:1)—he evidenced the orphic paradox of being trapped between the dead and the living.

The subject is constituted according to the way in which he interprets himself: consequently, Nietzsche was dead as his father's son and alive as his mother's son. Identification with the father (a dead man) meant that he, too, was dead: "My father's *wicked* heritage came to my aid at bottom, predestination to an early death" (EH III: HATH 4). Nietzsche showed a longing, according to Salomé, to "reinterpret his terrible fate, which threatened his human spirit" (2001, 148). However, he was incapable of reinterpreting his past starting out from the present.[23]

As his father's son, Nietzsche felt identified with the tragic figure of Christ, who was willing at first to accept his fatal destiny: to suffer agony and die on the cross in order to reach salvation for the glory of the Father and to be reunited with Him in the hereafter. The idea of death and suicide seems to represent his yearning for a final victory over the lost object, a liberation from grief and from his search for a God-father (see BGE 103; HATH 80). Nonetheless, at the same time Nietzsche wished to escape from the anguish of death: "Oh, how do I bear to go on living! And how could I bear to die now!" (Z III:2). Identification with the (M)other and Dionysus offered another path. Dionysus's myths about a double bird, death and rebirth, and a journey to the underworld made him a god capable of attracting those who wished to find a way to escape the anxieties of death.

Yet even while the (M)other represents a nondogmatic way of approaching existence, the submission to her is also a form of death as a subjective experience, for it requires the surrender and submergence of the ego or "death" of the identity (re-fusion). "If one shifts the center of gravity of life *out* of life into the 'Beyond,' " wrote Nietzsche in *The Antichrist,* "one has deprived life as such of its center of gravity." Nietzsche's "center of gravity" remained lost in the "Beyond," in the realm of the nocturnal Mother, where the dead father embraced her lunar mysteries. Therefore, the philosopher Jill Marsden concluded, "[Nietzsche's] religion . . . is a religion of the *night sun*" (2000, 263), that "demands self-annihilation" (ibid., 265).

Again Nietzsche was trapped by the necessity of sacrificing his existence, but on this occasion no longer to the Christian God or to an incarnation of his ideal in a paternal figure, but to a pagan god closely related to the (M)other: an immanent god who echoed his own essence. If we comprehend that the law of the Mother is not a moral law ("shalt" and "shalt not") but the imperative of the instincts (erotic or thanatic), we can better understand Nietzsche's unconscious incestuous longing for containment in the maternal abyss.

"Regression," writes Jung, "leads back apparently to the mother; in reality she is the gateway into the unconscious, into the 'realm of the Mothers.' Whoever sets foot in this realm submits his conscious ego-personality to the controlling influence of the unconscious" (CW 5:508). In response to the intolerable longing for liberation of his soul, Nietzsche fell back into the "mines," believing that he was exploring the depths of his own psyche, without knowing that, as in the case of Dionysus, in reality he was returning to the (M)other: "Drink back into myself the flames that shoot out of me" (Z II:9).[24] The dark and terrifying elements of the chthonian "realm of the Mothers" finally gained mastery over him.

Whatever form of salvation Nietzsche had chosen, the result would have been the same; he would always have lost: "Among you is also a mere conflict and cross between plant [or Mother] and ghost [or father]" (Z P:3). Whatever way out he imagined was only a path back to the labyrinth. Recognizing his incapacity to find real solutions, Nietzsche confessed to Köselitz in a letter dated August 26, 1883: "My drives and aims have become totally confused and labyrinthine, so that I no longer know how to find my way out." "Every passage outward," wrote Lou Salomé, "always led back to the depth of his self . . . every passage took him farther into his final depth and his decline" (2001, 28). Thus began Zarathustra's decline.

"I came from tragedy and to tragedy I go."

In Nietzsche's thought, the word "tragic" acquired a reiteration similar to that of a mantra. "Tragedy" would always be his reply, to the questions arising from the horrors of war confronted during his brief participation in it, or to the torments and paradoxes inherent to his personality and which he finally developed in *The Birth of Tragedy*.

Tragic thought draws back the veil of existence to show man in his complete solitude and brings to center stage our constitutional irrationality. Therefore, whereas the epic experience is an ethos of conquest, the tragic experience is one of pathos, marked by exile, the silence of the gods, and the omnipotence of fate (Moira). Tragedy is wound and abyss: it is a fatal absence that wants to be assumed, redeemed. The tragic consciousness is the consciousness of fate, chance, and destiny. In tragedy it is not the force and will of the hero, the conductor of the existential drama, but the force of fate that assigns man his life lot and exact proportion. "I came from tragedy and to tragedy I go," declared Nietzsche.

As a tragic man, he seems weighed down by the fatalist view of life typical of a passive-feminine attitude ("matriarchal consciousness"), contrary to that of a differentiated ego, which is a reflection of an active-masculine attitude ("patriarchal consciousness"). "The unconscious is fate," explained Jung, "the descent into the unconscious [realm of the Mothers] is a sort of fatality; one surrenders to fate" (SNZ II:1252). Even if he claimed to be the philosopher of self-creation, Nietzsche embraced fatalism from the beginning of his philosophical career until the very end of his lucid life. He began *Ecce Homo* by declaring, "The good fortune of my existence lies in its fatality," and the fatalistic view recurs throughout the book, for example in the chapter titled "Why I Am Destiny." In *Beyond Good and Evil*, he wrote of that "granite of spiritual fatum, or predetermined decision," and in his *Nachlass* he went to the extreme of declaring: "Everything has been directed along certain lines from the beginning" (WP 458). "*Amor fati* is my inmost nature," he confessed in *Ecce Homo*. Nietzsche decided to accept these given situations rather "than rebelling against them. . . . I displayed the 'Russian fatalism' [25] . . . by tenaciously clinging for years to all but intolerable situations, places, apartments, and society, merely because they happened to be given by accident" (EH 1:6). And Zarathustra is the advocate of chance (cf. Z III: "Before Sunrise," "Upon the Mount of Olives").

In *The Birth of Tragedy,* Nietzsche wanted to recreate the world in "thunder and lightning," and the mythical-imaginal drama of this recreation followed the internal dynamics of his personality. Nietzsche showed signs of an indomitable nature full of obscure enigmas, in which antagonistic forces constantly struggled for pre-eminence, giving rise to war between the light of consciousness and the darkness of the unconscious; between appearance and essence; between the moderation of the ego ideal, represented by the enlarged imago of the father, and the intoxication and ecstasy brought by the irrational world of the (M)other, always close by; between the father-self and the son-self; between his own inner vocation and the "sense of duty" to the spirits of his ancestors. Nietzsche expressed the conflict in the symbolic images of Apollo and Dionysus, whose eternal drama is the theme of tragedy, of his own tragedy.

As a tragic nature, Nietzsche made suffering his religion.[26] His pain and melancholy (*mortificatio*), the bases of tragedy, are essential to the Dionysian character. Tragedy is Dionysian: "Nothing like this has ever been written, felt, or suffered: thus suffers a god, a Dionysus" (EH Z:8). Nietzsche's eternal companion and savior—and that of Dionysus, the afflicted god—was suffering. Because the Orphic god affirms all that appears, even the bitterest suffering, he is able to understand the extreme agonies of a tormented man like Nietzsche in the way he suffered them in his own flesh: he had already experienced death from the beginning. Consequently, he also was able to provide meaning to Nietzsche's pathos. Dionysus became for Nietzsche the symbol of the affirmation of life with all its suffering and terror.[27]

"I too have been in the underworld, like Odysseus."

Unlike the patriarchal gods in Greek mythology, who reaffirmed their masculinity by killing their fathers and taking their places (Cronos with Uranus and Zeus with Cronos), Nietzsche "killed" his father but failed, as Zarathustra, to replace him with a new lawgiver (a new form of consciousness); instead, he returned to the telluric realm of the Great Goddess.[28] This return represents an incestuous regression, the ego's "re-immersion in the primordial state of 'participation mystique'" (Jung, CW 15:162). Indeed, Dionysus, as god of fertility, always returns to the (M)other and is therefore a regressive deity.

Dionysian worship promoted ecstatic self-transcendence, where all boundaries between humanity and nature are dissolved (cf. BT 1; WP 1050). Like the orgiastic divinity of tragedy, Nietzsche manifested a desire to submit to a "blissful *solutio* . . . the most dangerous one," as Edinger points out (1996, 49). He evidenced "a deadly longing for the abyss, a longing to drown in his own source. We can understand Nietzsche's willingness to radically "dissolve" his selfhood, considering the stages that led him to a theory of the fortuitous case: an experience that can qualify as a psychotic induction. As Nietzsche himself explained it, "1. I sought a new center; 2. Impossibility of this endeavor recognized; 3. Thereupon I advance further down the road of dissolution. . . . We have to be destroyers! . . . I perceived the state of dissolution, in which individual natures can perfect themselves as never before" (cited in Klossowski 1997, 219–20).

Nietzsche went from the forests of his adolescence to the seas in his adulthood,[29] a more regressive, more primitive stage of the psyche. Although forest and sea are symbols of the dark and mysterious unconscious, nonetheless the sea is a more primitive symbol than the forests: the sea is the *prima materia*. Nietzsche wanted to merge with the sea through a Dionysian dissolution of the ego. As Zarathustra, he yearned to go *under*, becoming fluid by merging with the sea: "Now my ultimate loneliness has begun. Alas, this black sorrowful sea below me! Alas, this pregnant nocturnal dismay! Alas, destiny and sea! To you I must go *down*! . . . deeper into pain than ever I have descended, down into its blackest flood. Thus my destiny wants it. Well, I am ready" (Z III:1). In this undifferentiated state Nietzsche risked being sucked down in the limitless waters of the unconscious world.

However, the yearning for dissolution in the "Primordial One" strengthens the terrible character of the Feminine. It would seem that Nietzsche's well-known doctrine of eternal recurrence, core of the Dionysian and Eleusinian mysteries, a passing of time without advancing (*circulus vitiosus deus*), which vivifies the experience of the uroboric circle, stems from Nietzsche's matriarchal level of consciousness.[30]

With the circle of eternal recurrence, Nietzsche yearned to place himself in a mythical time (a Dionysian time)[31] as an unhistorical subject. Thus history is disqualified as a conductor of meaning: "No one attains freedom," Nietzsche wrote, "without . . . an unhistorical condition" (HL

1). The mythic-cyclic time of "eternal recurrence" conceives a history without beginning or end (no genesis or conclusion), consequently rejecting any kind of teleology. Escape from the eschatological-linear time marked by the idea of sin allows, at the same time, an escape from threats, punishments, and hell.[32] Similarly, a belief in a transcendental God is no longer necessary: all transcendence becomes absurd, as does a repressive and castrating morality. With his "abysmal thought," Nietzsche seemed to be willing to escape the power of time in order to redeem his past and gain free will. According to him, man cannot obtain wholeness through the lineal becoming that aims to reach the teleological topos: wholeness can only be constituted in the constant return to the ambit of contradiction where opposites meet as such.

With respect to time it is necessary to consider that although linear time is saturnine (the time of a cruel, voracious, and inflexible god who devours his sons), nonetheless, only Saturn is capable of freeing us from the anguish of recurrence. In the vicious circle of the nihilism represented by the eternal recurrence, there is a constant return to the wound as an eternal déjà vu: there is no forgetting, there is no possibility of conquest. The past continues to hold a cruel and tyrannical power over the present. Not only man is the object of this return; his emotions, his pleasures and chagrins, and even his physical surroundings come back with him: "My past burst its tombs; many a pain that had been buried alive awoke, having merely slept, hidden in burial shrouds" (Z III:3).[33] How would Nietzsche's demon reply when asked the decisive question: "Do you desire this once more and innumerable times more?" (GS 341). In reply, would he "throw [himself] down and gnash [his] teeth and curse the demon who spoke thus?" (ibid.).

At times Nietzsche referred to his doctrine as "the eternal recurrence of *the same*."[34] Indeed, the soothsayer expresses to Zarathustra the implications of his "thought of thoughts" in the following words: "All is empty, all is the same, all has been. . . . we are still waking and living on—in tombs" (Z II:19). After these words are pronounced, Zarathustra "walked about sad and weary." Then the hermit prophet, in a melancholic mood, falls asleep and has a terrible gothic nightmare in which he sees himself as a guardian of tombs (cf. ibid.). Finally he is confronted by a black coffin that "burst and spewed out a thousandfold laughter." It can be interpreted that the contents of the coffin, dreamed by Nietzsche himself, are the souls of the past who come to sabotage the possibilities of the present.[35] It is possible to infer that the eternal return to the wound was the origin of Nietzsche's ambivalent approach to the possibility of "the same": he would suffer the recurrent pain of his father's death, his melancholic identification with the lost figure, his abject identification with his suffocating and castrating mother, and the guilty feelings caused before and after the "deed" (deicide). Also, it is worth pointing out that when Zarathustra conjures up his "most abysmal thought" he collapses and remains unconscious for seven days. Once again, Nietzsche constructed a labyrinthic thought with no way out: as a recursive loop, nothing can be superseded; all he could imagine was "the possibility of eternal damnation."

To live in the uroboric time of eternal return means that the ego has been dissolved. Being a thoughtful scholar, Nietzsche allows us to study dissolution through his identifications with and treatment of classic characters. For example, it seems important to highlight the fact that his "killing" of the father furthered his identification with Oedipus.[36] Nietzsche intuited the incestuous condition of the tragic character as a necessary means for acquiring wisdom. "There is an old popular belief . . . that a wise magus can be born only from incest" (BT 9). This belief, reported originally by Catullus, indicated that the magician, in order to transcend space and time, must violate social and natural law.

The melancholic philosopher showed great admiration for the Oedipus of Colonus in *The Birth of Tragedy*. He considered that Oedipus's lack of vision elevated him to the infinite transfiguration emanating from the "divine sphere," and praised his transformation from a passive sight to an active insight (cf. BT 9). From his youth, Nietzsche was possessed by an inner impulse capable of allowing him to take the gigantic leap from preconceived ideas to the vertigo of revelation. For Nietzsche, "truth" was not something that could be found in the great texts of humanity. In his conception, truth appears as a sudden revelation into the conscious realm: "What *I* find, what *I* am seeking—Was that ever in a book?" (HATH, "Among Friends").

The unconscious appears as an Other that reveals itself as opaque, mysterious, an enigma to be deciphered.[37] Nietzsche felt "impelled by his mission" to be "ensphinxed" (cf. Z IV:16) and to solve the "riddle of nature": "And how could I bear to be a man if man were not also a . . . guesser of riddles" (EH III: Z 8). He was driven to submerge himself totally in nature and to establish contact with the infinite through a passive surrender.[38]

While Plato searched for knowledge through the elevation of consciousness into the celestial spheres, Nietzsche sought wisdom through a descent into "the Dionysian abysses" (BT 14), into the very core of nature. Tragic knowledge places man before the abyss and the enigma. Nietzsche was driven toward the *ungrund* of being, between the crevices, where limits are dissolved, in order to demolish boundaries: he was not impelled toward the search for epistemological knowledge[39] but, with a restless and insatiable spirit, he desired to apprehend the tragic or esoteric knowledge that questions the innermost essence of things in the abyss where the mysterious and the enigmatic appear: where gods and demons are convoked and where both rapture and horror may be evoked.

Nietzsche was willing to risk hurling himself into the dark and Hesiodic chaos that gives birth to night and darkness for the sake of a "dancing star":[40] "I love only what a man has written with his blood" (Z 1:7). "It is just as if Nietzsche had been present at a performance of the mysteries," concluded Jung (CW I:210). Salomé suggested: "[Nietzsche] believed himself to be the fated, though sickly, medium through which humans would solve the riddle of existence and would become conscious of their essence. . . [e]mbodied in himself" (2001, 138).

"Pitilessly I went forward in my journey, a journey of knowledge at all costs," Nietzsche wrote in the summer of 1875. "I resemble an old, weatherproof fortress which contains many hidden cellars and deeper hiding places; in my dark journeys, I have not yet crawled down into the subterranean chambers. Don't they form the foundation of everything?" (cited in Salomé, 2001, 22). Wanting to be seduced to the inner recess of mysterious knowledge, he let himself be submerged in the chthonic realm like a "Don Juan of knowledge," who, "in the end, lusts after Hell—it is the last knowledge that *seduces*" (D 327). In his wild passion for ontological truth, Nietzsche was eager to cross the security zone in order to reach those regions in which knowledge becomes mortal. Based on his own experience, he related, in his philosophy, the search for truth with the thanatic drive: "The will for truth could be a disguised wish for death" (GS 344).

Oedipus is a personification of the Dionysian world of the unconscious,[41] for Dionysus, as Nietzsche himself pointed out, is behind Oedipus (cf. BT 10). One can thus infer that the voice to which Nietzsche refers in his work is the voice of the Sphinx-(M)other, who proposes seductive riddles. "Who of us is Oedipus here?" Nietzsche asked himself. "Who is the Sphinx?" (BGE I:1). In fact, he seemed to be both: at times, like Oedipus, he was a decipherer of riddles; at others, under the aegis of the Sphinx[42] and identified with the dark feminine, he proposed them: "I no longer know whether I am the Sphinx who poses the questions, or the renowned Oedipus, who is questioned—so I have two chances for the abyss" (Letter to Overbeck, May 7, 1885). He wanted, like Oedipus, to solve nature's ungraspable mystery, and as the tragic character he became "his father's murderer, his mother's lover, solver of the Sphinx's riddle" (BT 9), leaving him, like Oedipus, an outcast and exile.

Over and over Nietzsche killed the father, who was constantly dying like Dionysus, but he did not kill the devouring mother represented by the Sphinx ("monstricide"). The hero's struggle with the monster (an ensnaring, suffocating, and devouring maternal complex) could have allowed him to attain the rank of hero and granted him access to "the daughter of the king" (nonmaternal feminine) instead of the (M)other (incest). In the Oedipal myth, the Sphinx is not conquered by a direct confrontation but by an intellectual or Apollonian one. Oedipus does not kill her in hand-to-hand combat; she commits suicide. The French scholar Jean-Joseph Goux writes:

> In the struggle against the frightful beast, dragon, or Medusa, the hero develops his masculinity, he mobilizes inner forces that transform his infantile dependence into a concentrated and combative manhood. . . . In the case of Oedipus, it appears clearly that his full manhood has not been mobilized, that it is the intelligence of the head and not the courage of the chest . . . that made success possible. . . . Oedipus, by avoiding the trial of true

matricide . . . remain[s] entirely the prisoner of his own mother.
. . . His destiny remains tightly controlled by his mother. . . . It
is the absence of the monster-mother's murder, this nonmatri-
cide that pursues Oedipus. The liberation from the feminine
thus remains unaccomplished in Oedipus's destiny. He is the
one who does not liberate the bride. The suicide of the Sphinx
is a spiteful lover's anger, turned inward. (1993, 37–9)

He concludes that Oedipus's story is "a myth of failed or avoided initiation" (ibid., 23).[43]

Nietzsche's own failed initiation is further highlighted by his own reference to another mythological figure. During his voyage to the *nekyia*,
Nietzsche also liked to identify himself with Odysseus:[44] "I too have been
in the underworld, like Odysseus" (AOM 408).[45] However, Odysseus
confronted the dark feminine (Circe, Calliope, the Sirens, etc.) after
having fought for ten years in Troy and become a hero; or, in psychological terms, after having strengthened his ego through conflict. Nietzsche,
on the other hand, had not achieved this strengthening of the ego
through the resolution of conflicts. The sacrifice necessary in order to
achieve a greater degree of consciousness did not take place, because his
ego easily abandoned its position in the psychic system to serve the
Mother.

To become a hero, according to Jung, man must show that he is capable of "leaving the mother, the source of life, behind him"; yet Jung also
affirmed that by so doing man becomes "driven by an unconscious desire
to find her again, to return to her womb. Every obstacle that rises in his
path and hampers his ascent wears the shadowy features of the Terrible
Mother, who saps his strength with the poison of secret doubt and retrospective longing" (CW 5:611). But Nietzsche demonstrated from an
early age an incapacity to leave the (M)other behind him: when faced
with the obstacles of existence, he always showed regressive tendencies
toward the (M)other (*regressus ad uterum*), a womb without needs:[46]

> Hail, hail to the whale
> If he left his guest
> That well off. . . .

Hail to this belly
If it was as
Lovely an oasis belly. . . .
There I sit now,
In this smallest oasis. . . .
Drinking this most beautiful air,
My nostrils distend like cups,
Without future, without reminiscences. (Z IV:16)

It was a Dionysian regression, for in many versions of the myth, when the god was persecuted he would retire to where he felt at home: the deep, feminine sources of nature, either the forest or the depths of oceans, seas, and lakes—symbols of the dark and mysterious unconscious.

It is worth pointing out that Nietzsche's doctrine of eternal recurrence precluded choice and action because the future was already contained in the past and could not be changed in any respect, it could only be affirmed (*amor fati*). Dionysian knowledge kills action, which requires the "veils of illusion":

The Dionysian man resembles Hamlet: both have once looked truly into the essence of things, they have *gained knowledge*, and nausea inhibits action; for their action could not change anything in the eternal nature of things; they feel it to be ridiculous or humiliating that they should be asked to set right a world that is out of joint. Knowledge kills action; action requires the veils of illusion. (BT 7)

While Oedipus didn't know, Hamlet knew. Like Hamlet, Nietzsche was haunted by the ghost of his father: "Is Hamlet *understood*? No doubt, *certainty* is what drives one insane" (EH II:4). At the same time, confronted with the Gorgonian aspect of the dark feminine, like Shakespeare's character, Nietzsche proved to be incapable of taking action: in the face of external and internal vicissitudes, he tried to flee by yearning for a lethargic dream that expressed his desire "to be devoured."

The descent into the depths of the underworld constitutes the dramatic action of many of the initiatory mysteries. Jung indicated that the relation between the ego and the unconscious (underworld) can lead to three different situations: to a regressive restoration of the persona, a drowning by the Self, or individuation. Consequently, this perilous descent can have either a destructive or a redemptive outcome, depending on the strength of the ego. Plunging into darkness does not ensure redemption. We find an example of this in Orpheus, who submerged himself in darkness in a state of hubris (thanatic inflation), or in Oedipus, who "succeeded all by himself, without soliciting either sacred teachings or divine help, thereby claiming he could obtain on his own what was supposed to be conferred on him only by initiatory transmission" (Goux 1993, 88).

Nietzsche seems to have followed, like Orpheus and Oedipus, an inflated route, without being conscious of it and despite having become aware at some time of the inherent danger. The internal warning was made evident when he wrote: "There are many things we must leave in the Hades [unconscious] of half-conscious feeling, and not desire to redeem them out of their shadow existence, otherwise they will, as thoughts and words, become our daemonic masters and cruelly demand our blood from us" (AOM 374). However, he set aside his own prescription and, possessed by a Faustian desire, attempted to know the universal and archetypal "truths," the mysteries, to offer humanity the "new tablets of the law" and "break the history of humanity in two" (Letter to Strindberg, December 7, 1888). As an *anima naturaliter Faustiana* (cf. WP 124), from an early age Nietzsche seemed motivated by this search: "Immense is the breadth of knowledge, infinite the search for the truth!" he wrote in 1859.

With regard to the Faustian quest for knowledge, Jung wrote:

> The rational man, in order to live in this world, has to make a distinction between "himself" and what we might call the "eternal man." Although he is a unique individual, he also stands for "man" as a species, and thus he has a share in all movements of the collective unconscious. In other words, the "eternal" truths become dangerously disturbing factors when they suppress the unique ego of the individual and live at his expense. If our psychology is forced, owing to the special nature of its empirical material, to stress the importance of the unconscious, that does

not in any way diminish the importance of ego-consciousness. It is merely the one-sided over-valuation of the latter that has to be checked by a certain relativization of values. But this relativization should not be carried so far that the ego is completely fascinated and overpowered by the archetypal truths. The ego lives in space and time and must adapt itself to their laws if it is to exist at all. (CW 16:293)

"To get to the bottom of [the] mystery I went over the sea, and I have seen truth naked—verily, barefoot up to the throat" (Z II:18). Nietzsche, "the knower of eternal truths," did not free himself from the fate of Orpheus or the tragic Oedipus. Stripped of its mysteries, nature punishes the wise man with the wisdom acquired—tragic wisdom marked by the sufferings of he who has penetrated its sacred intimacy and has taken on this knowledge for himself. In Nietzsche's case, as occurred with Oedipus, so much wisdom ultimately causes blindness: "He who by means of his knowledge plunges nature into the abyss of destruction must also suffer the dissolution of nature in his own person" (BT 9).

"I am the eternally creative primordial mother."

Dionysus's close relationship with the Great Mother or *Magna Mater* encouraged him to share her inherent triple nature: creatrix, preserver or protector, and destroyer.[47] Because Dionysus is, at the same time, an erotic and thanatic image, his mythos expresses the natural cycle of birth, death, and rebirth. The ecstatic god is the embodiment of the affirmation as well as the annihilation of life: the *tremendus* and the *fascinans* are inextricably united in him. Like Dionysus, Nietzsche was in a continuous struggle between being and nothingness. Consequently, he showed the ambiguity inherent in the Dionysian self-generating/self-consuming dialectic.

As Nietzsche's ego gradually became identified with the (M)other, he also identified himself with the woman-mother in her role as creatrix; thus he sacralized the womb:[48] "I am the eternally creative primordial mother" (BT 17). The woman, mother, or pregnant woman knows the mystery, knows creation. Woman is the *temenos* for the dark (chthonian) mysteries of life: she is "Truth." Thus Nietzsche, in his identification with the matriarchal Mother Goddess,[49] resorted to a demonic partheno-genesis or "automaternity" (Klossowski's term) in order to give birth to his own *Übermensch*: "May I give birth to the overman!" (Z I:18).

Nietzsche characterized his *Zarathustra* in maternal terms: he confessed in *Ecce Homo* that after eighteen months of pregnancy, like a "female elephant," he gave birth to his magnum opus—in which he yearns to be "impregnated by Eternity" (Z III:16).

This self-creation superseded the idea of the despised Judeo-Christian God as creator, so that Nietzsche could attribute the power of creation to his new god. "The torment of the woman in labor" represents the world of Dionysus, a god who emerges from the shadow: "For eternal joy of creation to exist, for the will of life to affirm itself eternally, the 'torment of the woman in labor' must also exist eternally. . . . The word 'Dionysus' means all of this . . . the very path of life, procreation, is felt to be the holy path" (TI X:4).

Nietzsche's "will to power" is the will to procreate: he wanted to be the mother capable of giving birth to himself, of reproducing himself: "To be the child who is newly born, the creator must also want to be the mother who gives birth and the pangs of the birth-giver" (Z II:2). In his work *Daybreak* (522), Nietzsche gave maternity a holy status.

By identifying himself as woman, Nietzsche evaded any encounter with woman as an Other: in him the archetype of alterity became aberrant. Nietzsche preferred pregnant women, who, being certain of what there was within them, revealed the enigma and did not make it threatening—i.e., containing a child, and not an abyss, they seemed to ask nothing of him sexually.[50] Besides, Nietzsche believed in pregnancy as an instrument of domestication: "Everything about woman is a riddle, and everything about woman has one solution: that is pregnancy" (Z I:18). The emancipated women, whom Nietzsche despised, were women who, instead of children, seemed to yearn for a phallus, thus putting Nietzsche in an unbearable position. Having opined that *"Buona femina o mala femina vuol bastone* [Good and bad women want a stick]" (BGE 147), he had no "stick" to offer them.[51]

"Whence do you come, O Man-Woman?"

Nietzsche, like Dionysus, had something feminine in his nature. Unlike the traditional philosophers, Nietzsche promoted "feminine" values over the "masculine" or phallocentric ones. He valued body over mind, nature over culture, irrationality over reason, intuition over conceptualization, art over science. In an "Attempt at Self-Criticism" of *The Birth of Tragedy* (1886), Nietzsche himself judged his early work as "sugary . . . to the point of femininity."

Dionysus was a god mostly worshipped by women. Bachofen, in his *Matriarchy,* called Apollo "the advocate of father's right" and Dionysus "primarily the god of women [in whom] all aspects of female nature find satisfaction." With reference to Dionysus, Walter F. Otto, in his work *Dionysus: Myth and Cult*, cites such epithets as *ho gunnis* ("the woman-ly one"), *thêlumorphos* ("womanly stranger"), and *arsenothêlus* ("woman-ish-man"). Karl Kerényi, in *The Gods of the Greeks,* cites the same epi-thets and adds "the surname Dyalos, 'The Hybrid,' which must certainly refer to a hermaphroditic being and together with other names of the sort must be derived from hushed-up tales of the god's bisexuality." Lycurgus, one of the characters in Aeschylus's *Edoni,* when Dionysus appears onstage, asks: "Whence do you come, O Man-Woman?" His feminine traits, combined with his phallic nature, suggest an inherent androgyny. And the only man with whom Dionysus kept company was his tutor Silenus, a very effeminate personality.

However, despite the fact that Dionysus is at the same time a femi-nine and a masculine god, he is isolated from the sexuality that sur-rounds him. The reason for this lies in the fact that Dionysus's contribu-tion, as shown by the myth, is emotionality (fear, amazement, ecstasy, etc.) and not genitality, like Pan, for example. Therefore, although Dionysus was commonly represented by a phallus in cult practice (*pars pro toto*), the phalli stood in a disembodied (and castrated) state. Similarly, Jung concludes, "there is a lot of unrealized sexuality in Nietzsche" (SNZ I:242).

It should be added that the Dionysian consciousness reveals a charac-teristic mechanism for coping with the devouring mother,[52] a pathological introjection known in psychoanalytic theory as "identification with the aggressor." In *The Birth of Tragedy,* Nietzsche presented woman as Medusa, She of the petrifying gaze. It is worth noticing in this work an almost complete absence of the maenads, the female worshippers of

Dionysus. Nietzsche instead placed the attention on the chorus of male satyrs. The satyr was for him "the image of nature and its strongest urges" (BT 2). The notorious omission of the maenads seems to qualify as evidence of a fear of the effects of the feminine principle. In the revised text of part one, section three of *Ecce Homo*, Nietzsche presented the mother and sister as a "hell-machine" that wounded him in his "highest moments," a confession that implies a fear of castration by the feminine. The mother imago paralyzed him as if he were confronted by Medusa's head:[53]

> The treatment I always received from my mother and sister . . . fills me with unutterable horror: here a highly perfected, infernal machine is at work, one that operates with unfailing accuracy at the very moment when I am most vulnerable and most likely to bleed—during the supreme moments. (cited in Farrell Krell 1996, 216)

In his final work Nietzsche presented the "Eternal Feminine" in her dark aspect, as a source of evil: "Perhaps I am the first psychologist of the eternally feminine . . . the perfect woman tears to pieces when she loves—I know these charming maenads. . . . Woman is indescribably more evil than man . . . good nature is in a woman a form of degeneration" (EH III:5). In his lyrical composition "The Small Brig Called the "Little Angel,' " Nietzsche, in the guise of a woman's voice, revealed the demonic essence of the feminine hidden beneath the surface of the "Little Angel." From Nietzsche's various statements it is possible to infer that in order to avoid the suffering of a Dionysian *sparagamos*, he must deny the feminine or identify with it. With the decrease of consciousness that he experienced during his fall into a nihilistic state, the shadow returned and he finally became possessed by the Mother manifested in "anything secret, hidden, dark; the abyss, the world of the dead . . . anything that is terrifying and inescapable like fate" (Jung, CW 9 I:158).[54] In a rapturous state, he wrote in his *Zarathustra*: "Now that which has hitherto been your ultimate danger has become your ultimate refuge" (Z III:1). Nietzsche became unconsciously identified with the aggressor as a defense mechanism against maternal evil.

The "theatres of the body"

The Dionysian, pertaining to a god subordinated to the mother, relates to the immediacy of the body. For Nietzsche, the body was the conductive thread, the "great reason" (cf. Z I: "On the Despisers of the Body"; GS 11). Equally, his notion of the *Selbst* (cf. ibid.) is directly related to the primordial unity and the Dionysian. Nietzsche identified the *Selbst* with the body and presented it as the non-differentiated primal principle that contains and is being served by the spirit, by the soul, by reason, and by feelings. Frey-Rohn considered that as a result of the divided chaotic multiplicity of Nietzsche's psyche, his "consciousness could no longer fulfill a regulatory function. In such a case, the individual is left to his 'passions and instinctive impulses,' and the body is elevated to the position of being a basic source of knowledge and truth" (1988, 88).

Throughout Nietzsche's life, the conflict and pain that should have been verbalized were not expressed in his personal life but displaced through his writings and through the "theatres of the body."[55] If we take into account the term "psychosomatosis," which the psychoanalyst Joyce McDougall employs "to indicate mental organizations in which the leading, or sometimes the only, visible reactions to disturbing fantasies and experiences are of psychosomatic order" (1989, 18), we find that Nietzsche's body functioned as a container and signifier for his psychic pains. Psychosomatic illness was a significant trait of his entire personality.

The philosopher Siegfried Mandel recognized this trait when he wrote:

> Nietzsche experienced anxiety during his personal "anniversaries," and these often prompted claims in letters that he was at death's door. Certain dates, periods of year, chiming of church bells, midnight, and other recurrent "triggers" caused migrainous reflexes. Many of these forcibly drew him back to childhood with the persistent trauma of his father's burial and Christmas and New Year's festivities. A cluster of such anniversary neurosis and his somatic reactions almost finished him in 1879. (in Salomé 2002, xxxix)

It is worth noting that while "the body had gone mad" (McDougall), Nietzsche did not suffer severe psychotic episodes until the moment of his final breakdown. However, when his physical health reached its zenith, as he confessed in several letters written during his stay in Turin,[56] the early unconscious affective contents that had always been expressed through the somatic sphere transferred, in some mysterious way, to the psyche, which, given its fragility, was incapable of resisting the attack.

When it came to the female body, Nietzsche had to endure other difficulties in this respect: his libido adhered to the material corporeality of the mother, gradually converting the maternal trapping body into a phobic object, a circumstance that made him develop evident signs of "gynecophobia." Nietzsche wrote: "When we love a woman, we easily conceive a hatred for nature on account of all the repulsive natural functions to which every woman is subject. We prefer not to think of all this" (GS 59). In the Prologue of *The Gay Science*, Nietzsche called it a matter of "decency and shame" for women to keep their pudenda veiled.[57]

Yet it is important to note that for Nietzsche the body was also a source of transfiguration, particularly through music and dance. The misunderstood thinker lived and expressed himself from the vital, mysterious, and unfathomable depths from which emerge pure emotions and symbolic images of myths, dreams, and reveries, and which refuse to be condensed into rational language: "We need a new world of symbols; and the entire symbolism of the body is called into play" (BT 2). The body, during his final breakdown, became for Nietzsche his means of expression. Dancing is a frequently used metaphor, particularly in his *Zarathustra*. And dance and music are basic attributes of Dionysus's nature. Walter Otto tells us that Dionysus danced even in his mother's womb and Nietzsche "would believe only in a god who could dance" (Z I:7). For Nietzsche, music was the direct path to the tragic emotion that profoundly moves the body and places it on the verge of dissolution without needing the intervention of resources such as the figures and concepts used in other forms of art. The mythopoeic power of music arises, according to Nietzsche, as a direct expression of the essence of being, the Dionysian world (see BT 17). Zarathustra rebels against the prison of language. He wants to "dance his vision" and his speech becomes dithyrambic: a language of transfiguration capable of permitting a relationship with the world through the body, through feeling. "Only in the dance I know to tell the parable of the highest things" (Z II:11).

In dance, the dithyrambic philosopher conceived infinite possibilities of creation and transformation. This is why the multiple and unlimited movements of the Dionysian man appear throughout the entire Nietzschean opus. However, Nietzsche's dance is a maenadic dance of death. Seduced by the intoxicating vertigo of the abyss, he lets himself be drawn by the mysterious attraction of the precipice, from which his terrible fall will finally occur.

"The artificial paradise"

Dionysus is the god of addictions (alcohol or opiates). Although Nietzsche was not addicted to alcohol, he was addicted to opiates and, as he confessed to Salomé and Rée, considered opium to have a therapeutic effect (cf. Letter, mid-December 1882). Nietzsche found that the drug-induced delirium was capable of bringing on a change of perspective that helped him to obtain a "sensible insight into the state of things" (ibid.). In his poem "Rimus Remedium" (1882), he attempted to overcome his nihilistic attitude toward time through a poppy-induced hallucinogenic state. He wanted to establish a dialogue with his tormentor, "the witch, Time," to free himself from his existential illness brought about by consciousness and reality, by transcending temporality: "All joy wants eternity. Wants deep, deep eternity," said Zarathustra. In his poem "The Mysterious Bark" (1882), Nietzsche claimed that the peace of a "good conscience" could be brought about through a descent into a neurotoxic oblivion, the suspension of the laws of causality and temporality.

Opium, "the artificial paradise," extracted from poppy seeds, similar to the wine used in the Dionysian mysteries, lessens consciousness and puts the individual in a drunken stupor. Opium is a narcotic that dulls the rational world, and narcosis is a journey to oblivion.

"The Great Incognito"

Dionysus was also known as the "god of the mask": since the duality of life and death, inherent in Dionysus, "has its symbol in the mask" (Otto, 1993, 209), the mask was considered a manifestation of the god. "The galvanic entrance of the god and his inescapable presence," writes Walter Otto in his seminal book on Dionysus, "have found their expression in [the symbol of the mask,] an image out of which the perplexing riddle of his twofold nature stares—and with it, madness" (ibid., 86).

As for Nietzsche, he loved masks: "Whatever is profound loves masks" (BGE 40). He liked to call himself "The Great Incognito." Furthermore, he associated a good conscience with the use of masks: "As for ancient life! What can we understand of that as long as we do not understand the delight in masks and the good conscience in using any kind of mask!" (GS 77).[58]

Klossowski considered that "Nietzsche would treat his own necessary ego as a mask. . . . The mask hides the absence of a determinate physiognomy—and thus conceals Chaos" (1997, 224). Unable to find anyone to validate his Dionysian essence (Being), Nietzsche lived protected by an ideal Apollonian persona. Experiencing appearance and essence without existence, he lacked the opportunity to experience himself as a subject with a will to power. In Nietzsche there was a ground for a vertiginous superposition of masks that constituted the self-simulacrum of his hidden disintegration and plurality. Under each mask there was always another mask, never an individual he could call "I." It was instead as if he were a medium through which the contents of the unconscious came directly and involuntarily.

"The Wanderer"

Dionysus was a nomadic god: nowhere was he at home, an attribute shared by "the good European" Nietzsche, who was gripped by an extremely powerful wanderlust his entire life (see GS 377, Z II: "On the Land of Education," and his poems "Lost," "The Wanderer," "Autumn," "Isolated"). The tragic experience is the experience of exile, because it is located in the fissure that divides the mundane (ego) from the sacred. Tragical forces want to be constantly on the road, like a foreigner, fugitive, or expatriate. There is no homeland, because the homeland is the denial of the road. Nonetheless, the tragic road does not follow the direction of progress but rather of return. In the restlessness of the infinite roads, Nietzsche sought to lose himself (dis-identification from the "I"), and both the inner and the outer world became for him a place of exile.

Chapter 10

Theia mania: the Dionysian redemption

We make our destinies by our choices of Gods.

—Virgil

And now there begins a description of illuminations, ecstasies, elations, exaltations, feelings of divine power, which he takes as something atavistic, daemonically derivative from other, "stronger," states when man stood closer to the gods, states of being utterly exceptional, lifted far above the physical potentialities of our feeble, rational epoch.

—Thomas Mann, *Nietzsche's Philosophy in the Light of Recent History*

In *The Birth of Tragedy*, Nietzsche showed us three roads to redemption.

1. Apollonian redemption, through illusions and dreams: the archetypal capacity that allows us to live against the backdrop of incessant movement and change. A redemption based on the polarizing logic of the discriminating consciousness of the phenomenal world.
2. Dionysian redemption, through ecstasy, music, and dance, which prevents the fixation of appearances as truth and proves to be "liberating"

by invoking the forgetfulness of individuality through the submersion of consciousness in the indivisible reality of the noumenal world.

Both of the first two forms of redemption lead to unilateralism: either all bets are placed in favor of Apollonian consciousness (formal principle) or in favor of Dionysian unconsciousness (orgiastic energy): there is no recognition of alternation and, consequently, no possible commitment to it.

3. The third form, represented by the tragic redemption resulting from the alliance of two opposing forces,[1] the Apollonian and the Dionysian, makes it possible to find happiness in a balance of these opposites: "These two . . . drives must unfold their powers in a strict proportion according to the law of eternal justice" (BT 25).

In Nietzsche, who could not sustain ambivalence, there was no reconciliation between the two antagonistic forces or topographic worlds.[2] His inner "multiplicity of voices," which in many cases contradicted each other, came from the split complexes incapable of being reunited consciously under an organic unity: "I have been more a *battlefield* than a human being" (Letter to Gast, July 25, 1882).

From a Jungian perspective, it is well known that the conflicts in our lives are the conflicts among the gods (archetypes). In Nietzsche's case, this was represented by a conflict between the Father archetype (Apollo) and the Mother archetype (Dionysus):

> The *puer's* shadow is the *senex* . . . associated with the god Apollo—disciplined, controlled, responsible, rational, ordered. Conversely, the shadow of the *senex* is the *puer*, related to Dionysus—unbounded instinct, disorder, intoxication, whimsy. Whoever lives out one pattern to the exclusion of the other [as Nietzsche did] risks constellating the opposite. (Sharp 1991, 110)

Until almost the end of his lucid life, Nietzsche lived according to an Apollonian one-sidedness identified with the persona. Yet this world of appearance would seem to have been related to a false or inauthentic self, or the "as if" personality (in Winnicott's sense).[3] Hence the Apollonian world of the "veils of illusions" corroded him little by little:

> The idea that appearances are a necessity is something we hate more than death; and the constant rancor this causes makes us volcanic and threatening. From time to time we take revenge because of our forced concealment, our imposed reserve. We come out of our caverns then with a frightening attitude, our words and our deeds are explosions, and we may possibly annihilate ourselves. (Letter to his sister, January 1875)

Whereas in *The Birth of Tragedy* Nietzsche upheld the alliance between Apollo and Dionysus and warned of the dangers of promoting the Dionysian at the expense of the Apollonian (cf. BT 9), in his later writings, the Dionysian aspect, which he considered his true self, gradually took hold of his personality, with a fading out of the Apollonian:[4]

> For the eternal joy of creation to exist, for the will to life to affirm itself eternally. . . . The word "Dionysus" means all of this: I know of no higher symbolism than this Greek symbolism, the symbolism of the Dionysia. In it the most profound instinct of life, the instinct for the future of life, for eternity of life is felt in a religious way. . . . Saying yes to life, even in its strangest and hardest problems; the will to rejoicing in the sacrifice of its highest types to its own inexhaustibility—this is what I called Dionysian. . . . I, the last disciple of the philosopher Dionysus—I, the teacher of the eternal recurrence. (TI X:4–5)

In *Ecce Homo* he declared: "I obey my Dionysian nature, which does not know how to separate doing no from saying yes. I am the first immoralist" (IV: 2). In these writings Nietzsche confirmed that "in the Dionysian symbol the ultimate limit of affirmation is attained." Paradoxically, for Nietzsche reality was the subject of the unconscious and not in the "I," which he personified as Dionysus: "Our empirical existence," he stated, is just a "representation of the primal unity" (BT 4). Nietzsche presented the Dionysian true essence vis-à-vis the Apollonian appearance; possessed by the former, he wanted to become one with *das Ur-Eine*.[5]

Nietzsche constantly craved escape from the "human, all too human" world, which he experienced as hostile: "Rather would I be a day laborer in Hades among the shades of the past! Even the underwordly are plumper and fuller than you. . . . I can endure you neither naked or clothed, you men of today" (Z II:14). As a defender of the elements of the "mysterious doctrine of tragedy," he wanted to commune with its principles, i.e., "The fundamental knowledge of the oneness of everything existent, the conception of individuation as the primal cause of evil, and . . . the joyous hope that the spell of individuation may be broken in augury of restored oneness" (BT 10). It is possible to describe his psychic condition using the same description that he offered of the Dionysian artist: as a Dionysian man, Nietzsche "has identified himself with the primal unity, its pain and contradiction: [he has] surrendered his subjectivity on the Dionysian process. . . . The 'I' . . . therefore sounds from the depths of his being: its 'subjectivity' [was] a fiction" (BT 5).[6]

"The Dionysian suffering," wrote Nietzsche in *The Birth of Tragedy*, "is like a transformation into air, water, earth, and fire," a *katálisis* related to the thanatic drive, a phenomenon of regressing to primeval non-differentiation. He added: "We are therefore to regard the state of individuation as the origin and primal cause of all suffering, as something objectionable in itself."

Dionysus, the god of ecstasy, can annihilate "the ordinary bounds and limits of existence." The word *ecstasy* is derived from the Greek *ekstasis*, meaning rapture, displacement, or delirium; from *eksistánai*, whose meaning is to put out of place, to displace, that is, to shift toward another state of consciousness, "being-outside-oneself." And *Zarathustra*, according to Jung, "was the Dionysian experience par excellence. In the latter part, the Dionysian *ekstasis* comes in. *Zarathustra* really led [Nietzsche] up to a full realization of the mysteries of the cult of Dionysus: he already had ideas about it, but *Zarathustra* was the experience which made the whole thing real" (SNZ I:10).

Nietzsche's own theory of eternal recurrence seemed dreadful to him. He could not bear the weight of the recurrent past with all the pain, anger, desire for revenge and its concomitant guilt feelings, as God's murderer, coming back again and again. This may be why he identified eternal recurrence as the petrifying head of Medusa: an embodiment of the terrifying abyss that must be acknowledged but must not be stared in the face.

However, there was a way out: identification with the Dionysian,[7] because of its "*lethargic* element," was capable of eliminating memories of the past. By leading us to complete oblivion of ourselves, Dionysus frees man from old ties, dissolves past claims, and lifts the barriers that hide the invisible and infinite from ordinary consciousness. Nietzsche kept searching for the "bliss of forgetfulness," a theme which occupied a central place in his early works and continued in his writings: for him, life and forgetfulness were strongly interwoven notions. In "On the Uses and Disadvantages of History for Life" (Section 1), he called the ability to forget a "divine ability," and remarked: "It is altogether impossible to live at all without forgetting. . . . He who cannot sink down on the threshold of the moment and forget all the past, who cannot stand balanced like a goddess of victory without growing dizzy and afraid, will never know what happiness is."

In his Preface to *The Gay Science,* Nietzsche glorified forgetting as the highest wisdom. His desire for forgetfulness is also present in his poems:

> A.—Was I ill? I got well?
> Who was my doctor? Can you tell?
> B.—Only now you're truly well
> Those are well who have forgotten.
> —"Dialogue," from "Prelude in German Rhymes" (GS)

> Throw what is oppressive to you into the depths!
> Man, forget! Man, forget!
> The art of forgetting is divine!
> —"The Sun Sinks"

Therefore, the philosopher Allen S. Weiss concludes in this respect: "Nietzsche reverses the dictum 'Know thyself!' . . . for the sake of a style

of existence which is initiated by the prescription, 'Forget thyself!' "
(1983, 285).

The deicide was another attempt to "forget," in this case to forget his
guilt at having failed to live up to "God's" rules. "What? Never to be
allowed to be alone with oneself? Never again to be unobserved? . . . this
importunity from Heaven, this inescapable supernatural neighbor . . ."
(D 464). "This god had to die! Man cannot bear it that such a witness
should live," declared *Zarathustra's* Ugliest Man (Z IV:7). Therefore, to
Nietzsche's declaration that "God is dead" one could add a subtle hope:
"Ergo, I'm free!" Free of what? Principally, free of guilt. Without God
there is no moral import, because God is "the Chief Justice and Supreme
Auditor of the universe's moral account" (Wicks, 2002, 118). If there is
no God, then there is no accountability; without accountability, there is
no possibility for morality. The death of God implies the disappearance
of purpose, of goal, of the distinction between good and evil, and of the
permitted and the prohibited. There is no longer a need for His sanction,
approval, or repulsion.

However, having failed to reach his cherished ideal, the *Übermensch*,
Nietzsche could not occupy the place of the Law. As a result, he became
trapped in an overwhelming guilt complex without escape: the God
killed didn't disappear just because of Nietzsche's decree. He resurrect-
ed in Nietzsche's psyche as the dark side of Self (personified in Dionysus
Zagreus), and played a more oppressive part in his psychic economy than
the God Nietzsche had tried to escape.[8] The psychoanalyst Donald
Kalsched points out in this regard:

> The persecuting god is much more than the introjected father.
> He is a primitive, archaic, archetypal figure, personifying the ter-
> rifying dismembering rage of the catalyst psyche and, as such,
> represents *the dark side of the Self*. The outer catalyst for this
> inner figure may be the personal father [or the mother's animus],
> but the damage to the inner world is done by the psyche's
> Yahweh-like rage, directed back upon the Self. It was for this
> reason that neither Freud nor Jung were convinced that outer
> trauma alone was responsible for splitting the psyche. It was

rather an interior, psychological factor that ultimately did the worst damage. (1996, 17)

Like the Pale Criminal (cf. Z I:6), Nietzsche felt guilty before and after the deed (crime). If God lived, he felt guilt before God and "this thought becomes an instrument of torture to him. He apprehends in 'God' the ultimate opposition to his own inextinguishable animal-instincts; he regards these animal-instincts themselves as a kind of guilt before God" (GM II:22). Because God "saw everything: he saw man's depths and ultimate grounds, all his concealed disgrace and ugliness. . . . [God] crawled into [all of the] dirtiest nooks" (Z IV:7), He had to die. But declaring the death of God, Nietzsche's final act of self-assertion, proved a self-annihilation, for he could not bear the guilt, impossible to expiate, after the deed:[9]

> How shall we comfort ourselves, the murderers of all murderers? What was holiest and mightiest of all that the world has yet owned has bled to death under our knives: who will wipe this blood off us? What water is there for us to clean ourselves? What festivals of atonement, what sacred games shall we have to invent? (GS 125)

Because the death of God implies the disappearance of the distinction between good and evil, the "murder" of God leads ideally to a guilt-free conscience. But the image of this murder haunted Nietzsche:[10] "An image made this pale man pale. He was equal to his deed when he did it; but he could not bear its image after it was done" (Z 1:6).[11] Like the Pale Criminal, "Nietzsche's 'ugliest man,'" writes the philosopher Robert Wicks, "still lives in the 'shadows' of God, and has not stepped into what Nietzsche believes to be the guilt-free, more beautiful and healthy day-light, which is to say that Nietzsche's staunch advocacy of atheism prob-ably troubled him at times, for he saw himself as one of God's chief mur-derers" (2002, 59). Nietzsche himself, after declaring the death of God, suffered from a constant and overwhelming sense of irrational guilt.[12] It is important to highlight that even if in the eternal recurrence there is no room for redemption, compassion or sin, guilt always returns and, consequently, becomes eternal. Therefore, in *Ecce Homo,* Nietzsche concluded: "A god who would come to earth must not *do* anything except wrong: not to take the punishment upon oneself but the *guilt* would be divine" (EH I:5).

The guilt generated by a "murderer of the law" reflects the existential situation pictured by Arthur Rimbaud in his work *Un saison en enfer:*

> Condemnation is eternal! Is it not true that every man who wishes to mutilate himself is already condemned? I believe myself in hell, therefore I am in hell. It is the fulfillment of my catechism. I am a slave to my baptism. Parents, you have created my misfortune and yours. Poor innocent! Hell cannot attack pagans.

Nietzsche was aware of this inescapable reality when he wrote in 1863: "As a plant I was born near the cemetery; as a man in the home of a village pastor."[13] In spite of his great battle against congregational morality, the son of the "village pastor" did not seem able to forget his historical condition, the spiritual heritage of his Christian ancestry, by a mere act of will: "I have broken with the legacy of old times . . . the shadows of the church would cover me" (NP 23).[14] He could not be liberated from "sin, bad conscience and guilt," the traits he attributed to Christianity: "One cannot erase from the soul of a human being what his ancestors liked most and did most constantly. . . . It is simply not possible that a human being should *not* have the qualities and preferences of his parents and ancestors in his body" (BGE 264). When Nietzsche declared that "God is dead; but given the way of men, there may still be caves for thousands of years in which his shadow will be shown" (GS 108), we can infer that the persistence of this shadow is evidence of his unwillingness to suspend belief.[15]

It is worthwhile to notice that Nietzsche expressed the deed (the thought and the action) of the Pale Criminal in terms of madness: "Now for evermore he saw himself as the perpetrator of one deed. I call this madness" (Z I:6). Also it is through the words uttered by a madman that Nietzsche announced dramatically the death of God. The madman seems to represent Nietzsche's anticipation of the effect of the deicide already committed.[16]

Believing that "There is no redemption for one who suffers so of himself" (Z I:6), no resolution of this greatest guilt except by agreeing to relinquish everything (through death or madness),[17] the tragic thinker finally tried to forget completely the persecutory guilt for the crime of parricide;[18] madness represented that act of total detachment. Disintegration is the most desperate attempt of the ego to defend itself from extreme anxiety. "My ego is to me the great contempt of man" (Z I:6). According to Overbeck, who knew him so well, "Nietzsche's whole life was a preparation for madness" (Schain 2001, 103).

Beside death, the only way Nietzsche had to escape from the power of his Christian origin and of the "murdering" of God was the gift of oblivion. And Dionysian dissolution was capable of offering him total oblivion. Dionysian ecstasy means the extinction of the individual in the divinity: "When the Dionysian emotions awake . . . everything subjective vanishes into complete self-forgetfulness" (BT 1). Psychologically, it represents the dissolution of the ego in the objective psyche, that is, psychosis: the dissolution of time (eternal recurrence) and the "I," the triumph of forgetfulness. In other words, what is freed in the Dionysian ecstasy is not the body but the tyranny of the ego: "My Ego is something that shall be overcome" (Z I:6). This is the condemnation of the Pale Criminal, not by an external jury but by himself. There is an intimate connection between guilt and psychosis. And if it is accompanied by megalomania, the guilt is unbearable. The omnipotent subject, in this case Nietzsche, feels that all kinds of terrible things are his fault (negative inflation).

Death and madness are the most powerful agents providing forgetfulness of guilt (of the order of the superego) and shame (of the registrant of the ego ideal): "Under the charm of the Dionysian . . . the slave is a free man: now all the rigid, hostile barriers of necessity, caprice, or 'impudent convention' ["Naumburg convention"] are broken" (BT 1). Dionysus Mainomenos (the mad god) became Nietzsche's god and the cause of his madness through possession. At the same time, as mentioned previously, Dionysus, like all gods of fertility, always comes back to the (M)other; thus, ultimately, "madness" is the result of possession by the terrible (M)other, with her "mantic and orgiastic characteristics." Madness or dissolution of the personality forms part of the sphere of the Great Mother (the unconscious): "Insanity," writes Neumann, "is an ever-recurrent symptom of possession by her or by her representatives" (1991, 61). Consequently, the author considers: "The ecstatic, orgiastic nature of the Feminine . . . is manifested in relation with the women of Dionysus" (ibid., 72).

In choosing to follow the dangerous Dionysus-Zagreus,[19] the "great hunter," the "most psychiatric of the Greek Gods" (López-Pedraza 2000, 22), Nietzsche sealed his destiny. With this act he attempted to abandon the ego to such an extent that consciousness would see its agent abandoned. With Dionysus, Nietzsche wished to merge with the unknown, so as to establish his kingdom in the "other world" (collective unconscious): "My kingdom is no longer of this world," proclaimed Zarathustra (Z III:9).

In divine "mania" (*theia mania*), the spirit loses consciousness of itself so that it can be possessed by forces alien to the individual's consciousness. It is a case of madness "that does not stem from any human illness, but from a divine transposition, that makes man step out from his habitual state" (Plato, *Phaedrus*). "Divine transposition" should be understood to be the archetypal forces emerging from the collective unconscious. It is a state in which the subject is not active but passive: a surrender of self-control to achieve "being filled with the god." In this view, madness is not a disease but a cure: a refuge from guilt and shame. The philosopher felt a complicity between reason and morality, whereas madness relates to immorality; and in his opinion, he was "an immoralist."

The Dionysian energy began to take possession of Nietzsche's psyche, with results that find parallels in "some of the central emotional themes of *The Bacchae*—including the alternation, in both Pentheus ['man of sorrows'] and Dionysus, of submissiveness and effeminacy with megalomaniac fantasies of power, the sexual confusion, the vengeful, castrating, mannish mother, the boastfulness, the self-destructiveness, the uncontrollable affects" (Slater 1992, 303). In *Ecce Homo*, we can see that Nietzsche related the "Dionysian nature" exclusively in terms of the "joy in *annihilation*." [20]

"With Dionysus," López-Pedraza considers, "our imagination is connected immediately to the most archaic complexes in humankind" (2000, 14). This reality is eminently evident in Nietzsche's psyche. Combined with this, López-Pedraza adds, the dismemberment of Dionysus by the titans "is an image of horror and a well-known metaphor for madness: in the language of psychiatry, a psyche in pieces" (ibid.). The symbolic quartering of Dionysus occurs in the psyche of the one who profanes his mysteries. Nietzsche's reason was finally destroyed by the same Titans who defend chaos. Henderson was not too far from López-Pedraza's affirmation when he wrote that the dismemberment of Dionysus represents "a triumph of the matriarchal orgiastic principle, as the Way of Nature, over the patriarchal principle of Law and Order" (1967, 23).

Neumann suggests that the Dionysian attributes are generally associated with a maternal goddess, but of the most terrible variety:

> The male experiences this force that violates him not as something of his own, but something "other," alien, and therefore feminine . . . whether he is transformed into an animal . . . whether he is . . . castrated; or whether, dressed as a woman and identified with the Feminine . . . he fulfils the function of the Feminine. (1995, 91)

According to Nietzsche "each one of us . . . must organize the chaos within him" (UM II:10); however, in his case the step from chaos to cosmos (consciousness) was never taken. Nietzsche placed himself at the mercy of the alluring, wild, untamed, and uncontrollable forces of the archaic chaos, which took an absolute hold: "He wanted to make of chaos an object of affirmation" (Deleuze 1988, 388). By rejecting the Apollonian logos, which orders and structures the cosmos, Nietzsche became an anti-Platonic: the Apollonian cosmos was placed below the Dionysian chaos, whose attributes are the ecstatic, the dance, the dithyrambic chorus, and tragedy.

"The picture of madness stands at the end of Nietzsche's philosophy [and life]," wrote Lou Salomé, "the point of departure is formed by dissolving everything . . . and letting drive-like chaos dominate" (2001, 150). Therefore, Nietzsche's philosophy "creates the world in its own image; it cannot do otherwise" (BGE 9). He perceived the world as a reflection of his own internal Pandemonic condition: pointless, meaningless, or aimless, lacking regularity and self-identity. The world became for him void of all absolute *teloi*: a transient configuration, the product of chance, a complete chaos. "The total character of the world, however, is in all eternity chaos—in the sense of not a lack of necessity but a lack of order, arrangement, form, beauty, wisdom, and whatever other names there are for our aesthetic anthropomorphism" (GS 109).[21] And Dionysus, whose votary Nietzsche became, is that god of chaos and contradiction "from whose touch, everyone goes away . . . richer in himself, newer to himself than before, broken open, blown up and sounded out by a thawing wind" (BGE 295).

I consider that the concluding words of the philosopher María Zambrano are highly illuminating to understand Nietzsche's relation to Dionysus:

> That which is sacred was considered by Nietzsche as the first chaos. He returned to chaos in search of an altar where he could offer his sacrifice. . . . There, he discovered Dionysus, primary god of life, life itself in nascent form, unfurling in metamorphosis. . . . It was necessary to go back to chaos, to life without form, in order to correct man's destiny, so that man would not be that different being: endowed with a fixed being, consciousness, embedded between *good* and *evil*. It was necessary to fuse the human creature from the primary chaos of life with the warmth of Dionysus, so that he could be something that included everything: everything that was afterwards called "good" and "evil" by virtue of an "idea." (1973, 170)

Chapter 11

Ecce mulier

Who warms me, who still loves me?
Give hot hands!
Give coal warmers for the heart!
Stretched out, shuddering,
like a half-dead man whose feet one warms,
shaken, alas! by unknown fevers,
shivering with sharp, icy frost-arrows.
Hunted by you, O thought!
Unnameable, veiled, terrible one!
You hunter behind clouds!
Struck down by your lightning bolt,
you mocking eye that stares at me from the dark!
So I lie,
bending myself, twisting myself, tormented
by all eternal tortures,
hit by you, cruelest hunter,
you unknown—God!

Hit deeper!
Hit again, once more!
Sting, shatter this heart!
Why this torture
with blunt arrows?
Why do you stare again,
unwearied of human agony,
with gods' lightning eyes that delight in suffering?

You don't want to kill?
Only torture, torture?
Why—torture me,
you unknown god who delights in suffering? . . .

And you torture me, fool that you are,
torture my pride?
Give love to me—who warms me still?
Who loves me still?
Give hot hands,
give coal warmers for the heart,
give me, the loneliest one,
whom ice, alas, sevenfold ice
teaches to languish for enemies,
for enemies themselves,
give, yes, give me,
cruelest enemy,
—yourself! . . .

He has fled,
my only companion,
my great enemy,
my unknown,
my hangman-God! . . .

No!
Come back![1]
With all your tortures!
All my tears run
their course to you
and the last flame of my heart
glows upward to you.
O come back,
my unknown god! My pain!
My last happiness! . . .

A bolt of lightning. Dionysus
becomes visible in emerald beauty.[2]

Dionysus:
Be clever, Ariadne!
You have small ears,[3]
Put a clever word into them!—
Does not one first have to hate oneself if one is to love oneself?[4]
I am your labyrinth.

—F. NIETZSCHE, *Ariadne's Lament* (NP, 217)

A labyrinthine human being never seeks the truth,[5] but—
whatever he may try to tell us—
always and only his Ariadne.

—F. NIETZSCHE

I condoned my boredom at having
created a world. . . .
I, together with Ariadne, have only to be
the golden balance of all things.

—F. NIETZSCHE

THE ANIMA IS BOTH A personal complex and an archetypal image. According to Jung, it is the function of the anima to act as the overriding form of all the images of the feminine (cf. Jung, CW 9ii, 24) in a man's psyche, and to be mediatrix to the eternally unknowable; as psychopomp, the anima is "the one who shows the way" to the unknown (CW 12:74). Just as the persona functions as a bridge to the external world, the anima is the bridge between the ego and the inner world. It helps the ego to confront itself and to adapt to the demands of feelings, images, emotions, and intuitions derived from the unconscious ambit. A man in whom the anima does not fulfill its function of helping to cope with the overwhelming contents of the collective unconscious will be more seriously exposed to its destructive onslaught.[6]

As happens with all archetypes, the anima possesses a bipolar nature, described by Jung in the following terms: the anima not only represents "life's reasonable and useful aspects, but its frightful paradoxes and ambivalences where good and evil, success and ruin, hope and despair, counterbalance one another. Because she is his greatest danger she demands from a man his greatest, and if he has it in him she will receive it" (CW 9 II:24).[7] Like Dionysus, the anima represents the psyche's deepest erotic and thanatic drives.[8]

The anima is "much further away from consciousness" than the shadow "and in normal circumstances seldom if ever realized" (Jung, CW 9 I:19). Jung wrote that if the encounter with the shadow is the "apprentice-piece" in a man's development, then coming to terms with the anima is the "master-piece" (ibid., 61).

The mother, according to Jung, is the first bearer of the anima's image, and Nietzsche himself intuited this phenomenon when he wrote: "Everyone carries within him an image of a woman that he gets from his mother; that determines whether he will honor women in general, or despise them, or be generally indifferent to them" (HATH 380).[9] To carry out its mediating function, the anima must previously be differentiated from the maternal complex.

The development of a man's anima is reflected in how he relates to women. Nietzsche failed to come to terms with the feminine outside him and within him: he failed to effect a harmonious differentiation between his anima and the maternal complex. His personal mother did not perform the function of mirroring and reflection; hence the development of his anima was deficient, distorted. Nietzsche became dominated by a negative mother complex and could not make the shift of his libido from the mother through the anima to an actual woman. Consequently, he did not achieve a strengthened masculine ego, differentiated from the (M)other. In him, there was no "crystallization" of the anima of the maternal archetype; the feminine image didn't "extricate itself from the grip of the Terrible Mother" (Neumann 1995, 198). Thus, in addition to incomplete masculine development, he presented a conflictive anima development. His anima and, in turn, the potentiality to establish a relationship with the opposite sex was totally impeded by a powerful maternal complex: feminine love is "maternal love," Nietzsche concluded (cf. HATH 203). The mother archetype dominated him until the end of his life,[10] and his inability to break the incestuous bond made him incapable of any emotional progression. Nietzsche lost his capacity for a full

development of consciousness and the necessary inner connection with
the Self (the *imago Dei*), as they both depend on the anima's function.

We can perceive Nietzsche's difficulties with the feminine and the
anima in his life and writings. Even if his anima, as the figure of Life in his
Zarathustra (cf. Z III:15), saved the deflated old sage from being drowned
in the deep ocean of depression by pulling him out with a golden fishing
rod (cf. Z II:10),[11] Nietzsche-Zarathustra was unfaithful to her[12] and tried
to deceive her, hoping to secretly leave her to pursue eternity (Z III:15.2).[13]

Elsewhere Nietzsche declared:

> Truth is horror and kills action. (cf. BT 7)

> Truth is a woman. (GS P:4)

Consequently, in his mind it would seem possible to complete the syl-
logism as follows:

> Woman is horror and kills action.

In these terms we can understand Nietzsche's rejection of the feminine.
But, as we know, what is consciously denied does not necessarily cease to
exist: it just splits in the unconscious and eventually returns to demand its
due. The exiled feminine flooded Nietzsche's works, as Günter Schule
explained: Nietzsche's philosophy "showed itself to be that of the repressed
femininity of the male" (cited in Köhler 2002, XIV). Schule's comment
holds true, not only of Nietzsche's work, but also of his life.

Jung questioned himself: "And where has the feminine side, the soul,
disappeared to in Nietzsche?" (CW 10:434). In his seminar on Nietzsche's
Zarathustra, Jung wrote: "We have no anima in *Zarathustra*. . . . It takes the
whole development of *Zarathustra* to call Nietzsche's attention to the fact
that there is an anima" (SNZ, I:533).[14] Jung finally concluded that the
anima as mediatrix was absent in Nietzsche: "Helen has vanished in
Hades, and Eurydice will never return" (CW 19:434).[15]

In Nietzsche's case, the absence of the anima in her mediating function inevitably hurled him into the unconscious abyss. "In the pleasure
of facing into the Dionysian abysses" (BT 14), Nietzsche found ecstasy

and his source of inspiration. Neumann, however, warns: "The positive element of inspiration and the positive rapture of ecstasy may lead to the decline of the ego, possession and madness" (1991, 76).

Hillman was able to relate the experience of the abyss with the absence of the anima:

> Absence of anima opens one to the soul's immeasurable depths . . . revealing those depths as an abyss. Not only are the guide and the bridge gone, but so too is the possibility of a personal connection through personified representation. For it is through the anima that the autonomous systems of the psyche are experienced in personified form. Without her the depths become a void. . . . This happens because the anima who "personifies the collective unconscious" . . . is not there to mediate the depths in personified images with personal intentions. At the same time, the world outside is perceived without its depths, and losing perspective it becomes a soulless flatland. (1996a, 109)

Instead of becoming effectively related to his anima, Nietzsche got caught by this autonomous complex, with its concomitant symptoms: "We have there [in *Zarathustra*] a problem in itself," Jung pointed out, "namely, the identity of Zarathustra with the anima, and most probably an identity of the author with the anima" (SNZ I:31). Therefore, Jung concluded: "Nietzsche equals Zarathustra equals anima" (SNZ I:1165).

Jung also explained that the character of the anima is compensatory with regard to the persona: "The character of the soul can be deduced from that of the persona. "Everything that should normally be in the outer attitude, but is conspicuously absent, will invariably be found in the inner attitude" (CW 6:806). Nietzsche's persona was extremely luminous, Apollonian; and consequently it is to be expected that the attributes of his anima were dark, Dionysian, and chthonic.

Developing further Jung's ideas, the Jungian analyst Donald Sandner distinguished the two poles of the anima by naming them dominant anima and wounded anima.[16] He pointed out that, in practice, they have been observed to be experienced separately, as a "split anima," and in conflict with each other. In this regard, he wrote:

> The two poles are distinguished by their qualities. The dominant pole may be represented by a range of qualities—from harshness, rudeness, sadism, and maliciousness or even murderous intent to strong, positive, assertive leadership. The wounded anima is represented by weakness, disability, and illness, but also lovingness, sensitivity, and soulfulness. (1993, 221)

Following Sandner's observations, it is possible to say that in Nietzsche the dominant pole seems to have remained projected on the mother, the sister, Cosima Wagner, and Lou Salomé, as an undifferentiated anima of the maternal-filial imago, whereas his ego would appear to have been possessed by the unconscious wounded anima. The wounded anima is personified by Ariadne, who was betrayed by the solar hero Theseus.[17] She is the Ariadne of midnight, as in the poem, the Ariadne of the moment of darkness of the unconscious world. She is not the heroic Ariadne who gave Theseus the thread so he would not lose his way in the maze, but the one with whom Dionysus,[18] "the nocturnal one," would consummate a holy marriage. In "The Song of Melancholy," Zarathustra's soul, possessed by sorrow and melancholy, awaits the great redeemer who will come, as Dionysus, from the sea, symbol of the unconscious (cf. Z IV:14). "For this is the soul's secret: only when the hero has abandoned her, is she approached in a dream by an overhero" (Z II:13). His name is Dionysus: "I saw him," wrote Nietzsche, "his halcyonic smile, his honey eyes, now deepest and hooded, now green and slippery, a shimmering surface . . . the sea surges up in his eyes." He is writing as Ariadne, who no longer has to hand over the thread because she has been enticed to lose herself in the innermost recess of the labyrinth itself.

If Ariadne had been integrated with Nietzsche's consciousness, she could have acted in her positive aspect: the psychic energy she personified could have functioned as the mediatrix between Nietzsche's ego and his unconscious, as in the myth of the Minotaur and the labyrinth. For Nietzsche, the Minotaur, the trans-human subject, represented the truly "free spirit" who lost the belief in God and knew that "nothing is true" (cf. GM 24).[19] The labyrinth, on the other hand, usually symbolizes the source of archetypal feminine energy as chaos, the dangerous aspect of the unconscious that represents the risk of getting lost (devouring Mother). As keeper of the enigma of the labyrinth,[20] Ariadne knew the way out of the (M)other. Even if Theseus had enslaved the Minotaur by his own hands, he would have remained confined forever in the labyrinth had he not received Ariadne's help.

As we mentioned, however, for Nietzsche it was the tragic Ariadne who seemed to possess his ego.[21] As an autonomous complex, the anima constellates the negative aspect, which possesses a demonic power.[22] The more opposed and disintegrated the feminine aspect in the masculine consciousness, the greater its power of seduction. In the "Second Dance-Song," Zarathustra referred to the anima-life as a dangerous temptress: "Who would not hate you, great woman who binds us, enwinds us, seduces us, seeks us, finds us!"[23]

Like a bold seafarer, Nietzsche placed himself at the mercy of the vortices of an abysmal sea and was seduced there by "the songs of the Sirens" (the dark feminine).[24] The Sirens are mythological deities, endowed with the attribute of fulminating with the knowledge of eternal opposites; consequently, they may be considered the feminine equivalent of Dionysus.[25] "We know everything," sang Odysseus's Sirens. "They offer man the gift of memory, transcendent knowledge of the archetypal world" (Edinger 1994, 117), as Nietzsche himself seemed to experience when he wrote the following in the passage titled "Will and Wave":

How greedily this wave approaches, as if it were after something! How it crawls with terrifying haste into the inmost nooks of this labyrinthine cliff! It seems that it is trying to anticipate someone; it seems that something of value, high value, must be hidden there.—And now it comes back, a little more slowly but still quite white with excitement. . . . But already another wave is approaching, still more greedily and savagely than the first, and its soul, too, seems to be full of secrets and the lust to dig up treasures. . . . So? You mistrust me? You are angry with me, you beautiful monsters? Are you afraid that I might give away your whole secret? Well, be angry with me, arch your dangerous green bodies as high as you can, raise a wall between me and the sun—as you are doing now! Truly, even now nothing remains of the world but green twilight and green lightning. Carry on as you like . . . or dive again, pouring your emeralds down into the deepest depths, and throw your infinite white mane of foam and spray over them: everything suits me, for everything suits you so well, and I am so well-disposed toward you for everything: how could I think of betraying you? For—mark my word: I know you and your secret. (GS 310)

These "beautiful monsters" offer eternity:[26] "Never yet have I found the woman from whom I wanted children, unless it be this woman whom I love: for I love you, O eternity" (Z III:16).[27]

During his journey to *terra incognita,* to the omphalos of the chthonic universe, the mythical creatures finally trapped Nietzsche: he ran back to Mother Nature's dark and fatal embrace. Glory, fame, transcendence, and knowledge are ineffable enticements for human nature:

> "Then, replete with happiness, you can continue on your journey with a greater knowledge of more things," the Sirens repeated to Odysseus. And now we know what fascinated Odysseus as he approached the island of the Sirens; it was the unconscious psyche and its wondrous seductive power. To be sure, there is wisdom there, but for the naïve ego that is 'unsuspecting' . . . there is also the grave danger of *identifying* personally with the archetypal sources of knowledge . . . and any limited miserable human being who sails his ship of fate too close to the archetypes thinks he knows everything too. (Elder 1996, 195)

When man is satiated with wisdom, a situation occurs similar to that of the temptation by the serpent in Genesis, when it offers man divine wisdom: "Ye shall be as gods" (3:5). But when someone goes no further than this point, as occurred with Nietzsche, the *numinosum* turns negative and destructive.[28]

It is pertinent at this point to recall Jung's explanation of this phenomenon:

The unconscious anima is a creature without relationships, an autoerotic being whose one aim is to take total possession of the individual.[29] When this happens to a man he becomes strangely womanish in the worst sense, with a moody and uncontrolled disposition which, in time, has a deleterious effect even on the hitherto reliable functions—e.g., his intellect. (CW 16:504)

Nietzsche's anima, like a jealous and possessive demon, kept him from establishing any relation. However, the greatest danger lies in the *imitatio animae:* the identification with the archetype of the soul triggers the acting out of the dynamism inherent in the corresponding archaic image. Jung declared, "If the ego adopts the standpoint of the anima, adaptation to reality is severely compromised. . . . The anima's irruption into consciousness often amounts to a psychosis" (CW 7:521). In concert with Jung, Hillman asserts: "Union with anima also means union with my psychosis" (1996a, 135).

There was a sacred marriage in Nietzsche's delusional imagery. The *sponsus* and *sponsa* were Dionysus and Ariadne, a union representative of the central archetype. But the *hierosgamos* or union of opposites did not take place on a conscious level, bringing the mystical union to reality. It did not take place in "this world" but in the "other"; thus both figures sank once again into the unconscious, indicating that a "lesser *coniunctio*" had taken place. Unlike Odysseus, Nietzsche did not survive the thanatonic song of the Sirens, and his ego receded into the collective unconscious, into the timeless world of the primordial images. Thus Nietzsche's psyche became the *temenos* of the archetypal encounter. The psychopathological problem of incest is the aberrant natural form of the union of opposites, a union which has never been made conscious or has once more disappeared from view. As a result, Nietzsche's ego withdrew into an innermost idealized encapsulated nucleus: "The immature son-ego [was] eclipsed and threatened with destruction when it naively embrace[d] the maternal unconscious" (Edinger 1996, 212).

The Ariadne-Dionysus *coniunctio*[30] seems to have made way for Nietzsche's self-redemption when he let fall the last self-imposed mask: "That nethermost self which had, as it were, been buried and grown silent under the continual pressure of having to listen to other selves . . . awakened slowly, shyly, dubiously—but eventually it spoke again" (EH III: HATH 4). Nietzsche spoke then with the voice of a woman. In early January 1889, on the eve of his mental breakdown Nietzsche rewrote the "Magician's Song" (Z IV:5)[31] in the voice of a woman and titled it "Ariadne's Lament," adding also a new epilogue: the epiphany of Dionysus.[32] Nietzsche was then *Ecce mulier* and his name was Ariadne:[33] "Who besides me knows what Ariadne is!" (EH III: TSZ 8). This was the last of his riddles that no one, according to him, was able to decipher: "For all such riddles nobody so far had any solution; I doubt that anybody even saw any riddles here" (ibid.).

As Zarathustra, Nietzsche could only aspire to reach the object of his desire, Eternity. The philosopher T. K. Seung suggests: "In the 'Seven Seals,' [Nietzsche] is still desperately seeking the fulfillment of his love," and "the seven stanzas are meant to explain why his love is perpetually frustrated in the temporal world" (2005, xvi). However, with this *hieros-gamos*, and once his transformation into a woman was complete, the labyrinthine philosopher was able to take possession of his love object: Nietzsche as Ariadne submitted himself to the divine fecundation embodied by Eternity personified in Dionysus. Zarathustra already knew the god of wine and the mystical experience of Dionysian intoxication that transported him into the "well of eternity" while he fell into a brief but numinous sleep under a grove of grapevine: "Still! Still! Did not the world become perfect just now? What is happening to me? As a delicate wind dances unseen on an inlaid sea, light, feather-light, thus sleep dances on me. My eyes he does not close, my soul he leaves awake. . . . He touches me inwardly with caressing hands, he conquers me" (Z IV:10).

Following this experience, Nietzsche-Zarathustra longed for the assimilation of his soul into the eternal/archetypal sphere: "When will you drink my soul back into yourself?" (ibid.). Only through a betrayal of Life could Nietzsche consummate this mystical union in order to fulfill what he desired most: the subversion of lineal time (past, present, and future) by Eternity.[34] Gone were the chains holding him prisoner to mundane/conscious reality. His fragmentary self reached finally into the plenitude of the infinite, the transcendental-unconscious realm: in a letter addressed to Carl von Gersdorff (February 12, 1885), he referred to Part IV of his *Zarathustra* as "a sort of sublime finale."

In Nietzsche's case "the (male) one is lost, also the (female) other" (Irigaray 1991, 64). Due to her particular connection with Dionysus (unconscious), Ariadne not only becomes his bride, she also dies for him. Thus Ariadne no longer exists for Nietzsche, only Dionysus-Hades as the somber personification of Nietzsche's timeless domain: "Among the Hindus I have been Buddha, in Greece—Dionysus. Alexander and Caesar are my incarnations, as are Shakespeare's poet, Lord Bacon. Lastly, Voltaire and Napoleon, perhaps Richard Wagner also," he wrote to Cosima Wagner in January 1889, the year that marks his own dissolution. In another letter dated January 6, 1889, addressed to Jacob Burkhardt, he confessed: "Fundamentally, I am every name in history." With this, there becomes apparent an irrevocable dismemberment typical of Dionysus Zagreus: the total collapse of all boundaries, before the final plunge into the primeval abyss.

The biographer Werner Ross considers that this mythical union is the restitution, through Nietzsche's psyche, of the ancient Greek tragedy:

> *Incipit tragoedia:* this means the restitution of Greek tragedy in its own right, meaning also the resurrection of the god Dionysus, who returns in glory from the sea to redeem a mythical Ariadne. From that point of view, Nietzsche's madness is in effect something similar to the consummation, the celebration of a great festive finale. (1994, 737)

CHAPTER 12

The crossing of the Rubicon[1]

The [geniuses] are credited with a direct view into the essence of the world, as through a hole in the cloak of appearance, and as though able, without the toil or rigor of science, thanks to this miraculous seer's glance, to communicate something ultimate and decisive about man and the world. . . . At any rate, it is a dangerous sign when a man is overtaken by awe of himself . . . when the aroma of sacrifice, which by rights is offered only to a god, penetrates the genius's brain, so that he begins to waver, and to take himself for something superhuman. The eventual results are a feeling of . . . exceptional rights, the belief that he blesses merely through his company, and mad rage at the attempt to compare him to others, or, indeed, to judge him lower and reveal what is unsuccessful in his work. By ceasing to criticize himself, the pinions finally begin, one after the other, to fall out of his plumage. . . . In the case of every "genius" who believes in his divinity, the poison at last becomes apparent, to the degree that the "genius" grows old. One may recall Napoleon, for example: surely through that very belief in himself and his star, and through a scorn for men that flowed from him, his nature coalesced into the mighty unity that distinguishes him from all modern men, until finally this same belief turned into an almost mad fatalism, robbed him of his quick, penetrating eye, and became the cause of his downfall.

—F. NIETZSCHE, *Human, All Too Human* (164)

Has anyone had even an inkling of the real cause of my long sickness, which I have perhaps mastered now, in spite of everything? I have forty-three years behind me, and am just as alone as when I was a child.

—F. NIETZSCHE (Letter to Rohde, November 11, 1887)

NIETZSCHE'S INSANITY IS SURROUNDED BY mystery, around which several hypotheses have arisen: 1) There are those who believe that his mental breakdown was a result of the confluence of several factors: overwork, loneliness, and a marked dependence on chloral hydrate and a Javanese narcotic (Förster-Nietzsche).[2] 2) There is likewise the hypothesis that Nietzsche's mental illness was inherited, given the background of psychological disorders in the family (Möbious).[3] 3) Some are of the opinion that it was due to an unknown "biological factor" (Jaspers).[4] 4) Others suggest that he searched actively for madness as a means to enter the realm of the *ungrund* of being.[5] 5) The strangest testimony was that offered by his friends Overbeck and Köselitz: they considered Nietzsche's madness a farce (*Incipit parodia?*).[6] 6) There is the diagnosis of a schizophrenic disorder (Podach, Jung, Schain).[7] 7) Finally, the most widespread hypothesis about Nietzsche's mental degeneration and subsequent paralysis (paresia) holds that his disorder was the result of a syphilitic infection contracted between 1866 and 1867. However, based on the facts reviewed throughout this research, it can be maintained that even if the diagnosis of syphilis was correct, the tertiary syphilis would have only precipitated Nietzsche's mental illness, not caused it.[8]

Nearly all of the common themes that J. W. Perry (1974, 29–30) found present in the deep turmoil of the schizophrenic process were also present in Nietzsche, such as death (Dionysian dismemberment or sacrifice); return to beginnings (immersion into the waters of the abyss); cosmic conflict (the death of God, the triumph of Dionysus and the Antichrist); threat of opposites (identification with figures of the other sex: Ariadne); apotheosis (messianic feelings directed to saving, changing, or reforming society); sacred marriage (Dionysus-Ariadne); new birth (the coming of the overman); and a new society (envisioned by

Nietzsche as a result of the transvaluation of all values).[9] All are images of redemption, yet Nietzsche was not redeemed: in the end, it was a failed process of renewal.[10]

As we can conclude from the present investigation, the search for his father, the lost object, was the leitmotif of Nietzsche's life and works, and a focal point in the construction of his schizophrenic delusion. Like Zarathustra, Nietzsche carried a corpse on his shoulders throughout his life—that of his deceased father (cf. Z I:8).

From the perspective of current psychiatric classification, the schizophrenic mark was inscribed in Nietzsche's psyche even if he didn't show the psychotic breakdown until 1889.[11] There was in him a lack of the paternal function which, according to Samuels, plays a prime part in the following themes: "(1) the question of personal and social authority; (2) the evolution of ideals and values; (3) the development of sexuality and psychosexual identity; and (4) social and cultural role" (1985, 25). Hence, with the love object Nietzsche also lost, as a metaphorical equivalent, his freedom as "will to power," the capacity to adjust to the demands of the external and internal worlds, his sense of nationality, his necessary discriminatory power, the ability to live life following his own ideals and values, and his cultural meaning (nihilistic state).

In order to understand the etiology of his schizophrenic breakdown it is necessary to stress the kinship nexus between the Self, the father, and God. With the loss of the real or symbolic father, the images of the divine Father and of the Self as *imago Dei* are likewise affected, because the image of the archetypal father, of God with His paternal qualities, and that of the Self are analogically linked. According to Jung: "It is not possible to distinguish between symbols of God and symbols of the 'self' "(1975, 266); "the God-image is immediately related to, or identical with, the self" (CW 9ii:170).[12] The loss of Father as God points to the loss of Self, the transpersonal center. As a result, it would seem impossible to achieve the necessary dialectic relationship between the ego and the Self, *ergo* it is impossible to draw together heterogeneous psychic fragments or unite polarized opposites: "Only a unified personality can experience life, not that personality which is split up into partial aspects" (Jung, CW 12:105).

E. F. Edinger stated:

> When the personal father is missing . . . there is no layer of personal experience to mediate between the ego and the numinous image of the archetypal father. A kind of hole is left in the psyche through which emerge the powerful archetypal contents of the collective unconscious. Such a condition is a serious danger. It threatens inundation of the ego by dynamic forces of the unconscious, causing disorientation and loss of relation to external reality. (1992, 132)

Without the paternal function, Nietzsche's academic pursuits had allowed him to sustain a *sentiment du réel* by dispensing meaning and organizing his existence under the aegis of external reality and reason. However, upon losing his faith in God and in a surrogate father figure after Wagner's fall, Nietzsche abandoned the temple of knowledge and withdrew not only from the scholarly world but also from all relationships. Consequently, he also lost the paternal symbolic "prosthesis."

In Nietzsche's wounded soul suppurated the feeling of an uninhabited, inhospitable, and hostile world: "All the world is at odds with me" (EH II: D 2). His exacerbated sensibility and "uncanny *compulsion* to self-isolation" (Salomé 2001, 56) led him finally into a complete state of ostracism as self-defense until he became a "solitary mole":[13] "Any kind of stimulus from the outside has too vehement an effect and strikes too deep. One must avoid chance and outside stimuli as much as possible: a kind of walling oneself in belongs among the foremost instinctive precautions" (EH II:3). Living in a hermit's cell, in a complete state of solipsist's entrapment, Nietzsche followed his own prescription:[14] "As far I am concerned," he said, "what is there except myself? There is no externality." Identified with the *fictio* of his own *poesis*, he declared: "I live in my own light; I drink back into myself the flames that break out of me" (Z II:9). Having disentangled himself from society, he became trapped in an autistic world that led him to a state of complete affective isolation: "I live on my own credit" (EH P:1). By constantly feeding upon his very entrails, during this narcissistic withdrawal Nietzsche transformed himself into his own devourer: as he fed a regressive inner world, the normal energetic mechanism of regression-progression became paralyzed in a sort of "eternal return." A pathological activation of unconscious contents began: consciousness became overwhelmed by an abnormally intense intrusion of autonomous complexes that were split completely from conscious control, "swallowing" the ego and forcing it to act under the personification of mythical archetypal figures: "Night has come; now all fountains speak more loudly" (Z II:9).

Davide and Candida Fino, Nietzsche's landlords in Turin, described the strange behavior shown by their tenant in early January 1889: "The howling racket and the interminable, eccentric piano-playing kept them awake. Candida, peering through the keyhole, saw Nietzsche prancing naked round the room, enacting solitary Dionysian rites" (Chamberlain 1998, 216).[15] As Nietzsche himself suggested early in his career as a thinker, under the Dionysian intoxication the "entire symbolism of the body is called into play, not the mere symbolism of the lips, face, and speech but the whole pantomime of dancing, forcing every member into rhythmic movement" (BT 3). In this way the dithyrambic thinker became the actor in his own Bacchic dance described in *The Birth of Tragedy*: "Just as the animals now talk and the earth yields milk and honey, so there sounds from him something supernatural: he feels himself a God, he himself walks about ecstatic and uplifted, like the gods he saw walking in his dreams" (BT 1). It was a dance of complete liberation: "Now a god dances through me." Thus spoke Nietzsche. Through the ritual dance—a form of self-surrender—man and god are fused. Nietzsche as a "woman [who] wanted to be taken and accepted as a possession, [who] wanted to be absorbed into the concept of possession, possessed" (GS 363) is *entheos, plenus deo*, "full of the god." "Through his presence, Dionysus transfigures this world instead of tearing us from it" (Vernant and Vidal-Naquet 2002, 240). Already possessed by the mythic figure, Nietzsche wrote to Peter Gast: "To my maestro Pietro: Sing me a new song: the world is transfigured and all the heavens rejoice" (January 4, 1889).

Following an archetypal approach to the etiology of his mental illness, it is relevant to highlight that, according to the Orphic hymn, Dionysus Zagreus was born as a result of the union of Persephone and Zeus. Hera, infuriated by this betrayal, encouraged the Titans to dismember the child and to devour his limbs. Athena rescued the boy's heart and brought it to

Zeus, who swallowed it and gave life to the new Dionysus. As punishment, the Titans were struck by Zeus's lightning and reduced to ashes. The human race was then created from a mixture of those ashes and earth. Based on the Dionysian orphic myth, López-Pedraza concluded: "Human nature contains something of Dionysus and something of the Titans, forces that can be seen at the inner and outer level of reality: the divine Dionysus in conflict with Titanic forces" (2000, 5).

In Nietzsche's psyche, a pleromatic drama of divine contradictoriness took place: Dionysus and the matriarchal (the eternal recurrence and *amor fati*) and Prometheus and the patriarchal (the will to power and the *Übermensch*) struggled simultaneously for pre-eminence: a "primordial contradiction" between individuation and dissolution. Nietzsche acknowledged to Overbeck his unavailing efforts to master "a tension between opposing passions which I cannot cope with" (Letter dated December 25, 1882). In the end, Dionysus won the battle. Prometheus remained chained by his ideal: a world inhabited by overmen who never came to be.[16] Therefore, just as Zarathustra suffered a metamorphosis from the lawgiver who spoke in "Old and New Tablets" and proclaimed the coming of the overman to the advocate of suffering and the teacher of the eternal recurrence, so his will suffered a tragic reversal. In the final round Zarathustra linked the will with necessity, the Goddess Ananke (cf. Z III:12–30).[17] Consequently, the philosopher T. K. Seung concludes: "Prior to subsection 30, [Zarathustra] treated the will as an instrument of creation under his command. Now he treats it as his master. It is the master of necessity, before whom he feels powerless and helpless" (2005, 159).

Nonetheless, sanity has nothing to do with the mythical contents present in personal psychology. The way in which the ego relates to those contents and the way they are integrated into consciousness determines their beneficent or destructive (pathological) effects. In the latter case the ego shows a wrong relation to the affect-images in allowing itself to identify with them, or to be overwhelmed by the contents of the collective unconscious.

Nietzsche's fate appears to have been determined by an inadequate relationship with and integration of the unconscious contents: he was incapable of establishing a dialectical relationship between the ego and the collective unconscious to create a synthesis between both ambits (a transcendental function) in order to acquire a consciousness of whole-ness. The early damage done to the ego-Self axis was a result of the deci-sive stresses in his early childhood. Following Fordham's model, his psy-chosis can be assumed to be a disorder of the Self due to a permanent defect in the unifying principle and a consequent disorder of the deintegrative-reintegrative processes.[18] This led to a pathological splitting between the archetypal self-objects: "I regard myself as the victim of a disturbance in *nature*" (Letter to Gast, February 2, 1883).

Only by reinstating Dionysus and thus integrating the unconscious into consciousness is it possible for anyone to achieve wholeness.[19] However, in Nietzsche's case the inverse situation occurred in view of the damage previously mentioned: the ego was "swallowed up" by the Dionysian ambit of the collective unconscious and the psychosis appeared (phylogenic regression in schizophrenia).[20] "Luna is really the mother of the sun," suggests Jung, "which means, psychologically, that the unconscious is pregnant with consciousness and gives birth to it" (CW 14:219). But Nietzsche claimed: "When the moon rose yesterday I fancied that she wanted to give birth to a sun: so broad and pregnant she lay on the horizon. But she lied to me with her pregnancy" (Z II:15).

Thus spoke Zarathustra:

> O men, in the stone there sleeps an image, the image of my images. Alas, that it must sleep in the hardest, the ugliest stone! Now my hammer rages cruelly against its prison. Pieces of rock rain from the stone: what is that to me? I want to perfect it; for a shadow came to me. . . . The beauty of the overman came to me as a shadow. O my brother, what are the gods to me now? (Z II:2)

Unable to free the *Übermensch*, the divine spirit (Self) trapped in the "ugliest stone,"[21] Nietzsche became possessed by a superhuman power and took on the prerogatives of a deity. "The most fatal kind of megalo-mania there has ever been on earth," wrote Nietzsche, "[occurred when] man began to reverse values according to his own image, as if he were the meaning, the salt, the measure, and the standard of all the rest" (WP 202). Nonetheless, identified with the forces of the unconscious, he engaged in an *imitatio dei*: "Since the old God is abolished, I am pre-

pared to rule the world" (EH: Appendix). Jung explained that states of
inflation, like the one expressed in Nietzsche's words, follow after the
breakdown of any archetype. As in Nietzsche's case the archetype broken was the God-archetype itself, we can understand that the consequences had to be very serious. In this kind of situation, the ego personality takes on the qualities of God and the individual can feel like a god
or a "superman."[22]

"But what did Dionysus mean to Nietzsche?" Jung asked himself.
"There can be no doubt that he knew, in the preliminary stages of his
fatal illness, that the dismal fate of Zagreus was reserved for him.
Dionysus is the abyss of impassioned dissolution, where all human dis-
tinctions are merged in the animal divinity of the primordial psyche—a
blissful and terrible experience" (CW 12:118). Nietzsche was defeated
by the very archetypal force that he invoked. His destiny became solely
an expiation of his hubris. He was overtaken and punished by Nemesis,[23]
"righteous indignation," for his state of inflation. He lived his life far from
the "human, all too human" terms: he had a great deal of knowledge
regarding the "eternal truths," but not about his own truth.

Nietzsche—like Oedipus, the decipherer of the Sphinx's riddle concerning the abstract man—could not decipher the most important of all
enigmas: who he really was.[24] From an early age he suffered an ontological insecurity that he tried to hide behind a thousand masks[25] until he
became "every name in history":[26] "The minds of others I know well; but
who *I* am, I cannot tell" (GS, "Joke, Cunning, and Revenge," 25).[27] Even
if Nietzsche remained for himself a mystery, "a weary riddle," a "question
mark . . . between two nothings,"[28] he never stopped searching for himself in the abyss. His destiny and thought were the result of that quest:
" 'I thirst for myself'—this has really been the constant theme of my last
ten years," were Nietzsche's anguished words written to Marie
Baumgartner on August 30, 1877.

The personal relationship with the unconscious could have acted in
Nietzsche as a ritual of redemption, as in the initiatory mysteries.
However, given the insufficient differentiation of his ego in relation to
the Self, Nietzsche could not avoid being seized by the myths. His case
is reminiscent of Jacob and the angel: he had to wrestle with the old gods
(archetypes) in order not to become "possessed" by them. Yet Nietzsche,

instead of liberating himself, fatalistically delivered himself to the "old gods." He was psychically unable to understand the mythical images emerging from the unconscious in terms of his own personal reality: "To live archetypally is to live without limitations (Inflation)" (Samuels, Shorter and Plaut 1986, 26). Therefore, Zambrano concluded, "Nietzsche was the author of his own tragedy and, at the same time, its protagonist: as if Oedipus had written his fable instead of insinuating himself into Sophocles' consciousness" (1993, 153–54).

Nietzsche wrote his *Ecce Homo*,[29] his ultimate attempt to summarize his weltanschauung, in an uninhibited tone and belligerent mood. He confessed that he had been driven to write it by an overriding need to tell the world who he was in order to avoid being taken "for someone else" (EH P:1). However, in writing this work, all otherness was erased. Thus *Ecce Homo* turned out to be a circular testimony transmitted from himself to himself: "And so I tell my life to myself" (ibid.). Symbolically, Nietzsche, or his doppelgänger (shadow),[30] began to write this work on October 15, 1888, on his forty-fourth birthday, an age that marked the definitive end of his lucid life: "The *tragic* catastrophe of my life . . . begins with *Ecce*" (Letter to Gast, December 16, 1888).[31] Even though in his final soliloquy Nietzsche boasted of his excellent mental health, we can perceive that he had already crossed the threshold of sanity, that *Ecce Homo* was written under the effects of his megalomania (self-deification). Frey-Rohn notes that in *Ecce Homo* "Nietzsche's identification with the symbol of the self reaches its climax . . . the entire piece is the expression of his self-advancement, this untimeliness and his corresponding withdrawal from contemporary events. Loathing for humanity alternates with the glorification of his own greatness" (1988, 255).

Nietzsche's self-mythologizing can be appreciated just by reading the shocking chapter headings of *Ecce Homo*: "Why I Am So Wise," "Why I Am So Clever," "Why I Write Such Good Books," and "Why I Am Destiny."[32] However, the psychiatrist Anthony Storr posed the following consideration:

> Can people be regarded as psychotic merely because they hold eccentric beliefs about the universe and their own significance

as prophets and teachers? What are the boundaries between sanity and madness? What does labelling someone psychotic really mean? Are our current psychiatric classifications adequate? These are not merely academic questions raised by a skeptical psychiatrist. I want to make a serious attempt to show that our dividing lines between sanity and mental illness have been drawn in the wrong place. The sane are madder than we think; the mad are saner. (1996, 152)

Words that echo those written by Nietzsche when, casting a retrospective glance in the "Attempt at Self-Criticism" added to the third edition (1886) of *The Birth of Tragedy*, he asked: "Is madness perhaps not necessarily the symptom of degeneration, decline, and the final stage of culture? Are there perhaps—a question for psychiatrists—neuroses of *health*?"

Following these shifts in the traditional psychiatric perspective with respect to health and madness, it is valid to declare that although Nietzsche became a legend of insanity, he not only had the courage to "descend" to the abysmal depths (conscious of the dangers to which he was exposed), driven by his exalted passion for truth, but also was capable of articulating and transmitting his *nekyia* experiences through his writings. Nietzsche didn't want to obtain the ontological and topological truth through indirect inference or metonymy: he was willing to live the immediate experience of the primary *factum,* the primal unity, even if it represented his own dissolution as subject: *Fiat veritas, pereat vita.*[33]

Nietzsche made several voyages into the realm of the essences—the Absolute—from which he brought to light an "extraneous knowledge" concerning the groundless abyss (*Abgrund*) of being. Even if the subterranean thinker suggested essence as a "fictionalization" of appearance, his archaeology sought not only to create himself through parthenogenesis, but also to excavate the strata of consciousness, in order to launch a philosophy that emerged from the very source of the *humana conditio*: "It is out of the deepest depth that the highest must come to its height" (Z III:1).[34] Although Nietzsche knew that many years were to pass before his message would become intelligible, when he described himself as "posthumous," he was ready to pay with his blood for the search for knowledge of the *natura naturans,* and for the passing on of this knowledge:

> I, too, have been in the underworld, like Odysseus,
> and shall be there often yet;
> and not only rams have I sacrificed
> to be able to speak with a few of the dead,
> but I have not spared my own blood.
> —F. NIETZSCHE, *The Journey to Hades* (AOM 408)

Nietzsche was an explorer and cartographer of uncharted psychic territories: "Send your ships into uncharted seas" (GS 124). He gave form and coherence to the *archai* of the mystery world of the "Primordial One,"[35] not through opaque concepts or systems (patriarchal mode of expression or "directed thinking") characteristic of methodical rational inquiry, but mostly through mythical and mythopoeic images from both classical and archaic Hellas (matriarchal mode of expression or "nondirected thinking") in order to elucidate his key doctrines and convey his philosophical intuitions and *ur*-experiences. Since he knew about the contingency of language, his mode of expression left far behind those cultivated by modernity: he returned to the primordial words of the ancient oracles, riddles, and prophecies—for, according to Nietzsche, the ineffable that emerges from the enigmatic abyss cannot be apprehended, captured, or petrified as concepts (rigidified metaphors) that repress/suppress affection.[36]

Had his writings been the product of a madman, they would not have elicited as much reflection in the reader as they do, nor would they have had such a canonical influence in the Western world on core topics such as philosophy, literature, ethics, aesthetics, politics, and contemporary critical movements like deconstruction and revisionism. This influence was not widely recognized, however, until almost half a century after his death. Likewise, his highly influential anticipation of many of the discoveries of depth psychology has also been emphasized only in recent years.[37] It is as if Nietzsche's delirium assumed the level of extreme suprapersonal lucidity. He was a creative man and a philosopher of the extreme ("We immoralists—we are the most extreme," WP 749) and of the unconscious (the "Real"),[38] making him dangerous both for himself and for the readers of his time.[39]

A word on the creation of these works: as Erich Neumann described a "mythic or visionary ego,"[40] a creative ego "to which the world appears as a unitary world" (1979, 166), so Nietzsche described the "mysterious primordial unity" of the matriarchal-Dionysian world (BT 1). Neumann draws a distinction between "two creative and formative artistic processes, depending on whether the main emphasis lies with the archetype of the mother or of the father" (1989, 169). In matriarchal consciousness, Neumann explains, "fantasy, inspiration and 'sudden ideas' are the dominant influence, with the result that there is a spontaneous productivity of the unconscious." He continues by suggesting that a creative person, under matriarchal influence, processes the activation of the unconscious in "the form of inner growth, pregnancy and birth, or even as a breakthrough or an inundation in which the unconscious takes over the leading role" (ibid., 170), as in Nietzsche's case. Neumann concluded that "all forms of romantic, intuitive, and visionary art and almost all lyrical poetry belong to the sphere of the matriarchal" (ibid.), and constituted Nietzsche's means of expression.[41]

Neumann added: "Normal development involves to a large extent the surrender of the creative in favor of recognition of generally accepted cultural values and the sacrifice of individuality to an adjustment to the requirements of the collective" (ibid., 212): an ideal *coniunctio oppositorum* between the matriarchal and patriarchal principles.[42] However, in Nietzsche such reconciliation was not possible and he remained under the domination of the matriarchal principle. He surrendered his life to the archetypal world of the unconscious, to the unitary reality, the source of creativity: "I am the eternally creative primordial mother" (BT 17). Possessed by a Dionysian energy, the great rhapsodist wrote *The Case of Wagner* (May–August 1888),[43] *Twilight of the Idols* (September 1888), *The Antichrist* (September 1888), *Ecce Homo* (October–November 1888), and *Nietzsche contra Wagner* (December 1888). Writing seemed to be the only means capable of appeasing the volcanic plenitude of his soul: "In the [Dionysian state] we enrich everything out of our plenitude: whatever we see, whatever we want, we see swollen, crammed, strong, supercharged with energy. . . . The whole system of emotions is aroused and intensified: so that it discharges its every means of expression at one stroke" (TI IX:9–10). His eroticism, which could not find its natural means of expression, found an orgasmic apotheosis in every stroke of his pen. Gestation and creation occurred in the "god-intoxicated" Nietzsche at that time in one single instant, in a flash of lightning.

"While [the] attitude toward the god [Dionysus] is wholly one of service, it is nevertheless the highest, namely the Dionysian, expression of nature and therefore pronounces in its rapture, as nature does, oracles and wise sayings" (BT 8). Gripped by the inspiration *mantiké*, Nietzsche gave voice to Pythian words. There was no possibility for incubation. Rest was not permitted because time was of the essence; the scissors already shone in the hands of Atropos and the entrance to the kingdom of the shadows appeared quite near.[44] Nietzsche's voracious demon, which he could not master, denied him all rest: "I never had any choice" (EH: TSZ 3).[45] The compulsion he felt to fulfill his self-imposed mission, to be considered a point of inflection in the history of humanity, to mark a new chronology with his "transvaluation [subversion] of all values"[46] was, in a way, similar to that of Melville's Ahab when he accepted the self-imposed task of killing the whale. The tragic philosopher, like the fictional character, seemed to feel alienated by the self-consuming fervor of the religious faith placed in his mission.

By the end of December 1888, Nietzsche had finished the manuscript of *Dithyrambs of Dionysus*.[47] In addition, he had written innumerable comments in several notebooks for the project on the "transvaluation of all values"[48] and an outline for the political manifesto against Bismarck and the Hohenzollern Dynasty, *Promemoria*. Furthermore, "at this period," declared Elisabeth Förster-Nietzsche, "he covered some sheets of paper with the wildest fantasies, mingling the legend of Dionysus Zagreus with the story of the Passion" (1912, II:392). Unfortunately, all these papers were destroyed (Elisabeth blamed her mother for the deed, cf. ibid.).[49] In Nietzsche there was an overlapping of the Greek and Christian tragical: "Have I been understood?" he asks at the end of *Ecce Homo*, signing the work "Dionysus versus the Crucified."

Between the latter part of October 1888 and the first week of January 1889, the dithyrambic philosopher began to send to his friends, to

Cosima Wagner, to the ruling houses of Europe, to statesmen, "to the Polish," those postcards, notes, and letters which would later be known as *Letters from Madness*. He began signing his missives from this period with mystifying pseudonyms such as "The Phoenix," "The Monster," and "Nietzsche-Caesar"; later messages were signed with the epithets "The Crucified" and "Dionysus."[50]

Using Neumann's terminology, Nietzsche's conflict can be conceived of as a struggle between the "world-ego," "related to an external and human reality," and the "mythical ego" or "visionary ego." With the augmentation of the creative force in the last months of 1888, his extreme state of solipsistic self-containedness was a consequence of being stateless, loveless, homeless, and godless. In addition, the condemnation or dense silence imposed on him by his contemporaries provoked his conscious world-ego to recede in favor of the "prehistoric world of the mythical-ego" related to the "Mother-Goddess and the prepatriarchal level of the unconscious" (collective unconscious) (Neumann 1979, 245). Nietzsche fulfilled his own prophecy when, as Zarathustra, he warned his disciples about the perils of solitude: "But the time will come when solitude will make you weary, when your pride will double up, and your courage gnash its teeth. And you will cry, 'I am alone!'" (Z I:17). The desert's anchorite felt finally in a state of *participation mystique* that in an inexorable way led him into schizophrenia.[51] Jung wrote in this respect: "Nietzsche had lost the ground under his feet because he possessed nothing more than the inner world of his thoughts—which incidentally possessed him more than he it. He was uprooted and hovered above the earth, and therefore he succumbed to exaggeration and reality" (MDR 189).

Facilis descensus Averno: noctes atque dies patet atri ianua Dite; sed revocare gradum superasque evadere ad auras, hoc opus, hic labor est (Virgil, Aeneid VI, vv. 126–29).[52] If, in the years beforehand, Nietzsche had been able to find his way back from the underworld, by 1889 the gate allowing him to exit from this dismal place was forever closed: he remained trapped in the unconscious like Theseus in Hades and lost his self in the Dionysian depths. He finally succumbed to the "great danger of the matriarchal principle."[53] The bold incendiary of all the established truths and beliefs was immolated by his own creative fire, regressing from a matriarchal state of consciousness (where the ego has its center and greater area in primary identity with the Self) to the primordial and undifferentiated uroboric state (a state of primary ego-Self identity), remaining caught in the "quivering chaos" described by Neumann (1989, 171).

The flaming moments of creation engulfed him and he became a living pyre:

> Unsatiated like the flame
> I glow and consume myself . . .
> Flame I am assuredly
> —F. NIETZSCHE, fragment of the poem "Ecce Homo"

In Nietzsche's last works of 1888, we can observe the accentuated use of a style that became increasingly hyperbolic and apocalyptic: an immoderate rhetoric, characteristic of prophets, saviors, and redeemers. These last works are marked by a Cassandra-like consciousness and an incomparable dramatic element. In a supreme exaltation of strength, he let out the frenetic call of one who had never been heard, one who with desperate capers and bombastic language made a last attempt to defy the indifference that encircled him.[54] Nonetheless, the world, about which he wanted to know nothing, didn't want to know about him either:

> In Germany, although I am in my forty-fifth year,[55] and have published about fifteen books (including a *non plus ultra*, *Zarathustra*), there has not yet been a *single* even moderately reputable review of any *one* of my books. People help themselves out now with the phrases 'eccentric,' 'pathological,' 'psychiatric.'. . . . And in all the years no solace, not a drop of humanity, not a breath of love. (Letter to von Seydlitz, February 1888)[56]

During the first days of January 1889,[57] a tearful Nietzsche embraced a horse that was being mistreated by a coachman in the Piazza Carlos Alberto in Turin. As he did so, Nietzsche himself fell and briefly lost consciousness (cf. Chamberlain 1996, 208). It was as if, in addition to offering us the image of the harsh vicissitudes the visionary thinker would encounter throughout his existence, Nietzsche had given us in *Thus*

Spoke Zarathustra a premonitory image of his fateful end: the moment in which Zarathustra got up after the aforementioned midnight intoxication. Once this cosmic/archetypal fusion took place, he no longer felt "separate and individual" but "engulfed under the exploding flood of heavenly love" (Seung 2005, 336), which he professed toward all animals. This love was reciprocated, even by a fierce lion, which meekly lay at the feet of the anchorite. By then, Nietzsche-Zarathustra had already been transported to the mythical time of the unconscious: "All this lasted for a long time, or a short time: for properly speaking, there is *no* time on earth for such things" (Z IV:20). *"The sign [was] at hand"* (Z IV:20) when the episode with the horse took place.

Identified with the animal nature in this incident of the beaten horse, Nietzsche seems to have perceived a direct image of his own wound inflicted by the cruel deafness of his contemporaries:

> There is indeed a great *emptiness* around me. Literally, there is no one who could understand my situation. The worst thing is, without a doubt, not to have heard for ten years a single word that actually *got through* to me—*and* to be understanding about this, to understand it as something necessary! I have given humanity its profoundest book. . . . How one must atone for that! It places one outside all human intercourse, it brings unbearable tension and vulnerability—*one is a wild animal which is constantly being wounded.* The wound is not hearing any answer, and having to bear, most terribly, on one's own shoulders, alone, the burden which one would like to share, to shed (why else should one write?). (Letter to Meysenbug, end of July, 1888. Emphasis added)[58]

Confronted with the cruel beating of the frightened and exhausted horse, Nietzsche seems not to have been able, as in the final scene of his *Zarathustra*, to bear his *humanity* any longer: "Coarse I call all who only have one choice: to become evil beasts or evil tamers of beasts; among such men I would not build my house." Thus spoke Zarathustra. The compassionate man finally kissed the wounded animal and begged his forgiveness for the tribulations inflicted by the other beasts, men:[59]

Yesterday I dreamt up an image of *moralité larmoyante,* as Diderot calls it. Winter landscape. An ancient drayman, with an expression of the most brutal cynicism, harsher still than the winter that surrounds him, relieves himself upon his own horse. The horse—poor berated creature—looks about, grateful, very grateful. (Letter to von Seydlitz, May 1888)

Nietzsche suffered the annihilating intrusion of the Real: his nightmare became crystallized before his eyes. Davide Fino, his landlord and a witness to the horse scene, led the confused man home.

The septuagenarian Burckhardt, scandalized by the letters he received and fearing for Nietzsche's mental health, persuaded Overbeck to travel to Turin. Overbeck arrived on the night of January 7[60] and took his delirious friend back to Basel accompanied by Dr. Bettman, who had been hired for the trip: "Overbeck reported that scurrilous gestures, leaps, and dances accompanied Nietzsche's comments and songs" (Crawford 1999, 2).[61] Nietzsche was taken to the Basel psychiatric clinic and transferred during the night of January 17 to the Jena clinic, headed by Professor Otto Binswanger, where he remained as an inmate for the next fourteen months (cf. Janz 1987, IV:41).[62]

In his *alienation mentis,* Nietzsche finally did what he had loved most (and sacrificed) all his life: he took great pleasure in improvising for hours at the piano. The Basel hospital reported in January 1889 that when one asked about his state, he responded that he felt well, but that he could only express his state in music, his *Ursprache.*[63]

On May 13, 1890, Nietzsche went to live in his mother's house in Naumburg, where he stayed until her death on April 20, 1897. He was then taken care of by the "Faithful Lama"[64] in Weimar until his death. In this way Elisabeth's most intimate desire was fulfilled: to have her brother exclusively to herself.[65] Approaching his fifty-sixth year, Nietzsche succumbed to an attack of apoplexy on August 25, 1900.

The visionary thinker predicted his own end in premonitory dreams, in his correspondence, and in his works. In a letter sent to Peter Gast, written from Sils-Maria in August 1881, he stated: "Ah, my friend . . . a premonition crosses my mind that I am really living an extremely dangerous life, for I belong to those machines that can *explode!*" Nietzsche, through the *dramatis persona* of Zarathustra, says to the dying Tightrope Walker who, like him, showed a precarious equilibrium and eventually lost his balance: "Thy soul will sooner be dead than thy body!" (Z P:6). Nietzsche's soul had vanished in Dionysian mists and he never regained lucidity. Only his body had remained for eleven years as an empty shell. "And now your body returns, after the incomparable odyssey of your spirit, to your homeland," said Peter Gast before Nietzsche's tomb, located in the humble churchyard of Röcken bei Lützen, his birthplace (cited in Janz 1987, IV:283). "He went back into the grave, and the tombstone fell on it. The organ music ceased immediately." Fritz was finally reunited with his beloved father. Like the river, Nietzsche flowed back to his own source, the sea, after following an extremely tortuous course.

> Day of my life!
> the sun sinks. . . .
> Day of my life!
> Progression toward evening! . . .
> Cheerfulness, golden one, come!
> you, the most secret,
> sweetest foretaste of death!
> —Did I run my way too swiftly? . . .
>
> Whatever was difficult
> sank into blue forgetfulness. . . .
> Smooth lie soul and sea.
> *Seventh* loneliness!
> Never did I feel
> nearer my sweet security. . . .
> Silvery, light, a fish
> my bark now swims out . . .
> —F. Nietzsche, "The Sun Sinks" (PN 291)

Appendix A

Nietzsche's Writings

> Those thinkers in whom all stars move in cyclic orbits are not
> the most profound. Whoever looks into himself as into vast
> space and carries galaxies in himself, also knows how irregular
> all galaxies are; they lead into chaos and labyrinth of existence.

—F. Nieztsche, *The Gay Science* (322)

Early Writings: 1872–1876

The Birth of Tragedy (1872)

This first published essay is a work whose main topic is art and its development—aesthetics. Nonetheless, it may be approached from an ethical viewpoint, since Nietzschean aesthetics is basically an ethical posture: his "configure yourself" is an aesthetic requirement grounded on a distinctly ethical attitude. For the thinker "the existence of the world is *justified* only as an aesthetic phenomenon." In his first work, Nietzsche has bequeathed us an ethical lesson by giving voice to his instinct as a "defender of life"—the Dionysian forces of body, emotions, passions, the unconscious, contradictions, tragedy, etc.—which he considered to be in opposition to moral values. In the mythical figures of Apollo and Dionysus, Nietzsche attempts to capture the contrast between the light of consciousness and the darkness of the unconscious, and to reconcile these antagonistic forces through the birth or rather the rebirth of tragedy. The essence of the tragic that permeates Nietzschean thought focuses on the *coincidentia oppositorum* of the two archetypes, represented by Apollo and Dionysus.

Untimely Ones (1873–76)
>   This book is made up of four essays.

"David Strauss, the Confessor and the Writer" (1873)
>   In this first essay, Nietzsche attacks German "culture." He presents David Strauss, author of *The Old and the New Faith*, as the emblematic figure of the disdained image of the philistine.

"On the Uses and Disadvantages of History for Life" (1874)
>   In the philosopher's opinion, it is salutary to incorporate the past so that it can be used by the present culture: the assimilation of the past in the present changes the current experience, helping us to understand it more consciously. The recovery of natural and human history within the mystery of the whole extends our memory toward those things which are of value to recall. Nonetheless, Nietzsche warned us that this approach should be implemented with certain precautions: we must maintain a functional balance between Mnemosyne and Lethe, so that the result is living and acting: we want to serve history "insofar as it stands in the service of life" (Section 1).
>
>   Nietzsche considered that the study of pre-Socratic Greek civilization could be of great help for modern man (and even more so, we might say, for postmodern man and his limitless condition). Having received influences from other cultures that attempted to intimately permeate their civilization, the Greeks knew how to extract and assimilate only what they considered consonant with their own existential need, thus maintaining their cultural identity.

"Schopenhauer as Educator" (1874) and "Richard Wagner in Bayreuth" (1876)
>   In the third and fourth essays, Nietzsche proposed his ideal of culture. His paradigmatic examples are the pessimistic philosopher Arthur Schopenhauer and the famed composer Richard Wagner, respectively.

Middle-Period Writings: 1878–1882

Human, All Too Human: A Book for Free Spirits (1878)
>   This work initiated a new phase in Nietzsche's thought: it represents his release from the constrictive tutelage of Wagner's ideals and from the alien-

ation experienced as a professor at the University of Basel. With this work, he left behind his previous idealisms (Schopenhauer's philosophy and Wagner's aesthetic) and embraced realism (science and naturalistic explanation). In 1879, Nietzsche supplemented this work with a second part, *Mixed Opinions and Maxims* (1879).

The Wanderer and His Shadow (1880)[1] and *Daybreak: Reflections on Moral Prejudices* (1881)

These works reflect, as Nietzsche himself confessed, the "most painful periods of my life" (EH III: HATH 4), and also represent his attempt to "return to himself": "a supreme kind of recovery" (EH III: HATH 4). Although in *The Wanderer and His Shadow* Nietzsche made an attempt to recover those psychic aspects alienated from his personality by means of a dialogue between his ego and his "shadow," in *Daybreak* he began a campaign against morality, which he continued until the end of his lucid life. The book contains the seed of the doctrine of will to power that would appear explicitly for the first time in *Thus Spoke Zarathustra*.

The Gay Science (1882)

In this book, Nietzsche offered an astute diagnosis of the incapacity shown by the sciences to offer absolute knowledge. He attacked the mechanistic view of the world and the demand for certainty prevalent in his time, proposing in their place a "joyful science" that is aware of its own bias and limitation. Also, he offered here his existential proposal under the name of "the great health," his ideal of *amor fati* and the vision of the eternal recurrence. In *The Gay Science* Nietzsche also introduced his shocking announcement "God is dead."

Later Writings: 1883–1887

Thus Spoke Zarathustra: A Book for All and None (1883–85)

This was Nietzsche's manifesto of personal self-overcoming. As was indicated previously, in this work he presented, through the voice of the timeless figure of the great Persian prophet, his pivotal doctrines: the death of God, the eternal recurrence, the will to power, and the *Übermensch*. Like the historical prophet, Nietzsche's Zarathustra is a sage with a message directed to the contemporary world in hope of overcoming its crisis of nihilism.

Beyond Good and Evil: Prelude to a Philosophy of the Future (1886)
> This book represented a new phase of Nietzsche's work, focusing on the "revaluation of all values." Here Nietzsche centered his attention on a criticism of modernity (science, politics, and art) and challenged accepted values such as "good" and "evil," the judgmental moral categories employed as the fundamental terms in the Christian worldview.

On the Genealogy of Morals: A Polemic (1887)
> In this book Nietzsche continued his analysis of the origin of moral values. The work is based on the questioning of the birth of Christianity "out of the spirit of *ressentiment*." Nietzsche used psychological and sociological genealogy to destroy the authority of other means of explanation, by forcing his readers to question the psychic and social substrata of their reasoning. Genealogy, thus understood, takes on a historical-critical meaning. It was not his intention to search for a substratum that would serve as an all-inclusive explanation. It would be a task for criticism to unceasingly clarify all attempts to ultimately fix upon that which is real.

Final Writings of 1888

The Case of Wagner: A Musician's Problem (1888)
> If in *Untimely Meditations* Wagner was elevated to the pinnacle of Nietzsche's cultural ideal, in this work Nietzsche performed a "transvaluation of all values," casting the previously idealized figure into the "lowest depths of the abyss"; Wagner was now presented as "the Cagliostro of music," embodying the decadent culture of his time. Nietzsche went so far as to accuse Wagner of being one of the main causes of the evils that the philosopher perceived in the German nation. "To do justice to this essay," Nietzsche confessed, "one has to suffer of the fate of music as an open wound."

Twilight of the Idols, or How One Philosophizes with a Hammer (1888)
> The title of the book seems to be a mockery of one of Wagner's operas: *Twilight of the Gods*. In this work, Nietzsche presented topics he had previously addressed, such as his contempt for Christianity, "Morality as Anti-Nature." He continued his attacks against Socrates, Plato, Kant, and Christianity. "This little work," he confessed in the Preface, "is a *great declaration of war*" in order to fortify his doctrine of the "revaluation of all values."

Despite the apparent lack of connection among the different essays in the book there is a common axis: the fight against nihilism as an expression of decadence (of philosophy, religion, morality, politics, and art)—a decadence that, in his view, emerges as a result of the absence of will to power. At the same time, the thinker offered his ideal, Dionysian view of the world: his ideal world.

The Antichrist, Curse on Christianity (1888)

Despite the title, this portrait of the figure of Jesus is essentially positive. Nietzsche directed his attack at Christianity and particularly against St. Paul as the main organizer of the church. The book represents the highest point of Nietzsche's deliberation against Christianity. It is also considered his most blasphemous book.

Ecce Homo: How One Becomes What One Is (1888)

This autobiographical work was written a few months before Nietzsche's final breakdown. In it the tragic philosopher attempted "to tell the story of his life to himself," as he confessed. He also revealed how and why each of his works was written. However, Nietzsche conveyed in this book a new and idealized version of himself: it does not reflect the man who retired from his professorship at age thirty-five, or the man who was deceived by his significant others (his mother, sister, Wagner, Lou Salomé, Paul Rée, colleagues, students, readers, etc.). Instead he portrays a man who is "clever," one who writes "such good books" and is a "destiny."

Ecce Homo was written in 1888 but was not published until 1908, in accordance with express orders from his sister Elisabeth, who had censored it in view of Nietzsche's virulent criticisms against her and her mother. It is important to highlight the fact that Nietzsche initiated and concluded his opus with autobiographical works.

Nietzsche contra Wagner, Out of the Files of a Psychologist (1888)

In his last book, completed only a month before his collapse, Nietzsche extracted some passages from his works published between 1878 and 1887. Though coming out against Wagner and charging that the composer had been corrupted by Christianity, he also confessed to admiring some of Wagner's compositions for their deep expression of the Dionysian consciousness—characterized by loneliness and suffering—which he admitted was impossible for him to articulate.

Appendix B

Chronology of Friedrich W. Nietzsche's Life and Works

1844 October 15: Friedrich Wilhelm Nietzsche is born in the village of Röcken in Saxony. His parents, Pastor Karl Ludwig (1813–1849) and Franziska Oehler (1826–1897), who were married in 1843, name their firstborn after King Friedrich Wilhelm IV, whose birth-date their son shares.

1846 July 10: Therese Elisabeth Alexandra is born and baptized in honor of the three princesses of Altenburg, whom Karl Ludwig tutored. Growing up, she is known by her middle name and its shorter versions, Lisbeth and Linchen. Her brother calls her "Lama."

1848 February 27: Ludwig Joseph, the third child, is born. Toward the latter part of August, Karl Ludwig becomes seriously ill with nervous seizures.

1849 July 30: Karl Ludwig dies from an illness diagnosed as "softening of the brain."

1850 January 9: following Friedrich's premonitory dream, "Little Joseph" dies just a few weeks before his second birthday. The paternal grandmother, Erdmuthe (1778–1856), decides to move the family (the widow with her two children and two single paternal aunts) to Naumburg an der Saale. Around Easter time, Friedrich begins to attend the local school. He spends the first of many summer vacations in Pobles, with his maternal grandparents.

1851 Nietzsche begins to attend the private academic institute of Professor Weber, where he studies Latin, Greek, and religion. He becomes friends with Weber's two other students, Wilhelm Pinder and Gustav Krug.

1854 First attempts at composing music and writing poetry.

1855 Summer: Auguste, Nietzsche's paternal aunt, dies.

1856	Nietzsche begins a diary and his memoirs. April: Erdmuthe dies; Franziska moves out with her two children.
1857	Nietzsche begins to suffer severe headaches, a malady that will accompany him for the rest of his life. This, together with deteriorating eyesight, keeps him from attending his last semester of classes.
1858	Nietzsche resumes his studies and becomes an outstanding student. In summer, he moves with his mother and sister to another house in Naumburg, which will be his mother's permanent residence until her death in 1897. Thanks to his excellent academic achievements, the city of Naumburg offers him a scholarship to attend school at Pforta. On October 5 Nietzsche enters the elite boarding school located in the Saale River valley, an hour's walking distance from Naumburg. He writes the poem "Verloren" ("Lost"), which portrays his feeling of alienation.
1859	Friendship with Paul Deussen. Carl von Gersdorff enters Pforta. On December 17, after another premonitory dream, David Oehler, Nietzsche's maternal grandfather, dies. Nietzsche writes the melancholic poem "Ohne Heimat" ("Without Homeland"), which manifests his feelings of desolation and uprooting.
1860	Sadness and abandonment are evident in Nietzsche's poem "Entflohn die holden Träume" ("Fled Are the Lovely Dreams"). He spends the summer vacation in Jena with Pinder at the home of his maternal uncle, Pastor Edmund Oehler. On July 25, together with Pinder and Gustav Krug, solemnly founds the literary and musical club Germania in the Schönburg tower.
1861	March 10: Nietzsche is confirmed. He composes essays on Hölderlin and Byron, declares the former his favorite poet, and is consequently criticized by his professor, the literary historian Koberstein, who advises him in vain to dedicate himself to a more wholesome, more intelligible, and more German poet.
1862	Critical (and secretive) reflections on Christianity. Marked deterioration of health (considerable increase in the number of entries in the official medical log at Pforta). Migraines intensify and Nietzsche is sent home to recuperate. April: writes essays "Fatum and History" and "Free Will and Fate." Writes "On Moods," a composition that shows the stormy conflict between the new and old views of the world. July: writes the fragment "Euphorion." Follows up with musical compositions. Reads Machiavelli and Emerson. Poems and songs continue to reflect a profound nostalgia for death and a restless isolation.

1863	The literary and musical club Germania breaks up due to economic difficulties and, in particular, because of Nietzsche's severe criticism of his friends' essays. Rift in friendship between Pinder and Krug. Nietzsche writes a historical-critical study of Gospel texts. The poem "Jetzt und ehedem" ("Now and Formerly"), shows his state of despair and alienation at having "broken with the legacy of old times . . . with whatever held me in my childish faith."
1864	Graduates on September 7 and leaves Schulpforta. Vacations with Deussen on the Rhine. In mid-October, studies theology and philology at the University of Bonn. Joins the Franconia fraternity.
1865	August 9: runs away from Bonn "like a fugitive." Two months in Naumburg due to rheumatism attacks. Mid-October: arrives in Leipzig to begin studies in classical philology under the direction of Professor Friedrich Ritschl (1806–1876). Toward the end of October and beginning of November, discovers the pivotal work of Schopenhauer, which impacts him strongly. December: founds the "Philological Association."
1866	Begins to attend the University of Leipzig. Prepares lectures for the Philological Association. Commences friendship with Erwin Rohde (1845–1898). Discovers Lange's *Geschichte des Materialismus*. Receives university prize for his work on the sources of Diogenes Laercio.
1867	Makes plans to move to Berlin for the following winter semester. In the summer, travels with Rohde through the Bohemian and Thuringian forests to Meiningen and Wartburg. Called to Naumburg to fulfill military service, precluding plans to move to Berlin. October 9: commences service in the Cavalry of the fourth Field Artillery Regiment.
1868	March: falls from his horse and is seriously hurt, breaking his breastbone and rupturing his pectoral muscles. Five months of convalescence. August: Naumburg. Mid-October: continues his studies in Leipzig. Works on his philosophical notes on Democritus, Kant, Hesiod, Homer, and Diogenes Laercio. Publication of his works in *Rheinisches Museum* and *Litterarisches Centralblatt*. Beginning of November: first meeting with Richard Wagner (1813–1883) at the Leipzig home of the Brockhaus family.
1869	February: with Professor Ritschl's recommendation, awarded the chair in classical philology at the University of Basel. April 19: settles in Basel. Renounces his Prussian citizenship and becomes a Swiss citizen. May: visits the Wagners for the first time (and without announcing himself) in their villa in Tribschen. Gives his inau-

gural lecture, "Homer and Classical Philology." Summer session: lectures on Aeschylus, *Choephorae*, and Greek poets. Awarded doctorate by the University of Leipzig based on his works published in the *Rheinisches Museum*. Comes into contact with two renowned colleagues of the "paternal" generation: Jacob Burckhardt (1818–1897) and Johann Jakob Bachofen (1815–1887). Winter semester: Latin grammar. Visits the Wagners during the Christmas holidays.

1870   January: delivers a public lecture, "The Greek Musical Drama." February: delivers another lecture, "Socrates and Tragedy." April: promotion to full professorship. Summer session: lectures on Sophocles, *Oedipus Rex*. Meets the German theologian Franz Overbeck (1837–1905), who becomes his friend and neighbor. Works on "The Dionysian Worldview," a text that serves as a prelude to his first published book. June 19: the Franco-Prussian War breaks out. Nietzsche volunteers his services to the German army and asks Councilor Vischer (*ordinarius* for classical philology, high official at the University of Basel, and president of the Institute of Education) to grant him leave from work. Enlists as a nurse; however, a week later he becomes ill with dysentery and diphtheria. Convalesces at his mother's home in Naumburg. November: returns to his teaching post and continues the winter semester, lecturing on metrics and Hesiod's *Works and Days*. Once again he is invited to spend Christmas and New Year's with the Wagners.

1871   January: applies for a chair in philosophy at Basel. March: Lugano, working on *The Birth of Tragedy*. Summer session: seminar on the study of classical philology. Winter semester: introductory seminar on the Platonic dialogues; introductory seminar on Latin epigraphy. December: *The Birth of Tragedy* in print. Spends Christmas holidays in Basel.

1872   January 2: *The Birth of Tragedy* appears in bookstores, published in Leipzig by E. W. Fritsch, who was also Wagner's publisher. As a result of the publication of this work, Professor Ritschl begins to distance himself from Nietzsche, who continues teaching philology at the university. January–March: gives five public lectures on "The Future of Our Educational Institutions." April: composes *Manfred Meditations* for the piano, dedicated to Hans von Bülow. Writes the fragment "Oedipus: Conversations of the Last Philosopher with Himself." Makes his last visit to the idyllic Tribschen; the Wagners move to Bayreuth. May: goes with Rohde to Bayreuth. Begins a friendship with Hugo von Senger, a musician from Geneva. Rohde introduces *The Birth of Tragedy* to the literary world through the publication of a review in the *Norddeutsche Allgemeine Zeitung*. The work is fiercely criticized by the German philologist Ulrich von Wilamowitz (1848–1931) in a fiery pamphlet. At the end of May, Nietzsche begins to review the text of his unpublished essay "On Truth and Lies in a Nonmoral Sense." In June, Wagner's letter refuting von Wilamowitz appears in the *Norddeutsche Allgemeine Zeitung*. In August, Nietzsche meets in Bayreuth the cosmopolitan German feminist, writer, and fervent admirer of Wagner, Malwida von Meysenbug (1816–1903). Summer session: lectures on pre-Platonic philosophy, Aeschylus, *Choephorae*. On October 15, Rohde's reply to von Wilamowitz appears; however, the damage has been done: no students register for the winter semester. Christmas in Naumburg.

1873   Continues with his classes at the University of Basel. Forced by worsening eyesight to memorize his lectures for some time. Plans for a project to be called "The Philosopher as Physician of Culture" fall through. At the beginning of April, goes to Bayreuth to discuss with the Wagners and Rohde his *Philosophy in the Tragic Age of the Greeks* and what was to be the first of the *Untimely Meditations*, a diatribe against David Friedrich Strauss, which is published on August 8. Summer session: lectures on pre-Platonic philosophy. Carl von Gersdorff and Dr. Paul Rée (1849–1901) sit in on these lectures as auditors. Mid-August: begins to write the second of his *Untimely Meditations*. Financial problems in Bayreuth. Wagner pressures him to act as promoter. Winter semester: classes canceled because of vision problems. Christmas and New Year's in Naumburg.

1874   Continues with his lectures on philology. In February, the second of the *Untimely Meditations*, "On the Use and Disadvantage of History for Life," is published by E. W. Fristsch. Begins to work on the manuscript of what will be the third of the *Untimely Meditations*. The second edition of *The Birth of Tragedy* is printed (but not distributed until 1878). March 29: meets Marie Baumgartner at the home of her son, one of his students. April: creates first draft of the musical composition "Hymnus auf die Freundschafft" ("Hymn to Friendship"), which will take him two years to complete. Resumes the reading of Emerson's works. Winter semester: lectures on history of Greek literature and Aristotle's *Rhetoric*. Health deteriorates (migraines, vision problems, vomiting, and gastric ailments). Accepts his sister's offer to move to Basel to take care of him. October: visits from Rohde and Gersdorff. October 15: Schmitzner publishes the third of his *Untimely Meditations*, "Schopenhauer as Educator." He again spends Christmas and New Year's in Naumburg.

1875 Continues teaching at the university. Writes a fragment on Judeo-Christian religion. Begins to sketch what he hopes will be the fourth of his *Untimely Meditations*, "We Philologists," a project he will later abandon in favor of "Richard Wagner in Bayreuth." The third of the *Untimely Meditations* is translated into French by M. Baumgartner. Moves to a larger apartment and Elisabeth takes over the reins of the new home. Winter semester: lectures on antiquities of Greek religion and history of Greek literature. Heinrich Köselitz (1854–1918), who changed his name to Peter Gast, goes to Basel to attend the lectures. December: reads the Buddhist text *Sutta Nipáta*. Health continues to deteriorate; collapses at Christmastime in Naumburg and fears having succumbed to "some cerebral illness" (cf. letter to Gersdorff, January 18, 1876).

1876 Requests that the authorities excuse him, in light of his precarious state of health, from his responsibilities at the Teachers' College. Continues with his classes at the university. March: convalesces in Montreux and Chillon. First week of April: visits the composer Hugo von Senger in Geneva. Finds himself in an exalted mood. April 11: proposes marriage in a letter to Matilde Trampedach (the secret mistress of Hugo von Senger), whom he had met five days before. His proposal is turned down. Friendship with Hugo von Senger comes to a definite end. Rohde announces his engagement. Nietzsche writes his poem on the lonely traveler. Closer contact with Köselitz. On July 19, "Richard Wagner in Bayreuth" appears as the fourth of his *Untimely Meditations*. Summer session: lectures on the pre-Platonic philosophers; Plato's life and teachings. July–August: two brief stays in Bayreuth to attend the first Wagner music festival. Leaves the city suddenly before the close of the festival, plagued by worsening health and intolerance for both the ostentation of the festival and Wagner's indifference toward him. Begins to write *Human, All Too Human*. October: the university grants him a year of sick leave. Begins his vacation with Rée and Brenner, taking a tour of Italy (Genoa, Livorno, Pisa, Naples, and Sorrento). They are the guests of Malwida von Meysenbug at Villa Rubinacci in Sorrento. April: Rée and Brenner abandon the community of free spirits. November: last encounter with the Wagners in Sorrento. Overbeck and Ida Rothpelz are married. December: "Richard Wagner in Bayreuth" is translated into French by M. Baumgartner. Reads Voltaire and other French moralists.

1877   Between January and May: Villa Rubinacci in Sorrento. March: visit to Pompeii and Capri. Rohde's wedding. May: undergoes cure in baths of Bad Ragaz in Switzerland. September: resumes teaching at the University of Basel and works on the manuscript of *Human, All Too Human* with the help of Peter Gast. Shares his living quarters with Elisabeth. Agrees to be examined by Dr. Otto Eiser, who forbids him to read and write. Wagner requests information regarding Nietzsche's health and receives a confidential report from the doctor. Wagner responds, attributing Nietzsche's illness to compulsive onanism and pederasty (Nietzsche does not hear of this exchange until 1883). Winter semester: lectures on religious antiquities of the Greeks. December: breaks off with von Gersdorff. Christmas in Basel.

1878   Continues as professor at the University of Basel. January: Wagner sends him the score of his *Parsifal*. Nietzsche's ailments take a turn for the worse. Treatment in Baden-Baden. End of April: Part One of *Human, All Too Human* goes to press. Köselitz moves to Venice. May: Nietzsche sends a copy of his new book to Wagner, dedicated in memory of Voltaire. Definite breakup with Wagner and Wagnerians. July: Elisabeth returns to Naumburg. August: Wagner attacks Nietzsche underhandedly with his article "Publicum und Popularität," which appears in the *Bayreuther Blätter*. December: Nietzsche moves to a small furnished apartment. Close relationship with Overbeck and his wife. Winter semester: lectures on Greek lyric poets; introductory lessons on Plato. Christmas and New Year's in Basel, working on "Assorted of Opinions and Maxims."

1879   January–March: continues teaching at the university, in very poor health. March: "A Miscellany of Opinions and Maxims" appears as an appendix in *Human, All Too Human*. March: stops teaching completely. May: requests retirement pension. Closes up his last apartment in Basel with the help of Elisabeth, who comes from Naumburg for this purpose. Toward the end of June, leaves for St. Moritz, where he stays until mid-September. Writes *The Wanderer and His Shadow*, included in Part Two of *Human, All Too Human*. His resignation from Basel University is accepted. September: returns to Naumburg. Struggles against debilitating physical symptoms and depressions. Reads Twain, Poe, Lermontov, Gogol, Janssen. Christmas and New Year's in Naumburg; once again he is seriously ill during the holiday season. He adds up 118 days of terrible migraine attacks during this year.

1880   January: Naumburg, visited by Rée. February: in Riva on Lago di Garda, with Peter Gast. March–June: Venice. June: Marienbad, Bohemia. Reads Mérimée and Sainte-Beuve. September: returns to Naumburg for five weeks. October: goes for a checkup with Dr. Eiser in Frankfurt and visits Overbeck in Basel. Travels to Stresa on Lago Maggiore. November: Genoa. Works on the manuscript of his work *Daybreak*.

1881   Remains in Genoa until March. March: sends manuscript of *Daybreak* to Schmeitzner. Constant migraines. End of April–May: with Gast in Recoaro. End of June: *Daybreak* is published. July: travels via St. Moritz to Sils-Maria; remains for three months. Discovers the philosophy of Spinoza. Beginning of August: revelation of his most profound thought, the eternal recurrence of the same, at Surlej in Silvaplana. August: the name Zarathustra appears for the first time in his notes. Estrangement from friends causes him unbearable physical and emotional pain: "five times I have called for Doctor Death." October: returns to Genoa. November: hears Bizet's opera *Carmen* for the first time.

1882   January: works on *The Gay Science*. February–March: visited in Genoa by Rée, who brings him a typewriter. March: Nietzsche and Rée take a tour to Monaco. March: goes to Messina (Sicily) by boat. Writes "Idylls of Messina" and Book Four of *The Gay Science*, "Sanctus Januarius." April: travels to Rome to meet with Rée and Malwida von Meysenbug. Meets Lou Salomé in Saint Peter's Basilica. May: excursion with Lou to the Monte Sacro in Orta. May: visits the Overbecks in Basel. Meets with Lou in Lucerne. Visits Tribschen. During those days, the famous photograph of Lou, Rée, and Nietzsche is taken. Proposes marriage to Lou, who declines. July–August: spends the summer in Tautenburg Forest, accompanied by Lou and Elisabeth during part of this time. August 20: publication of *The Gay Science*; Nietzsche is back in Naumburg. Escapes to Leipzig after a serious argument with his mother, who was informed by Elisabeth of the affair with Lou. September: with Rée and Lou in Leipzig. Breaks off with Rée and Lou. Meets Heinrich von Stein. November: travels to Genoa via Basel. November: arrives in Santa Margherita in Rapallo. December: breaks off correspondence with his mother. Becomes seriously depressed. Consumes large doses of opium.

1883   January: Composes the first part of *Zarathustra* in Rapallo. February 13: Wagner dies in Venice. Nietzsche returns to Genoa, where he remains until the first week of May. March: profound depression. Writes to Malwida von Meysenbug: "I am . . . the Antichrist." End of April: Part One of *Thus Spoke Zarathustra* is published. May 4–June 16: meets with Malwida von Meysenbug in Rome and reconciles himself with Elisabeth. June: lives in Sils-Maria. Works on Part Two of *Zarathustra*. Breaks off once again with Elisabeth due to their frequent arguments regarding the Lou affair. August: in a letter to Overbeck, confesses his hatred toward his sister and adds that his desire for revenge "is bringing me step by step closer to *madness*." September: Naumburg. Elisabeth becomes engaged to Bernhard Förster. October: visits the Overbecks in Basel. Continues on to Genoa. Works on Part Three of *Thus Spoke Zarathustra*. November: travels to Nice, where he remains until the following spring. Continues working on Part Three of *Zarathustra*.

1884   January: in Nice, composes Part Three of *Thus Spoke Zarathustra*, published on April 10. February 22: writes to Rohde, "Friend Nietzsche, you are completely alone now!" End of April: in Venice, as the guest of Peter Gast. Mid-June: visits Overbeck in Basel. July: Zurich, meeting with the Swiss feminist aristocrat Meta von Salis. Mid-July to end of September: in Sils-Maria, where he is visited by Heinrich von Stein. "One good day in every ten," he reports to Peter Gast (September 2, 1884). October: new reconciliation with Elisabeth in Zurich. November: Part Four of *Zarathustra*. December: returns to Nice.

1885   January: in Nice. Finishes Part Four of *Zarathustra*. Reads St. Augustine's *Confessions*. Considers spending the summer in a Roman monastery. April: in Venice with Gast. Mid-April: publication of the last part of *Zarathustra*, private printing (forty copies) financed by Nietzsche. May 22: wedding of Elisabeth and Bernhard Förster (Nietzsche does not attend). Beginning of June: Sils-Maria. Writes *Beyond Good and Evil*. Prepares a second edition with a new preface for *Human, All Too Human*. Mid-September: brief stay in Naumburg. Beginning of October: Leipzig. Beginning of November: Munich and Florence. Mid-November: Nice. December: writes to his mother asking her to order a new gravestone for his father's tomb, financed with the money obtained from the suit filed against Schmeitzner (who is on the brink of bankruptcy) to recover his copyrights. Spends Christmas Day walking to Cap St. Jean.

1886   January: in Nice, working on *Beyond Good and Evil* and the preface of the new edition of *Human, All Too Human*. February: Elisabeth leaves with her husband for La Plata, Paraguay, to establish a German colony ("New Germania"). April: a week alone in Venice. May: in Munich, tries to organize a performance of Gast's comic opera *The Lion of Venice*. Mid-May: Naumburg and Leipzig, where he visits Rohde, then a professor at the University of Leipzig (last meeting). End of June: Sils-Maria. Works on a project, the tentative title of which is *The Will to Power: Attempt at a Transvaluation of All Values*. August: publication of *Beyond Good and Evil*, privately printed by C. G. Naumann. Beginning of August: the publisher Ernest Fritsch buys the copyright of Nietzsche's early works. End of September: Genoa, Ruta Ligure, Santa Margherita, and Rapallo. October: Nice. Works on a new preface to the second edition of *Daybreak*; extends the "Idylls from Messina" to the "Songs of the Outlaw Prince," so as to include them in the extended second edition of *The Gay Science*. Works on other prefaces for new editions of his books.

1887   Mid-January: attends a concert in Monte Carlo, where he hears the orchestral arrangement of *Parsifal* for the first time and feels overtaken by sublime sentiments. End of February: earthquake in Nice (on the threshold of madness, he assumes that the publication of his *Twilight of the Idols* will provoke a similar earthquake in Turin [cf. Letter to Meta von Salis, November 14, 1888]). May: Lou Salomé announces her engagement to Friedrich Carl Andreas. Beginning of April: starts out for Sils-Maria, via Cannobio, Zurich, Ammden, Chur, Lenzerheide. Mid-June to mid-September: Sils-Maria. Argument with Erwin Rohde by correspondence. July 17: sends manuscript of *On the Genealogy of Morals* to Naumann. Heinrich von Stein dies. Works on the final version of the "Hymn to Life," with lyrics by Lou Salomé and orchestration by Gast (the score is printed on October 20 by Fritzsch)—the only musical composition published by Nietzsche. Beginning of September: visited in Sils-Maria by Paul Deussen and his wife. End of September: Venice. Last visit to Gast. End of October: Nice. November 10: a private printing of *On the Genealogy of Morals*. November 26: receives a letter from the Danish writer and academic Georg Brandes (1842–1927), announcing his intention of giving a course on his philosophy. Resumes correspondence with Gersdorff. Unsuccessful efforts to arrange for a performance of his "Hymn to Life."

1888   January–February: Nice. Marked estrangement from his sister and mother. Letters in which he emphasizes his deplorable condition and proximity to death. Oppressive loneliness: "I am alone now . . . in . . . my relentless underground struggle against everything that human beings till now have revered and loved" (Letter to Seydlitz, February 12). Brandes is lecturing on his philosophy to three hundred students at the University of Copenhagen. Acknowledges Wagner and Baudelaire as "kindred spirits." Works on *The Antichrist.* March: discontent with Bismarck's Germany and the anti-Semitism of Adolf Stoecker. April: Arrives in Turin. Rents a room on Via Carlo Alberto 6 on the corner of Piazza Carlo Alberto and across from Palazzo Carignano. Attends a performance of *Carmen* and is moved to the point of tears. Hears of Brandes's lectures. Works on *The Case of Wagner.* Gast is hired as private musical tutor in Berlin. May: reads the French translation of the *Laws of Manu,* "which supplements [his] views on religion in the most remarkable way." June: travels to Sils-Maria via Milan. Remains for six weeks. Complains of the climate and its effects on his health. July: sends the manuscript of *The Case of Wagner* to Naumann, who, finding it illegible, rejects it. Sends rewritten manuscript toward the end of August. September: sends the manuscript of *The Twilight of the Idols* to the printer. Mid-September: publication of *The Case of Wagner.* End of September: returns to Turin. Completes the manuscript of *The Antichrist* (published in 1895). Sudden return of physical and mental health: highly euphoric. October: begins to write *Ecce Homo* on the day of his forty-fourth birthday. Fears the confiscation of his autobiography by authorities. Unexpected breaking off of relations with Hans von Bülow and Malwida von Meysenbug over Wagner, whom Nietzsche accuses Malwida of confusing with Michelangelo. November: cancels trip to Nice and declares Turin his place of permanent residence. Receives the first copies of *Twilight of the Idols,* printed by Naumann. December 7: sends the final manuscript of *Ecce Homo* to Naumann. December 10–11: sends the manuscript of *Nietzsche contra Wagner,* made up of excerpts from previous works. Mid-December: sends the manuscript of *Dithyrambs of Dionysus* to his publisher. End of November–December: with Dr. Brandes as intermediary, begins corresponding with the Swedish playwright August Strindberg (1849–1912), " 'the true genius'—only rather mad." December: manifests in several letters "significant coincidences." Confesses to Gast that with *Ecce Homo* he attempts to divide "the history of mankind in two." Corrects proofs of *The Antichrist*. Begins to send "the letters from madness," messages to Umberto, King of Italy, the House of Hohenzollern, the Vatican State Secretary.

1889	January 3: breakdown in the Piazza Carlos Alberto. January 4: last postcards to Gast, Brandes, Overbeck, Burckhardt, Cosima Wagner. January 8: shocked by Nietzsche's incoherent letters, Overbeck arrives in Turin. January 9–10: Overbeck and Miescher travel with Nietzsche to Basel and take him to a psychiatric hospital. January 13: Nietzsche's mother arrives in Basel. January 17: transferred to Jena Psychiatric Clinic. Placed under the care of Otto Binswanger. End of January: publication of *The Twilight of the Idols*. Spring: a private edition of *Nietzsche contra Wagner* appears.
1890	End of March: released into his mother's custody. Mid-May: brief stay in Jena and then on to Naumburg; Elisabeth returns from Paraguay in the autumn.
1892	Peter Gast begins to prepare an edition of Nietzsche's complete works, printed by Naumann in Leipzig. Mother reports worsening of her son's mental condition.
1894	After severe disputes with her mother, whom she threatened with lawsuits, Elisabeth gradually takes over the publication rights of Nietzsche's works. She founds the first Nietzsche Archive in her mother's home. In the autumn she moves the archive to another house.
1895	*The Antichrist* and *Nietzsche contra Wagner* are published. Elisabeth arranges to acquire all the rights to Nietzsche's works, excluding her mother. Manifestations of paralysis in the patient.
1896	Elisabeth moves to Weimar with the Nietzsche Archive.
1897	Franziska dies. Elisabeth takes her brother, together with the archives, to Weimar, to the "Silberblick" villa.
1900	August 25: after two strokes and a bout of pneumonia, Nietzsche dies. His remains are buried on August 28 at 4:00 P.M. in Röcken, next to the tombs of his father, his mother, and "Little Joseph."
1901–13	Important edition of Nietzsche's complete works in Leipzig.
1905	Death of Nietzsche's faithful friend, Franz Overbeck.
1908	*Ecce Homo* is published for the first time in a limited edition. The Nietzsche Archive becomes a foundation.
1920–29	Musarion Edition of Nietzsche's Complete Works (Munich).

1934	On October 15, in Weimar, and in Hitler's presence, solemn commemoration of the ninetieth anniversary of Nietzsche's birth.
1935	Elisabeth dies.
1937	A new building is constructed for the Nietzsche Archive.
1945	The Red Army occupies Weimar and takes over the management of the Nietzsche Archive.
1947	The Nietzsche Archive is included in commemoration and research activities of classical literature in Weimar.
1954	Nietzsche's letters, manuscripts, documents, diaries, books, etc. are opened for research purposes in Weimar. Serious discussions encouraged by Karl Schlechta regarding falsifications introduced by Elisabeth in all prior editions of his works and, in particular, in his correspondence.
1956	Publication by Karl Schlechta of Nietzsche's works in three volumes.
1964	Publication of what appears to be the last and definitive edition of Nietzsche's Complete Works, directed by the Italians Giorgio Colli and Mazzino Montinari.

NOTES

INTRODUCTION

1. Jung highlighted the relation between madness and creativity when he wrote: "The visionary material [from the creative person] exhibits peculiarities which are observed in the fantasy of the insane. Conversely, psychotic products often contain a wealth of meaning such as is ordinarily found only in the works of a genius" (CW 15:144).

2. Nietzsche himself was aware of the effect of the "Terrible Mother," the destructive aspect of the unconscious, when he wrote: "Loneliness surrounds him, curls round him, ever more threatening, strangling, heart-constricting, that fearful goddess and *mater saeva cupidinum* [wild mother of the passions]" (HATH P:3).

3. Scholars have established numerous guidelines for a psychobiography. Among them it is worth noting those offered by Freud in his analysis of Leonardo da Vinci (recalling that, with this research, the father of psychoanalysis founded the psychobiographical discipline); by Erik Erikson in his works *Young Man Luther: A Study in Psychoanalysis and History* (1958) and *Gandhi's Truth and Insight and Responsibility* (1969); by Alan C. Elms in his work *Uncovering Lives: The Uneasy Alliance of Biography and Psychology* (1994); by Irving E. Alexander in *Personology: Method and Content in Personality Assessment and Psychobiography* (1990); by William McKinley Runyan in *Life Histories and Psychobiography: Explorations in Theory and Method* (1984); Lloyd Demause's *Foundations of Psychohistory* (1982); and *Readings in the Method of Psychology, Psychoanalysis and History* (1987). The philosopher Walter Kaufmann, in his work *Discovering the Mind*, Vol. III (1990), claims Nietzsche's right to be recognized as the father of psychohistory, since he was a pioneer in this field. Although Nietzsche had not written a monograph on a personality from the past, Kaufmann cites Nietzsche's psychological analysis of the position assumed by St. Paul, the first Christian, to demonstrate that the philosopher had applied depth psychology when analyzing various historical figures (D 68). Nietzsche also presented a psychological analysis of the life of Jesus in his work *The Anti-christ*, and likewise analyzed the events surrounding the emergence of Christianity from a psychohistorical point of view.

4. The philosopher Lawrence J. Hatab wrote: "Nietzsche's posture subverts the traditional notion of an absolute, uniform, stable truth. There is no freestanding truth or purely objective, disinterested knowledge; there are only perspectives of different and conflicting instances of will to power" (2005, 144).

5. One of the most didactic examples I find in this respect is that offered by William McKinley Runyan in his essay "Why Did Van Gogh Cut Off His Ear?" The author states that thirteen different psychological explanations, with "supporting evidence for each," have been offered as to the cause of this self-mutilation by the artist. Once they have all been presented, Runyan goes on to explain the reasons why some hypotheses are more valid than others, based on a "critical testing of the claims and implications of [the] various explanations" (1984, 129).

6. "Imago" is a term introduced by Jung and inspired by the title of a 1906 novel by Carl Spittler.

> When "imago" is used instead of "image," this is to underline the fact that images are generated subjectively, particularly those of other people. That is, the object is perceived according to the internal state and dynamics of the subject. There is the additional specific point that many images (e.g., of parents) do not arise out of actual personal experiences of parents of a particular character, but are based on unconscious fantasies or derived from the activities of the archetype. (Samuels, Shorter and Plaut, 1986, 73–74)

7. In the case of Nietzsche it is particularly important to limit my work primarily to Greek mythology since, with the exception of Zarathustra, he unconsciously identified most of his own psychic manifestations and used as a representation of the ideas he wanted to convey through his writings the images of Dionysus, Ariadne, Apollo, Prometheus, Silenus, Satyrs, Baubo, and Oedipus.

CHAPTER 1

1. Since his date of birth, October 15, coincided with that of their sovereign, King Friedrich Wilhelm IV, his father named his firstborn son after the King.

2. Nietzsche wrote in a letter, dated October 1887 and addressed to Hermann Levi, a famous orchestra director: ". . . there has never been a philosopher who has been in his essence a musician to such an extent as I am."

3. According to Jung, "the real god of the Protestant communities is respectability. . . . That means observance of the laws, a lower point of view which has nothing to do with Christian love. It is Christian fear" (SNZ II:922). Therefore, he concluded that behind every true Protestant there is "a good old Jew" (a "Jewish complex"). And, according to Jung, "the Jewish standpoint was morality, obedience, the observance of the law; and the wrathful God was revengeful" (ibid., 917).

4. "The general picture Nietzsche gives us of his father is of a perfect being, not really of this earth and destined to move rapidly away from it. . . . There is nowhere in his youthful writings (which date from age twelve on) anything which presents his father as other than wonderful and perfect" (Strong 1985, 322).

5. The child "lives in a prepersonal world, i.e., a world essentially conditioned by the archetypes, a world whose unity is not yet, as in a developed consciousness, split into an outward physical reality and an inward psychic reality. Consequently, everything that happens to his still undeveloped personality has a numinous, mythical character" (Neumann 1974, 7). Neumann adds: "Precisely because the child, with the undeveloped consciousness, still lives in the mythical world of the primordial images . . . [he or she] has a 'mythological apperception' of the world [and] the profoundest strata [that] can be expressed" (ibid., 24).

6. In this regard Jung wrote: "The whole dream-work is essentially subjective, and a dream is a theatre in which the dreamer is himself the scene, the player, the prompter, the producer, the author, the public, and the critic. This simple truth forms the basis for a conception of the dream's meaning which I have called *interpretation on the subjective level*" (CW 8:509).

7. Jung considered that prospective dreams "are merely an anticipatory combination of probabilities" (CW 8:493). He recommended that the dream "should be taken as a *preliminary* map or a plan *roughed out* in advance rather than as a prophecy" (Samuels, Shorter, Plaut, 1986, 49).

8. "This does not mean that all unconscious contents appear symbolically as feminine. The unconscious contains masculine as well as feminine forces, tendencies, complexes, instincts, and archetypes. . . . But in general consciousness sees the unconscious symbolized as feminine and itself as masculine" (Neumann 1991, 148).

9. Father-Uranus, who, like Jehovah, represents that which is most primitive.

10. The Titans were twelve in number, six daughters and six sons, and were imprisoned in Tartarus, an abyss located in the bowels of the earth.

11. The spirit confined by matter-body is an archetypal theme. It is present in multiple religious writings as well as philosophical works. Plato is the best-known representative of this position.

12. An anecdote narrated by his sister will serve as an example of his docile character:

> One day, just as school was over, there was a heavy downpour of rain, and we looked out along the Priestergasse for our Fritz. All the boys were running like mad to their homes—at last little Fritz also appeared, walking slowly along, with his cap covering his slate and his little handkerchief spread over the whole. Mamma waved and called out to him when he was some way off: "Run, child, run!" The sheets of rain prevented us from catching his reply. When our mother remonstrated with him for coming home soaked to the skin, he replied seriously: "But,

Mamma, in the rules of the school, boys are forbidden to jump and run about in the street, but must walk quietly and decorously to their homes." (Förster-Nietzsche 1912, I:25)

13. "The Church . . . stands between the ego and the divine mysteries [collective unconscious] in the same relation as the soul [anima] stands between the ego and the mystical communion with God [Self]" (Fordham 1958, 120).
14. At the age of twelve he had already interpreted several of Beethoven's sonatas and orchestral works, and had tried his hand at composing.

CHAPTER 2

1. "In Christian theology the God-image of Yahweh has undergone a transformation by the Incarnation . . . in the process of that incarnation he takes on a one-sided goodness. He becomes exclusively the loving, benevolent God who has no darkness in him" (Edinger 1992, 12). This understanding of the transformation of the God-image is not peculiar to Jung and his followers; notwithstanding, it does not necessarily find support among orthodox Christian theologians.
2. It was Nietzsche "who anticipated so many psychoanalytic discoveries, [who] spoke of *das typische Erlebnis* (the typical experience). He wanted to say that an experience in life, which repeats itself with striking similarity, is not accidental but is complementary to our character, and unconsciously sought by us. As is well known, Freud rediscovered the same phenomenon and named it 'repetition compulsion.' Particularly in cases in which we maneuver ourselves repeatedly into painful experiences" (Stern 1985, 96).
3. Hillman explains that when the *senex-puer* complex is "cut off from its own child and fool . . . the feminine may be kept imprisoned in a secret, or may be Dame Melancholy, a moody consort" (1994, 21).
4. Between the ages of fourteen and twenty, Nietzsche wrote at least half a dozen different accounts of the great loss suffered through his father's death. The emotional tone transmitted by these accounts is evidence that the pain of this loss remained always fresh in Nietzsche's memory. His life, his entire philosophy, and his final breakdown revolved around the father figure.
5. For a child, death and abandonment are equivalent terms.
6. In his essay entitled "*Senex and Puer*" (1979), Hillman indicates that the *senex* is present in the psyche from the beginning, in a potential manner, ready to be incarnated according to existential circumstances and innate predispositions. Consequently, it can be incarnated at any age.
7. The Neoplatonic Florentine philosopher Marsilio Ficino (1433–1499) described the onset of the saturnine spirit as follows: "We are subjected to Saturn through leisure, solitude, and sickness, through theology, secret philosophy, superstition, magic . . . and withdrawal" (cited in Moore 1989, 174).

8. Samuels presents the *puer aeternus* (eternal youth) and *senex* (old man) as "emotional outlooks" (1989, 3): "the *puer* suggests the possibility of a new beginning, revolution, renewal, and creativity generally. The *senex* refers us to qualities such as balance, steadiness, generosity towards others, wisdom, far-sightedness" (ibid.). However, Samuels describes the consequences of the dis-association of the *puer-senex* archetype: "Each of these positions can become pathological—unmitigated *puer* is redolent of impatience, overspiritualization, lack of realism, naïve idealism, tendencies ever to start anew, being untouched by age and given to flights of imagination. Pure *senex* is excessively cautious and conservative, authoritarian, obsessional, overgrounded, melancholic, and lacking imagination" (ibid.). Eventually, Nietzsche's spirit of melancholy will be personified, in his adulthood, by the "spirit of gravity" while the *puer* will represent the necessary courage to oppose that spirit, the dwarf who wants to drag Zarathustra down toward the abyss (cf. Z III:2).

9. The feeling of homelessness would always accompany him (see "We who are homeless," GS 377).

10. Nietzsche, in his later years, declared himself to be a "master of suspicion."

11. Cf. Jung CW 7:92, 275; CW 8:159; CW 16:330.

12. Music, along with literary and poetic compositions, allowed Nietzsche to escape from the monotony and orthodoxy of the boarding school. It would seem that these private creative activities had the power to placate his inner turmoil. They can also be seen as a searching for initiation, a rite of passage, through participation in a secret society.

13. Regarding this, Elisabeth Förster-Nietzsche recounts the following: "On August 2, 1859, we were celebrating grandpapa Oehler's seventieth birthday. Children, stepchildren, and grandchildren all came together in great numbers. When, on the following morning, I left my room rather early, Fritz, who was already in the garden, came to meet me, and told me that he had awakened very early because he had had an extraordinary dream. He had seen the whole parsonage of Pobles lying in ruins, and our dear grandmother sitting alone beneath its shattered framework amid the debris. This dream had made him give vent to such heartbreaking tears and sobs that he had not been able to go to sleep again. Our mother forbade us to mention this dream. Besides, our dear grandfather was so fresh and vigorous that anyone would have given him another twenty years to live. Late in the summer, however, he caught such a violent cold that he fell seriously ill. . . . And towards the middle of the win-ter, the man we all loved so deeply departed this world and left an irreparable breach in our midst" (Förster-Nietzsche 1912, I:87–88).

14 . "The devouring Feminine is connected in various ways with the destructive Masculine . . . it can appear in male form; for example, as a mother's brother, who represents the authority and punishment complex" (Neumann 1991, 178).

15. Until 1861, at the time of his confirmation, Nietzsche appeared to be of a pious nature. His friend Deussen wrote of this period, trying to capture the feelings he and Nietzsche experienced at that time, "I still very clearly remem-

ber the holy, otherworldly feelings, which filled us during the weeks before and after confirmation. We would have been completely ready to, at once, leave this world for the purpose of being with Christ, and all our thinking, feeling and striving were filled with an otherworldly joy" (cited in Brobjer 2000, 3).

16.

Fled are the lovely dreams
Fled is the past
The present is horrible
The future gloomy and far away
I have never experienced
the joy and happiness of life.
I look back sadly
upon times that are long vanished
I do not know what I love
I have no place to rest
I do not know what I believe
or why I'm still living
For what?
I would like to die, die.
—F. Nietzsche, fragment of the poem "Fled Are the Lovely Dreams" (1860, in NP 1986, 15). Cf. also the poems "Now and Formerly" (1863, NP 22) and "Return" (AML 129).

17.

I have broken with the legacy
of old times
which the happiness of childhood
admonishingly called into memory,
I have broken with whatever held me
in my childish faith.
—F. Nietzsche, fragment of the poem "Now and Formerly," 1863

18. This piece was preserved because it was sent to his classmate Granier. Nietzsche, and subsequently his sister, destroyed almost all his literary works, byproducts from his early crises.

19. Could the image of "beast tied to the millstone" be an anticipation of the Nietzschean figure of the great wheel of the eternal recurrence of the same, his "thought of thoughts"?

20. The psychotherapist Stephen Larsen suggested that "Psychologically, if the central unitive principle of the ego has lost control, a cacophony of inner voices and subpersons emerges; we are literally self-devoured by our own plurality" (1996, 185).

CHAPTER 3

1. This seems, once again, a form of expression of the spirit encapsulated in matter. Lisandro López-Herrera, a well-known Venezuelan medical doctor, has published the results of his penetrating research on physical ailments and their correlative psychological disorder in a work titled *La alquimia del sufrimiento*. With regard to headaches and rheumatism, he states:

   > Repressed anger is the predominant feeling in headaches and rheuma-tism. The typical migraine . . . disguises itself very subtly, because the person . . . requires the assurance represented by the esteem and approval of those around him; his desire for autonomy does not totally overcome the need for maternal protection, and this makes him more refined and diplomatic in controlling his hostility. Rage is understand-able in a person with rheumatism who has already experienced loss of affection and fears insecurity and desolation. This fury also usually has its roots in a difficult childhood, where there has been abandonment or a hunger for affection . . . the rheumatic person tries to disguise at all costs what would be a degrading manifestation of tears and lamen-tations due to a lack of affection, as well as the unacceptable feeling of envy of others. Consequently, he tries to dispense totally with links of affection, to the point that he gives up all hedonistic pleasure, making asceticism and austerity his way of life. (1996, 267)

2. Salomé concluded in this respect: "Suffering is *natural* and necessary to Nietzsche's existence" (2001, 14).
3. "As a general rule, visions are born of extreme personal alienation" (Samuels, Shorter and Plaut, 1986, 159).
4. The time seems to have come when the Self appeared in the personification of Zarathustra: "Around noon . . . when the captain and his men were together again, they suddenly saw a man approach through the air, and a voice said dis-tinctly: 'It is time! It is high time!' And when the shape had come close to them— and it flew by swiftly as a shadow in the direction of the fire-spewing mountain— they realized with a great sense of shock that it was Zarathustra" (Z II:18).
5. John Weir Perry, in his work *The Far Side of Madness* (1992), describes the common emergence of this ritual drama in patients who present psychotic episodes.
6. It is necessary to point out that Nietzsche's somatic illnesses worsen on spe-cial dates, particularly at Christmas and on New Year's Eve, throughout his life: "The Christmas and New Year season—associated in his mind with the annual 'going-under' (*Untergang*) of the dying year . . . had always been a dif-ficult period for Nietzsche" (Cate 2002, 564).
7. This search represents the gestation of a concern that will be fully developed in his essay "On Truth and Lies in a Nonmoral Sense" (1873).

8.   Nietzsche's reply to his sister argues the following logic:

> Is it really so difficult simply to accept everything in which one has been brought up, which gradually becomes deeply rooted in oneself, which holds true among relatives and among many good people, which does moreover really comfort and elevate man? Is that more difficult than to take new paths, struggling against habituation, uncertain of one's independent course, amid frequent vacillations of the heart, and even of the conscience, often comfortless, but always pursuing the eternal goal of the true, the beautiful, the good? . . . I write this to you, dear Lisbeth, only in order to counter the most usual proof of believing people, who invoke the evidence of their inner experiences and deduce from it the infallibility of their faith. Every true faith is indeed infallible; it performs what the believing person hopes to find in it, but does not offer the least support for the establishing of an objective truth. Here the ways of men divide. If you want to achieve peace of mind and happiness, then have faith; if you want to be a disciple of truth, then search. (June 1865)

9.   Nonetheless, in a letter sent to his mother on May 29, 1865, he stated that the reason for his going to Leipzig was that Ritschl had been transferred to that city: "that has been the main reason for my decision."

CHAPTER 4

1.   Nietzsche continuously provided evidence of being divided between two polarities: the "elected one" and the "outcast." His life is the result of the conflictive oscillations between these existential antipodes.

2.   It is worth highlighting that archetypically, seven is the number indicating the departure from the known and entrance into the unknown: "It is a transition to a new stage of becoming" (Jacoby 1985, 205).

3.   From an early age, Nietzsche felt identified with nature, particularly with lightning and thunder: "From infancy I sought solitude. I felt best in those places where, without being disturbed, I could be myself. This generally happened in the open temple of nature, where I experienced the greatest of joys. A storm has always produced a very beautiful impression on me; the distant rumbling of thunder and the threatening brightness of lightning" (AML 48).

4.   Schopenhauer was one of the first philosophers to recognize the privileged place occupied by music among all the arts. To Nietzsche, the tragic seemed consubstantial with music, which was an experience of Dionysian immediacy. Music seemed to offer him the articulation of instinctual life and of undomesticated passions.

5.   According to Nietzsche those traits were also present in Wagner's personality.

6. Nietzsche's "revaluation of all the values" has its central point in placing the body over the spirit. The primordial inversion is the primacy of the unconscious over the conscious. The latter is always coarser and simpler and is submitted to the plurality of unconscious forces, where representations, motivations, and emotions are born. This inversion has its origin in Nietzsche's existential reality, a spirit trapped in the abysmal whereabouts of irrational nature, "imprisoned" in matter. The Name of the Father is replaced by the body of the mother. That is why Nietzsche stated that he found himself "on home ground in these obscure regions" of the unconscious.

7. The Jungian analyst Murray Stein calls Hermes the god of *significant passages* of our existence: he is the archetype present *between or in the midst of* the various phases of psychological development, particularly during transition phases. He manifests himself through synchronistic events, and that is why Stein personified "the experience of synchronicity" as Hermes (1996, 19).

8. With respect to Schopenhauer, Nietzsche wrote: "It is true that I only found a book [not Schopenhauer himself], and that was a great lack. But I made all the more effort to see beyond the book and to picture the man whose great testament I had to read, the man who promised to make his heirs only those who wished to be and were capable of being more than just his readers: mainly, his sons and pupils" (UM III).

9. Thus when von Gersdorff lost his brother Ernest, the new "convert" wrote him suggesting that he should look for support in the doctrines of the *Pater philosophus*:

> This is a time in which you can test for yourself what truth there is in Schopenhauer's doctrine. If the fourth book of his chief work makes on you now an ugly, dark, burdensome impression, if it does not have the power to raise you up and lead you through and beyond the outward violent grief, to that sad but happy mood which takes hold of us when we hear noble music, to that mood in which one sees the earthly veils pull away from oneself—then I too want to have nothing more to do with this philosophy. He alone who is himself filled with grief can decide on such things: we others in the midst of the stream of things and of life, merely longing for that negation of the will as an isle of the blessed, cannot judge whether the solace of such philosophy is enough also for times of deep mourning. (January 16, 1867)

10. It is worth noting that demonology is probably the predecessor of psychopathology. "*Demonology*—the belief in the existence of spirits, demons or devils," writes the clinical psychologist Stephen A. Diamond, "is probably the primeval prototype of the modern science of *psychopathology*: both paradigms seek to make sense of mental illness and aberrant human behavior" (1996, 64). From time immemorial, demons have acted as willing scapegoats. They are ideal personifications to bear the shadow. Consequently, they embody

those fearful aspects of our nature that are difficult to integrate into consciousness because of their terrible and despicable nature.

11. Plato referred to Socrates' demon, his "occult self," as a supernatural voice within the mind of the thinker, that made itself heard each time the philosopher was required to make a decision.

12. Some time afterwards, while improvising at the piano in a dark room in Bayreuth with his friend Rohde, Nietzsche suddenly cried out: "There's a spirit coming." Rohde, however, perceived nothing.

13. "The superego is the representative for us of every moral restriction, the advocate of the striving for perfection—it is, in short, as much as we have been able to grasp psychologically of what is described as the higher side of human life" (Freud 1973, XXII:66–67). Nonetheless, J. W. Perry voices a warning not to confuse guilt with the Freudian superego. In this regard, he writes: "While Jungians might borrow this term from time to time for colloquial purposes, it does not properly fit into the Jungian schema of the psyche, which has no great triad of ego, superego, and id. We see in this guilt not one complex but many" (1976, 53).

14. The resentment will be extrapolated by Nietzsche's personality in his philosophical writings. Resentment and guilt are the pivotal axes around which he will build his work *On the Genealogy of Morals*.

15. Perhaps that is why, in his deranged state, he gave free rein to his contained aggressiveness. In the reports of the psychiatrist from Jena, where he was taken after the mental breakdown he suffered in Turin in 1889, there are descriptions of Nietzsche's numerous displays of rage. For this reason he was isolated and put under surveillance on several occasions (see Crawford 1995, 179).

16. Author of *The Greek Novel* (1876) and *Psyche: The Cult of Souls and Belief in Immortality among the Ancient Greeks* (1894).

17. It should likewise be added that the shadow does not consist exclusively of negative aspects (the negative shadow). There are also positive aspects: the instincts, abilities, and moral qualities repressed for a long time or never conscious. The positive shadow constitutes a source of potentialities. The somber positive aspects are also projected, and the bearer of our projections also will be the illusory bearer of our admiration and idealization.

18. In 1869, when Nietzsche accepted the professorship in classical philology in Basel, Rohde traveled to Kiel, where he obtained his doctorate. In 1870 he was named professor at the University of Kiel, and in 1876 he was named "ordinary" professor in Jena. He then went on to Turinga, Leipzig, and finally Heidelberg, where he remained until his death in 1898. Nietzsche did not meet again with Rohde until ten years after their separation, in 1886, when he became fully aware of the distance between them (cf. Diethe 1999, 182–83).

19. We can also see this sublimated form of the Eros in Nietzsche's description of the feeling evoked by his friendship with Wilhelm Pinder during his stay at Pforta. In a note written recalling the summer spent with his friend in 1859,

he wrote: "Is there possibly a greater pleasure than going through the world like this, together? Friendship, faithfulness! The breath of this wonderful summer night, the perfume of the flowers and the sunset! Don't your thoughts rise rejoicing like the lark to the throne of clouds surrounded by gold?" (AML 135). It would seem that the initiation archetype was oriented toward the father.

20. According to Hillman, Eros and Soul are two distinct psychic instances and consequently reflect different phenomenologies, in contrast to Jung, who considers that "The anima [soul] corresponds to the maternal Eros" (CW 9, II:29).

21. Mythologically there also exists a distinction between Aphrodite Urania and the Celestial, represented by platonic and asexual love, and Aphrodite Pandemos, embodiment of profane, sexualized love. In a letter addressed to his friend Rohde, dated May 1876, Nietzsche wrote: "Eros . . . in the best period, is pederastic love; the view of Eros which you call 'somewhat high-flown,' according to which the Aphrodite aspect of Eros is not essential but only occasional and accidental."

22. Subsequently, Nietzsche attributed this friendly relationship to the "Goddess of Friendship," whom he honored in his poetic work:

> Goddess of friendship, listen favorably to the song
> we intone to friendship,
> where the gaze of friends appears
> filled with the joy of friendship.
> Kindly bring us
> the dawn in your eyes and
> faithful guarantee of eternal youth in your sacred right hand. (1875)

For his part, the philosopher Robert C. Salomon concluded: "But there is one kind of love that . . . is the truest of the true love that Nietzsche would defend. That is friendship, *philia*, which may or may not contain an erotic component . . . but in any case represents a kind of ideal of Being-with-Others for Nietzsche. If erotic love is too obsessive and Christian love too banal, friendship gets it just right. Nietzsche [had] a model of friendship. However, that is quite idealized. . . . It thus resembles the *Eros* that some of Plato's characters describe in the *Symposium*" (2003, 95). It is important to highlight that Nietzsche's father called his son "his little friend" (Förster-Nietzsche 1912, 9).

CHAPTER 5

1. However, Nietzsche would let himself be constrained for another five years until sickness rescued him.

2. It was Overbeck, seven years his senior, who went to Turin when Nietzsche suffered his psychotic outburst, in order to bring him back (cf. chapter 12).

He was also Nietzsche's unconditional friend during his period of madness, despite the fact that, by mid-1880, he no longer shared his friend's philosophical views.

3. "[Overbeck] approached the Book not as revealed wisdom, but as an historical-philosophical document. This provoked a breaking away from an essential basic premise of the Christian faith, but it was not a violent break nor a dispute, nor an existential problem as in the case of Nietzsche. It occurred thus, due simply to his intellectual disposition" (Janz 1987, II:76).

4. "An accident had already freed him from military service as an artilleryman. Once again, a small accident—a dislocation of his foot—would free him from greater ills. After a few days, his illness would free Nietzsche from the absurd war experience, for which he was in no way prepared, due to his hypersensitivity" (Janz 1987, II:114).

5. At that time, Wagner was "living in sin" with Cosima von Bülow, the illegitimate daughter of Franz Liszt. Born in 1837, the second of the three illegitimate children the famous composer had with Marie d'Agoult, Cosima was not raised by her parents but was brought up to idolize her father. She was attracted to men involved in the world of music, as if expecting to win through them the paternal love that had been denied her. It is possible that she married the conductor Hans Guido von Bülow because he was an admirer of Liszt's music as well as Wagner's. Although he was an excellent conductor, von Bülow was not a creative genius like her father. He was also an insecure and depressive man. Cosima eventually decided to direct her amorous darts toward her husband's other hero, Richard Wagner, whom she had met while visiting Zurich in 1857 on her honeymoon. She finally became his mistress in 1863.

    Cosima had found in Wagner the incarnation of her father's idealized figure. While still married to Hans von Bülow, she gave Wagner two daughters. When she began to live with the composer in Tribschen in 1868, she became his right hand: she was his secretary, public relations officer, and agent. She was nearing the end of her third pregnancy when Nietzsche met her on May 17, 1869. Siegfried, her last child, was born on the first night of his second visit. This was quite an embarrassing situation for the young "pastor," given his puritanical background. He even hid this last pregnancy from his sister, who was surprised when she first visited the Wagner home and found a newborn infant. Consequently, Nietzsche was extremely pleased when Richard and Cosima were legally wed in August 1870 (see Köhler 1998, 21–31).

6. Joachim Köhler, author of *Nietzsche and Wagner*, considers the mystification by Nietzsche of his visits to Tribschen and his "intimate relationship with Wagner" a "Dionysian fantasy," totally removed from reality. "The sky above them in Tribschen . . . was generally overcast and often exploded in a storm, with Wagner hurling down his thunderbolts. Tribschen was never an idyllic place" (1998, 37).

7. "Wagner's whole life is patriarchal in nature," wrote Nietzsche.

8. The word "mana" is of Melanesian origin and is used in anthropological lan-

guage to refer to those individuals or objects from which extraordinary powers emanate. The mana personality, according to Jung, "is a dominant of the collective unconscious, the well-known archetype of the mighty man in the form of hero, chief, magician" (CW 7:377). And he adds: "Historically, the mana personality evolves into the hero and the godlike being, whose earthly form is the priest" (CW 7:389). A priest, like Nietzsche's father: a divinized paternal imago.

9. "The upper ranks were occupied by those he remembered as the 'little Bülow children,' Elsa, Isolde, Senta, and Siegfried, while in the highest rank of all stood 'the wise noble Frau von Bülow'" (Köhler 1998, 46–47).

10. Fascination hinders all reflection. Only with the fall of the ideal, and of that fascination, did Nietzsche become aware of his actual role in Wagner's life: "The 'false omnipotence' created something 'tyrannical' in Wagner. . . . The tyrant did not allow any individuality but his own or that of his intimate circle to take a leading role" (Ross 1994, 419).

11. Cosima records these plans in her intimate diary. On November 5, 1869, she wrote: "We shall have to send Siegfried away." Her husband had pointed out that their son, approaching manhood, would have to " 'meet other people, get to know adversity, have fun, and misbehave himself; otherwise he will become a dreamer, maybe an idiot. . . .' 'But where?' " she inquired of Wagner. " 'With Nietzsche . . . and we shall watch from afar, as Wotan watches the education of Siegfried. He will have a free meal twice a week with Nietzsche, and every Saturday we shall expect a report' " (1997, 43).

12. However, in Cosima's diary, Nietzsche is cited around two hundred times between 1869 and 1877.

13. Nietzsche received his copy of *Parsifal* several months before sending his final manuscript of *Human, All Too Human* (see Borchmeyer, 1992, 338–39).

14. With the repudiation of Wagner, Nietzsche also abandoned Schopenhauer's philosophy. To the Schopenhauerian "no to life" he opposed a "yes to life," and to Schopenhauer's despised "will" he opposed the "will to power."

15. Nietzsche also seemed to envy Wagner for his collective recognition as a genius and the preeminent position that he had established in the German-speaking world. Unable to draw any attention to his own works, Nietzsche wrote a letter to Peter Gast dated February 19, 1883 (a few months after Wagner's death): "I shall be in good measure his heir. . . . Last summer I felt that he had taken away from me all the people in Germany worth influencing." Five years later, in the same vein, he wrote to Malwida von Meysenbug: "The old seducer Wagner, even after his death, is taking from me the few remaining people on whom I could have some influence."

16. While Nietzsche's book was a passionate work with no footnotes and no bibliography, Rohde's work *Psyche* (also about Apollo and Dionysus) is a scholarly work: it contains references, appendices, and numerous readings.

17. In one year, Nietzsche had lost three friends—Overbeck, Rohde, and Gersdorff—to marriage or engagement, despite his determination to sustain the friendships. In the last lines of a letter sent to Gersdorff in December

1873, he stated: "We are united and we are going to continue being faithful, even though between us there be hundreds of kilometers or also women."

18. These lines contain a tinge of reproach: the "eternal loner" and wanderer stops his roving, seduced by the appearance of the bird-Rohde.

19. The relationship with Rohde—to whom Nietzsche signed some of his letters *Frater Fredericus*—was one of total symmetry. The relationship with Wagner, whom Nietzsche called his *Pater Seraphicus*, was asymmetrical, as that of a disciple with his "dearest master." Furthermore, his relationship with Wagner "only reduced him to another form of subjugation, one as disastrous to his fragile self-esteem as the drudgery of his work in Basel had been to his health" (Köhler 1998, 59).

20. Nietzsche had taken a year's vacation because of his precarious health. He spent most of this time in Sorrento without informing Rohde of his new address (cf. Janz 1978, II:375).

21. Emotionalism is characteristic of the activity of a complex, possibly of a homo-erotic complex in which the sexual element is secondary ("narcissistic" or "pre-Oedipal" homoeroticism). Jung, in his theory on complexes, established that the emotional tone of the complex points to where the pathology lies. Robert H. Hopcke, in turn, clarifies in *Jung, Jungians, and Homosexuality* that homoeroticism, from Jung's viewpoint, "is as much a psychic state of same-sex attraction as the behavioral expression of this sexual attraction with another man or woman" (1989, 25). It can thus be inferred that the attraction reflects a state of the soul in its own right and independent of genitality.

22. Depersonalization is "a condition in which an individual feels himself thoroughly changed in regard to his former state of being. This change encompasses both the ego and the external world and results in the individual not recognizing himself as a personality. His actions seem to him automatic. As an onlooker he observes his activities and deeds. The outer world appears alien and new and has lost its reality" (Paul Schilder, 1914, quoted and translated by James Hillman, 1996, 101). James Hillman, on his part, states that depersonalization "can be distinguished from depression since depersonalization is less the inhibition of vital functions and narrowing of focus than it is a loss of personal involvement with and attachment to self and world" (ibid., 105). "Depersonalization presents a striking similarity with what anthropology has called 'loss of soul' " (ibid., 107).

23. An example of this occurred on July 24, 1876. When Nietzsche arrived in Bayreuth to attend a festival, he experienced "a profound alienation from everything that surrounded me . . . as if I was dreaming! Where was I? There was nothing I recognized; I scarcely recognized Wagner" (EH: H2). In a letter written to Carl Fuchs in December 1887, he stated: "I need, above all, a new estrangement, a still more intense *depersonalization*. . . . What age am I? I do not know."

24. Nietzsche continued the letter as follows: "Frankly, you have never mentioned anything to me that might have allowed me to suppose you knew *what* it is

that lies upon me! Have I ever reproached you for this? Never, not even in my heart. . . . Has anyone had even an inkling of the real cause of my long sickness, which I have perhaps mastered now, in spite of everything? I have forty-three years behind me, and am just as alone as when I was a child."

25. Daniel Halévy, Nietzsche's biographer, states that "Peter Gast assisted him with touching kindness; he accompanied him on his walks, read to him and played his favorite pieces" (2000, 198).

26. A reversal of roles occurred: in Rohde's case, Nietzsche had surrendered himself completely to him. "You are always the one who gives," Rohde wrote to Nietzsche when he received *The Wanderer and His Shadow*, "I, the one who always receives."

27. Lesley Chamberlain suggests that "[Nietzsche's] fantasy took an odd toll on Köselitz, whose friendship with Nietzsche was his only claim to fame besides a marching song written for the First World War. He was forty-six when Nietzsche died in 1900, and although he and Nietzsche only briefly lived side by side, for thirteen years he let himself be dominated by Nietzsche's needs. Then six days after Nietzsche was buried Köselitz married" (1996, 239n).

28. "On the Land of Education," in the second part of *Zarathustra*, where Nietzsche suggests that educated men are sterile beings, shows the author's scorn toward the scholarly milieu (cf. Z II:14).

29. The hermetic doctrine is based on intimate and mysterious relationships between the visible and the invisible universe, and particularly between the universe (macrocosm) and man (microcosm) (see Edinger 1996, 230–32).

30. "Our professional calling depends on the paranoid ability to detect, suspect, and interpret, to make strange connections among events. We must 'see through' the screens of appearances into their meanings, and listen with a third ear" (Hillman 1998, 34).

31. Archetypes, according to Jung, possess a transgressive character: they are not limited to the psychic realm (cf. CW 8:964).

32. Nietzsche "relinquish[ed] his German citizenship in 1869, but because of 'continuous residence' requirements he never became a Swiss citizen either" (Mandel in Salomé 2001, ix).

33. His traveling took him to Nice (during winters), to the Swiss alpine village of Sils-Maria (during the summers), to Turin, Genoa, Recoaro, Messina, Rappallo, Florence, Venice, and Rome (see Farrell Krell and Bates, 1997).

CHAPTER 6

1. Lou, according to her biographer, H. F. Peters, "was born under the rising star of freedom" (1974, 26). The author explains: "Her birth coincided almost to the day with one of the major events in modern Russian history: the emancipations of the serfs. There was great rejoicing. . . . Everywhere freedom bells were ringing, everywhere the traditional division of society into masters and slaves was being challenged" (ibid.).

2.   Gillot, twenty-five years her senior, the married father of two daughters of approximately the same age as his disciple Lou, was so fascinated by the young lady's extraordinary intellect and beauty that he went so far as to attempt to dissolve his marriage in order to ask Lou to become his wife. An unconditional defender of her freedom, Lou rejected the mature professor's proposal (see Peters 1974, 56; Ross 1994, 631–32). The main reason for her rejection, according to Peters, was that "she was not ready for marriage. 'My persistent childlikeness, a result of the Nordic late development of my body, forced him [Gillot] to conceal from me at first that he had already made all the necessary preparations for our union.' The poignancy of her love for Gillot was that she loved as a child. He stirred but failed to rouse the woman in her" (Peters 1974, 57).

3.   Kinkel had struggled in favor of women's rights, particularly in the academic field.

4.   Lou recalls this first encounter in the following words: "On a March evening in Rome, in the year 1882, while a few friends were gathered at Malwida von Meysenbug's, the doorbell rang and Malwida's faithful servant Trina came rushing in and whispered to her agitatedly—upon which Malwida hurried to her desk, scraped some money together, and left the room. Although she was laughing when she returned, the fine black silk scarf about her head was still trembling a bit from excitement. The young Paul Rée entered with her: a friend of some years whom she loved like a son, who—having come helter-skelter from Monte Carlo—was in a rush to send the waiter the money he had borrowed from him for the journey, since he had lost everything, literally every last penny, gambling. Surprisingly enough, this funny and somewhat sensational debut scarcely disturbed me: we made friends immediately—indeed, the fact that Paul Rée stood out because of it, as if he were on a dunce's stool, sharply separated from the others, may have played a role" (Andreas-Salomé 1991, 44).

5.   "Lou was by nature self-centered. She was determined to live her life regardless of the consequences to herself or to others," suggests Peters (1974, 73).

6.   After the profound pain caused by their final separation, Nietzsche, full of resentment, had turned over the whip to Lou (a phallic element as a symbol of power and authority, and also an attribute of Hecate, personification of the fearful dark-feminine). In the chapter "On Little Old and Young Women" in his *Zarathustra*, the "little old woman" [Hecate?] says to him,

> "Zarathustra knows women little, and yet he is right about them. Is this because nothing is impossible with women? And now, as a token of gratitude, accept a little truth. . . . Wrap it up and hold your hand over its mouth: else it will cry overloudly, this little truth." Then I said: "Woman, give me your little truth." And thus spoke the little old woman: "You are going to women? Do not forget the whip!"

It was less than a year after his breakup with Lou that Nietzsche would compose the celebrated line. Resa von Schrinhofer claimed that Nietzsche confessed to her, shortly after the publication of *Thus Spoke Zarathustra*, that he was referring to Lou Salomé in this passage (cf. Gilman 1987, 151). Bertrand Russell wrote with respect to this line: " 'Forget not thy whip'—but nine women out of ten would get the whip away from him, and he knew it, so he kept away from women, and soothed his wounded vanity with unkind remarks" (1945, 767).

7. Rée himself confessed to Lou this new reality in a letter dated May 1882: "I was thinking . . . that my relationship with Nietzsche is not very frank and open since a certain young lady appeared on the horizon." Malwida von Meysenbug also intuited the fatidic consequences of their bold plan. In a letter she advised Lou: "This Trinity. No matter how much I believe in your neutrality, the experience of a long life and my knowledge of human nature tells me that it is not possible without at best cruelly hurting one heart and, at worst, destroying a friendship" (cited in Peters 1974, 108).

8. He uses a metaphor similar to that utilized to refer to Rohde.

9. The eagle is considered traditionally as a masculine, celestial, and solar symbol, also a symbol of the direct perception of intellective light. The eagle symbolized Zeus, Odin, and Christ. Nietzsche chose the eagle, "the proudest among animals," as one of the companions of the solitary sage Zarathustra. In the autobiographical notes of his youth, he wrote in his poem "Homeless" a line that evidenced his most intimate desire: to be *free as the eagle!*

10. "Sister" and "Brother" are recurrent terms in Nietzsche and Lou's correspondence.

11. It is worthwhile to note that Nietzsche was convinced Lou was condemned by poor health to an early death (cf. Peters 1974, 112; 134).

12. The free spirits are, for Nietzsche, represented by those individuals capable of freeing themselves of the most solid bonds: their duties, their tradition, their homeland, and the religion in which they were educated. Therefore they must become sacrilegious, destroyers (see HATH P:4–5).

13. With respect to their differences, Peters wrote: "Like Kriembild and Brunhild, they came from different worlds and represented diametrically opposite ideals. Bold and unconventional one—self-righteous and petty the other. They were fated to clash, even if they had met under more favorable circumstances" (1974, 113).

14. Elisabeth had read the phrase on the twilight of Zarathustra in *The Gay Science*, where, at the end of the fourth book, Zarathustra appears for the first time.

15. Letter from Nietzsche to Lou, dated November 1882: "But Lou, what letters you write! That is how spiteful little schoolgirls write. What shall I do with such pettiness? Understand this: I want you to rise in stature before me, not lower yourself even more. . . . Such a poem 'to pain' is a profound untruth coming from your lips. In these things I detest all *superficiality*. . . . How your dignity, as well as that of our friend Rée, diminishes! How you have become impoverished as regards respect, appreciation, piety, admiration—modesty—not to mention

more elevated things. What would you answer if I were to ask you: are you good? Are you incapable of betrayal? Are you not aware that a man like me, next to you, must have a keen desire for self-improvement? Do you know that he does not wish to hear your voice even if you ask me? . . . I want you to judge yourself and set your own punishment. . . . If you let free all the meanness of your nature: who can stand you? You have done damage, you have *hurt*—not only me but all those who loved me: this sword is hanging over you" (Nietzsche, Salomé and Rée 1982, 183–84).

16. "Strictly speaking there was never a 'Lou Affair.' It was a 'Nietzsche Affair' from beginning to end. How little Lou was affected by it can be seen from an entry she made in her diary at the end of 1882. Summing up the events of that fateful year, she writes only of Rée" (Peters 1974, 138).

17. Nevertheless, while Lou's book was an immediate success, Rée's was a failure (cf. Peters 1987, 166).

18. Rée, however, felt forsaken and betrayed when Lou accepted Andreas's proposal of marriage.

19. Lou was sexually inhibited until she met the poet Rilke at thirty-six: "She felt no trace of erotic attraction [to Andreas]. 'My emotional responses were totally different from those of a woman,' she recalled. . . . Chastity was an unshakeable principle of her marriage. . . . Not until years after marriage to Andreas did Lou experience her sexual dawning—mostly with men considerably younger than herself" (Köhler 2002, 207).

20. "You are 'an understander par excellence,'" Freud wrote to her.

21. "I am faithful to memories forever, I shall never be faithful to men," confessed Lou (cited in Peters 1974, 243).

22. According to Peters, "Nietzsche paved the way to her work with Freud a quarter of a century later" (1987, 147). The author explains: "Nietzsche had told her that it was not the intellect that matters but hidden and subconscious drives. In her work with Freud she learned that this was indeed the case" (ibid.).

23. Among Lou's works she bequeathed us her psychological interpretation of Nietzsche's oeuvre, under the title of *Friedrich Nietzsche in seinen Werken* (1894), and several novels, among which we can mention *Ruth* (1895) and *Ma* (1901). In the short story "Fenitschka" (1898), we can catch a glimpse, indirectly, of the effect of her encounter with Nietzsche. She wrote numerous articles and reviews and an essay on feminine sexuality, *"Die Erotik"* (1910).

24. Repression constitutes a secondary-order or more mature defense mechanism. However, in Nietzsche's case, a more primitive defense mechanism, such as denial, primitive idealization / denigration, splitting, primitive withdrawal, projection, or introjection / projective identification, seems to operate.

25. Among which we can read sentences such as the following: "I have long known that people of my mother's and sister's kind must be my enemies: there is nothing to change in this, it lies in the very nature of things." Then again similarly to Overbeck: "I do not like my mother, and hearing my sister's voice

upsets me; I have always fallen ill when together with them." In August 1883 he wrote again to Overbeck: "the whole return trip I was lost to evil black sentiments, including true hate for my sister, who for one year now has deprived me of all self-control with ill-timed silence and ill-timed talk: so that I wound up a prey to pitiless vengefulness, whereas my innermost way of thinking precisely rejects all avenging and punishing:—*this* conflict in me is driving me step by step to madness."

26. In the first edition published after Nietzsche's mental breakdown, Elisabeth eliminated this revealing fragment, so as to offer the world the image of a totally idyllic family relationship.

27. Evocative of the way Nietzsche described the appearance of Lou in his life. Nietzsche was referring to Lou when he wrote the following lines in his *Zarathustra*: "Once I craved happy moments from the birds: then you led a monster of an owl [Athena's bird] across my way, a revolting one" (Z II:11).

28. Athena never was in a woman's womb. Therefore, in *The Eumenides*, Apollo says to Athena: "There can be a father without a mother. There she stands, the living witness, daughter of Olympian Zeus, she who was never fostered in the dark of the womb."

CHAPTER 7

1. It is possible that Nietzsche was alluding to his lady friend Lou Salomé.

2. Zarathustra says to his followers: "I taught them to work on the future and to redeem with their creation all that *has been*" (Z III:12.3).

3. In *Zarathustra* we are able to find innumerable alchemic images such as chaos, the sleeping spirit in the stone, fire, sun and moon, dragon, serpent, uroborus, lead, gold, the emergence of the child, etc. Zarathustra also receives a present from his disciple: a staff topped by a serpent (chthonic power), coiled around a golden orb representing the sun (celestial power). Also in numerous letters and notes Nietzsche represents himself as an alchemist or goldmaker.

4. "The dragon in mythology always represents the thing that must be overcome or killed in order that something may be liberated; it is always guarding a stolen treasure which really belongs to man. Then the hero has to overcome the dragon in order to liberate the treasure. . . . The treasure . . . is a symbol for value and life" (Jung, SNZ I:264).

5. The first part of *Zarathustra* was finished on February 13, 1883, "exactly at the holy hour" at which Richard Wagner died in Venice. In another ten days, from June 26 to July 6, 1883, he wrote the second part. The third book was written in Nice from January 8 to January 20, 1884. With this third part Nietzsche considered his most beloved work concluded. However, a year later he wrote the fourth and last part.

6. With respect to Nietzsche's *Zarathustra* and Goethe's *Faust II*, Jung wrote:

> These works positively force themselves upon the author; his hand is as if it were seized, his pen writes things that his mind contemplates with amazement. The work brings with it its own form. . . . He can only obey the apparently alien impulse within him and follow where it leads, sensing that his work is greater than himself, and wields a power which is not his and which he cannot command. Here the artist is not identical with the process of creation; he is aware that he is subordinate to his work or stands outside it, as though he were a second person, who had fallen within the magic circle of an alien will. (CW 15:110)

Consequently, Jung concluded that "Every creative person is a duality or synthesis of paradoxical qualities. *On the one hand he is human and personal; on the other hand he is an impersonal, creative process*" (CW 15:157). When writing *Answer to Job*, Jung had an experience similar to Nietzsche's: "The experience of the book was for me a drama that was not mine to control. I felt myself utterly the *causa ministerialis* of my book. It came upon me suddenly and unexpectedly during a feverish illness. I feel its content as the unfolding of the divine consciousness in which I participate, like it or not" (LJ II:112). Like Nietzsche in respect to his *Zarathustra*, Jung regarded his *Answer to Job* as his magnum opus: "In his old age, Jung remarked that he wished he could rewrite all of his books except this one. With this book he was completely satisfied" (Edinger 1983, 60).

7. In the second section of the prologue, Zarathustra meets a saintly hermit. The hermit has isolated himself from all men because, according to him, he needs only his animals for company and God above for praise. Zarathustra was aware of not sharing the hermit's worldview. "Could it be possible?" he asked himself after leaving the saint. "This old saint in the forest has not yet heard anything of this, that *God is dead!*"

8. "Enantiodromia" is the emergence of the unconscious opposite over time: "This characteristic phenomenon practically always occurs when an extreme, one-sided tendency dominates conscious life; in time an equally powerful counterposition is built up, which inhibits the conscious performance and subsequently breaks through the conscious control" (Jung, CW 6:709).

9. When Zarathustra summons his most "abysmal thought," the eternal recurrence, and proclaims that it is nothing outside himself, his animals constellate for him a "sphere" whose "center is everywhere" (Z III:13); a metaphor that was originally used to describe the Christian God (*Liber XXIV philosophorum*). Jung, on his part, described the Self, in its condition of *imago Dei*, in the same way (CW 12:44).

10. "Like the anima," wrote Jung, Zarathustra is "an immortal daemon that pierces the chaotic darkness of brute life with the light of meaning" (CW 9 I:77). Jung also states: "Zarathustra is more for Nietzsche than a poetic figure; he is an involuntary confession, a testament. Nietzsche too had lost his way in the darkness of a life that turned its back upon God and Christianity, and that is the

way there came to him the revealer and enlightener, the speaking fountainhead of his soul. Here is the source of the hieratic language of Zarathustra, for that is the style of this archetype" (ibid.). Jung also interpreted the image of the "golden ball" (Z I:22), the "dancing star" (Z P:5), and the "wheel which rolls out of itself" (Z I:1) as symbols of the Self (cf. SNZ I: 107, 708; II: 781). Nietzsche declared that "All opposites are in Zarathustra bound together into a new unity" (EH: TSZ-6).

11. Zarathustra spoke to the sun: "For ten years you have climbed to my cave: you would have tired of your light and your journey had it not been for me and my eagle and my serpent" (Z P:1). Based on the previous lines, the contemporary scholar Douglas Thomas concludes that "the sun, literally, existed for, and because of, Zarathustra" (1999, 117).

12. Zarathustra had already appeared to Nietzsche in a dream when he was a boy.

13. Jung went through an experience similar to Nietzsche's, the experience of the animated unconscious:

> Through No. 1's eyes I saw myself as a rather disagreeable and moderately gifted young man with vaulting ambitions, and undisciplined temperament, and dubious manners, alternating between naïve enthusiasm and fits of childish disappointment, in his innermost essence a hermit and obscurantist. . . . No. 2 . . . was a *vita peracta*, born, living, dead, everything in one; a total vision of life. . . . Here were meaning and historical continuity, in strong contrast to the incoherent fortuitousness of No. 1's life, which had no real points of contact with its environment. (MDR, 86–87)

Similarly, in the case of Goethe, Jung considers that Personality No. 2 was represented by Faust.

14. Coincides with the age at which Jesus begins to preach the Gospel (Luke 3:23.).

15. The cave is the symbolic locus of the unconscious. Hillman writes: "By living in a cave—the burial place of the old religion—the desert saint performed a mimesis of death" (2000, 120). Marie-Louise von Franz similarly suggested that, like Zarathustra, "the image of the spirit of the mountain evokes Saturn, who symbolizes in alchemy the confused, not too visible position and as yet not thought out, which has to be brought up [or lowered] to consciousness. . . . The cult of the temple in the interior of the mountain is dangerous, because it is exposed to the collective unconscious" (1993, 191).

16. "God is dead; but given the way of men, there may still be caves for thousands of years in which his shadow will be shown" (GS 108). Therefore, the death of God never came to completion; his shadow (under numerous guises) continues to govern human destinies.

17. There are several parallels between Zarathustra and Moses. In Exodus (19:23), Moses says to God, "You yourself warned us to set limits around the

mountain and keep it holy." Zarathustra says: "I draw circles around me and sacred boundaries . . . on ever higher mountains" (Z III:12). When God speaks to Moses, there is "thunder and lightning, the sound of the trumpet, and the mountain smoking" (Exodus 24:3,7). Zarathustra's word comes as lightning and thunder in the "Seven Seals." Like Moses, who, when he comes down from the mountain, observes his followers adoring a golden calf and becomes angry, Zarathustra is also infuriated when he sees his people kneeling "like children," in an attitude of adoration before an ass. As the hermit prophet, following Moses' example, Zarathustra is another new lawgiver who brings new tablets to humankind.

18. With respect to Zarathustra's descent to the human world, Thomas considers the following: "It is with a sense of emergence and emergency that Zarathustra leaves the mountains to return to the world. His desire is unexplained: Zarathustra does not tire of 'his spirit and his solitude' until 'finally . . . a change came over his heart'" (1999, 116). Therefore, Thomas concludes: "We are signaled by a sense of completion, a sense that Zarathustra's desire to return to civilization is not a product of thought, desire or intention, but, rather, one of necessity" (ibid.). Zarathustra's necessity, in his view, is "to experience time," in other words, to be human. However, Zarathustra remained "caught in the trap of time" (ibid., 120) when he declared the spirit of gravity, "the spirit of time, of temporality" (ibid.), his "archenemy" and confronted him with an ultimatum: "It is you or I" (Z III:2).

19. James Hillman and other archetypalists have made a clear distinction between the spirit and the soul. Despite the occasional overlapping of both, they are to be considered completely different entities with diametrically opposed movements. Whereas the spirit always attempts to rise toward the light and the heights, the soul is more pagan. It does not look for heights but rather for vales and depths (cf. Hillman 2000, 119). Thus, while the spirit yearns for intellectual contemplation, starting out from pure abstraction and consequently divorcing itself from the body and all that is concrete, the soul, on the contrary, lodges deeply in the darkness of the body, of matter, as a vehicle of that which is transcendental. In his flight, Nietzsche once again missed the opportunity of "making soul." Jung wrote: "If Zarathustra could remain with the town he would remain with Nietzsche—and Nietzsche would remain" (SNZ I:169).

20. The philosopher T. K. Seung associates the "spirit of gravity," Zarathustra's "sworn enemy, archenemy, primordial enemy" (Z III:11.1), with human worries and anxieties: "The spirit of gravity is Dame Care (*Frau Sorge*), a familiar figure in German folklore. . . . [It is] the chthonic force of Mother Nature . . . the ultimate source of earthly concerns and anxieties" (2005, 153).

21. For a discussion on the vertical movement and its relation to the sacred see *Shamanism: Archaic Techniques of Ecstasy* by Mircea Eliade (1970).

22. "We are the Hyperboreans." With these words Nietzsche began *The Antichrist*. The "Hyperborean" is a metaphor widely used by Nietzsche: he

used it in *Human, All Too Human* (1:2), in his *Dithyrambs of Dionysus*, and in the outline for the *Will to Power*. According to the ancient Greek texts the Hyperborean was a mythical realm (similar to the "blessed isle") where the inhabitants, worshippers of the god Apollo, lived a utopian existence at the edge of the world. In the *Pythian 10*, Pindar says of the Hyperboreans that "they live, escaping the rigid rule of Nemesis," goddess of righteous indignation and divine retribution. In other words, the Hyperboreans lived "beyond good and evil."

23. "But then he recalled his friends when he had left; and, as if he had wronged them with his thoughts, he was angry with himself for his thoughts. And soon it happened that he who had laughed wept: from wrath and longing Zarathustra wept bitterly" (Z II:22).

24. "Thus, adjusting my step to that of my guide, I was able to emerge from the smoky clouds, when the sun barely touched the peaks" (Dante Alighieri, *The Divine Comedy*: Purgatory, canto XVII).

25. Nietzsche was an especially labyrinthine man, according to his own description.

26. It should be recalled that the shadow contains hidden or unconscious aspects of oneself, positive as well as negative, denied, repressed, or never recognized by the ego. The realization of the shadow is inhibited by the persona, because both psychic instances stand in a compensatory relationship. And if the persona shown by Nietzsche is complacent, servile, and tied to conventions, the appearance of a shadow of a personified Promethean nature can be expected. In Nietzsche's case, this occurs through the *Übermensch*. Jung asks himself: "Is God really dead, because Nietzsche declared that he had not been heard of for a long time? May he not have come back in the guise of the superman?" (CW 12:559).

27. The "Higher Men" and the "Ugliest Man" described by Nietzsche express, according to Jung, the self-regulatory nature of the psyche: "The 'higher' men want to drag Zarathustra down to the collective sphere of average humanity as it always has been, while the 'ugliest' man is actually the personification of the counteraction" (CW 8:162). Nonetheless, Zarathustra's moral conscience suppresses the self-regulatory function: "The roaring lion of Zarathustra's moral conviction forces all these influences . . . back again into the cave of the unconscious. Thus, the regulating influence is suppressed" (ibid.). Jung perceived in Nietzsche's Zarathustra "a good example of the suppression of the unconscious regulating influence" (CW 8:162).

28. The "Voluntary Beggar" seems to be Nietzsche's personification of the historical Jesus as he appears characterized in *The Antichrist*: a pacific man, a preacher in the mountains.

29. The first three parts of *Zarathustra*, published separately, caused absolutely no repercussions among Nietzsche's colleagues, for none of them read his masterpiece. Having estranged himself from his editor, Nietzsche was forced to finance, out of his own scant resources, the publication of forty copies of the fourth part (in which the chapter of the Voluntary Beggar appears) (cf. Cate

2002, 462). Nietzsche was right when he wrote that he considered himself to be a posthumous writer: thirty years after the initial publication of *Zarathustra*, 150,000 copies were printed by the German government and suggested as inspirational reading for young soldiers during World War I (cf. ibid., 573).

30. The Shadow is the image of the wandering free spirit who, tired from the destruction of values, has no strength to create new ones.

31. "Thus spoke the shadow, and Zarathustra's face grew long as he listened. 'You are my shadow,' he finally said sadly." This phrase is reminiscent of that expressed in Shakespeare's *The Tempest* when Prospero says: "That dark thing I recognize as my own."

32. Over the years Jung gave different interpretations to the snake of Nietzsche's *Zarathustra*. In *Symbols of Transformation*, Jung interpreted the vision as a symbol of psychic renewal (CW 5:596). In his *Visions* seminar Jung wrote: "the black snake is the earth factor in man, and we might assume that it is seeking rebirth, or perhaps it penetrates the body as a sort of phallic demon in order to impregnate it, or to transform it" (VS I:291). In his seminar on Nietzsche's *Zarathustra*, Jung suggested that the snake is "The *deus absconditus*, the god concealed in darkness. . . . This is the dark god and the god that dies. The god that Nietzsche declared to be non-existent" (SNZ II:1295). He declared that "the snake is the symbol of the savior, the *agathodaimon*, the good daimon, the redeemer that forms the bridge between heaven and hell, or between the world and god, between the conscious and the unconscious" (SNZ II: 1299–1300). See also the essay of the philosopher Nickolas Pappas titled "The Eternal Serpentine" (2004, 71).

33. However, it is worth noting that the image of the snake introducing itself phallically into the shepherd's mouth evokes the idea of fellatio. Nietzsche as Zarathustra seems to desire and fear fellatio simultaneously: the scene shows the impulse to take the snake in, symbolically being impregnated by his father, while at the same time Zarathustra defends himself against the snake by biting its head.

CHAPTER 8

1. In Nietzsche's case it is evident that the paternal function is reduced to the image of the father. Nietzsche assigned decidedly paternal roles to several people during his adolescence, youth, and early adulthood: Ritschl, Schopenhauer, Bachofen, Burckhardt, and especially Wagner.

2. Either in the form of a god, a demon, a genius, a redeemer of mankind, or the *Übermensch*.

3. Nietzsche could relate closely only with those objects he could idealize: "I do not love my neighbor near, but wish he were high up and far. How else could he become my star?" (GS, "Joke, Cunning, and Revenge," 30). According to Nietzsche's sister,

[Nietzsche] placed Wagner upon a pedestal far transcending anything human and found his highest consolation in so doing. . . . Now his idol [lay] in ruins at his feet—an idol who tyrannically wished to prohibit any intellectual tendency other than his own, now enfeebled by age and weakness. Looking back upon this painful experience, my brother [cried] out in very anguish of heart: "I shuddered as I went on my way alone; I was ill, or rather more than ill. I was weary—made so by the inevitable disappointment in all that [remained] to kindle enthusiasm in us modern men; weary at the thought of all the power, work, hope, love, youth flung to the winds; weary with disgust at the effeminacy and undisciplined rhapsody of this romanticism, at the whole tissue of idealistic lies and enervation of conscience, which here again had won a victory over bitterness and harrowing suspicion that, from now on, I was doomed to distrust more deeply, to despise more deeply, and to be more *deeply alone* than ever before. For I had never had any one but Richard Wagner." (Förster-Nietzsche 1949, 310)

4. Nietzsche believed that sounds, gestures, and images are the best way to apprehend immediate sensual reality. Music was very close to the essence of his being. He also considered that the Dionysian music was the only means capable of crossing the borders of image and language and of conveying the vitality of the life force of the primordial abyss. At the onset of his mental breakdown, when image and language reached their limits and Wagner's music became "sick," he laughed, then shouted, and finally fell silent for the rest of his life.

5. "Primitive devaluation is only the inevitable downside of the need to idealize. Since nothing in human life is perfect, archaic modes of idealization are doomed to disappointment. The more an object is idealized, the more radical the devaluation to which it will eventually be subject; the bigger one's illusions are, the harder they fall" (McWilliams, 1994, 106). In his *Zarathustra*, Nietzsche wrote: "This god whom I created was man-made and madness. . . . Man he was, and only a poor specimen of man and ego" (Z I:3).

6. Jung noted that paradoxically Wagner's *Parsifal* and Nietzsche's *Zarathustra* deal with the same problem, which was also Nietzsche's: "the idea of the cure of the incurable wound." The difference lies, according to Jung, in the fact that "Wagner remained very much in the tradition, using a legend which was well known and still much appreciated. And he only went back to the Middle Ages, while Nietzsche made a much further regression, going back into the eighth or ninth century B.C., to fetch his figure or analogy, his myth" (SNZ II:1365).

7. Yet Nietzsche at times wrote of *Parsifal* in enthusiastic, even exalted terms. In a letter written to Gast on January 21, 1887, we read: "I have recently heard for the first time the introduction to *Parsifal*. . . . Did Wagner com-

pose anything better? The finest psychological intelligence and definition must be said here, expressed, *communicated*, the briefest and most direct form for it. . . . A sublime and extraordinary feeling, experience, happening of the soul at the basis of the music, which does Wagner the highest credit." In yet another letter addressed to his sister that same year, he wrote the following with reference to *Parsifal*: "I can only think of this work with emotion, to the point that I felt elevated and moved. It is as if, after several years, someone, at last, spoke to me of the problem that concerns me." There also seems to be a tinge of envy at not having been able to achieve the mastery required to compose a work such as *Parsifal*. In a letter to Elizabeth, dated July 25, 1882, he stated: "Precisely this kind of music is what I was writing when I was a boy, at the time when I wrote my oratorio; and then I took out the old manuscript and, after all these years, played it—the *identity* of mood and *expression* was fabulous! Yes, a few parts . . . seemed to us more moving than anything we had played from *Parsifal* and yet they were very wholly Parsifalesque! I confess that it gave me a real fright to realize *how* closely I am *akin* to Wagner."

8.   Nonetheless, it should be pointed out that there are much more complex factors underlying the breakup of the relationship with Wagner. The composer's alliance with German nationalism and the beginning of the *Parsifal* stage seem to be only the "tip of the iceberg"; it is impossible to speak of a specific moment or a single and concrete reason for the breakup. The feeling of abandonment experienced by Nietzsche during the first Bayreuth festivals, where the philosopher found himself excruciatingly alone among the group of great personalities who venerated Wagner, was definitely another triggering factor. Also, in August 1878, Nietzsche was judged and criticized by an anonymous author in a Bayreuth newspaper as a result of the publication of his book "for free spirits." Nietzsche believed this to be the work of Wagner. But the wound most profoundly felt was that which Nietzsche qualified as a "mortal offense" on the maestro's part in a letter addressed to Overbeck on February 22, 1883, and which referred to the information exchanged between Wagner and Eiser, Nietzsche's physician. In that correspondence, the former attributed the philosopher's physiological disorders to the frequency of his masturbatory practices. This information also reached Cosima's ears and those of other close acquaintances of the famous couple, causing painful feelings of betrayal and humiliation in Nietzsche. "Wagner has insulted me in a *deadly* fashion," Nietzsche confessed. In a letter to Peter Gast (April 21, 1883), he seemed to explain the nature of the insult. One passage reads, "Cosima has spoken of me as one would of a spy who insinuated himself into the trust of others and who absconded once he obtained what he wanted. Wagner is rich with evil ideas. But would you believe that these ideas are part of his correspondence (even with my doctors) in order to express his *conviction* that my changed way of thinking was the consequence of unnatural deviation, pointing to pederasty?" Perhaps it

was due to this low blow that in *The Case of Wagner: A Musician's Problem,* Nietzsche attacked the maestro's music, using, either consciously or unconsciously, "physiological" objections.

9. This fragment may lead us to ask with Jung: "Which of them 'broke down before the cross'—Wagner or Nietzsche?" (CW 7:43). History has been Nietzsche's executor and witness and has given us the answer.

10. It is worth recalling that Nietzsche addressed Wagner as a personification of the celestial realm, calling him *Pater Seraphicus* and Jupiter.

11. It is interesting to note that Nietzsche describes the ascetic priest, whom he attacks brutally in *The Genealogy of Morals,* in the same words he applies to his father in *Ecce Homo.* He calls them "delicate, kind, and morbid" (EH I:1). He wrote venomous diatribes against Christianity and ended *The Antichrist* with a terrible curse on that religion (see A 62). We see too how the image of his initial dream, in which the father ends the life of the child by pulling him toward the tomb, becomes real for Nietzsche. From an early age, he had a death wish, feeling he had been seized from life. Consequently, father, God, and death came to be equivalent terms for him. This reality can be glimpsed, amongst many other examples, in the following passage: "God degenerated to the *contradiction of life,* instead of being its transfiguration and eternal Yes! In God a declaration of hostility towards life, nature, the will to life!" (A 140). And in *Beyond Good and Evil* Nietzsche states: "Christianity gave Eros poison to drink." Since the Self as the archetype of totality is, by definition, a *complexio oppositorum,* therefore, according to Jung, "the Antichrist would correspond to the shadow of the self" (CW 9 II:76), Nietzsche's destructive, dark, and threatening side.

12. Possessed by Zarathustra, the archetype of the wise man, Nietzsche derived the nonexistence of God or gods from his own desire to be God: "If there were gods, how could I endure not to be a god! *Hence* there are no gods" (Z II:2).

13. "Without freedom there is no real morality; there is only law abidingness, more or less complete obedience based upon the principle of 'thou shalt' " (Jung, SNZ I:264).

14. Nietzsche echoes this phrase through the voice of the shadow of Zarathustra: "Nothing is true, all is permitted" (Z IV:9).

15. After his break with Wagner, Nietzsche replaced his aesthetic consideration of the world with an ontological consideration in which the will to power took center stage. The will to power was considered by Nietzsche as the basic drive in all life: "Where I found a living creature, there I found the will to power" (Z II:12).

16. Jung considered that Nietzsche "cannot stand the idea of God, because God would anticipate the creative man Nietzsche to such an extent that he could not make the creative effort" (SNZ II:932).

17. Jung suggests the following: "The sea which is supposed to be unlimited is therefore . . . a symbol of the collective unconscious which has no boundary anywhere" (SNZ I:14).

18. It should be highlighted that the image of embarking on a ship into an infinite ocean (GS 124) directly precedes the madman passage announcing the "death of God."

19. Therefore, Nietzsche proposed not only the "death of God" but also the "death of man": "Man is something which should be overcome" (Z P:3).

20. Cf. *Euphorion* (1862), where Nietzsche portrayed the Euphorion character of Goethe's *Faust II*, and his poem "Between Birds of Prey." While Jung speaks of the necessity of "discovering" the Self, Nietzsche speaks of creating himself from the void that emerges from the deconstruction. Therefore he showed great admiration for Goethe, because he considered that the German man of letters "created himself" (TI: IX).

21. Nietzsche questioned himself in this regard: "What could one create if gods existed?" (Z II:2).

22. "[Zarathustra,] you [are] my last refuge," is the anguished cry of the Ugliest Man, the "Murderer of God."

23. Nietzsche never abandoned the sermonic voice, the preaching voice of his father.

24. Zarathustra refers to himself as the "connoisseur-executioner of himself," and the Pale Criminal shows a murderous lust when he confesses that "he thirsted after the bliss of the knife" (Z II:6). In a posthumous fragment written in the summer of 1878, Nietzsche referred to his "self-annihilation." He was an expert at self-mortification. In tragedy, according to Nietzsche, Dionysus was both the victim and the murderer. The shadow side of the Dionysian ecstasy is the cruel, excessive, and violent aspect evidenced in the phenomenon of self-torture.

25. Among the innumerable examples of this condition, it is worth mentioning the case of the youth (a part of Nietzsche's personality) who "cried with violent gestures" to Zarathustra: "It is the envy of you that has destroyed me" (Z I:8).

26. Jung made the distinction between "identification" and "imitation": "Identification differs from imitation in that it is an unconscious imitation, whereas imitation is a conscious copying" (CW 6:742).

27. Nietzsche raised his hammer against Pauline Christianity; however, he showed empathy toward the figure of Christ (cf. A 39). Additionally, his identification with Christ is implicit particularly in his letters from madness, some of which he signs "The Crucified One"; in others, like the one sent to Cosima Wagner in January 1889, he states: "I also hung on the cross." Like Christ, Nietzsche created an image of an all-loving father. Like Christ, Nietzsche wanted to become a Messiah, the "redeemer of the redeemed."

28. "It is possible that underneath the holy fable and disguise of Jesus's life there lies concealed one of the most painful of the martyrdoms of *knowledge about love*: the martyrdom of the most innocent and desirous heart, never sated by any human love; *demanding* love, to be loved and nothing else, with hardness, with insanity, with terrible eruptions against those who denied him love; the story of a poor fellow, unsated and insatiable in love, who had to invent hell in order to send to it those who did not *want* to love him. . . . Anyone who feels that way, who *knows* this about love—*seeks* death" (BGE 269).

29. In *The Birth of Tragedy*, Nietzsche posed the questions and appealed to Silenus's wisdom for an answer. The work begins with the question: "What makes life worth living?" and ends with "What pushes us to live the next instant?" Silenus proposes the wisdom of suffering. Each time man perceives the horrible and absurd aspect of existence, he recognizes the wisdom of Dionysus's companion and tutor, which finds its aesthetic expression in art. Consequently, in his first work, the only justification that Nietzsche offers for life is the aesthetic phenomenon, that is, the creative act.

30. An image that evokes the detachment of the ego from the transpersonal center of the psyche.

31. The ambivalent feelings toward his father would be projected in his relationship to God. Thus Nietzsche showed a constant struggle between supplicating adoration and hateful rejection of God.

32. This is the same ambivalent attitude Nietzsche showed toward his father: in *Ecce Homo*, he exalts his father's ancestral ties to the Polish nobility, while at the same time blaming him for his wicked heritage.

CHAPTER 9

1. The Christian theologian Rudolf Otto introduces in *The Idea of the Holy* (1958) the phrase *mysterium tremendum* to identify the specific emotional constellation inherent to numinous experience.

2. In *Ecce Homo* there are passages in which Nietzsche claimed that his philosophy was based on his personal encounter with the Dionysian (cf. EH: BT 2, 4).

3. Zarathustra encountered on his way the Voluntary Beggar, a personification of Nietzsche's shadow, who was forced to live with cows because he was rejected by men.

4. Many times Nietzsche referred to the "Unknown God," and upon his graduation from Pforta (September 7, 1864), he wrote a poem dedicated to the "Unknown God." In an "Attempt at Self-Criticism" of *The Birth of Tragedy*, he confessed that he was possessed by a still "Unknown God" when he wrote his first book, and in his *Zarathustra* he included a heartfelt poem dedicated to an "Unknown God" (cf. Z IV:5).

5. The idealized Father is pure disembodied spirit, and his shadow is body and emotion (attributes of Dionysus). Christian religion is the supreme rejection of instinctuality and, consequently, of the body. By rejecting, conquering, and controlling the body, the mind will rise toward the supreme Logos (Father-God). The body (and the feminine) then becomes the dominion of the devil. Christianity has repressed the chthonic, i.e., instincts and emotions (Pan and Dionysus). E. F. Edinger said in this regard: "When the ego is identified with the spirit, nature becomes demonic—Pan and Dionysus were recast as versions of the devil by Christian mentality" (1986, 97).

6. It is important to highlight that Nietzsche sacrificed the paternity of his own voice in his "firstborn," *The Birth of Tragedy*, transferring it to his god-Wagner,

to whom he dedicated the work, having written it with Wagner, for Wagner, and in support of Wagner. He appears in this first book as an initiate, the chosen adept, the apostle of a God whom he thought incarnate in Wagner. However, when casting a retrospective glance at *The Birth of Tragedy*, in an "Attempt at Self-Criticism" (section 3) added to the third edition (1886), Nietzsche admitted being the legitimate father of his "firstborn": "What finds expression here [in *The Birth of Tragedy*] in any case was a *strange* voice, the disciple of a still 'unknown God,' one who concealed himself for the time being . . . under the bad manners of the Wagnerian." Therefore, in his autobiographical work *Ecce Homo*, Nietzsche declared: "In all psychologically decisive places of 'Wagner in Bayreuth' one could substitute for 'Wagner,' without hesitation, my name or the word 'Zarathustra' " (EH IV:4).

7. Dionysus knows death before being born; he has experienced suffering, death, and rebirth before his birth. In one of the stories regarding the birth of Dionysus, it is said that Zeus, his father, loved the mortal Semele, daughter of the king of Thebes. When Hera, Zeus's wife, discovered the betrayal, she took revenge on the girl. Taking on the appearance of the princess's wet nurse, she persuaded the innocent girl to request that Zeus show himself before her in his true aspect as a god. At the unsuspecting princess's entreaty, Zeus appeared before his beloved in all his glory. The palace then caught fire, and Semele died in the flames, carrying their son Dionysus in her womb. With the aid of Hephaestus, Zeus removed Dionysus from Semele's womb and sewed him in his own thigh so that the gestation period could be completed. When the moment came, Dionysus tore open the god's thigh and emerged into life.

8. In "On Great Events" (Z II:18), Zarathustra flies to the island regarded by the people as the gate of the underworld. When he hears a ghost voice (his own shadow) crying, "It is time! It is high time!" he pays a visit to a fire-spewing monster from whom he wants to learn about the great events. The people are worried, thinking that Zarathustra has been taken by the devil. His disciples, however, laugh, knowing that instead "Zarathustra has taken the devil." When the sailors praise his heroic journey to the underworld, Zarathustra replies that they must have seen his shadow and draws a distinction between the "wanderer and his shadow." During his voyage to the *nekyia*, Zarathustra's ghost "has seen truth naked—verily, barefoot up to the throat."

9. Perhaps this is why he later detached himself from the metaphysical notion of a "Spirit in itself." With the death of God, Nietzsche felt the need to create himself and to give meaning to his own self-creation or, rather, self-procreation. Creation, in turn, emerges from Chaos, from the "realm of the Mothers" (the collective unconscious). In traditional cosmologies, the order of the world emerges from Chaos: a state before any creation. The realm of the Mothers, related to Chaos, is a world both fascinating and terrifying, and is beautifully described by Goethe, when Mephistopheles says to Faust:

I dislike letting out one of the higher secrets. There are goddesses enthroned in solitude, outside of place, outside of time. It makes me

uneasy even to talk about them. They are the Mothers. . . . When you
come to a glowing tripod you'll know you're as far down as you can go.
By the light it throws you'll see the Mothers. Some sitting, some stand-
ing or walking about. It just depends. Formation, transformation, the
eternal mind eternally communing with itself, surrounded by the forms
of all creation. (*Faust*, Part II)

In this regard, Jung points out: "The 'realm of the Mothers' has not a few connections with the womb, with the matrix, which frequently symbolizes the
creative aspect of the unconscious" (CW 5:180).

10. Nietzsche regarded the self-conscious ego as a social construct: "My idea is
    . . . that consciousness does not really belong to man's individual existence
    but rather to his social or herd nature. . . . Consequently, given the best will
    in the world to understand ourselves as individually as possible, 'to know our-
    selves,' each of us will always succeed in becoming conscious only of what is
    not individual but 'average' " (GS 354).

11. When Nietzsche was possessed by a state of inflation as his ego was over-
    whelmed by unconscious contents, he considered that the highest type of
    philosopher was a kind of fusion of animal and god (TI I:3). And in *Beyond
    Good and Evil*, he considered that the man of knowledge "may readily feel
    himself to be like the god who becomes animal" (BGE 101).

12. In his "Attempt at Self-Criticism" (section 7) in *The Birth of Tragedy*, Nietzsche
    wrote: "That Dionysian monster who bears the name of Zarathustra."

13. Jung describes the danger of the Dionysian experience as follows: "The redis-
    covered unconscious often has a really dangerous effect on the ego. In the
    same way that the ego suppressed the unconscious before, a liberated uncon-
    scious can thrust the ego aside and overwhelm it. There is a danger of the ego
    losing its head, so to speak, that it will not be able to defend itself against the
    pressure of affective factors" (CW 10:183).

14. As a reflection of this ambivalence, Nietzsche's thoughts continuously swung
    in antithetic motion between a strong misogynous tendency and the deification
    of the feminine in its condition of matrix-creatrix. Statements such as "You are
    going to women? Do not forget the whip!" (Z I:18) and "When a woman has
    scholarly inclinations, there is usually something wrong with her sexually"
    (BGE 144), among others, caused him to be known as a "misogynist," despite
    his having also declared that "misogynists actually hated themselves" (D 165).
    Yet he was also able to idealize womanhood: "The perfect woman is a higher
    type of human than the perfect man" (HATH 377). Nietzsche used the femi-
    nine as a polyvalent metaphor by means of which he represented cherished
    aspects and decisive themes of his philosophy. For Nietzsche woman was a
    symbol of wisdom, of music, of life, of nature, of happiness, yet likewise of
    error: "[Woman] does not want the truth: what is truth to a woman? From the
    beginning, nothing has been more alien, repugnant, and hostile to woman than
    truth—her great art is the lie" (BGE 232). Reading Nietzsche one always runs
    the risk of being trapped in his labyrinths; for example, truth and error are

interchangeable terms throughout his entire philosophical corpus, because in his view the history of truth is nothing but the history of an error.

15. Nietzsche yearned to escape his own genealogy. In his last work, *Nietzsche contra Wagner*, we find the following poem: "Who is father and mother to me? / is not Prince Abundance father / to me and quiet laughter mother?"

16. An atheist would not search for redemption the way Nietzsche yearns for it. Nietzsche wrote: "Yes, my friends, believe with me in the Dionysian life and the rebirth of tragedy . . . put out wreaths of ivy, put the thyrsus into your hand, and do not be surprised when tigers and panthers lie down, fawning, at your feet. Only dare to be a tragic man; for you are to be redeemed . . . believe in the miracles of your god" (BT 21). Nietzsche envisioned the redeeming and redeemed man as follows:

> He must yet come to us, the *redeeming* man of great love and con-
> tempt, the creative spirit whose compelling strength will not let him
> rest in any aloofness or any beyond, whose isolation is misunderstood
> by the people as if it were flight from reality—while it is only his
> absorption, immersion, penetration *into* reality, so that he one day
> emerges again into the light, he may bring home the redemption of this
> reality, its redemption from the curse that the hitherto reigning ideal
> has laid upon him. (GM 96)

17. In *Will to Power*, Nietzsche asked himself: "Whence comes the seductive charm of such an emasculated ideal of man? Why are we not disgusted by it as we are perhaps disgusted by the idea of a castrato?" And he immediately replied: "the voice of a castrato does not disgust us, despite the cruel mutilation that is its condition: it has grown sweeter—Just because the 'male organ' has been amputated from virtue, a feminine note has been brought to the voice of virtue that it did not have before" (WP 204).

18. Represented by the thyrsus, the phallic wand of Dionysus.

19. "The self is not only the center, but also the whole circumference which embraces both conscious and unconscious; it is the center of the totality, just as the ego is the center of consciousness" (Jung, CW 12:44). For Jung the experience of the self possesses a numinosity similar to religious revelation and therefore can be described also as the *imago Dei*.

20. In the myth of Dionysus, the Terrible Mother is represented by Hera, who instigates the Titans to attack and devour the illegitimate infant child of Zeus. Furthermore, it is Hera who induces madness in Hercules and in Dionysus himself.

21. The mother should act as a mirror of her child's selfhood. For Lacan, the "mirror stage" represents a fundamental aspect of the structure of subjectivity. The mirror stage describes the way the ego is formed as a result of identifying with one's specular image. We can evidence a distortion in the mirror stage in a passage from his *Zarathustra* where Nietzsche describes the reaction to the image reflected in the mirror held up by a child: "When I looked into the mir-

ror I cried out, and my heart was shaken: for it was not myself I saw, but the devil's grimace and scornful laughter" (Z II:1). Nietzsche failed to assume this image as his own.

22. "The man who, from lack of eternal enemies and resistance and forcibly confined to the oppressive narrowness and punctiliousness of custom, impatiently lacerated, persecuted, gnawed at, assaulted, and maltreated himself; this animal that rubbed itself raw against the bars of its cage as one tried to 'tame' it; this deprived creature, racked with homesickness for the wild, who had to turn himself into an adventure, a torture chamber, an uncertain and dangerous wilderness—this fool, this yearning and desperate prisoner became the inventor of the 'bad conscience' " (GM 16). Nietzsche related "bad conscience" to feelings of revenge, *ressentiment*, and madness. In a letter sent to Peter Gast on August 26, 1883, he wrote: "The curious danger of this summer is . . . insanity. . . . It could come to something that I have never thought possible in my case: that I should become mentally deranged . . . [beset by such] feelings of revenge and *ressentiment*."

23. Yet in Part III of *Zarathustra*, the prophet himself "realized that interpreting the present from a perspective that gives primacy to the past is both psychologically devastating and unnecessary" (Higgins 1987, 152). Still, Nietzsche wished to redeem his past (cf. Z II:20). Finding this impossible, he wanted to cut himself off from the past. In a letter to Paul Deussen (January 3, 1888), he wrote: "Basically, as concerns me, all is now epochmaking; my entire past crumbles away from me and when I add up what I have done in the last two years it appears to me now as always one and the same piece of work: to isolate myself from my past, to cut the umbilical cord between me and it."

24. "In the latter part of *Zarathustra* . . . Nietzsche describes how he was digging down into himself, working into his own shaft; there you can see how intensely he experienced the going into himself, till suddenly it produced the explosion of the most original form of spirit, the Dionysian" (Jung, SNZ I:369).

25. "I call *Russian fatalism* that fatalism without revolt" (EH I:6).

26. In *Beyond Good and Evil* (225), Nietzsche declared: "The discipline of suffering, of great suffering—do you not know that only *this* discipline has created all enhancements of man so far? That tension of the soul in unhappiness which cultivates its strength, its shudders face to face with great ruin, its inventiveness and courage in enduring, persevering, interpreting and exploiting suffering and whatever has been granted to it of profundity, secret, mask, spirit, cunning, greatness—was it not granted to it through suffering, through the discipline of great suffering?"

27. Nietzsche suggested that even if Christ and Dionysus share the condition of martyrdom, there exists a significant difference between their sufferings: "The god on the cross is a curse on life, a signpost to seek redemption from life[, while] Dionysus cut to pieces is a *promise* of life" (WP 1052). Therefore he distinguished between the tragic man (follower of Dionysus) who "affirms even the harshest suffering [because] he is sufficiently strong, rich, and capa-

ble of deifying to do so[, while] the Christian denies even the happiest lot on earth: he is sufficiently weak, poor, disinherited to suffer from life in whatever form he meets it" (ibid.).

28. Cf. GS 109; WP 1067, 1050, 433 (the Dionysian world); Z (the overman as the "meaning of the earth").

29. Cfr. images of the sea in A 314, 423, 575; CJ 279, 283, 343, 371, 374, 382; Z P1, "Before Sunrise," "The Honey Sacrifice," "The Sign," "The Seven Seals": 1, 5, 7.

30. In 1860, Nietzsche showed through his lyrical escapes his longing for a world that anticipated his doctrine of "eternal recurrence." In his juvenilia poem "Fled Are the Lovely Dreams" he wrote: "The eternal wheels of the universe / Roll in a circular path / The rusty spring of the earth's globe / Winds itself up again and again. . . . In the pit of my stomach / I would overcome infinity / And would then prove with a thousand reasons / That word and time are finite."

31. Dionysus's eternal cycle of death and rebirth makes him the conveyer of the mythical-religious idea of circularity. Apollo and Dionysus represent the contrast between historical time and mythical time.

32. The belief in future punishment or reward for past actions depends on a linear conception of time: the past recurs infinitely so the future is already contained in the past. When the Tightrope Walker is afraid that the devil will drag him to hell, Zarathustra tells him that there is no hell.

33. These are the words Zarathustra speaks after proclaiming the doctrine of the eternal recurrence. And in Nietzsche's final autobiographical work we can perceive that the past recurred to him over and over again: "Everything hurts . . . memory becomes a festering wound" (EH II:6). It is worth highlighting that Freud in *Beyond the Pleasure Principle* uses the phrase "eternal recurrence of the same" to convey an example of repetition compulsion.

34. The philosopher Farrell Krell wrote in this respect: "Nietzsche, within the space of a few months, weeks, days, or perhaps even moments, both promulgate[s the] eternal recurrence 'of the same' and decr[ies] every appeal to 'the same' as the most flagrant error" (1996, 158). Krell observed that in Nietzsche's notes relating to his pivotal doctrine there are "twenty-five notes [that] affirm eternal recurrence of the same, while twenty-nine excoriate any and every notion of the same" (ibid.). Therefore, he concludes that as a permanent trait of his agonistic nature Nietzsche once more "oscillate[s] between two positions" (ibid., 159).

35. The dream also alerted Nietzsche to the danger inherent to the *katabasis* toward which he was voluntarily moving as he became more and more fascinated by, and attracted to, the unknown.

36. "OEDIPUS. Conversation of the last philosopher with himself. A fragment of the history of posterity: I call myself the last philosopher. Because I am the last man. No one speaks with me but myself, and my voice comes to me like the voice of a dying man! Let me associate for but one hour more with you, dear voice, with you, the last trace of memory of all human happiness. With you I escape loneliness through self-delusion. . . . I cannot bear the shudder of the loneliest loneliness, and so it forces me to speak as if I were two. . . .

And yet, I still hear you, dear voice! Something else dies, something other than me, the last man in this universe. The last sigh, your sigh, dies with me. The drawn-out 'Alas! Alas!' sighed for me, Oedipus, the last miserable man" (Nietzsche, *Notebooks of the Early 1870s*).

37. In Nietzsche-Zarathustra's words: "Still is the bottom of my sea; who would guess that it harbors sportive monsters? Imperturbable is my depth, but it sparkles with swimming riddles" (Z II:13).

38. It is worth noting that Polyhymnos, guide and pathfinder, made Dionysus promise complete female surrender in order to show him the path to the Underworld.

39. Nietzsche rejected knowledge that generates codes. Also, it is obvious to Nietzsche that the traditional gnoseological structures are incapable of providing an entry to the abysmal dimension of hazardous human existence, to the "Primordial One" (equivalent to the Schopenhauerian will and the Kantian thing-in-itself). These structures, he concludes in *The Birth of Tragedy*, have rather proven to be illusory and luminous masks of the Apollonian dimension, whose purpose is to hide the horrors of existence, in which the only reason for the subsistence of human life is as an aesthetical phenomenon. Such was his conclusion in the "Attempt at Self-Criticism" in *The Birth of Tragedy*.

40. He wanted to "live *experimentally* and to offer himself to adventure" (HATH P:4).

41. "Hades and Dionysus are the same," said Heraclitus (frag. 15). For the Greeks of antiquity, the world of the deep unconscious was the chthonic realm. Due to his connection with death, Dionysus also has a strong connection with depression.

42. It should be pointed out here that the Sphinx of the Oedipus myth was the result of a punishment imposed by Hera on Thebes for the kidnapping of young Chrysippus by Laius (Oedipus's father), in order to make him his lover. Hera considered this act an attack upon the institution of marriage, of which she was the protectress. In Egypt the Sphinx guarded temples and graves. In a dream reported in his *Zarathustra* (Z II:19), Nietzsche sees himself as a "guardian of tombs."

43. Goux also suggests that in Oedipus's myth there are three fundamental acts: "1) Eviction of the Father; 2) Promotion of Man (and the Ego); 3) Possession of the Mother." The author is struck by the parallelism found between the myth and Nietzsche's doctrines represented by: "1) The death of God; 2) The advent of the Superman; 3) The total domination of the Earth" (ibid., 172–73).

44. For Nietzsche, Odysseus, Oedipus, and Prometheus are only masks of Dionysus.

45. The passage continues, indicating that Nietzsche was "able to speak with a few of the dead," among whom he listed Epicurus and Montaigne, Goethe and Spinoza, Plato and Rousseau, Pascal and Schopenhauer. "With this I must come to terms when I have long wandered alone . . . the living forgive me that occasionally *they* appear to me as shades, so pale and somber, so restless and, alas, so lusting for life—while those men then seem so alive to me, as if now *after* death, they could never again grow weary of life."

46. The literalization of his yearning is obvious in the following lines from a letter sent to Heinrich Köselitz on September 11, 1879, when he is close to his thirty-sixth birthday and thinks that upon arriving at that age (the age at which his father died) he too will meet his end: "I am at the end of my thirty-fifth year. . . . And now in the very midst of life I am so 'surrounded by death' that it could seize me at any hour . . . I'm in a state where it seems more suitable to settle down close to my Mother, my hometown, and my childhood memories."

47. Prayer to Kali: "Thou art the Beginning of all: creatrix, protectress, and destroyer that Thou art."

48. Walter Otto associates Dionysus with maternity through the figures of the maenads, stating, "these women are mothers and nurses. . . . We have found the origin of the Dionysian women in the element of water, from which the spirit of womanliness rises, together with . . . motherliness, music, prophecy, and death" (1993, 178).

49. Whereas he rejects all other forms of femininity (cf. Woman as mother in EH 5; BGE 163, 177, and 232; HATH 197, BT 16, OGM III 8).

50. "My brother's ideal," suggested Elisabeth Förster-Nietzsche, "was in fact the ideal cherished by every man of high character. . . . the healthy, beautiful woman who brings strong, healthy children into the world and gives them all that a mother's love and care can provide. In other words, it was the ideal hitherto glorified by every artist . . . [the] mother with her child should always be for us the most moving of all pictures. . . . This is the ideal which my brother always regarded and treated with the tenderest reverence. He considered that a grave danger was involved if . . . this ideal of mother and child were no longer looked upon as the highest" (1912, 304–05).

51. Due to the absence of the paternal function, there was no phallic transmission corresponding to the identification of the son with the father. Nor was there the imago of a powerful father capable of depriving the mother of his phallic attribute. (Rather, the father's imago was associated with death and decline, "wicked heritage.") Consequently, it became impossible for Nietzsche to transfer from the condition of *being* the imaginary phallus of the mother to that of *possessing* it. It is through the father-son relationship that gender consciousness emerges, and Nietzsche's deprivation probably drew him close to Dionysus, because Dionysus—whose infancy also lacked objects for masculine identification—does not possess a solar phallus: he is a chthonian-phallic god. Under the tutelage of the Great Mother, he is, like Nietzsche, the imaginary phallus of the mother.

52. The personal mother (along with Nietzsche's sister) became "the very image of life in its most despicable and detested form," as described in *Ecce Homo*. Nietzsche refers to his mother and sister in terms such as "venomous vermin," referring to the "unspeakable horror" they aroused.

53. In a short text dating from 1922, Freud suggests that the symbol of Medusa's head is a symbolism of castration: "To decapitate = to castrate. The fear of Medusa is also the fear of castration, which is linked to a gaze."

54. It is worth highlighting that, four years after having written the "Magician's Song" in his *Zarathustra*, Nietzsche rewrote the poem with very few changes and retitled it "Ariadne's Lament." The changes he did introduce, however, were significant: 1) He altered the sex roles of the poet-narrator, replacing the male magician (a caricature of Wagner) with the mythical Ariadne, and 2) He added an epilogue to the poem in which the god who had disappeared in the first version reappeared in an epiphany, personified as Dionysus.

55. Based on *Zarathustra's* chapter entitled "On the Despisers of the Body," Jung concluded that Nietzsche made a mistakenly one-sided identification of the Self with body: "If he identifies the body with the self, he brings the self into the body or the body up into the self, and that produces an inflation of the body. . . . The body is extraordinarily important but that is an overrating" (SNZ I:394).

56. "I have just seen myself in the mirror—never have I looked so well. In exemplary condition, well nourished and ten years younger than I should be." Letter to Peter Gast from Turin, dated October 30, 1888. And to Carl Fuchs, Nietzsche wrote on December 18, 1888: "The most amazing tasks as easy as a game; my health, like the weather, coming up every day with boundless brilliance and certainty."

57. In the Preface (4) to *The Gay Science,* Nietzsche identified "Truth" with Baubo, the Greek mythological vaginal goddess: a personification of the female genitalia. It was in the vaginal abyss that Nietzsche sought truth, while at the same time he was horrified by the primal opening of the woman's body.

58. The passages written by Nietzsche regarding masks are numerous (for example, cf. BGE 4, 5, 25, 40, 47, 204, 221, 225, 230, 270, 278, 289).

CHAPTER 10

1. Apollo and Dionysus passed from "art deities" to ontological principles, as is evident in subsequent works.

2. This condition would appear to be reflected also in his musical "predilection for discords." For Nietzsche, the pleasure generated by the tragic worldview represented in the Dionysian was similar to the pleasure produced by musical dissonance. In response to his *Manfred-Meditation* composition for piano, which Nietzsche sent to Hans von Bülow as a sign of gratitude for the performances of *Tristan*, the maestro wrote to Nietzsche: "I could not discover in it the least of Apollonian elements, and, as for the Dionysian, to tell you frankly, it made me think of the morning after a bacchanalian orgy rather than of an orgy itself." And he ended the letter, dated July 24, 1872, with a harsh verdict: "[Your composition is] a kind of rape of Euterpe." According to the philosopher Hatab, "Dionysian energy alone is not 'creative' in the sense of culture formation, it supplies the underlying power of becoming in life, but without the Apollonian such becoming would be more chaotic than creative" (2005, 136).

3. According to D. W. Winnicott, the false self is a defense mechanism that

results from a deficient relation with a mother who fails to perform empathic attuning and mirroring due to "an inability to sense her infant's needs" (1965, 145). As a consequence, there is a failure in the capacity of the child to recognize and enact spontaneous needs of self-expression. Winnicott asserts that "Whereas a True Self feels real, the existence of a False Self results in a feeling of unreality or a sense of futility" (ibid., 148).

4.   "Wherever the Dionysian prevailed, the Apollonian was checked and destroyed," declared Nietzsche (BT 4). Apollo acts as a symbol for the spirit within the psyche (see Kerényi 1983). When Nietzsche dismissed the world of the father, he detached himself from the metaphysical notion of a "Spirit in itself" that he had once sustained, and with it Apollo was also dismissed.

5.   Therefore, unlike Jung, Nietzsche esteemed the broadening of consciousness as a risk: "Whatever becomes conscious *becomes* by the same token shallow, thin, relatively stupid, general, sign and herd signal: all becoming conscious involves great and thorough corruption, falsification, reduction to superficialities, and generalization. Ultimately, the growth of consciousness becomes a danger" (GS 354).

6.   For Nietzsche, subjectivity is an effect rather than a cause: the unconscious speaks through the "individual": "A thought comes when 'it' wants, not when 'I' want it; so that it is a *falsification* of the fact to say: the subject 'I' is the condition of the predicate 'think.' It thinks: but that this 'it' is precisely that famous old 'I' is, to put it mildly, only an assumption, an assertion, above all not an 'immediate' certainty" (BGE 17).

7.   It is worth highlighting that Nietzsche associated Medusa's head with the Dionysian power (BT2). He seems to have tried and failed to use this power as an apotropaic device to fend off the Gorgon's head.

8.   Therefore, Jung suggested that even if Nietzsche's *Zarathustra* "begins, practically, with the statement that God is dead . . . you can see throughout the book that Nietzsche never gets rid of him" (SNZ I:843).

9.   Perhaps this was the guilt of young Fritz, the child who wished the death of his father to free him from his suffering and whose desire came true: "My father had to suffer terrible pains, but the illness did not abate; on the contrary, with each day, it intensified. In the end, it even deprived him of his sight, so that he had to bear the rest of his torment in eternal darkness. This situation continued until July 1849; then the day of freedom arrived" (AML 43). For the magical childish imagination, wish and fact are equivalent terms. In *Totem and Taboo*, Freud states that for the primitive psyche there is no difference between imagining an action and carrying it out. He adds that not even the memory of having helped the patient with the greatest dedication is enough to put an end to the torment of the person who experiences pathological mourning. With his declaration of the death of God, Nietzsche had killed his father twice, and he carried this burden with a tragic guilt.

The persecutory guilt concomitant to pathological mourning creates a paradox: the object is not felt as dead but as malignly alive, and as a menace to the rest of the ego. Thus Nietzsche perceived the murdered god/father as a wrathful and revengeful being: "For *that man be delivered from revenge,* that is for me the bridge to the highest hope, and a rainbow after long storms." Thus spoke Nietzsche (Z II:7). J. W. Perry draws a distinction between the guilt that emerges from personal history and archetypal guilt. "The guilt with which parents endow their child," he states, "is most hurtful when it damages and severely distorts both the personal and archetypal self-image, that is, the self-image of the ego and of the central archetype, thus creating a strong sense of unwholeness and inner strife" (ibid., 54). As to the archetypal level,

> . . .guilt is based on a less familiar principle, belonging to the ways of the archaic mind and not so easily recognizable to our modern consciousness. Yet I find it as prevalent in the problem of the schizoid personality. . . . This kind of guilt is analogous to the primordial view found in tribal societies that only acts performed according to the prescribed ways of the ancestors are right, meaningful and endowed with truth. . . . The other, profane ways are those initiated by the individual ego, which, unlike adherence to the strict sanctions of the collective and of the ancestral tradition, assumes the privilege of making its own choices, according to its personal needs and views. . . . For the mother-bound personality, his guilt was very binding. From the point of view of the mother figure, either the personal mother with her demanding animus, or the primordial Great Mother, who holds all order and wisdom in herself, guilt is inevitable if the ego chooses to act on its own. . . . There must be no change. Such ego grows to be mortally afraid of action that might lead to error and to making mistakes, which threaten to bring down shame; such an ego has an inordinate need for absolute rightness. On the other hand, another kind of guilt ensues if the ego does not find freedom from the mother and does not learn to act on its own. (1976, 54–55)

10. The parricide, and Nietzsche's pathological guilt, showed the condition inherent to an inflated ego: "I kill God," "I deprive the world of God," "I caused all this."
11. Nietzsche made a distinction between the "thought," the "deed," and the "image of the deed." It was not the thought or the deed but the image of the deed that the Pale Criminal could not bear (cf. Z I:6).
12. Nietzsche could not find forgiveness in himself or in others. "If God wished to become an object of love, he should have given up judging . . . first of all; a judge, even a merciful judge, is no object of love" (GS 140). "My unconscious is reinscribable beyond the gift that an other presents me by not judging my actions," suggests the French psychoanalyst Julia Kristeva, adding, "Forgiveness does not cleanse actions. It raises the unconscious from beneath the actions and has it meet its loving other—another who does not judge but hears my truth in the availability of love, and for that very reason allows me to be reborn" (1989, 205). She concludes: "Whoever is in the realm of forgiveness—who forgives and who accepts forgiveness—is capable

of identifying with a loving father, an imaginary father, with whom, consequently, he is ready to be reconciled, with a new symbolic law in mind"
(ibid., 207).

13. Nietzsche was not only the son of a village pastor, but also the grandson of
    pastors on both sides: "Almost all the particular lines of succession of the
    Nietzschean genealogical tree lead . . . to one very concrete profession: that
    of (Protestant) pastor" (Janz 1987, I:27). The philosopher Fraser adds that
    "Nietzsche's cousin, Max Oehler, worked out that some twenty per cent of his
    ninety-eight known male ancestors were pastors" (2002, 31).

14. Nietzsche also declared: "I have tried to deny everything. Oh, it is easy to tear
    down, but to build up! And even tearing down seems easer than it is: the
    impressions of our childhood, the influence of our parents, our education
    determine us to our inmost depths, so that these deeply rooted prejudices are
    not so easily weeded out by rational grounds or sheer will" (cited in Fraser
    2002, 32).

15. If he had suspended belief, he would not have felt harassed by guilt or perse-
    cutory feelings, nor would he have sought redemption (see Z IV:7). In a letter
    addressed to H. Albert, Paul Valéry wrote about Nietzsche's attack on
    Christianity: "His criticisms of Christianity are shadows brushing the shadow
    of a Christian" (August 1903).

16. In reference to the chapter "Of the Pale Criminal," we can appreciate Jung's
    negative emotional reaction when he wrote:

    > [This chapter] is exceedingly disgusting to my feeling. . . . From an
    > intellectual point of view, it is unspeakably intricate; a sort of intellec-
    > tual devil is all over. . . . Here really Nietzsche becomes an intellectu-
    > al criminal. That is the disgusting thing—he reaches here one of the
    > pre-stages of his own madness. . . . You are stopped dead when you
    > begin to read it. Your feeling refuses to touch upon that thing because
    > it is altogether too pathological. . . . You see, you have to deal with a
    > man who is doomed to madness, preparing himself for it. (SNZ I:459)

    Freud used the case of the Pale Criminal too in his essay on "Criminality
    from a Sense of Guilt," in which he stated: "Paradoxical as it may sound, I
    must maintain that the sense of guilt was present prior to the transgression,
    that it did not arise from this, but counterwise—the transgression from the
    sense of guilt. These persons we might justifiably describe as criminals from
    a sense of guilt" (1953, 342). However, Freud assumed that after the deed had
    been committed "the oppression was mitigated" (ibid.). That was not the case
    with Nietzsche, whose oppression became unbearable.

17. The philosopher Kathleen Marie Higgins considers that the doctrine of eter-
    nal recurrence proposed by Nietzsche was an attempt to free himself from the
    Christian doctrine of sin:

    According to Nietzsche, the Christian doctrine of sin promotes a certain perspective on our activities in time. . . . The Christian conception that we are sinful is focused on *past* actions. . . . We are sinful from birth because our first parents sinned originally. . . . Moreover, the sin that always demonstrates our personal guilt is always embedded in our personal past. We feel guilty because of what we *have* done. . . . Recognition that one's past includes events that might have inspired guilt is a precondition to adopting the Christian route of salvation. . . . The doctrine of eternal recurrence, by contrast with the Christian moral doctrine, focuses on the significance of the present. . . . After all, according to the doctrine every moment recurs eternally, and in this respect the present moment is no different from any other. (1987, 166–69)

Consequently, the doctrine of eternal recurrence breaks with the linear conception of time to take its place in a cyclical or uroboric time (time of the unconscious) and the past will recur in a distant future. Punishment and reward for past actions have no room or meaning in this model of time; therefore, with this doctrine, the Christian idea of redemption is eliminated. It is precisely in the chapter titled "On Redemption" that Nietzsche described in terms of madness the idea of "this law of time that it must devour its children" (Z II:20).

18. The main emotions involved in persecutory guilt are resentment, pain, despair, fear, and self-reproach. The extreme cases of persecutory guilt are schizophrenia and melancholia (pathological mourning). We must not forget that in melancholia such as Nietzsche's, the self-reproach and loss of self-esteem characteristic of pathological mourning often culminate in a delusional expectation of punishment, because the person suffering from melancholia is incapable of repairing the objects. "Only in Christendom," wrote Nietzsche, "did everything become punishment, well-deserved punishment: it also makes the sufferer's imagination suffer, so that with every misfortune he feels himself morally reprehensible and cast out" (D 78). Similarly, his attempt to abolish the Christian idea of sin and guilt was also a frustrated desire: "Let us do away with the concept *sin* and let us quickly send after it the concept *punishment*" (D 202). One must recall that the feeling of guilt is preponderant in the etiology of neurosis and, particularly, of psychosis. A stronger and more integrated ego is capable of bearing guilt, whereas an immature ego, as in Nietzsche's case, cannot free itself of persecutory guilt and its concomitant anguish.

M. Klein, in her work *Envy and Gratitude* (1957), points out that unlike "persecutory guilt," "depressive guilt," inherent to a more integrated ego, involves the capacity to bear the suffering caused by the guilt and develop the corresponding defenses, in particular the tendency to repair. Nietzsche tried unsuccessfully to project the guilt and accuse the object that had become the persecutor (priests and God, among others). In Freud's view, on the other hand, the superego transforms itself into an implacable persecutor and the ego surrenders (dies) because it feels hated by the superego.

19. "The mythology of a later period distinguished the Zagreus, who was the child of Zeus and Persephone and who was destroyed by the Titans, as an earlier manifestation of the real Dionysus, the son of Semele, whom Zeus called into life to take the place of Dionysus-Zagreus. This by no means did the old myth an injustice. In it too, a horrible death precedes the reappearance of the god, and in it the dying god is also related to the powers of the underworld. But in the original conception both are one. The god, with his multiplicity of forms, the lord and first-born child of life and death, is born of Semele as well as of Persephone, and entered Hades as well as Olympus" (Otto 1993, 196).

20. He also commented that in the Dionysian dissolution, "We have become, as it were, only the infinite primordial joy in existence" (BT 17).

21. Therefore, while in *The Gay Science* the eternal recurrence invites an existential or ethical reading, in *Will to Power* (36) the doctrine presented a call for a cosmological reading: the eternal recurrence would be for Nietzsche the fundamental dynamics of the universe and "the most scientific of all possible hypotheses."

CHAPTER 11

1. " 'Come, come, come, Dionysus!' is the sort of invocation that pertains to most Dionysiac religions" (López-Pedraza 2000, 51).

2. Edinger considers that when the ego is in a state of "blackness," the images that emerge from the unconscious are usually green in color (cf. 1995, 269). As in Euripides' *Bacchae*, Dionysus appeared to Nietzsche-Ariadne as a sudden irruption. In Euripides' drama the first word uttered by Dionysus is *hêkô*, meaning, "Here I am, I have come." It is also worth pointing out that Nietzsche described the overman in terms of the Dionysian when he wrote: "Behold, I teach you the overman: he is [the] lightning, he is [the] frenzy" (Z I:P3).

3. In his writings, Nietzsche continuously alluded to "the labyrinth of an ear" and made a distinction with regard to the selectivity of hearing of "small ears" vis-à-vis the indiscriminate hearing represented by "the big ears of a donkey." In *Ecce Homo* he wrote: "We all know—indeed, some of us know from experience—what a long-ear is. Splendid, I dare to assert that I have the smallest ears [like the Ariadne of the poem]. I am the antijackass *par excellence*, and am thereby a world-historical beastie—I am, in Greek, and not only in Greek, the Antichrist." Nietzsche made reference to "ears for something outrageous." Ariadne needs small ears to hear that Dionysus is her own labyrinth. Also, Nietzsche contrasted the Apollonian "rapture of the eye" with the Dionysian ecstasy. In "The Drunken Song" of the fourth part of his *Zarathustra*, Nietzsche showed that the prophet has "awakened" to the mystery of eternity while the others remain asleep, oblivious to it. Their ears are deaf to the mystery causing pain to Zarathustra: "The heedful ear is lacking in their limbs," Zarathustra says regretfully. Also, in the final chapter Zarathustra abandons

the higher men who sleep in his cave. He regards them as "not my proper companions" because "the ear that listens for [him], the *heedful* ear is lacking in their limbs" (Z IV:20). Regarding the ear we should remember Theophrastus's remark that hearing is the most emotive of all senses.

4. In the essay "Psychology of Hatred and Cruelty" in *Sadism and Masochism*, the psychoanalyst Wilhelm Stekel refers to his conception of hatred and, seeking the answer to the question of whether love or hatred is the primary feeling, concludes that it is hatred. For Stekel, though love constitutes the central strength of existence, hatred is in reality the motor of all. Freud confirms Stekel's assertion in "The Predisposition to Obsessive Neurosis" (1913), agreeing that hatred, and not love, is the primary bond among human beings.

5. Regarding Nietzsche's conception of truth, the philosopher Giles Fraser suggests that "although one has to be aware that Nietzsche uses the word true in a number of different ways without necessarily signaling to the reader the sense in which he is using it, for the most part he is not interested in what we might call philosophical truth" (2002, 59).

6. According to Paul Bishop, "Nietzschean imagery and Jungian psychology [came] together to produce the archetype of the anima" (1995, 202).

7. Nietzsche's anima spoke to him in the following words: "But I am merely changeable and wild, and a woman in every way, and not virtuous—even if you men call me profound, faithful, eternal, and mysterious" (Z II:10).

8. Jung relates anima, Life, and Dionysus.

9. Nietzsche also prefigured Jung's notion of the animus. After quoting Goethe's well-known phrase "the eternal womanly draws us *upward*," Nietzsche adds: "I do not doubt that every nobler woman will resist the belief, for *that* is precisely what she believes of the eternal manly" (BGE 236).

10. "Once a man's thoughts have gone beyond the demands of custom, he might consider whether nature and reason do not dictate that he marry several times in succession, so that first, aged twenty-two years, he marry an older girl who is spiritually and morally superior to him and can guide him through the dangers of his twenties (ambition, hatred, self-contempt, passions of all kinds). This woman's love would later be completely transformed into maternal feelings, and she would not only tolerate it, but promote it in the most salutary way, if the man in his thirties made an alliance with a quite young girl, whose education he himself would take in hand. For one's twenties, marriage is a necessary institution; for one's thirties, it is useful, but not necessary; for later life, it often becomes harmful and promotes a husband's spiritual regression" (HATH 421). On his part, the philosopher Farrell Krell confessed that "when *Postponements* first appeared, I asked a psychoanalyst friend whether Nietzsche's misogyny troubled her. Her reply silenced me. 'It doesn't trouble me at all,' she said. 'Whenever Nietzsche uses the word *woman* I substitute the words *my mother*, and then I have no difficulty accepting what he says'" (1996, 243). Finally, I would like to add that I completely disagree with Curtis Cate when he begins his biographical work on Nietzsche with the following

statement: "[Nietzsche] will always remain an enigma for neo-Freudians, since contrary to the standard X-pattern of attraction, he adored and idolized his father and never suffered from a mother complex" (2002, 1).

11. Zarathustra was tormented by the loss of the dreams and ideals of his youth, when he had seen all things as divine and holy (cf. Z II:11).

12. "The anima is the *archetype of life itself*" (Jung, CW 9 I: 66).

13. Zarathustra calls Life "a supple snake and a slippery witch" (Z III:15).

14. It is relevant to note that no female figures are invited into Zarathustra's cave of "higher men."

15. We can evidence Nietzsche-Zarathustra's final encounter with the anima in Part III (see Z III:14–15). In Part IV we can appreciate the absence of anima.

16. J. W. Perry (1970) also described the anima's bipolar nature. The two poles interact in different ways: one is aligned with the ego while the other is projected out upon an object emotionally related to the subject.

17. Theseus's abandonment of Ariadne is a tale of betrayal, deceit, and disloyalty. If Nietzsche had reached the rank of "hero," like Theseus, perhaps he would have been capable of liberating his anima from the labyrinth (unconscious), associated with the monster.

18. Theseus led Ariadne to grief. Only thus was it possible for her to establish a connection with Dionysus. "The women with whom he [Dionysus] is most intimately associated [Semele and Ariadne] reach a state of glory only by passing through deep sorrow" (Otto 1993, 185).

19. In the essay "Traces of the Beast: Becoming Nietzsche, Becoming Animal, and the Figure of the Transhuman," the philosopher Jami Weinstein concludes: "All four trans-human figures issuing from the sojourn into becoming Nietzsche—the nomadic subject [Deleuze and Guattari], Dasein [Heidegger], the genealogical subject [Foucault], and le *féminin* [Irigaray]—require the additional performance of a becoming-animal to reach their tectonic profundity" (2004, 314).

20. The anima, according to Jung, has " 'occult' connections with 'mysteries,' with the world of darkness in general" (CW 9 I:354), a reality that is even more decisive when it appears personified by Ariadne. "Ariadne 'carries' the important surname of Persephone—the untouchably pure, the most holy. This name indicates that Ariadne has a dark underworld character; therefore, she also knows the way into the underworld labyrinth" (Fierz-David 1993, 22).

21. "Ariadne gains ascendancy during the years 1886–89," points out the philosopher David Farrell Krell (1986, 13), adding: "And we know that the manuscript of *Thus Spoke Zarathustra*, Part III, had as the title of the episode now called 'On the Great Longing' (which begins, 'O my soul . . .') the name Ariadne. We also know that preceding the words of the title 'The Other Dance Song' appeared the rubric *Vita femina*. . . . By the autumn of 1888, when Nietzsche composes *Ecce Homo*, Ariadne is omnipresent. 'In the midst of martyrdoms . . .' writes Nietzsche in 'Why I Am so Wise' . . . applying in the story of his own illness the vocabulary of Ariadne's lament" (ibid., 26). In January 1889, only a few

days before his mental breakdown, a euphoric Nietzsche sent the *Dionysian Dithyrambs* to the printers. The poem titled "Ariadne's Lament" is included among these. It appears finally in the letters addressed to Ariadne and sent to Cosima Wagner.

There has been a great deal of speculation regarding whether Nietzsche felt a secret love for Cosima, based on the letters he addressed to her during his final alienation from reality, in Turin in 1889. These letters bear the heading "To Princess Ariadne, my beloved" and are signed "Dionysus." Furthermore, he stated that he had been brought to the psychiatric hospital in Jena by "Cosima, his wife." Nonetheless, there does not seem to be any evidence of an attraction, sexual or otherwise, on Nietzsche's part. When he wrote to Cosima calling her Ariadne, his ego had already identified with the mythical figure abandoned by the hero Theseus-Wagner. Absorbed by Dionysus, god of dissolution, Nietzsche manifested a complete absence of identity. Just as he declared himself to be Shakespeare, Voltaire, or Dionysus, he also believed he was Wagner, thus taking the place of the previously venerated numinous figure. What his letters "from madness" seem to reveal is his identification, and ensuing state of inflation, with Wagner's genius: "Even psychologically all decisive traits of my own nature are projected into Wagner's," he wrote in *Ecce Homo*. His note beginning "Ariadne, my love" seemed to show his desire to be either with or in the place of the genius, rather than a genuine amorous desire for the wife of the greatest musical phenomenon of his time. His attitude could be interpreted in a context of rivalry, in view of his own frustrated vocational desire. Nietzsche seemed to be more in love with the place occupied by Wagner's wife in the life of the brilliant composer than with Cosima. "Nietzsche falls in love with Wagner," claims the philosopher Tomas Abraham. "What other expression can describe this relationship? Can we say, as does Lou Andreas-Salomé, that with Wagner Nietzsche frees his feminine side? . . . Nietzsche falls in love with Wagner as a troubadour loves his mistress, his only wish is that his master look at him. Everything revolves around the gaze of his master, of its direction" (Abraham 1996, 44).

Following this same train of thought, there is also evidence of Nietzsche's identification with Wagner at other moments of his existence. Regarding his work "Richard Wagner in Bayreuth," he included the following reflection in *Ecce Homo*:

> In my essay on Wagner in Bayreuth: In all psychologically decisive places I alone am discussed—and no one need hesitate to put down my name or the word "Zarathustra" where the text has the word "Wagner." The entire picture of the dithyrambic artist is a picture of the pre-existent poet of Zarathustra, sketched with abysmal profundity and without touching even for a moment the Wagnerian reality. Wagner himself had some notion of that; he did not recognize himself in this essay. (EH III: BT 4)

The biographer Joachim Köhler concluded:

> In the flush of exaltation that accompanied his mental breakdown, he felt sublime sensations of divinity and, like Dionysus, his role model, exchanged one persona for another at will. At one moment he saw himself as Shakespeare or Caesar, at the next as King of Italy or as Wagner, a mortal enemy he pursued with all the savagery he had at his command. And these figures all revealed themselves to him as incarnations of the one god, the god Dionysus, with whom he knew himself to be identical. (1998, 3)

As for the biographer Janz, he suggested the following: "Ariadne possibly represented the greatest psychic burden for Nietzsche. One cannot gaily limit oneself to calling it 'madness.' Nietzsche established with her a symbol for the dominating *fatum* in his life and in his work, but we do not have a clear understanding of that. It remains only as a sign of warning" (1985, IV:27).

22. The heroic ego, personified by Wagner, is what Nietzsche as Ariadne wants to kill. In the following lines that Nietzsche wrote for a satyr-play, we can read: "'Theseus is becoming absurd,' said Ariadne. 'Theseus is becoming virtuous.' Theseus is jealous because of Ariadne's dream. The hero marveling at himself, becoming absurd. Plaint of Ariadne. Dionysus devoid of jealousy: 'The thing I love about you—how could Theseus love that?' Last Act: Marriage of Dionysus and Ariadne. 'One is not jealous when one is god . . .' 'Ariadne,' said Dionysus, 'you are a labyrinth. Theseus got lost in you, he no longer holds the thread; what good does it do him now that the Minotaur did not devour him? . . .' 'You flatter me,' replied Ariadne. 'But I weary of my pity; all heroes should perish on account of me. That is my ultimate love for Theseus: I shall see to it that he perishes' " (cited in Farrell Krell 1986, 81–82).

23. Jung, like Nietzsche, presented the anima as a cunning temptress: "With her cunning play of illusions the soul lures into life the inertness of matter that does not want to live. She makes us believe incredible things, that life may be lived. She is full of snares and traps, in order that Man should fall, should reach the earth, entangle himself there, and stay caught, so that life should be lived" (CW 9 I:56).

24. Paradoxically, it is in the place that Homer assigns to the dark feminine, the Strait of Messina in Sicily, where Nietzsche is inspired to write the collection of poems entitled *The Idylls from Messina* (1882). He wrote to Gast that in Messina "I have arrived at my 'end of the world' where, according to Homer, happiness is to be found." These poems reveal a fascination with the tenebrous feminine, particularly the one titled "Sils-Maria," which shows a splitting into two selves during his encounter with eternity: "Then suddenly . . . one turns into two." The same occurs with the meaningful poem "The Mysterious Bark," in which the dithyrambic philosopher evokes what seems to be a passage to Hades (the unconscious).

25. In Argolis, there exists the traditional belief that Dionysus arrived from Naxos with Ariadne, from the sea, accompanied by the Sirens. In Nietzsche's imagery, the Sirens and Dionysus appear as "green lightning." In his poem "Ariadne's Lament," "Dionysus becomes visible in emerald beauty." Euripides makes Tiresias claim that Dionysus is also a god of ecstatic prophecy. So, like the Sirens, he is a provider of foreknowledge.

26. Jung considers "eternity" as "a quality predicated by the unconscious" (CW 12:135). Hillman offers a similar view when he writes: "When we consider the House of Hades, we must remember that the myths . . . tell us that there is no time in the underworld. There is no decay, no progress, no change of any sort because time has nothing to do with the underworld" (1979, 29). Hillman suggested that our "beliefs in personal immortality . . . rest upon personifying, which in turn is an effect of the anima archetype" (1996a, 109).

27. Edinger warns about the seduction of the Sirens, the anima in her dark aspect: "The hazardousness in listening to them corresponds psychologically to the danger in being lured into the unconscious out of desire to know about the mysteries. For an underdeveloped ego to succumb to that lure is to expose it to dissolution into the archetypal. As the myth warns, it is safe to listen to the sources of divine knowledge only when one is solidly lashed to the mast of reality: Peril lies in the exploration of the unconscious, for the archetypal symbolism and images can be exciting and provocative, opening up vistas that seem enlarging and valuable; yet they can overwhelm any ego that is not grounded in reality" (1994, 117).

28. The "numinosum," a term coined by Rudolf Otto and adapted by Jung, refers, according to the psychoanalyst Donald Kalsched, to a "peculiar alteration in consciousness brought about by the ego's contact with transpersonal psychic energies which overwhelm it—whether these energies be daimonic or sub-lime. . . . Numinous experience dissolves ego-boundaries and therefore many people with shaky ego-boundaries [as in the case of Nietzsche] seek it out to escape the pain and humiliation that inevitably accompany the disillusioning process of coming into being as a limited, time-bound, definite, embodied individual. . . . It has been my intention to show that this defense is in itself a rather miraculous creation, but a deadly one as well. Jung did not suffi-ciently emphasize this daimonic, diabolical side of the numinous and its insidious, corrosive effect within the world of fantasy. He described it beau-tifully as the ambivalence of the archaic Godhead, but left the problem in the realm of religion, with its clinical applications to be worked out by those of us who follow" (2000, 207–08).

29. Under the stern command of an angry mistress, "Zarathustra must return once more to his solitude; but this time the bear goes back to his cave without joy." And Zarathustra asks himself: "What happened to me? Who ordered this? Alas, my angry mistress wants it, she spoke to me" (Z II:22). Zarathustra calls his "stillest hour" his "terrifying mistress," the mistress who seduces him into a complete solitude. He does not wish to abandon the "human" world, but his anima has given him her final instruction to return to his solitude again. The

philosopher T. K. Seung identified the "stillest hour" with the lady of the night, with Life:

> We have encountered her on three occasions. First she was represent-ed as night or rather as the kingdom of silence and darkness in "The Night Song." The voiceless voice is the voice of her silence. Second, she appeared as the lady who came to Zarathustra's rescue in "The Dancing Song." This episode explains why she now talks to him in "The Stillest Hour" not as a stranger, but as someone who has already secured her lordship over him. There is no other lady who fits the role except for Life (2005, 111).

The author concludes: "[Zarathustra's] encounter with Life turns out to be the most critical event in his epic journey" (ibid., 117). Farrell Krell reminds us that "in the original manuscript [of Zarathustra] . . . his soul bears the name of *Ariadne*" (1986, 55).

30. The *coniunctio* process or union of opposites should be preceded by the *sep-aratio*, so as to distinguish all the components and undifferentiated parts of the psyche—of the subject and object, of the I and non-I. This process did not take place in Nietzsche; consequently, in his case there was a "lesser *coniunc-tio*," as Edinger calls it. As a result, the *numinosum* turned negative and destructive. Instead of going "beyond good and evil" as Nietzsche sought to do, he inhabited a world before their distinction.

31. Grudlehner suggests that "the magician is a Wagnerian caricature who seeks to entice his listeners into a moribund state by his histrionic talents" (1896, 214). His suggestion is supported by many descriptions of Wagner made by Nietzsche himself. For example, in *The Case of Wagner*, Nietzsche describes the composer as the "old magician" (TCW 2). In the "Magician's Song," Nietzsche seems to identify Wagner with the magician Klingsor in *Parsifal*, who controls everyone and everything through his sorcerer's arts and demands that his orders be obeyed. As Parsifal, despite all his efforts, is unable to free himself from the spell of the wicked magician, so Nietzsche can never free himself from Wagner's influence.

32. Grudlehner dates the rewriting of the "Magician's Song" into "Ariadne's Lament" to early January 1889 (1986, 227). On his part, David Farrell Krell dates it to "the last days of 1888 or the first days of 1889" (1986, 15).

33. "I began a second time, taking up Karl Reinhardt's analysis of Ariadne's lament. Reinhardt's thesis . . . is that in Nietzsche's later philosophy he tried to become woman. He tried to reach Dionysus by exposing himself without reserve to all the agonies and vulnerabilities of Ariadne" (Farrell Krell 1986, 50). It is worth remembering that in Euripides' *Bacchae*, Dionysus transforms the masculine Pentheus into a woman by making him wear the robes of his devotees. Thus Pentheus appears completely transformed into a woman and willing to accept his feminine role. Dionysus says to him: "When I see you

[dressed as a woman], I seem to be looking at your mothers and aunts." Jung, reading some passages of Nietzsche's *Zarathustra*, noticed the fact that "Nietzsche uses words as if he were a woman. . . . It was quite obvious that he was transformed into his anima by identification. . . . And . . . we must theoretically at least conclude that he is in the role of femininity" (SNZ II:863).

34. Just as Wisdom vanished in the second part of Nietzsche's magnum opus, Life vanishes completely after "The Other Dancing Song" and never appears again.

CHAPTER 12

1. By leading an army across this river, contrary to the prohibition of the civil government in Rome, Caesar precipitated the civil war that resulted in the death of Pompey and the overthrow of the senate; hence the phrase "to cross the Rubicon" signifies a decisive step by which one is committed to a hazardous enterprise from which there is no retreat. In a note sent to Peter Gast on December 31, 1888, Nietzsche announced that by then he was crossing the "famous Rubicon." He ended the note confessing: "I no longer know my address: let us suppose that it will soon be the Palazzo del Quirinale." Christopher Middleton considers that Nietzsche's reference to crossing the Rubicon "could be taken to indicate that N[ietzsche] had gone out of his mind shortly before writing this note to Gast" (1996, 344n). Lesley Chamberlain also connects the crossing of the Rubicon with Nietzsche's mental collapse. The author adds that even though "[Nietzsche] could see it . . . he couldn't stop it" (1996, 210).

2. Elisabeth Förster-Nietzsche offered her own diagnosis regarding her brother's breakdown: "The correct diagnosis, perhaps, would be this: a brain exhausted by overstrain of the nerves of head and eye could no longer resist taking drugs to excess, and became disabled" (1912, II:402).

3. Nietzsche's father died of "softening of the brain." Several maternal aunts and uncles also presented mental problems: one aunt committed suicide and another was mentally ill. One of his mother's brothers, at sixty-eight years of age, suffered from psychic disorders. And, on one occasion, his mother admitted that one of her brothers had died in a "sanatorium for patients with nervous problems." This interpretation was sustained mainly by the neurologist and psychiatrist Dr. Paul Möbious in his work *Über das Pathologische bei Nietzsche* (J. F. Bergmann, Wiesbaden 1902). Dr. Möbious also revealed the diagnosis of syphilis and offered a very harsh comment: "If you find pearls do not imagine that it is all one chain of pearls. Be distrustful, for this man [Nietzsche] has a diseased brain" (cited in Podach, 1931, 61). However, it is worth pointing out that Möbious had previously written a book called *On the Physiological Weak-Mindedness of Women,* and that his description of pathological subjects included Jesus and Shakespeare.

4. The psychiatrist and philosopher Karl Jaspers attributed Nietzsche's illness to

a "biological factor" that had not yet been discovered and that "eventually may come to be recognized as psychiatry advances." In his opinion, this factor "affects Nietzsche's entire constitution: the exulting feelings and rapturous states assume the form of *seizures* or *attacks* that lead one to think that they are brought about by non-psychical causes" (1997, 96).

5.   "Quite early Nietzsche had brooded over the meaning of madness . . . that may have led the ancients to discern a sign of divine election," concluded Lou Salomé (2001, 145). Salomé considered that Nietzsche chose the road of madness in order to "go down into the chaotic, dark, and inexhaustible under-ground of life—not only into that of past mankind but even further down to the source from which even it developed initially" (2001, 145). She explained the reason for Nietzsche's search as follows: "What [Nietzsche] needed [was] a much more real, effective, and even more terrible experiencing, namely through orgiastic Dionysian conditions and the chaos of frenzied passions— yes, *madness* itself as a means of sinking back down to the mass of entwined feelings and imaginings. This seemed for Nietzsche the last road into the pri-mal depths imbedded within us" (ibid.). In his philosophical and lyrical writ-ings, Nietzsche deified madness by elevating it to a category of epistemic priv-ilege. Nietzsche himself had declared that "All superior men who were irre-sistibly drawn to throw off the yoke of any kind of morality and to frame new laws had, *if they were not actually mad*, no alternative but to make themselves or pretend to be mad" (D 14).

6.   After visiting Nietzsche at the asylum in Jena one year after his collapse, Köselitz wrote the following to Overbeck on February 20, 1890: "The question of whether one would be doing Nietzsche a favor if one reawakened him to life must be left aside. . . . I have seen Nietzsche in certain conditions where it seemed to me—a terrible thought!—that he was *faking* madness, as if he were glad that it had ended *thus*. It is highly probable that he could have writ-ten his philosophy of Dionysus only as a madman—it is admittedly not yet written, although he thinks he has sketched it out at least."

Overbeck had the same impression on various occasions. His criterion regarding Nietzsche's insanity was as follows: "It came every now and then to vacillate, in that I could not help having the horrifying thought, at least momentarily—though this happened during several of the periods in which I witnessed Nietzsche's mental illness—that his madness was simulated. An impression that is fully explicable only on the basis of the experience I had in general of Nietzsche's self-maskings" (cited in Parkes 1994, 373). The hypoth-esis of the fake insanity was also shared by the philosopher Claudia Crawford. In her book *To Nietzsche: Dionysus, I Love You! Ariadne*, the author explores the possibility that Nietzsche simulated his madness as a form of "voluntary death." In section 36 of *The Twilight of the Idols*, the subversive philosopher wrote: "To die proudly when it is no longer possible to live proudly. Death freely chosen, death at the right time, brightly and cheerfully. . . . From love of *life*, one should desire a different death: free, conscious, without accident, without ambush." But Nietzsche didn't commit suicide. Instead, according to Crawford, he chose madness. "Did Nietzsche choose the act of 'madness' so that he could be both dead to induce oathtakers and yet alive for a while to see it happen?" she asks. And answers, "Madness is much more uncanny than death. Someone like Nietzsche dies and it is to be expected, but someone like Nietzsche goes 'mad' and the world continually tries to mediate such a catastrophe." She concludes: "On the eve of 1889 Nietzsche takes the actions of his voluntary death, not as a martyr, but victoriously, like Caesar, weighing all the calamitous and beneficial consequences, with the belief that it would be a historically significant death, a conquering death" (1999, 136–37).

7. By 1930, a German philologist named Erich Podach had obtained a copy from the missing records of Nietzsche's case in Jena. After sending all available records of Nietzsche's illness to several well-known doctors so as to obtain their opinions, he concluded:

> The entry "syphilitic infection" has raised more dust than necessary. There is no certain evidence of such an infection. Nor is there any sure evidence of Nietzsche's "paralysis." . . . If the problem of the diagnosis of Nietzsche's illness were to be re-opened once more, it would be necessary to investigate the accuracy of the entries relating to cases of paralysis in general in the Jena records round about the year 1889. Dr. Stutz found many cases of "paralysis" entered in the Basel records of the period, which would certainly be diagnosed as schizophrenia today. Dr. A. Kronfeld has also pointed out that the Jena records were obviously made by persons who had paralysis in mind all the time. (1931, 235–36)

It is also worth drawing attention to the fact that Lou Salomé, fearing the destruction of Nietzsche's letters and the famous Lucerne photograph after her death, made Podach the recipient of these important documents (cf. Peters 1974, 296). Continuing with the syphilis question, it is relevant to highlight that despite his assumption that Nietzsche was infected with syphilis, basing his certainty on the image of a toad provided by Nietzsche himself, it is evident that Jung interpreted Nietzsche's insanity as a form of schizophrenia; for Nietzsche was completely possessed by the unconscious contents that his ego could not integrate in a coherent manner. Jung explains:

> When different aspects of a personality become so independent of each other that they are able to manifest themselves one after the other, with no control and no inner consistency of relatedness, there is justifiable suspicion of a sort of schizophrenic condition. And that is the case with Nietzsche. Of course the disease which followed has been understood as general paralysis of the insane, which is without exception a syphilitic infection of the brain. His case was not typical, however. According to my idea, there is plenty of evidence that it was more a schizophrenic than a paralytic condition; probably both dis-

eases existed in a peculiar mix, for through the whole course of development of his disease, there were numbers of indications which
would not point to the usual diagnosis of paralysis only. He often
behaved very queerly and said very strange things, which one is
unlikely to hear from anyone with general paralysis of the insane.
(SNZ II:1319)

However, the frog and the toad were animals Zarathustra associated with
the spirit of revenge. When a "vain fool" blasphemed against the inhabitants
of the great city, Zarathustra shouted, after comparing him with a frog and a
toad, that his desire for revenge came from the fact that, as was the case with
Nietzsche himself, "nobody flattered [him] sufficiently" (Z III:7). Richard
Schain, after carefully researching the clinical records of Nietzsche's illness
and the numerous medical hypotheses surrounding his final breakdown, came
to the final conclusion that Nietzsche suffered from a schizophrenic disorder:

All the information available regarding Nietzsche's condition fits a
diagnosis of "endogenous" psychosis, that is, originating within his personality structure rather than being introduced by an outside agent.
The healthy and pathological coexistence of thought processes, the evidence of persecutory delusions, the incoherence of speech, the man-
neristic grimacing, the automatic obedience, the echolalia, the verbig-
eration, the volitional blunting, the social withdrawal, the regression to
a vegetative state are all features of schizophrenic disorder. (2001, 102)

8.   According to his biographer Janz, Nietzsche reported to the psychiatrists in
Basel that he had twice been treated for syphilitic infection while in Leipzig
(cf. 1987 IV:12). However, Richard Schain considered that there was a mis-
understanding when Nietzsche reported that he "was infected twice": the doctors, due to a frequent euphemism, assumed that he was referring to a
syphilitic infection.

Cholera broke out in Naumburg while Nietzsche was home on vacation, causing him and his mother to flee to a neighboring town. His sister told the story that Nietzsche thought he was infected on two different occasions by cholera and cured himself through drinking large
quantities of hot water. Memories of these two "infections" may have
been in his mind over twenty years later when, totally psychotic in a
Basel institution, he claimed to have been infected twice. The Basel
psychiatrists thought he meant syphilis. (2001, 14)

Regarding the diagnosis of syphilis itself, Richard Schain suggested the
following: "In 1913, the advent of the Wasserman test for syphilis forever
alter[ed] the diagnosis of this disease at all its stages. . . . It became evident

that paresis had become an overdiagnosed disorder although specific details of the extent of overdiagnosis are hard to come by. Perhaps the most telling disclosure came from Kraepelin himself who confessed that after the availability of laboratory diagnosis, the percentage of paralytics in his clinic fell from thirty percent to eight to nine percent. This was an astonishing admission from the founder of descriptive clinical psychiatry" (2001, 73).

Alice Miller considers that the popularity of this hypothesis is based on a moralizing zeal: "Historians locate the cause of this tragic ending in a venereal disease he supposedly contracted as an adolescent. The outcome is in keeping with our moral standards: the just, though delayed, punishment, in the form of a fatal disease, for having visited a prostitute. This is similar to the present attitude toward AIDS. Everything seems to turn out for the best, and hypocritical morality is restored" (1991, 77).

9. The only theme that seems absent in Nietzsche's delirium is the fourfold structure of the world or cosmos. However, he thought he had created a world characterized by a golden equilibrium: "I condone my boredom at having created a world. . . . I, together with Ariadne, have only to be the golden equilibrium of all things" (Letter to Burckhardt, postmarked Turin, January 4, 1889).

10. Bishop suggests that for Jung "the rites of Dionysus are held to be the most impressive example of the psychological process of renewal" (1995, 212–13).

11. Those closest to him began to observe signs of insanity in Nietzsche and even to predict a tragic end, several years before the appearance of his clinical case of psychosis. Thus, in a letter addressed to Franz Overbeck and dated May 24, 1878, Wagner indicated: "Anyone . . . who has been observing [Nietzsche] for several years with his psychic torments, cannot have but confirmed that a catastrophe was underway, a catastrophe long feared and not at all unexpected."

12. Similarly, in *Mysterium Coniunctionis* Jung wrote: "The extraordinary difficulty in this experience is that the Self can be distinguished only conceptually from what has always been referred to as 'God,' but not practically. Both concepts apparently rest on an identical numinous factor which is a condition of reality" (CW 14:546).

13. See Debra B. Bergoffen's essay "On Nietzsche's Moles."

14. "The schizoid person," writes Anthony Storr, "is concerned to withdraw as much as possible from other people, because he fears their destructive influence upon himself. Only by isolating himself can he preserve himself and the illusion of omnipotence. They may lead him to construct a new world order . . . a world which he has himself created, into which, if possible, no disturbing or alien factors are allowed to enter" (1993, 103–04).

J. W. Perry considered that when the "consciousness is overwhelmed by the deepest level of the psyche . . . the individual finds himself living in a psychic modality different from his surroundings. He is immersed in a myth world. He [may] feel suddenly isolated because he finds no understanding of it on the part of those around him. The fear of this overwhelmingness and of this isolation causes a wave of panic, which sends him into an acute withdrawal. His emotions no longer connect with ordinary things, but drop into concerns and titanic involvements with an entire inner world of myth and image" (1992, 8).

According to the philosopher Daniel W. Conway, Nietzsche, like Odysseus, "sought to advance the recognized frontiers of the human condition." Like the epic hero, Nietzsche longed for "an experience previously unknown to mortals: to survive the thanatonic song of the sirens" (2002, 251). However, unlike Odysseus, who, knowing his own weakness, instructed his crew to bind him to the mast while he sailed through the Sirens' realm, Nietzsche untied himself completely from the mast—i.e., from any reality outside himself—in order to "pursue a transfigurative experience" through the "reveries of sirenic intoxication" without acknowledging his "all-too-human limitations" (2002, 251). Without reason to hold him, and overwhelmed by the "world of myth and image," Nietzsche was drawn as if by a magnet toward the vertiginous nothingness represented by the bottomless abyss of the *Abgrund* of being. He painfully confessed to Overbeck in a letter sent during the summer of 1883 from Sils-Maria: "I have no support from *outside*; on the contrary, everything seems to conspire to keep me imprisoned in my abyss."

Even the animals of *Zarathustra* (instinctual side) urge the prophet to connect with life by leaving his unhealthy isolation: "Step out of your cave," they tell him. "The world awaits you like a garden. . . . Step out of your cave! All things would be your physicians" (Z III:13). The philosopher Kathleen Marie Higgins writes in this respect: "The animals' advice is the advice of Dionysian insight. Zarathustra's words and thoughts have become a painful disease because they have become detached from the unruly immediacy of life. The cure for this cannot be achieved through further thought, but it can be achieved through encountering the world in immediacy and feeling one's own vital connection with it" (1987, 154). In the end, however, Zarathustra rejected the advice of his instinctual side and instead abandoned the world to become lost in the solitary mountains.

Jung suggested that Nietzsche "suffered from an overintensity of consciousness, which is always the case if one is anachronistic, if one lives in a time when one is not meant to live, because one finds no understanding contemporaries. . . . [As a result of his isolation] the unconscious came up with all its extravertion" (SNZ I:144–45). R. D. Laing wrote in this respect: "The [schizoid] individual is frightened of the world, afraid that any impingement will be total, will be implosive, penetrative, fragmenting, and engulfing" (1990, 83). This kind of withdrawal "can be understood as an attempt to preserve a being that is precariously structured. . . . But the tragic paradox is that the more the self is defended in this way, the more it is destroyed" (ibid.), because "*the reality of the world and of the self are mutually potentiated by the direct relationship between self and other*" (ibid., 82).

15. For his part, Walter Otto points out: "The deep emotion with which [the] madness announces itself finds its expression in music and dance" (1993, 143).

16. We can evidence that in his *Zarathustra* Nietzsche begins as the teacher of the *Übermensch*, which requires a linear concept of time, but ends as the teacher

of the eternal return, which requires a cyclical concept of time. Also, while in the beginning he shows himself as an incarnation of some new Prometheus, at the end he discovers the "midnight wisdom" and Zarathustra welcomes the return of Dionysus.

17. For an in-depth study on Ananke see Hillman 1991, 5–22.

18. According to Jung the Self is "the container and organizer of all opposites" (CW 16:536). Thus the Self can be regarded as a mediator of opposites.

19. In this respect, Edinger states: "The union of opposites in the vessel of the ego is the essential feature of consciousness" (1984, 21). According to James Hillman, to accept Dionysus (conscious incorporation of the Dionysian) means "to take back into the psyche what has been put into the body, to take back centuries of misogyny, to take back into consciousness the physical, the feminine and the inferior. This is the redemption of what is called . . . 'the earth, darkness, the abysmal side of bodily man with his animal passions and instinctual nature' and . . . matter in general" (1969, 395).

20. "Psychosis" is defined by the *Critical Dictionary of Jungian Analysis* as "a personality state in which an unknown 'something' takes possession of the psyche to a greater or lesser degree and asserts its existence undeterred by logic, persuasion or will. . . . The unconscious invades, assuming control of the conscious ego, and, since the unconscious has no organized or centralized functions, the consequence is that there is psychic confusion and chaos" (Samuels, Shorter and Plaut 1986, 123).

21. When Edinger relates *sublimatio* to the extraction procedure, he quotes the following from an early alchemical text: "Go to the waters of the Nile and there you will find a stone that has a spirit (*pneuma*). Take this, divide it, thrust in your hand and draw out its heart: for its soul (*psyche*) is in its heart" (1996, 122). The author explains that psychologically the extraction of the spirit hidden in the matter "refers to the redemption of the Self from its unconscious process" (ibid., 123).

22. We can see that after Nietzsche-Zarathustra announced the death of God to the old man in Part I (Z I:2), he immediately announced the coming of the overman (Z I:3). When Nietzsche lost the connection with his personal world he also lost the "connection of the imagery with its emotional context, for the reason that the complex has become as nuclear components of the complexes" (Perry 1974, 22).

23. Nemesis is the defender of the natural law and of the norm, and with her anger she attacks hubris, bringing calamities on the man who shows this weakness.

24. Individuation, according to Nietzsche, knows one law: "measure," which demands "self-knowledge" (Apollo's precept) in order to maintain it. "The overweening pride and excess" of the Titans and barbarians are the result of the forgetting of the precepts of Apollo, "know thyself" and "nothing in excess" (BT 4).

25. As philologist, historian, poet, philosopher, psychologist, artist, educator, cultural physician, master of the eternal recurrence, immoralist, disciple of the god Dionysus, etc.

26. "Whoever speaks in primordial images speaks with a thousand voices" (Jung, CW 15:129). About the necessity of distinctiveness, Jung wrote in *Septem Sermones ad Mortuous*:

> Distinctiveness is creatura. It is distinct. Distinctiveness is its essence, and therefore it distinguishes. Therefore man discriminateth because his nature is distinctiveness. . . . If we do not distinguish ["I am every name in history"], we get beyond our own nature, away from creatura. We fall into indistinctiveness. . . . We fall into the pleroma itself and cease to be creatures. We are given over to dissolution into nothingness. This is the death of the creature. (MDR, 480)

27. Nietzsche wrote: "We do not know ourselves, we men of knowledge, and we ourselves are unknown to ourselves" (GM, *Preface*). And, possessed by Zarathustra, he spoke about the "one who was sublime": "He subdued monsters, he solved riddles: but he must still redeem his own monsters and riddles" (Z II:13).

28.
> Now—huddled up
> between two nothings,
> a question mark,
> a weary riddle
> a riddle for birds of prey . . .
> —they will surely "solve" you
> they hunger already for your "solution"
> they flutter already around you, their riddle,
> around you, you hanged one! . . .
> O Zarathustra! . . .
> Self-knower!
> Self-hangman!
> —F. Nietzsche, "Between Birds of Prey" (cited in Grundlehner, 1986, 203–5)

29. *Ecce Homo*—the words that Pontius Pilate, the Roman governor of Judea, uttered in presenting Jesus Christ to his accusers (John 19:5): "Behold that man." The title shows once more Nietzsche's identification with the figure of Christ. In relation to his autobiographical book, Nietzsche wrote to von Salis (November 14, 1888): "This *Homo*, you will understand, is myself, including the *Ecce*."

30. "I am a doppelgänger," wrote Nietzsche in *Ecce Homo* (EH II:3).

31. According to R. D. Laing, when an extremely schizoid individual feels the urgency "to escape from its shut-upness, to end the pretense, to be honest, to reveal and declare and let itself be known without equivocation, one may be witness to the onset of an acute psychosis" (1990, 147).

32. In the preface to *Ecce Homo*, Nietzsche wrote: "It was not in vain that I

buried my forty-fourth year today: I had the right to bury it—what was life in it is saved, is immortal."

33.

> Thus I myself once sank
> from my craze for truth
> from my daytime longings
> weary of the day, sick from the light
> sank downward, down toward evening, toward shadows
> burned and parched
> by one truth
> do you still remember, do you still, hot heart
> how you thirsted then?
> *let me be banished*
> *from all truth*
> *Only* fool! *Only* poet! (PN 191)

34. Inspired by his search for the primal being in a state of purity, Nietzsche was forced, first of all, to take on the task of demolishing the moral values so as to tear off the masks that cover this primal being: "To translate man back into nature . . . the basic text of *homo natura* must again be recognized" (BGE 229). In a late preface added to his *Daybreak*, Nietzsche wrote:

> In this book you will discover a "subterranean man" at work, one who tunnels and mines and undermines. You will see him—presupposing you have eyes capable of seeing this work in the depths—going forward slowly, cautiously, gently inexorable, without betraying very much of the distress which any protracted deprivation of light and air must entail; you might even call him contented, working there in the dark. . . . He who proceeds on his own path in this fashion encounters no one. . . . No one comes along to help him. . . . At that time I undertook something not everyone may undertake: I descended into the depths, I tunneled into the foundation.

35. The "free spirit" proposed by Nietzsche searches to "think without *arkhé* and act without *télos*," in order to "throw himself to the adventure to experiment with all the values" (Cragnolini 1998, 119). Nonetheless, Nietzsche knew that the free spirit is an unreachable ideal, only a fiction necessary to entertain a solitary and godless wanderer (HATH: P).

36. "There is no greater danger than that the *spoken language* will awaken the theoretical man in us and thereby heave us over into the other, nonmythical sphere; so that in the end we should not through the employment of words have understood more clearly what has taken place before us, but, on the contrary, have failed to understand it at all. That is why [I have] forced language

back to a primordial state in which it hardly thinks in concepts and in which it is itself still poetry, image, and feeling" (UM IV: 9).

Nietzsche cast the strongest doubt on language itself, particularly when it needs to express the irrational and chaotic world of Dionysian impulses. In his early essay "On the Truth and Lies in a Nonmoral Sense" he wrote: "The word is not made for intuitions: man is silent when he sees them, or he talks in forbidden metaphors in a very distorted grammar in order to creatively respond to the powerful, present intuition at least by destroying and disregarding the old tower of concepts." Nietzsche wished to address the world through pathos rather than logos, he wanted to arouse in his readers feelings and emotions while communicating "an inward tension of pathos" (EH 3:4). "Regarding my *Zarathustra*, for example," Nietzsche explained, "I do not allow that anyone knows that book who has not at some time been profoundly wounded and at some time profoundly delighted by every word in it: for only then may he enjoy the privilege of reverentially sharing in the halcyon element out of which that book was born" (GM P:8).

37. Nietzsche's anticipation of the discoveries of depth psychology and his influence on this discipline have been researched by Henri L. Ellenberger in *The Discovery of the Unconscious: The History and Evolution of Dynamic Psychiatry* (New York: Basic Books, 1970); Didier Anzieu in *Freud's Self-Analysis* (London: The Hogarth Press, 1986); Walter Kaufmann in *Nietzsche: Philosopher, Psychologist, Antichrist* (Princeton, NJ: Princeton University Press, 1950); Daniel Chapelle in *Nietzsche and Psychoanalysis* (New York: State University of New York Press, 1993); Paul-Laurent Assoun in *Freud et Nietzsche* (Paris: Presses Universitaires de France, 1980); Ronald Lehrer in *Nietzsche's Presence in Freud's Life and Thought* (Albany, NY: State University of New York Press, 1995); Paul Bishop in *The Dionysian Self: C. G. Jung's Reception of Friedrich Nietzsche* (Berlin: Walter de Gruyter, 1995); Graham Parkes in *Composing the Soul: Reaches of Nietzsche's Psychology* (Chicago and London: University of Chicago Press, 1994); and in *Nietzsche and Depth Psychology* (New York: State University of New York Press, 1999, edited by J. Golomb, W. Santaniello, and R. Lehrer); among others. It should be kept in mind that Nietzsche had anticipated the important discoveries of depth psychology, which would be developed in subsequent decades by Freud, Adler, and Jung. Thus Ellenberger affirms that "Nietzsche may be considered the common source of Freud, Adler, and Jung" (1970, 276). Paul Bishop, in his work *The Dionysian Self: C. G. Jung's Reception of Friedrich Nietzsche*, suggests that "Jung's intellectual development can be read in detail as a reception of Nietzsche's thinking" (1995, 20). In that same work, the author includes the recognition afforded by other scholars to Nietzsche's contributions in the field of psychology (cf. ibid., 19).

38. "If we are prepared to describe the unitary reality [the Dionysian "Primordial One"] as the real, [Nietzsche as a] creative man [was] endowed by nature with a greater proximity to the wholeness of reality—though this may perfectly well go hand in hand with an inferior 'sense of reality' in that term by our conscious

minds, which often identify reality with the outside world" (Neumann 1989, 101). Nietzsche realized a Hegelian inversion: for him the "Real is not the rational."

39. An example is the review written by Josef Victor Widmann, editor of *Der Bund*, and reported by Nietzsche to Malwida von Meysenbug (September 24, 1886): "Heading: Nietzsche's Dangerous Book. The sticks of dynamite used for the building of the Gotthard Tunnel were marked by a black flag, indicating mortal danger. Exclusively in this sense do we speak of the new book by the philosopher Nietzsche as a dangerous book. . . .? There is dynamite here!'" (see also 3:1). Jung, on his part, wrote that Nietzsche's contemporaries "thought that *Zarathustra* was the work of a madman. . . . And at the same time they were frightened because they felt an amazing amount of truth in what he said" (SNZ II:1358–59). However, even Jung considered *Zarathustra* a dangerous book that "should not have been published, but should have been worked over and carefully concealed . . . because of the evil or morbid influence such a book can have" (SNZ I:483). Nietzsche tried to justify the attacks of his contemporaries by saying that "Ultimately, nobody can get more out of things, including books, than he already knows. For what one lacks access to from experience one will have no ear for" (EH 3:1).

40. Jung realized that great artists are almost always exceptional individuals for whom normal psychological development may not apply. Nietzsche's *Zarathustra* lent Jung support for this observation (cf. CW 15:111).

41. The other mode of creative expression that Neumann described is the result of a preponderance of the father archetype: "The dominance of the father-archetype, in complete contrast to that of the mother, invariably entails an accentuation of all those aspects of the material that are bound up with the affirmation and development of the conscious mind. In this sense patriarchal art is a celebration of the principle of light and of the hero, [it is a] glorification of the highest values of the cultural canon" (1989, 171). As is evident throughout this investigation, the patriarchal type of creativity was alien to Nietzsche's nature. Neumann adds: "If the great danger of the matriarchal principle is to be found in quivering chaos, the great danger of the patriarchal principle, bound up as it is by its very nature with the ethos and will of the conscious mind and with law, order, and strict form, is to be found in rigidity" (ibid.). Neumann also made a distinction between creation and madness: "When we call a man creative as opposed to pathological, we are thinking of a person who, in spite of [his] unusual psychological constellation and in spite of his difficulties in making a 'collective' adaptation to the world, produces an achievement or a work that is an expression of his own self-realization and is at the same time significant for the human species as a whole. It is a matter of indifference whether the contemporary representatives of the cultural canon either fail to grasp or deny the significance of a work of this kind" (1979, 207).

42. Or, in Freudian terms, the raw and chaotic materials that arise by the primary process must be given form through the secondary process characteristic of ego-activity in order to become communicable or aesthetic.

43. Correspondence with his closest friends (Baron Seydlitz, Krug, Malwida von Meysenbug) was brusquely interrupted, in particular because of the publication of his polemic work *The Case of Wagner* (see letter to Brandes, dated October 20, 1888).

44. Nietzsche seemed conscious of his near decline when he ended his philosophical career with an autobiographical book, *Ecce Homo*, in which he described himself as "a follower of the philosopher Dionysus." In this last work, as a kind of farewell, he was eager to let the world know who he really was and what each of his writings signified for him. As *Nietzsche contra Wagner* consists of a short selection of passages extracted from his 1878–1887 published works, *Ecce Homo* can be considered his last original work. Lesley Chamberlain considers it his "auto-obituary" (1996, 159).

45. "I am hard at work . . . and the outlines of an unquestionably immense task before me are emerging more and more clearly from the mists. . . . I know that I cannot escape by going backward or to the right or to the left; I have no *choice*" (Letter to Overbeck February 3, 1888). It is worth highlighting that Jung defines the anima as a demon: "Soul is the life-giving daemon who plays his elfin game and is above human existence" (CW 9 I:56).

46. Nietzsche dated a loose folio, which he later added to *The Antichrist*, as follows: "Given on the day of salvation, on the first day of year one (September 30, 1888 of the false chronology)." And in a letter dated December 1888, Nietzsche wrote to Brandes: "We have just entered the great politics, even very great. . . . I am preparing an event that will probably break history in two parts, so that a new calendar will be needed, where the year 1888 will be the year 1."

47. Most of these, which provided Jung with a symbolic representation of the introversion of the libido, were written in the fall of 1884, and were published just a few days before his mental breakdown. In 1899, Nietzsche wrote the following motto in his manuscript of the *Dithyrambs of Dionysus*: "These are the songs of Zarathustra which he sang to himself to endure his ultimate loneliness."

48. Compiled by his sister posthumously under the title *Will to Power*.

49. "It is extremely regrettable . . . from the standpoint of psychology," lamented Jung, "that the fragmentary writings . . . which were found in Turin after the onset of [Nietzsche's] malady should have met with destruction in deference to moral and aesthetic scruples" (CW 6:242).

50. It is worth highlighting that in the letters sent in his last months of lucid life, Nietzsche confessed to having experienced numerous phenomena of "meaningful coincidences," which seems to indicate a lowering of the level of consciousness or *abaissement du niveau mental* (see letters to his mother dated November 3, 1888; to Georg Brandes on November 20, 1888; to August Strindberg on December 7, 1888; and to Franz Overbeck on Christmas, 1888). The danger of the *abaissement du niveau mental* lies in the possibility for the emergence of latent psychotic tendencies.

51. J. W. Perry suggests that "because of an activation of the unconscious and a

collapse of the ego, consciousness is overwhelmed by the deepest levels of the psyche, and the individual finds himself living in a psychic modality quite different from his surroundings. He is immersed in a myth world. He feels suddenly isolated because he finds no understanding of it on the part of those around him. The fear of this overwhelmingness and of this isolation causes a wave of panic, which sends him into an acute withdrawal. His emotions no longer connect with ordinary things, but drop into concerns and titanic involvements with an entire inner world of myth and image" (1974, 8).

52. "The descent to Avernus presents no difficulty; Pluto's door is open night and day. But to return, and view the cheerful skies, in this task a mighty labor lies."

53. "The nocturnal domination of the . . . Night-Mother is the time of mental darkness, of gentle madness, and of the intoxicated slumber in which the ego goes down, while the other, visionary, mythical ego that creates the poetry comes into view. Such an overwhelming power on the part of the Great Mother, which appears psychologically in the form of the overmastering superiority of the archetypal mythical, archaic world, is invariably associated with an immature ego that has not achieved its complete masculinity—with a 'youthful,' juvenile ego, in fact. The tragic conflicts that are played out between the 'Great Mother' and her 'youthful son,' his impotence in relation to her, his vain resistance to incest with the Mother, his attempts to liberate himself as a 'struggler' in the secret society of the males, and his final downfall in addiction, madness, and self-destruction are—both in myth and in the psychic reality of mankind—typical expressions of the inferiority of the masculine vis-à-vis the matriarchal" (Neumann 1979, 196–97).

54. Nietzsche showed great sensibility and difficulty in tolerating rejection. Rejection created in him a sense of void, in which he became immersed. His words never found any echo: there were no friends or adversaries. Nobody listened to him because he was completely alone. This was the real tragedy of Nietzsche's life. Nietzsche's plunge into the unconscious was mostly generated by the lack of recognition from his contemporaries. Unluckily for this new prophet, his contemporaries were not ready to digest his message: "I have come too early . . . my time is not yet" (CS 125), the madman shouted, to the astonishment of his listeners. In his writings solipsism contracts to its ultimate, leaving Nietzsche both priest and idol of his own Dionysian cult. Jung offered an explanation in this regard:

> [Nietzsche] was moved by the childish hope of finding people who would be able to share his ecstasies and could grasp his "transvaluation of all values." But he found only educated Philistines—tragicomically, he was one himself. Like the rest of them, he did not understand himself when he fell head first into the unutterable mystery and wanted to sing its praises to the dull, godforsaken masses. That was the reason for the bombastic language, the piling up of metaphors, the hymnlike raptures—all a vain attempt to catch the ear of a world which had sold its soul for a mass of disconnected facts. . . . He did not know his way

about in this world and was a like a man possessed, one who could be handled only with the utmost caution. (MDR 103)

In the opinion of the Spanish philosopher María Zambrano, Nietzsche's inability to bequeath his message to "disciples" was the cause of his mental deterioration:

Nietzsche lived and consumed his freedom, far from impassability, only humanly. The natural thing would have been for him to accept the tragic freedom of a Kierkegaard or Unamuno. But the tragedy of free-dom, or freedom lived tragically, requires *someone* to whom to offer it. Every tragedy is a sacrifice; its protagonist needs someone to whom he can offer his agony. And in this radical solitude, before which the soli-tude of the Cartesian consciousness disappears, Nietzsche drained the tragedy of human liberty. He had no one to whom to offer his sacrifice. And that is where his destruction began. (1993, 169)

Zambrano's conclusion finds echo in the following observation of J. W. Perry: when an individual experiences hurtful feelings of rejection,

a change is initiated. The psychic energy, the libido, is attracted to the archetypal level of the psyche, where a process of very high energy-charge starts moving, reorganizing the central archetype and hence reconstituting the self-image. It appears that this recession of the libido leaves the higher levels of the psyche stripped of the usual energy-charge, and hence in a state of disorganization. Both the ego-consciousness and the complexes are left in a state of fragmentation. (1992, 27)

It seems that when Nietzsche wrote in his *Zarathustra* that he did not want disciples and in *Ecce Homo* that he was not looking for "believers," he was just emulating La Fontaine's fable of "The Fox and the Grapes." In his *Zarathustra* he made evident his yearning for pupils who could embark with him on his voyage through terrible seas and be able to accept his new worldview: "To you, the bold searchers, researchers, and whoever embarks with cunning sails on terrible seas—to you, drunk with riddles, glad of the twilight, whose soul flutes lure astray to every whirlpool, because you do not want to grope along a thread with cowardly hand; and where you can *guess*, you hate to *deduce*—to you alone I tell the riddle that I *saw*, the vision of the loneliest" (Z III:2.1). And in several letters he made the same claim: "I need disciples, *while I am still alive*, and if the books that I have written so far are not effective as fish-ing hooks, then they have 'missed their calling' " (Letter to Overbeck, November 1884). Again: "My yearning for pupils and heirs makes me impa-tient now and then and even seems to have led me to do some foolish things during the last years" (Letter to Overbeck, August 1885). Concerning his *Zarathustra*, Nietzsche remarked: "Not to hear a sound of an answer after such an appeal from my innermost soul, that is a *terrible* experience. . . . It lifted me out of all bonds with living men" (Letter to Overbeck, June 1887). *Ecce Homo* is practically a diatribe against his contemporaries for the indifference shown when they received his magnum opus: "I have a duty against my habits, even more the pride of the instincts, revolt at bottom—namely to say: *Hear me!*" (EH P:1). Zarathustra even manifested a vengeful spirit by wishing to harm those who refused to accept his wisdom:

> They received from me, but do I touch their souls? . . . a hunger grows out of my beauty: I should like to hurt those for whom I shine; I should like to rob those to whom I give; thus do I hunger for malice. To withdraw my hand when the other hand already reaches out to it; to linger like the waterfall, which lingers even while it plunges: thus I hunger for malice. Such revenge my fullness plots: such spite wells up out of my loneliness. (Z II:9)

And in 1887 he wrote to Overbeck: "It *hurts* frightfully that in these fifteen years not one single person has 'discovered' me, has needed me, has loved me."

Only two men showed interest in him as a thinker: Georg Brandes (Morris Cohen, 1842–1927), who was the first scholar who presented Nietzsche in the academic milieu. Brandes gave two public lectures on Nietzsche's philosophy at Copenhagen University. However, Nietzsche's sister deplored his contact with the Jewish scholar: "[My sister] wrote me with the utmost scorn [saying] what a scum I sought for company—Jews, who have been around licking all the plates, like Georg Brandes" (Letter to Overbeck, Christmas 1888). The other man was the Swedish dramatist August Strindberg (1948–1912), with whom Nietzsche began a correspondence through Brandes. Strindberg, born in Stockholm, wrote numerous novels, plays, poems, and over seven thousand letters. Among his most important works are *Fräulein Julie*, *The Road to Damascus*, *Master Olof*, and *Inferno Legends*. In the 1890s he dedicated himself to the study of alchemy, occultism, and religion. A misogynist who shared Nietzsche's antifeminist views and experienced continuous paranoid crises, Strindberg was a polemic character until the end of his days. I am in concordance with the French philosopher Pierre Klossowski, who suggested that the appearance of Strindberg in Nietzsche's life brought about a worsening of his already precarious mental condition. Contact was established barely a few weeks prior to his total breakdown:

> For the first time Nietzsche could dialogue (if only in letters) with an equal, a *genius* whose own temporary delirium had had the same scope as Nietzsche's—now embryonic but soon to become definitive. Strindberg not only provided Nietzsche with evidence, along with Brandes's lectures, of the growing recognition of his authority; even better, Strindberg—unwittingly, it is true—confirmed Nietzsche in his Turinesque vision of the world, and thereby helped prepare for Nietzsche's own transfiguration into an absolutely fabulous region. (1997, 226)

In the correspondence they exchanged during the brief period from November 1888 to January 1889, we can see how both assign themselves grandiose titles such as "Nietzsche-Caesar" and "The Crucified," on Nietzsche's part; as for Strindberg, he was wont to sign "Strindberg (*Deus optimus maximus*)." Similarly, in what appears to be a euphoric state, Strindberg induces the idea of madness in a letter sent in early January 1889: *"Thelo, Thelo manenai"* (I want, I want to be mad) and *"Interdum juvat insanire!"* (Meanwhile, let us rejoice in our madness).

55. Nietzsche seems to have lost track of his age: he was forty-three years old when he wrote this letter. At forty-five he was already "eccentric," "pathological," "psychiatric."

56. J. W. Perry suggests: "the schizophrenic person . . . becomes highly suggestible and identifies with any powerful impact from inside and outside. So, when society says to him, 'You're too different, a menace, sick, . . . he feels correspondingly crazy and reprehensible, dangerous and unmanageable. Hence, he reflects like a mirror what is expected of him" (1974, 110).

57. January 3 was the date established by Eric Podach; however, Karl Strecker, author of *Nietzsche und Strindberg* (1921), visited Turin in 1913 and spoke to some of the people who had known Nietzsche. They indicated that the incident with the horse had occurred several days before the collapse. "Otto tells us," writes the philosopher Claudia Crawford, "that the winter epiphany of the god Dionysus was celebrated on the Island of Andros on the Nones of January 5. Therefore, 'it is precisely in winter, when the sun gets ready to start on its new course, that Dionysus makes his most tumultuous entry.' It is no coincidence that Nietzsche/Dionysus plays out his Dionysian 'madness' and comedy of spring and eternal renewal at the beginning of January" (1999, 304).

58. In a letter sent to Meta von Salis on December 29, 1888, Nietzsche again identified himself with a beast. Lesley Chamberlain wrote about Nietzsche's relation with the animal:

> [Nietzsche cultivated] the animal in himself as much as the *Übermensch* and this is, I believe, one reason why he liked to refer to himself as "a beast." In July he had spoken of himself to Malwida as an animal who was constantly being hurt and who received no human word. He had pity for himself as an animal, for by the mark of illness he was one cast out of civilization and its comforts, though a creature of sensitivity and feeling. (1996, 207)

59. Nietzsche wrote: "The animal has as much a right as any human being; let it run about freely. And you, my dear fellow man, are also still an animal in spite of everything" (GS 77).

60. He provided the following description of how Nietzsche looked to him when he first saw him: "I saw Nietzsche in a sofa corner, crouched down and reading—as it turned out, the last proof of *N[ietzsche] contra Wagner*—he looked horribly decrepit; recognizing me, he threw himself upon me and embraced

me strongly, breaking into a torrent of tears, then sinking back onto the sofa. I too could hardly stand upright from the shock. Had he at this moment recognized the abyss opening in front of him or in which he was actually plunged? In any case, the moment did not return. . . . Scarcely had he started moaning and quivering again when he was given some bromine water. . . . In a moment, he was calm again and smiling, he began to speak of the great reception that was prepared for the evening. So he was in the grip of delusional ideas which never left while I was with him. He broke forth into loud singing and frenzied piano playing, fragments out of the mental world in which he had been recently living and interspersed with indescribably uttered expressions, sublime, wonderfully insightful and unspeakably horrible things about himself as the successor to a dead God, all punctuated by chords from the piano after which convulsions and outbursts of unspeakable suffering followed . . . in general, they were outweighed by the profession of his vocation to be the comic character of the new eternity, although he, the incomparable master of expression, was incapable of expressing the rapture of his happiness other than with trivial expressions or comical dancing and jumping" (cited in Janz 1987, IV:32–3).

61. "The Venetian Song," a Dionysian mode of expression.

Lately I stood at the bridge
In the brown night
From far off came a song
As of golden droplets it welled
Over the quivering surface
Gondolas, lights, music
Drunken it swam out into the dusk. . . .
My soul, a stringed instrument
Sang to itself, invisibly touched
A secret barcarole
Quivering with colorful bliss
Did anyone listen to it?

At the end of the third part of *Zarathustra* we can read the following words uttered by the hermit sage when he "jumped with both feet into golden-emerald delight": "Throw yourself around, out, back, you who are light! Sing! Speak no more! Are not the words made for the grave and heavy? Are not all words lies to those who are light? Sing! Speak no more!" (Z III:16.7).

62. Nietzsche was accompanied by his mother when he was transferred from Basel to Jena. During the first part of the trip he was quiet: he read newspapers and ate rolls. However, during the second part of the trip he fell into a rage directed against his mother. She had to complete the trip in another compartment (cf. Ross 1994, 824).

63. Nietzsche, as Schopenhauer, considered "absolute music" (melody without

words) to be a direct expression of the Dionysian essence (abysmal passions). He described music as "an unconscious force of a natural instinct" (see EH: BT 4). His musical legacy, presented for the first time in 1976 by Curt Paul Janz, consists of seventy-four compositions at different levels of completion.

64. Following the disappearance of her husband, Elisabeth divided her time between commercial activities in South America and proselytism in her native land. "She tried to make a national hero of her husband, but in vain," writes Walter Kaufmann. "She only provoked more and more attacks from disillusioned colonists who considered themselves swindled and ruined by the Försters. Then, suddenly, she realized that her brother's star had meanwhile begun its steep ascent—and Frau Förster turned into Elisabeth Förster-Nietzsche, became her brother's chief apostle, and began to fashion the Nietzsche legend" (1974, 4). After violently confronting her mother and threatening to take her to court alleging incompetence, Elisabeth was able to convince her to cede to her all rights to the literary inheritance of the delirious brother. Thus, to Nietzsche's misfortune, Elisabeth became his legal guardian. "I have a terrible fear," Nietzsche confessed in *Ecce Homo*, "that one day I will be pronounced *holy*: you will guess why I publish this book *before*; it shall prevent people from doing mischief of me" (EH IV:1). The irony of fate was that his sister, the person closest to him, was the one who hurt him most regarding his fear of the inappropriate use that could be made of his philosophy. She was the one responsible for Nietzsche's name being used to convoke, even today, barbaric ghosts. She drew his name into the world of Nationalist Socialist ideology. In 1934, encouraged by Elisabeth, Hitler paid three visits to the Nietzsche Archive located in the "Villa Silberblick" in Weimar and proclaimed it to be a "center of National-Socialist ideology." Elisabeth was likewise responsible for the delay in the publication of *Ecce Homo*, in view of the fact that this work contained explicit repudiation of many of the ideas attributed to Nietzsche which continued to be associated with him even in the mid-twentieth century. She also treacherously manipulated Nietzsche's *Nachlass*. And, not content with this, and against her brother's explicit wish, she tried to transform his image of a demented man into that of a "holy" prophet. To achieve this purpose, Elisabeth turned Nietzsche's home into a place of pilgrimage and dressed the inhabitant of the world of darkness in a white robe so that all visitors could contemplate this new prophet face to face (see Peters 1977).

65. Elisabeth declared that the last word pronounced by Nietzsche was her name (cf. Förster-Nietzsche 1912, 410). Hayden suggests that "there is rumor that Elisabeth arranged to have her brother's gravestone moved so that it would be over her own grave" (1999, 309).

Appendix A

1. It became the third part of *Human, All Too Human* in 1880. The three parts were published together in 1886.

BIBLIOGRAPHY

Abraham, T. 1996. *El último oficio de Nietzsche y la polémica sobre El Nacimiento de la Tragedia.* Buenos Aires: Editorial Sudamericana.

Andreas-Salomé, L. 1991. *Looking back memoirs.* Ed. B. Mitchell. New York: Paragon House.

Anzieu, D. 1986. *Freud's self-analysis.* London: The Hogarth Press.

Bachelard, G. 1968. *The psychoanalysis of fire.* Tr. A. C. M. Ross. Boston: Beacon Press.

———. 1997. *El aire y los sueños.* México: Fondo de Cultura Económica.

Bergoffen, D. B. 2004. On Nietzsche's moles. In *A Nietzschean bestiary: becoming animal beyond docile and brutal.* Ed. C. D. and R. R. Acampora. Lanham, Boulder, New York, Toronto, and Oxford: Rowman and Littlefield Publishers, Inc.

Binion, R. 1968. *Frau Lou: Nietzsche's wayward disciple.* Princeton: Princeton University Press.

Bishop, P. 1995. The Dionysian self: C. G. Jung's reception of Friedrich Nietzsche. Berlin: Walter de Gruyter.

Blanchot, M. 1998. The limits of experience. In *The new Nietzsche.* Ed. D. B. Allison. Cambridge, MA: MIT Press.

Bloss, P. 1985. *Son and father.* New York: Free Press.

Borchmeyer, D. 1992. Wagner and Nietzsche. In *Wagner handbook.* Ed. U. Müller, tr. J. Deathridge. Cambridge, MA: Harvard University Press.

Breuilly, J., ed. 2001. *Nineteenth-century Germany: politics, culture and society 1780–1918.* London: Edward Arnold (Publishers) Ltd.

Brobjer, T. 2000. Nietzsche's atheism. In *Nietzsche and the divine.* Ed. J. Lippitt and J. Urpeth. Manchester: Clinamen Press Ltd.

Campbell, J. 1968. *The hero with a thousand faces.* Princeton: Princeton University Press.

Cardew, A. 2004. The dioscuri: Nietzsche and Rohde. In *Nietzsche and antiquity: his reaction and response to the classical tradition.* Ed. P. Bishop. New York: Camden House.

Cate, C. 2002. *Friedrich Nietzsche.* London: Hutchinson.

Chamberlain, L. 1998. *Nietzsche in Turin.* New York: Picador.

Clegg, J. S. 2001. Life in the shadow of Christ: Nietzsche on *pistis* versus *gnosis*. In *Nietzsche and the gods*. Ed. W. Santaniello. New York: State University of New York Press.

Cocks, G., and Crosby, T. L., eds. 1987. *Readings in the method of psychology, psychoanalysis and history.* New Haven and London: Yale University Press.

Colli, G. 1988. *Después de Nietzsche.* Barcelona: Editorial Anagrama.

Collins, A. 1994. *Fatherson: a self psychology of the archetypal masculine.* Wilmette, IL: Chiron Publications.

Conforti, M. 1999. *Fate, form and field: patterns in mind, nature and psyche.* Woodstock: Spring Publications, Inc.

Conway, D. W. 2002. *Nietzsche's dangerous game: philosophy in the twilight of the idols.* Cambridge, UK: Cambridge University Press.

Corbin, H. L. 1964. *L'imagination symbolique.* Paris: P.U.F.

Cowan, L. 1997. *Masochism: a Jungian view.* Woodstock: Spring Publications, Inc.

Cragnolini, M. B. 1998. *Nietzsche, camino y demora.* 2nd ed. Buenos Aires: Editorial Biblos.

Crawford, C. 1999. Nietzsche's psychology and rhetoric of world redemption: Dionysus versus the Crucified. In *Nietzsche and depth psychology.* Ed. J. Golom, W. Santaniello, and R. Lehrer. Albany: State University of New York Press.

Deleuze, G. 1983. *Nietzsche and philosophy.* Tr. H. Tomlinson. New York: Columbia University Press.

———. 1988. *Sobre la diferencia y la repetición.* Madrid: Jicar.

———. 1993. *Nietzsche y la filosofía.* 3rd ed. Barcelona: Editorial Anagrama.

———.1994. *La lógica del sentido.* Barcelona: Planeta-Agostini.

Demause, L. 1982. *Foundations of psychohistory.* New York: Creative Roots Pub.

Derrida, J. 1979. *Spurs: Nietzsche's styles.* Tr. B. Harlow. Chicago and London: The University of Chicago Press.

Diamond, S. 1996. *Anger, madness and the daimonic.* Albany: State University of New York Press.

Diethe, C. 1999. *Historical dictionary of Nietzscheanism.* Lanham, MD: Scarecrow Press, Inc.

Dodds, E. R. 1984. *The Greeks and the irrational.* California: University of California Press.

Edinger, E. F. 1983. *The creation of consciousness: Jung's myth for modern man.* Toronto: Inner City Books.

———. 1986. *The Bible and the psyche: individuation symbolism in the Old Testament.* Toronto: Inner City Books.

———. 1987. *The Christian archetype: a Jungian commentary on the life of Christ.* Toronto: Inner City Books.

———. 1990. *Goethe's Faust: notes for a Jungian commentary.* Toronto: Inner City Books.

———. 1992. *Ego and archetype: individuation and the religious function of the psyche.* Boston: Shambhala Publications.

———.1994. *The eternal drama: the inner meaning of Greek mythology.* Boston: Shambhala Publications.

———. 1995. *The mysterium lectures*. Ed. J. D. Blackmer. Toronto: Inner City Books.

———. 1996. *Anatomy of the psyche*. 7th ed. Chicago and La Salle: Open Court.

———. 1999. *Archetype of the apocalypse*. Chicago and La Salle: Open Court.

Elder, G. R. 1996. *The body: an encyclopedia of archetypal symbolism*. Boston: Shambhala Publications.

Eliade, M. 1970. *Shamanism: archaic techniques of ecstasy*. Princeton: Princeton University Press.

———. 1991. *The myth of the eternal return*. Princeton: Princeton University Press (Bollingen Series XLVI).

Ellenberger, H. F. 1970. *The discovery of the unconscious: the history and evolution of dynamic psychiatry*. New York: Basic Books.

Elms, A. C. 1994. *Uncovering lives: the uneasy alliance of biography and psychology*. New York and Oxford: Oxford University Press.

Erikson, E. 1964. *Insight and responsibility: lectures on the ethical implications of psychoanalytic insight*. New York: W. W. Norton & Company.

Farrell Krell, D. 1986. *Postponements: woman, sensuality and death in Nietzsche*. Bloomington: Indiana University Press.

———. 1996. *Infectious Nietzsche*. Bloomington: Indiana University Press.

Fierz-David, L. 1993. *Women's Dionysian initiation: the villa of mysteries in Pompeii*. Dallas: Spring Publications.

Fordham, M. 1958. *The objective psyche*. London: Routledge and Kegan Paul.

Förster-Nietzsche, E. 1912. *The life of Nietzsche*, 2 vols. Tr. A. M. Ludovici. New York: Sturgis and Walton Company.

Foucault, M. 1986. Dreams, imagination, and existence. In *Review of existential psychology and psychiatry* 11:1.

Fraser, G. 2002. *Redeeming Nietzsche: on the piety of unbelief*. London and New York: Routledge.

Freud, E. L., ed. 1970. *The letters of Sigmund Freud and Arnold Zweig*. Tr. E. and W. Robson-Scott. New York: Harcourt, Brace and World, Inc.

Freud, S. 1953. Mourning and melancholy. In *Collected papers*, Vol. 4. Ed. E. Jones, tr. J. Riviere. 7th printing. London: Hogarth Press and The Institute of Psycho-Analysis.

———. 1989. Femininity. In *New introductory lectures on psycho-analysis*. Ed. and tr. J. Strachey. New York and London: W. W. Norton & Company.

———. 1989. The question of a weltanschauung. In *New introductory lectures on psycho-analysis*. Ed. and tr. J. Strachey. New York and London: W. W. Norton & Company.

———. 1989b. Acciones obsesivas y prácticas religiosas in *Sigmund Freud: obras completas*, Vol. 9. Buenos Aires: Amorrortu Editores.

———. 1994. *The Freud journal of Lou Andreas Salomé*. New York: Basic Books, Inc.

Freud, D., and Jung, C. G. (1974). *The Freud/Jung letters: the correspondence between Sigmund Freud and C. G. Jung*. Ed. W. McGuire, tr. R. Manheim and R. F. C. Hull. Princeton: Princeton University Press.

Frey-Rohn, L. 1988. *Friedrich Nietzsche: a psychological approach to his life and work.* Tr. G. Massey, ed. L. Fischli and R. Hinshaw. Zürich: Daimon Verlag.

Gad, I. 1994. *Tarot and individuation.* York Beach, ME: Nicolas-Hays, Inc.

———. 1996. The couple in fairy tales: when father's daughter meets mother's son. In *Psyche's stories: modern Jungian interpretations of fairy tales.* Ed. M. Stein and L. Corbett. Wilmette, IL: Chiron Publications.

Geer, G. 1996. The white snake. In *Psyche's stories*, Vol. 2. Ed. M. Stein and L. Corbett. Wilmette, IL: Chiron Publications.

Gordon, R. 1995. *Bridges: psychic structures, functions, and processes.* New Brunswick and London: Transaction Publishers.

———. 2000. *Dying and creating.* London: Karnac Books.

Goux, J. J. 1993. *Oedipus, philosopher.* Tr. C. Porter. Stanford: Stanford University Press.

Grundlehner, P. 1986. *The poetry of Friedrich Nietzsche.* New York: Oxford University Press, Inc.

Guettel Cole, S. 1993. Dionysus and the dead. In *Masks of Dionysus.* Ed. Y. H. Carpenter and C. A. Faraone. Ithaca and London: Cornell University Press.

Guggenbühl-Craig, A. 1977. *Marriage—dead or alive.* Zurich: Spring Publications.

Halévy, D. 2000. *Vida de Nietzsche.* Buenos Aires: Emecé Editores, S.A.

Hall, N. 1980. *The moon and the virgin: reflections on the archetypal feminine.* New York: Harper and Row.

Harding, E. 1963. *Psychic energy: its source and its transformation.* New York: Pantheon Books.

———. 1965. *The parental image: its injury and reconstruction.* New York: G. P. Putnam's Sons for the C. G. Jung Foundation for Analytical Psychology.

———. 1976. *Women's mysteries.* New York: Harper Colophon Books. Harper and Row.

Hatab, L. J. 2005. *Nietzsche's life sentence: coming to terms with eternal recurrence.* New York and London: Routledge.

Hayden, D. 1999. Nietzsche's secrets. In *Nietzsche and depth psychology.* Ed. J. Golomb, W. Santaniello, and R. Lehrer. Albany: State University of New York Press.

Heller, E. 1976. *The poet's self and the poem.* London: The Athelone Press, University of London.

———.1988. *The importance of Nietzsche: ten essays.* Chicago: The University of Chicago Press.

Henderson, J. L. 1967. *Thresholds of initiation.* Middleton, CT: Wesleyan University Press.

———. 1990. *Shadow and self: selected papers in analytical psychology.* Wilmette, IL: Chiron Publications.

———, and Sherwood, D. N. 2003. *Transformation of the psyche: the symbolic alchemy of the splendor solis.* Hove and New York: Brunner-Routledge.

Henrich, A. 1996. He has a god in him. In *Masks of Dionysus.* Ed. T. H. Carpenter and C. A. Faraone. 2nd printing. Ithaca and London: Cornell University Press.

Higgins, K. M. 1987. *Nietzsche's Zarathustra.* Philadelphia: Temple University Press.

———. 2004. Nietzsche and the mystery of the ass. In *A Nietzschean bestiary: becoming animal beyond docile and brutal.* Ed. C. D. and R. R. Acampora. Lanham, Boulder, New York, Toronto, and Oxford: Rowman and Littlefield Publishers, Inc.

Hillman, J. 1969. First Adam, then Eve. In *Eranos-Jahrbuch,* 38, 349–403.

———. 1978. *The myth of analysis: three essays in archetypal psychology.* New York: Harper and Row Publishers, Inc.

———. 1979. *The dream and the underworld.* New York: Harper and Row Publishers, Inc.

———, ed. 1980a. On the necessity of abnormal psychology. In *Facing the gods.* Dallas: Spring Publications.

———, ed. 1980b. Dionysus in Jung's writings. In *Facing the gods.* Dallas: Spring Publications.

———, ed. 1980c. The Amazon problem. In *Facing the gods.* Dallas: Spring Publications.

———. 1983. The bad mother. *In Spring.* Dallas: Spring Publications.

———, and K. Kerenyi, eds. 1989. Oedipus variations: studies in literature and psychoanalysis. In *Oedipus revisited.* Dallas: Spring Publications.

———. 1990. The Great Mother's son, her hero, and the *puer.* In *Fathers and mothers.* Ed. P. Berry. Dallas: Spring Publications.

———, ed. 1991. The Amazon problem. In *Facing the Gods.* Fifth printing. Dallas: Spring Publications.

———. 1994a. Introduction. In *The long journey home: re-visioning the myth of Demeter and Persephone for our times.* Ed. C. Downing. Boston: Shambhala Publications.

———. 1994b. *Insearch: psychology and religion,* Woodstock: Spring Publications.

———. 1994c. *Puer papers.* Dallas: Spring Publications.

———. 1996a. *Anima: an anatomy of a personified notion.* Woodstock: Spring Publications.

———. 1996b. *The soul's code.* New York: Random House.

———. 1998. *On paranoia.* Dallas: Spring Publications.

———. 2000. Peaks and vales. In *Working with images.* Ed. B. Selles. Woodstock: Spring Publications.

Hopcke, R. H. 1989. *Jung, Jungians, and homosexuality.* Boston: Shambhala Publications.

Huskinson, L. 2004. *Nietzsche and Jung: the whole self in the union of opposites.* Hove and New York: Brunner-Routledge.

Irigaray, L. 1991. *Marine lover of Friedrich Nietzsche.* Tr. G. C. Gill. New York: Columbia University Press.

Jacobi, J. 1968. C. G. Jung. *International encyclopaedia of the social sciences,* Vol. 8. New York: Macmillan/The Free Press.

Jacoby, M. A. 1985. *Longing for paradise: psychological perspectives on an archetype.* Tr. M. Gubitz. Boston: Sigo Press.

Jaffé, A. 1984. *Jung's last years.* Tr. R. F. C. Hull and M. Stein. Dallas: Spring Publications.

Jameson, M. 1996. The asexuality of Dionysus. In *Masks of Dionysus.* Ed. T. H. Carpenter and C. A. Faraone. 2nd printing. Ithaca and London: Cornell University Press.

Janz, C. P. 1987. *Friedrich Nietzsche,* 4 vols. Madrid: Alianza Editorial.

Jaspers, K. 1997. *Nietzsche: an introduction to the understanding of his philosophical activity.* Tr. C. F. Wallraff and F. J. Schmitz. Baltimore and London: The Johns Hopkins University Press.

Jung, C. G. 1955. *Modern man in search of a soul.* San Diego, New York, and London: Harvest Book.

———. 1965. *Memories, dreams, reflections.* Ed. A. Jaffé, tr. R. and C. Winston. New York: Vintage Books.

———. 1973. *Letters, volume 1: 1906–1950.* Ed. G. Adler and A. Jaffé, tr. R. F. C. Hull. Princeton: Princeton University Press.

———. 1975. *The myth of meaning.* Tr. R. F. C. Hull. London: Penguin Books.

———. 1979. *Collected works.* 20 vols. Ed. Sir H. Read, M. Fordham, G. Adler, and W. McGuire. Princeton: Princeton University Press (Bollingen Series XX). References are to the *Collected works* (CW), by volume and paragraph number.

———. 1988. *"Nietzsche's Zarathustra": notes from the seminar given in 1934–1939,* 2 vols. Ed. J. L. Jarrett. Princeton: Princeton University Press (Bollingen Series XCIX).

———. 1989. *Analytical psychology: notes from the seminar given in 1925.* Princeton: Princeton University Press.

———. 1997. *Visions: notes from the seminars given in 1930–1934,* 2 vols. Ed. C. Douglas. Princeton: Princeton University Press (Bollingen Series XCIX).

Kalsched, D. 2000. *The inner world of trauma: archetypal defenses of the personal spirit.* 3rd printing. London and New York: Routledge.

Kast, V. 1992. *The dynamics of symbols.* New York: Fromm International Publishing Corporation.

Kaufmann, W. 1974. *Nietzsche: philosopher, psychologist, Antichrist.* 4th ed. Princeton: Princeton University Press.

———. 1990. *Discovering the mind,* Vol. 1. New Brunswick: Transaction Publishers.

Kerényi, K. 1983. *Apollo: the wind, the spirit, and the god.* Tr. J. Solomon. Dallas: Spring Publications.

———. 1991. *Prometheus: archetypal image of human existence.* Tr. R. Manheim. Princeton: Princeton University Press (Bollingen Series LXV).

———. 1996. *Dionysus: archetypal image of indestructible life.* Princeton: Princeton University Press.

Klein, M. 1957. *Envy and gratitude.* London: Tavistock Publications Ltd.

Klossowski, P. 1963. *Un destin si funeste.* Paris: Gallimard.

———. 1997. *Nietzsche and the vicious circle.* Tr. D. W. Smith. Chicago: The University of Chicago Press.

Knox, B. M. W. 1957/1966. *Oedipus at Thebes.* New Haven and London: Yale University Press.

Köhler, J. 1998. *Nietzsche and Wagner: a lesson in subjugation.* Tr. R. Taylor. New Haven: Yale University Press.

———. 2002. *Zarathustra's secret: the interior life of Friedrich Nietzsche.* Tr. R. Taylor. New Haven and London: Yale University Press.

Kristeva, J. 1989. *Black sun: depression and melancholia.* New York: Columbia University Press.

Lacan, J. 1989. Seminar 7: *La ética del psicoanálisis.* Buenos Aires, Barcelona, and México: Ediciones Paidós.

Laing, R. D. 1990. *The divided self: an existential study in sanity and madness.* London: Penguin Books.

Larsen, S. 1996. *The mythic imagination.* Rochester, VT: Inner Traditions International.

Lavrin, J. 1971. *Nietzsche: a biographical introduction.* New York: Charles Scribner's Sons.

López-Herrera, L. 1996. *La alquimia del sufrimiento.* Bogotá: Editorial Oveja Negra.

López-Pedraza, R. 2000. *Dionysus in exile: on the repression of the body and emotions.* Wilmette, IL: Chiron Publications.

MacIntyre, B. 1992. *Forgotten fatherland: the search for Elisabeth Nietzsche.* New York: Farrar, Straus and Giroux.

Maffei, G. 1991. *Jung in modern perspective: the master and his legacy.* Ed. R. K. Papadopoulos and G. S. Saayman. Dorset, UK: Prism Press.

Magee, B. 1988. *Aspects of Wagner.* Oxford: Oxford University Press.

———. 2000. *Wagner and philosophy.* London: Penguin Books.

Marcuse, H. 1966. *Eros and civilization: a philosophical inquiry into Freud.* Boston: Beacon Press.

Marsden, J. 2000. Lunar rapture: Nietzsche's religion of the night sun. In *Nietzsche and the divine.* Ed. J. Lippitt and J. Urpeth. Manchester: Clinamen Press Ltd.

McDougall, J. 1989. *Theatres of the body: a psychoanalytic approach to psychosomatic illness.* New York and London: W. W. Norton & Company.

McGahey, R. 1994. *The orphic moment: shaman to poet-thinker in Plato, Nietzsche and Mallarmé.* Albany: State University of New York Press.

McWilliams, N. 1994. *Psychoanalytic diagnosis.* New York and London: Guilford Publications.

Megill, A. 1985. *Prophets of extremity: Nietzsche, Heidegger, Foucault, Derrida.* California: University of California Press.

Meyerhoff, H. 1987. On psychoanalysis as history. In *Psychohistory: readings on the method of psychology, psychoanalysis, and history.* Ed. G. Cocks and T. L. Crosby. New Haven: Yale University Press.

Miller, A. 1991. *The untouched key: tracing childhood trauma in creativity and destructiveness.* New York: Anchor Books.

Mogenson, G. 1989. *God is a trauma: vicarious religion and soul-making.* Dallas: Spring Publications.

Montaigne, M. de. 1943. *The essays of Montaigne.* Tr. E. J. Trechmann. New York: The Modern Library.

Moon, B., ed. 1997. *An encyclopedia of archetypal symbolism.* Vol. 1. Boston and London: Shambhala Publications.

Moore, T. 1989. *The planets within: the astrological psychology of Marsilio Ficino.* New York: Lindisfarne Books.

Nesbitt Oppel, F. 2005. *Nietzsche on gender: beyond man and woman.* Charlottesville and London: University of Virginia Press.

Neumann, E. 1974. *Art and the creative unconscious.* 3rd ed. Tr. R. Manheim. Princeton: Princeton University Press (Bollingen Series LXI).

———. 1976. *The child.* New York, Hagerstown, San Francisco, London: Harper Colophon Books. Harper and Row.

———. 1979. *Creative man: five essays.* Vol. 2. Tr. E. Rolfe. Princeton: Princeton University Press (Bollingen Series LXI.2).

———. 1989. *The place of creation.* Tr. H. Nagel, E. Rolfe, J. van Heurck, and K. Winston. Princeton: Princeton University Press (Bollingen Series LXI.3).

———. 1991. *The Great Mother.* 7th ed. Tr. R. Manheim. Princeton: Princeton University Press (Bollingen Series XLVII).

———. 1995. *The origins and history of consciousness.* 11th ed. Tr. R. F. C. Hull. Princeton: Princeton University Press (Bollingen Series XLII).

Nietzsche, F., Wagner, R. 1949. *The Nietzsche-Wagner correspondence.* Ed. Förster-Nietzsche, tr. C. V. Kerr. New York: Liveright.

Nietzsche, F. 1921. *Selected letters of Friedrich Nietzsche.* Ed. O. Levy, tr. A. M. Ludovici. Garden City, New York, and Toronto: Doubleday, Page and Company.

———. (1951). *Correspondencia.* Madrid, Buenos Aires y México: Ediciones Aguilar.

———. 1959. *Nietzsche: unpublished letters.* Ed. and tr. K. F. Leidecker. New York: Philosophical Library.

———. 1974. *The gay science.* Tr. W. Kaufmann. New York: Vintage Books.

———. 1978. *Thus spoke Zarathustra.* Tr. W. Kaufmann. New York: Penguin Books.

———. 1991. *Untimely meditations.* Ed. and tr. R. J. Hollingdale. Cambridge, UK: Cambridge University Press.

———. 1992. *Assorted opinions and maxims.* Ed. and tr. W. Kaufmann. In *Basic writings of Nietzsche.* New York: The Modern Library.

———. 1992. *Ecce Homo.* Ed. and tr. W. Kaufmann. In *Basic writings of Nietzsche.* New York: The Modern Library.

———. 1992. *On the genealogy of morals.* Ed. and tr. W. Kaufmann. In *Basic writings of Nietzsche.* New York: The Modern Library.

———. 1992. *The case of Wagner.* Ed. and tr. W. Kaufmann. In *Basic writings of Nietzsche.* New York: The Modern Library.

———. 1992. *The wanderer and his shadow.* Ed. and tr. W. Kaufmann. In *Basic writings of Nietzsche.* New York: The Modern Library.

———. 1994. On the truth and lies in a nonmoral sense. Ed. and tr. D. Breazeale. In *Philosophy and truth.* Atlantic Highlands, NJ: Humanities Press International, Inc.

———. 1992. *Beyond good and evil.* Ed. and tr. W. Kaufmann. In *Basic writings of Nietzsche.* New York: The Modern Library.

———. 1992. *The Birth of Tragedy.* Ed. and tr. W. Kaufmann. In *Basic Writings of Nietzsche.* New York: The Modern Library.

————. 1996. *Human, all too human.* Tr. M. Faber and S. Lehman. Lincoln: University of Nebraska Press.

————. 1996. *Selected letters of Friedrich Nietzsche.* Ed. and tr. C. Middleton. Indianapolis and Cambridge, MA: Hackett Publishing Company, Inc.

————. 1997. *De mi vida. Escritos autobiográficos de mi juventud* (1856–1869). Madrid: Edición Valdemar.

————. 1998. *Twilight of the idols.* Tr. D. Large. Oxford and New York: Oxford University Press.

————. 1998. *Philosophy in the tragic age of the Greeks.* Tr. M. Cowan. Washington, D.C.: Regnery Publishing, Inc.

————. 2000. *The Antichrist.* Tr. A. M. Ludovici. New York: Prometheus Books.

————. 2000. *Daybreak.* Tr. R. J. Hollingdale, ed. M. Clark and B. Leiter. Cambridge, UK: Cambridge University Press.

————. 2001. *Dithyrambs of Dionysus.* Tr. R. J. Hollingdale. London: Anvil Press Poetry.

————. 2003. *Writings from the late notebooks.* Tr. K. Sturge, ed. R. Bittner. Cambridge, UK: Cambridge University Press.

Nietzsche, F., L. Salomé, and P. Rée. 1982. *Documentos de un encuentro (Die Dokumenten ihrer Begegnung).* 2nd ed. Barcelona: Laertes S. A. de Ediciones.

Ornestein, P. H. (ed.) 1991. Introspection, empathy, and the semicircle of mental health. In *The search for the self: selected writings of Heinz Kohut, 1978–1981.* Madison, CT: International University Press.

Otto, W. F. 1993. *Dionysus: myth and cult.* Tr. R. B. Palmer. 5th printing. Dallas: Spring Publications.

————. 1958. *The idea of the holy.* Tr. J. W. Harvey. New York: Oxford University Press.

Padel, R. 1995. *Whom gods destroy: elements of Greek and tragic madness.* Princeton: Princeton University Press.

Paglia, C. 1990. *Sexual personae.* New Haven, CT: Yale University Press.

Pappas, N. 2004. The eternal-serpentine. In *A Nietzschean bestiary: becoming animal beyond docile and brutal.* Ed. C. D. and R. R. Acampora. Lanham, Boulder, New York, Toronto, and Oxford: Rowman and Littlefield Publishers, Inc.

Parkes, G. 1994. *Composing the soul: reaches of Nietzsche's psychology.* Chicago: University of Chicago Press.

Pautrat, B. 1990. Nietzsche medused. In *Looking after Nietzsche.* Ed. L. A. Rickels. Albany: State University of New York Press.

Perry, J. W. 1970. Emotions and object relations. In *Journal of analytical psychology* 13 (1):1–12.

————. 1976. *Roots of renewal in myth and madness.* San Francisco, Washington, London: Jossey-Bass Publishers.

————. 1992. *The far side of madness.* 2nd printing. Dallas: Spring Publications.

Peters, H. F. 1974. *My sister, my spouse: a biography of Lou Andreas-Salomé.* New York: W. W. Norton & Company, Inc.

————. 1977. *Zarathustra's sister: the case of Elisabeth and Friedrich Nietzsche.* New York: Crown Publishers, Inc.

Plato. 1965. *Symposium*. Tr. E. R. Dodds. In *Pagan and Christian in an age of anxiety: some aspects of religious experience from Marcus Aurelius to Constantine*. Cambridge, UK: Cambridge University Press.

Pletsch, C. 1991. *Young Nietzsche: becoming a genius*. New York: The Free Press.

Podach, E. F. 1931. *The madness of Nietzsche*. Tr. F. A. Voigt. New York: Putnam.

Ricoeur, P. 1970. *Freud and philosophy*. New Haven and London: Yale University Press.

Roazen, P. 1992. *Freud and his followers*. New York: Da Capo Press.

Rollo, M. 1981. *Freedom and destiny*. New York: W. W. Norton & Company.

Ross, W. 1994. *El águila angustiada. Una biografía*. Barcelona, Buenos Aires, México: Ediciones Paidós Ibérica, S.A.

Russell, B. 1945. *A history of western philosophy*. New York: Simon & Schuster, Inc.

Safranski, R. 2002. *Nietzsche: a philosophical biography*. Tr. S. Frisch. New York and London: W. W. Norton & Company.

Sallis, J. 1988. Dionysus—in excess of metaphysics. In *Exceedingly Nietzsche: aspects of contemporary Nietzsche interpretation*. Ed. D. Farrell Krell and D. Wood. London and New York: Routledge.

Salomé, L. 2001. *Nietzsche*. Ed. and tr. S. Mandel. Urbana and Chicago: University of Illinois Press.

Samuels, A. 1985. Introduction. In *The father: contemporary Jungian perspectives*. Ed. A. Samuels. New York: New York University Press.

———. 1989. *The plural psyche: personality, morality and the father*. London and New York: Routledge.

———. 1997a. Jung and the post-Jungians. In *The Cambridge companion to Jung*. Ed. P. Young-Eisendrath and T. Dawson. Cambridge, UK: Cambridge University Press.

———. 1997b. *Jung and the post-Jungians*. London and New York: Routledge.

Samuels, A., B. Shorter, and F. Plaut. 1986. *A critical dictionary of Jungian analysis*. London and New York: Routledge & Kegan Paul.

Sandner, D. 1993. The role of the anima in same-sex love between men. In *Same-sex love and the path of wholeness*. Ed. R. H. Hopcke, K. L. Carrington, and S. Wirth. Boston: Shambhala Publications.

Sanford, J. A. 1998. *Evil: the shadow side of reality*. New York: The Crossroad Publishing Company.

Schain, R. 2001. *The legend of Nietzsche's syphilis*. Westport, CT: Greenwood Press.

Seung, T. K. 2005. *Nietzsche's epic of the soul: thus spoke Zarathustra*. Lanham, Boulder, New York, Toronto, and Oxford: Lexington Books.

Shapiro, G. 1991. *Alcyone: Nietzsche on gifts, noise, and women*. Albany: State University of New York Press.

Sharp, D. 1991. *C. G. Jung lexicon: a primer of terms and concepts*. Toronto: Inner City Books.

Shearer, A. 2001. The wanderer: archetype for the times? In *Harvest: journal for Jungian studies* 47 (1). London: Karnac Books.

Sidoli, M. 1993. When the meaning gets lost in the body. In *Journal of analytical psychology* 38 (2): 175–190.

Slater, P. E. 1992. *The glory of Hera: Greek mythology and the Greek family.* Princeton: Princeton University Press.

Solomon, R. C. 2003. *Living with Nietzsche.* Oxford and New York: Oxford University Press.

Stambaugh, J. 1994. *The other Nietzsche.* Albany: State University of New York Press.

Stein, M. 1996. *In midlife.* Woodstock: Spring Publications.

Steiner, G. 2002. *Grammars of creation.* New Haven and London: Yale University Press.

Stern, K. 1985. *The flight from woman.* 2nd ed. St. Paul, MN: Paragon House.

Stevens, A. 1997. *The two-million-year-old self.* New York: Fromm International Publishing Corp.

———. 1999. *On Jung.* 2nd ed. Princeton: Princeton University Press.

Storr, A. 1973. *C. G. Jung.* New York: Viking Press.

———. 1993. *The dynamics of creation.* New York: Ballantine Books, Inc.

———. 1996. *Feet of clay: saints, sinners, and madmen: a study of gurus.* New York, London, Toronto, Sydney, and Singapore: Free Press.

Strong, T. B. 1985. Oedipus as hero: family and family metaphors in Nietzsche. In *Why Nietzsche now?* Ed. D. T. O'Hara. Bloomington: Indiana University Press.

Thomas, D. 1999. *Reading Nietzsche rhetorically.* New York and London: Guilford Publications.

Vasseleu, C. 1993. Not drowning, sailing. In *Nietzsche's feminism and political theory.* Ed. P. Patton. London and New York: Routledge.

Vernant, J. P. 2002. Dioniso enmascarado en las *Bacantes* de Eurípides. In J. P. Vernant and P. Vidal-Naquet, *Mito y tragedia en la Grecia antigua,* Vol. 2. Barcelona and Buenos Aires: Ediciones Paidós Ibérica, S.A. and Editorial Paidós.

von Franz, M. L. 1995. *Projection and re-collection in Jungian psychology.* Tr. W. H. Kennedy. Chicago and La Salle, IL: Open Court.

———. 1993. *Érase una vez. (Once upon a time).* Barcelona: Ediciones Luciérnaga.

———. 1998. *The cat: a tale of feminine redemption.* Ed. D. Sharp. Toronto: University of Toronto Press.

Wagner, C. 1997. *Cosima Wagner's diaries.* Ed. G. Skelton. Harcourt Brace Jovanovich, Inc.

Weinstein, J. 2004. Traces of the beast: becoming Nietzsche, becoming animal, and the figure of the transhuman. In *A Nietzschean bestiary: becoming animal beyond docile and brutal.* Ed. C. D. and R. R. Acampora. Lanham, Boulder, New York, Toronto, and Oxford: Rowman and Littlefield Publishers, Inc.

Weiss, A. S. 1983. The body Dionysian: Nietzsche, Freud, Merleau-Ponty. In *The great year of Zarathustra (1881–1981).* Ed. D. Goicoechea. Lanham, New York and London: University Press of America.

White, V. 1953. *God and the unconscious.* London: The Harvill Press.

Whitmont, E. C. 1969. *The symbolic quest: basic concepts of analytical psychology.* New York: Putnam.

———. 1992. *Return of the goddess.* New York: The Crossroad Publishing Company.

Wicks, R. 2002. *Nietzsche.* Oxford, UK: Oneworld Publications.

Williamson, G. S. 2004. *The longing for myth in Germany: religion and aesthetic culture from romanticism to Nietzsche.* Chicago and London: The University of Chicago Press.

Winnicott, D. W. 1965. Ego distortions in terms of true and false self. In *The maturational process and the facilitating environment.* New York: International University Press, Inc.

Wood, D. 1988. Nietzsche's transvaluation of time. In *Exceedingly Nietzsche: aspects of contemporary Nietzsche interpretation.* Ed. D. Farrell Krell and D. Wood. London and New York: Routledge.

Zambrano, M. 1993. *El hombre y lo divino.* México: Fondo de Cultura Económica.

Index

www.ingramcontent.com/pod-product-compliance
Lightning Source LLC
Chambersburg PA
CBHW050224270326
41914CB00003BA/567